CONFR AMERICAN DILEMMA OF RACE

The Second Generation
Black American Sociologists

Edited by
Robert E. Washington
Donald Cunnigen

University Press of America,® Inc.
Lanham · New York · Oxford

Copyright © 2002 by
University Press of America,® Inc.
4720 Boston Way
Lanham, Maryland 20706
UPA Acquisitions Department (301) 459-3366

12 Hid's Copse Rd.
Cumnor Hill, Oxford OX2 9JJ

British Library Cataloging in Publication Information Available

Library of Congress Cataloging-in-Publication Data

Confronting the American dilemma of race : the second
generation Black American sociologists /
edited by Robert E. Washington, Donald Cunnigen.
p.   cm
Includes bibliographical references.
1. African American sociologists—Biography. 2. United States—
Race relations—History. I. Washington. Robert E., 1941-
II. Cunnigen, Donald.

HM478 .C66 2002
301'.089'960730092—dc21   2002020299 CIP

ISBN 0-7618-2289-5 (clothbound : alk. ppr.)
ISBN 0-7618-2290-9 (paperback : alk. ppr.)

⊖™The paper used in this publication meets the minimum
requirements of American National Standard for Information
Sciences—Permanence of Paper for Printed Library Materials,
ANSI Z39.48—1984

Dedicated to our fathers,

Ernest D. Washington, Sr.

and

Oliver Wendell Cunnigen, Jr.

CONTENTS

LIST OF FIGURES

INTRODUCTION

Second Generation Black Sociologists Discover a "Place" in American Sociology

Donald Cunnigen

This book grew out of a session on the contributions of "Lesser Known Black Sociologists" during the 1980 Eastern Sociological Society (ESS) meetings. The session, which presented a broad range of papers on the unique sociological contributions of African Americans, aimed to expose contemporary sociologists to the varied contributions of African American sociologists whose works have been largely ignored by scholars. Due to the positive responses regarding the 1980 session, we organized several other sessions over subsequent years for the Association of Black Sociologists (ABS), the Society for the Study of Social Problems (SSSP), the Southern Sociological Society (SSS), and the ESS meetings.

In 1993, we were approached by an editor interested in publishing the papers as a book. We agreed to pursue that objective because we felt the papers provided invaluable information about a neglected group of scholars. Unlike the two previous books on African American sociologists (Blackwell and Janowitz 1974; Bracey, Meier, and Rudwick 1971) which provided significant historical insights into the careers of African American sociologists, with special emphasis on the works of W. E. B. DuBois, Charles S. Johnson, and E. Franklin Frazier, our goal is to focus on the theoretical worldview which characterized the second generation of African American sociologists and to call attention to the careers of some of its lesser known members.

In the spirit of Alvin Gouldner's critical analysis of mainstream American sociology (1970), the papers in this book examine the works of second-generation African-American sociologists in light of varied influences: graduate training in elite departments; Robert Park and the Chicago School of Sociology; the Great Depression; the caste-class theoretical school; Gunnar Myrdal's famous study of American race relations; the post war ascendance of functionalist social theory; the changing structure of American universities; and sociology's increased legitimacy as an academic discipline.

We agree with Douglas Davidson's (1977: 46) suggestion that it is impossible to determine the impact and influence of African American sociologists "without assessing critically the larger society and the politics of the discipline." Simply put, if we are to comprehend these African American sociologists' worldview, we must understand their historical development as an intellectual community in relationship to both "mainstream" sociological scholarship and the surrounding society.

Periods of the African American Sociological Tradition

John H. Stanfield, II (1993: ix) described a sociological generation as a collection of "people born into sequential birth cohorts who gain a sense of collective identity by going through the same dramatic historical events." On the other hand, Gordon D. Morgan (1994: 1) suggested "academic generations may not correspond precisely to chronological generations." By using Stanfield and Morgan, African American sociologists may be placed in an analytical context which allows an understanding of individuals with various birth dates, schooling experiences, and professional experiences.

The African American sociological tradition has been characterized by four distinct periods: first-generation, 1895-1930; second-generation, 1931-1959; third-generation, 1960-1975; and fourth-generation, 1976 to present. These periods are based on the time of Ph.D. acquisition, which various scholars have suggested is a crucial consideration in assessing the influence on African American scholarship.[1] Others have attempted to classify African American sociologists according to generational groupings, but we need not dwell on the differences among these classifications, because all such typologies are arbitrary. The key question is whether the typology serves to clarify the patterns of intellectual influences being studied. We believe the above typology satisfies that criterion.

Though we realize the disadvantages of restricting this volume to a specific period, we decided to focus on second-generation African American sociologists because their experiences reveal important insights into the impact of racial segregation on the development black sociology. Trained between 1930 and 1950, these African American sociologists embarked on their careers during the time when mainstream American sociology, and American society in general, was embedded in a racial caste system.

While some have suggested African American intellectuals, in response to racial obstacles, produced subversive texts that undermined the prevailing white intellectual paradigms (e. g., Jerry Ward on African American poets), we cannot make such a claim in reference to second-generation African American sociologists who, with few exceptions, embraced an assimilationist theoretical perspective. Nevertheless, we do maintain that they possessed a distinctive worldview.

Key (1978: 35-48) has identified seven unique characteristics of the second-generation African American sociologists: (1) their professional careers usually began after 1931; (2) they manifested little interest in professionally refuting the racist assumptions present in the intellectual discourse of the late nineteenth and early twentieth centuries; (3) they focused their research on the conditions which immediately affected the African American community and larger society; (4) their work utilized more sociological methods and supporting documentation than did that of the first generation; (5) they attempted to be more objective and scientifically oriented; (6) they tended to avoid direct social action; and (7) they gained greater acceptance from some segments of the white sociological community.

It should also be noted, as Ralph Hines (1967: 30-35) has pointed out, that they suffered from the contradictions between their professional status and their racial status. Focusing their energies almost exclusively on race relations, they embraced the pragmatic views of such scholars as Ernest Burgess and Robert E. Park. The white sociological community's greater acceptance of the second generation black sociologists no doubt was influenced by the latter's acquiescence to the prevailing mainstream theoretical paradigms, a matter we will elaborate later in our discussion of the Chicago School's influence.

The Development of Sociology and the Study of American Race
Relations

American Sociology developed as a discipline during an era of racial and ethnic conflicts and mounting urban social problems in 1890s America. The historian Rayford W. Logan (1957) labeled the period from

1895 to 1910 the "Nadir" of American history because of the racial abuses suffered by African Americans. Logan's "Nadir" argument notwithstanding, the period evidencing the most egregious white American hostility toward African Americans extended over the three decades from 1889 and 1931, which witnessed bitter strife between white and black workers, evidenced in the eruption of race riots in urban areas, and the lynching of some 2,800 African Americans.

Though widespread, racial problems were hardly the only problems then plaguing American society. There were also numerous urban problems spawned by the massive immigration of poor European peasants into American cities. It was during this period of worsening racial antagonisms and urban social problems that a small group of white American male scholars attempted to launch the discipline of academic sociology, and develop a theoretically grounded agenda for practical social reform. Most of the central ideas of their sociological outlook derived from Europe.

It was nineteenth century European scholars who developed academic sociology's domain assumptions, which in the words of Alvin Gouldner (1970: 52), emphasized "the potency of society and the subordination of [people] to it [as] an historical product . . ." which embodied "historical truth." Gouldner suggests that sociology developed the concepts of society and culture when the world was being transformed by revolution and people were able to see the contradictions in social changes they created. The concepts of society and culture, notes Gouldner, developed as ambiguous terms connoting human invention. As a discourse focused on the nature of these human inventions, sociology emerged as an academic discipline, which attempted to find a solution to the Europeans' "estrangement from themselves," the void of personal insecurity and anxiety that previously was filled by religion and metaphysics (Gouldner 1970: 53).

As new intellectual, social, and political changes, and the accompanying Industrial Revolution swept across Europe and obliterated traditional European society, giving birth to the modern world, sociology took its first halting steps toward defining itself with a European worldview. This European worldview was soon imported into the United States, marking the fledgling emergence of American sociology.

The late nineteenth century was a critical period for the development of American sociology. The first sociology courses were offered at Yale University and Colby College. The first department of sociology was established at the University of Chicago in 1892. The first sociology textbook was published in 1894. The first sociological journal, the *American Journal of Sociology*, was published in 1895. Throughout the early twentieth century, sociology continued to gain legitimacy in American academic circles which was accelerated by the organization of the American Sociological Association in 1905.

During these early years, American sociologists confronted a prickly dilemma. They were attempting to achieve both credibility as academic professionals and efficacy as social critics. Social criticism was a driving force behind American sociology's formation. According to Thomas F. Pettigrew (1980: xiii-xxxiii), the insider/outsider role of many sociologists as social critics derived from their social backgrounds, particularly the religious influences of their youthful socialization. Many of these early sociologists such as William Graham Sumner, Albion Small, and W. I. Thomas were either ordained clergymen or the sons of clergymen. Though they moved beyond theological discourse in their intellectual work, these religious influences led to their preoccupation with social problems, which they sought to resolve through the secular intellectual discipline of sociology.

Despite witnessing the worsening problems of race relations that plagued American society, the early white sociologists failed paradoxically to challenge the racist beliefs about African Americans that permeated American society. Insofar as they focused on racial problems, they did so from a perspective that reflected the racist attitudes of the surrounding white society.

Rhett Jones (1992: 16) has argued that white sociology failed to deal realistically with race relations, because it failed to take into account African American awareness of their racial disadvantages relative to white Americans. Jones provides an invaluable analysis of American sociology's shortcomings that illuminates the domain assumptions of white sociological scholarship. Those domain assumptions corresponded to what John H. Stanfield (1985: 3) has described as the "societal conditioning factors which shape the origins and development of social science disciplines, communities, and institutions" [and reproduce] the "societal patterns of class, gender, and racial inequality."

In a similar vein, Steven J. Rosenthal (1976: 1) has suggested that American sociology, throughout its formative years, was embedded in racist assumptions. The first American sociology texts by Henry Hughes and George Fitzhugh, observes Rosenthal, "were Comtean pre-Civil War defenses of the morality of [African] slavery." Rosenthal also notes that Sumner (1906) introduced [American sociologists to the] concept that 'legislation cannot make mores,' because mores must evolve through the slow accretion of tradition. Laws, thus, were thought to be useless as a means to promote Reconstruction and racial equality. Using this and similar arguments, leading American sociologists helped legitimate the idea that "government[al] protection of civil rights [was] futile 'interference'."

Rosenthal (1976: 1) goes on to note that these sociologists also helped to legitimate "Social Darwinist" thinking in reference to race relations, which justified the "reimposition of slave-like conditions on [African-Americans] and on the working class as a whole." Similarly, Key (1975) notes the pervasive covert nature of these early white sociologists' racial views. As he puts it, "the expression of racism among the 'pioneering sociologists' [was] so subtle it [was] difficult to recognize." Which is to say, it was often woven so deeply into the tapestry of their sociological arguments it was seldom perceived as racial ideology.

William Graham Sumner's perspective on mores provides an excellent example of these covert racial views in the dominant strain of sociological thought that buttressed conservative thinking about race relations. In *Folkway–A Study of the Sociological Importance of Usages, Manners, Mores and Morals* (1906 [1959]: 77-78), Sumner wrote:

> In our southern states, before the Civil War, whites and blacks had formed habits of action and feeling toward each other. They lived in peace and concord, and grew up in the ways which were traditional and customary. The Civil War abolished legal rights and left the two races to learn how to live together under other relations than before. The whites have never been converted from the old mores. Those who still survive look back with regret and affection to old social usages and customary sentiments and feelings. The two races have not yet made new mores. Vain attempts have been made to control the new order by legislation. The only result is the proof that legislation cannot make mores...some are anxious to interfere and try to control. They take their stands on ethical views of what is going on. It is evidently impossible for anyone to interfere. We are like spectators at a great natural convulsion.

In effect, Sumner regarded the racial mores of ante-bellum southern domination and exploitation of blacks under slavery as a social arrangement in which the races "lived in peace and accord."

Paralleling Sumner's racial views, Franklin H. Giddings presented a theoretical perspective on race which emphasized "consciousness of kind." Giddings thus wrote:

> In its widest extension the consciousness of kind marks off the animate from the inanimate. Within the wide class of animate it next marks off species and races. Within racial lines, the consciousness of kind underlies the more definite ethnical and political groupings it is the basis of class distinctions of innumerable forms of alliance, of rules of intercourse and of peculiarities of policy. Our conduct towards those whom we feel to be most like ourselves is instinctively and rationally different from our conduct towards others, whom we

xvi

believe to be less like ourselves. (Giddings 1921: 18)

Giddings' *The Principles of Sociology* was published in 1921, during a time of mass black urbanization and the subjection of African Americans to *de facto* and *de jure* segregation, because they were viewed by white Americans as being racially inferior. Support for this belief was evidenced in Giddings' influential book.

It is sometimes said that we ought not to assert that the lower races have not the capacity for social evolution, because we do not know what they could do if they had the opportunity. They have been in existence, however, much longer than the European races, and have accomplished immeasurably less. We are therefore, warranted in saying that they have not the same inherent abilities. (Giddings 1921: 328-329)

Giddings and other white sociologists' racial views derived from widely accepted notions about a hierarchy in human evolution. As Herman and Julia Schwendinger have noted, the early American and European social scientists maintained "simple racial schemes of gradation." (1977:100) The top of the racial schema consisted of the more "evolved" Anglo-Saxon and Germanic races. The very bottom of the racial schema consisted of the "savage" races such as Africans, Asians, Indians, and Mexicans. These ideas had a profound impact on the participants in the discipline. As members of one of the so-called "savage" races, second-generation African-American sociologists had the dubious honor of becoming members of a discipline based on domain assumptions that alleged their racial inferiority.

In light of those racial assumptions, it is hardly surprising that white sociological inquiry developed with little attention to the African American community or the scholarly works of African Americans. Mainstream sociological discourse focused primarily on Euro-Americans, while the problems of race relations were largely ignored by scholars. There was a lack of both financial resources and interests to stimulate research on racial problems (Pettigrew 1980: xii-xxiii), and this disinterest in race relations extended to the scholarly works of African American sociologists.

Jennifer Platt (1996: 225, 247) suggested the obscurity of African American sociologists was so obvious that she only made an oblique reference to any African American contribution in the area of research methodology. While some white scholarship failed to consider any African American scholarship (Eisenstadt 1976), the diminution of African American sociologists as obscure and minor scholarly figures in

xvii

the shadow of eminent whites (Abbott 1999; Fine 1995) continues in most major contemporary works on American sociology.

A World of Their Own: Sociology in the African-American Community

As "mainstream" sociology developed in the racially segregated white academic community, a parallel African American sociological tradition developed in the African-American academic community. As early as 1894, Morgan College (now Morgan State University) provided a course consisting of eight lectures on social science. In 1897, Atlanta University offered sociology courses as DuBois began his Atlanta University sociological studies of African-American life. By 1917, 23 African-American colleges/universities reportedly were offering sociology courses (Himes 1949: 17-32). In 1931, a survey of departments found 232 different sociology courses listed, the most popular courses being rural sociology, educational sociology, and race (Doyle 1933: 11-13).

As African-American college and university sociology programs were being taught, more African-Americans acquired advanced degrees in the field. James Robert Lincoln Diggs received the first Ph.D. in sociology from Illinois Wesleyan University in 1906 (Greene 1946: 561). Although Diggs is acknowledged as the first African American sociology Ph.D. recipient, George Edmund Haynes' doctorate from Columbia University (Columbia) in 1912 is often viewed as having been a more significant development, because he played such a pivotal role in fostering the sociology department of Fisk University, his alma mater, which became an important base of African American sociological work (Himes 1949: 21).

It was during this early period (1899-1930) that the first-generation of African American sociologists made their mark. Not all who made important research contributions were trained in sociology. The most outstanding example being DuBois, who in 1899 published his classic community study, *The Philadelphia Negro*, which was the first major sociological study of an African American community directed by an African American and funded by a major philanthropic foundation. Yet another example was Monroe Nathan Work, who became the director of the Bureau of Records at Tuskegee Institute in 1911, and subsequently published a series of statistical volumes on African American life, *Negro Yearbook* (Himes 1949: 19-21; McMurry 1985).

It is important to recall that these first-generation African American sociologists were trained and practiced their craft in isolation from the white sociological community. Employed in segregated African American colleges and universities, they faced formidable obstacles in trying to do

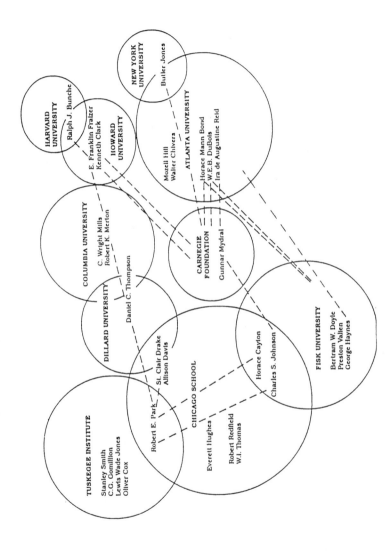

Figure 1. Intellectual Influences on African American Sociologists

research because they typically lacked administrative and financial support.

The 1930s and 1940s witnessed the emergence of the second generation black sociologists who had closer ties to white sociologists and reflected more mainstream white sociological influence in their work. Though white sociology departments persisted in their segregationist hiring practices up to the late 1960s, these second generation African American sociologists made significant scholarly achievements (Banks 1996: 121).

Exemplary works of the period included E. Franklin Frazier's *Negro Family in Chicago* (1932) and *Negro Family in the United States (1939), Allison Davis and John Dollard's Children of Bondage: The Personality Development of Urban Youth in the Urban South* (1940), Charles S. Johnson's *Shadow of the Plantation* (1934) and *Growing Up in the Black Belt* (1941), Ira deAugustine Reid's *In A Minor Key* (1940), St. Clair Drake and Horace Cayton's *Dark Metropolis: A Study of Negro Life in a Northern City* (1945), Oliver C. Cox's *Caste, Class and Race* (1945) and Hylan Lewis' *Blackways of Kent* (1955) were all published during the three decade period between 1930 and 1960.

The second generation consisted of 103 individuals, which included Charles Johnson, E. Franklin Frazier, Oliver Cox, Horace Cayton, St. Clair Drake, Walter Chivers, Daniel Thompson, Butler Jones, Joseph Himes, Hylan Lewis, Ira deAgustine Reid, G. Franklin Edwards, Albert McQueen, Charles Parrish, James E. Blackwell, Charles Willie, and Mozell Hill. [See appendix for a complete list of the second generation sociologists, the place of their graduate training, and the date of their doctorate degrees.]

Utilizing a modified version of Carl Jorgensen's network diagram of intellectual influences on African American sociologists, we can discern source and range of mainstream white sociologists' influences on second generation sociologists.

It is important to recognize that the network was also shaped by the relationships and influences flowing from the first to the younger African American sociologists. Atlanta University scholars -- particularly DuBois -- played a significant role in infusing African American scholarship with earlier African American research experiences. For example, as a student Butler A. Jones was influenced not only by DuBois, but also, and more importantly, by Walter Chivers, who taught him at Morehouse College.

Later, during his own professional career, Jones maintained professional contacts with Oliver Cox, Mozell Hill, and other members of the generation. We lack detailed information about these relationships but the few biographical accounts of second generation African American sociologists we have suggests they were extensive.

Even more important than the Atlanta University-Morehouse College axis was the influence of the Chicago School. St. Clair Drake was influenced strongly by W. Lloyd Warner, Robert Redfield, Everett C. Hughes, Louis Wirth, and Allison Davis, who taught him at Hampton Institute (now Hampton University) and later at the University of Chicago. Drake collaborated with Horace Cayton on a major research project and maintained contacts with other second-generation African American scholars. Horace Cayton, in turn, was influenced strongly by Robert E. Park, Ernest Burgess, Robert McKenzie, and Louis Wirth.

Other second generation African-American sociologists studied at such leading eastern universities as Harvard and Columbia, which fostered a smaller group within the second-generation. Daniel C. Thompson studied at Columbia and was influenced by Robert K. Merton. Ira de Augustine Reid, another Columbia graduate, was influenced by diverse range of scholars, including DuBois and Myrdal. As a scholar from Sweden, Myrdal influenced the second generation black sociologist primarily through his position as director of the pioneering study of race relations which resulted in the publication of *An American Dilemma,* an influence we will say more about later.

As we noted earlier, the assimilationist model prevailed as the dominant theoretical paradigm used by white sociologists of the period to explain race relations. Since many of the second-generation African American sociologists studied under Robert Park, the leading proponent of the assimilationist model, they incorporated all -- or significant parts -- of the model in their research. Which is to say, they acquiesced to the influence of mainstream white sociologists.

Although the period "between the First World War and the mid 1930s" is typically thought to be the highpoint of the Chicago School (Abbott 1997: 1153; Abbott 1999: 198-222), its influence, in the works of African American sociologists, extended well beyond the 1930s. Many African-American sociologists incorporated the Chicago School influences in their research. Accepting the Chicago School's emphasis on the importance of contextualizing social facts in social (and often geographic) space and social time" (Abbott 1997: 115), second-generation African American sociologists, in their research on racial issues, combined both the Chicago School's assimilationist and ecological models. The Chicago School influenced African American intellectuals in a broad range of arenas. William J. Maxwell (1999: 160-162) indicated that the Chicago School's students and faculty such as E. Franklin Frazier, Louis and Mary Wirth, Robert Redfield, and most notably Robert E. Park shaped the views of African American writers such as Richard Wright. Through African American sociologists such as Horace Cayton, St. Clair Drake, Charles S. Johnson, Frazier, the Chicago School was an important and influential component of what later became the "Black Chicago

Renaissance," the period between mid-1930s and the early 1950s in which the African American community of Chicago had a high level of cultural activity. Thus, Park's shadow and the Chicago School were ever present. As Alford Young (1993: 107) has noted in his study of Frazier and Johnson, the publications of many African American sociologists of this period were influenced by Park. Park's "views on the culture of African Americans and Africans as well as his race relations cycle" strongly influenced Johnson and Frazier (Young 1993: 109). Frazier's work, Young argues, represented a methodological and theoretical extension and revision of Park's ideas. Seeing an even broader impact, Gordon Morgan (1973: 106-119) suggests that the entire second-generation of African American sociologists was influenced by Park and/or the caste and class school of thought. Except for their assessment of Oliver Cox's work, both Young's and Morgan's views are consistent with Key's contention that the second-generation African-American sociologists operated under an assimilationist-accommodationist model which did not challenge profoundly the domain assumptions of sociology. As marginalized scholars, these African American sociologists viewed their commitment to the discipline's shibboleths as a mark of being well-trained and a requirement for full acceptance by their mainstream peers. The assimilationist perspective of second-generation African American sociologists eschewed racial essentialism. Like their intellectual counterparts in Africa and the Caribbean such as C. L. R. James, their intellectual perspective attempted to find a factual universality. The degree to which they accomplished or failed to accomplish their objective is the primary focus of this volume. Despite this attachment to the discipline's perspective on American social realities, they remained cognizant of personal experiences of racism they could not address within the prevailing white sociological paradigms on race relations. This was evidenced perhaps most dramatically in the experiences of Horace Cayton.

To a greater extent than the older generation of black scholars, the second-generation embodied what DuBois termed "dual consciousness," which resulted from living simultaneously in black and white social worlds. Anthony Platt (1990: 51-52) has suggested Frazier resolved the conflict in his written work by effecting two diverging writing styles, i. e., a scholarly style which exhibited "a sociological language in his academic publications" and an advocacy style which exhibited "[a] polemical language...[used] in [popular] journals like the *Messenger*." The Frazier writing technique for managing this conflict was evidenced in the writings of other sociologists, who maintained a rigid separation between their professional personae and their political personae, a maneuver essential to their professional survival. They had to project an intellectual outlook that was acceptable to mainstream sociologists in order to get access to research support and publishing outlets.

Gunnar Myrdal and the African-American Sociologist

As the most important sociological project during the interwar years, Gunnar Myrdal's Carnegie Foundation sponsored study of American race relations, **An American Dilemma--The Negro Problem and Modern Democracy**, (1944) perhaps best revealed mainstream sociology's relationship to the second generation African-American sociologists. While providing opportunities that helped to launch the careers of such young white scholars as Arnold Rose, Richard Sterner, Edward Shils, Donald Young, Samuel Stouffer, William Ogburn, Herbert Goldhammer, and Louis Wirth, Myrdal's study gave African American scholars few tangible career benefits. Some commentators have praised Myrdal for including African American scholars in the project (Jackson 1990; Southern 1987), but Myrdal actually allowed them only token participation. This reflected the Carnegie Foundation's plan, which considered "one colored social scientist" to be sufficient representation. The critical issue for Myrdal thus became that of selecting a competent "colored social scientist," and this turned out to be Ralph J. Bunche, the noted Howard political scientist.

Though initially Myrdal had intended to select Charles S. Johnson as a co-author for the study (Jackson, 1990; Southern, 1987), he chose Bunche over the more eminent Charles S. Johnson and E. Franklin Frazier because, in John Stanfield words (1985: 181, fn. 95), " he [Myrdal was] interest[ed] in controlling the interpretations of the Afro-American experience." As experienced African American scholars who had published significant works on the African American community, Johnson and Frazier probably would have opposed some of Myrdal's accounts of African American behavior.   Bunche's selection marked an important development that broadened the scholarly participation in the study, because Bunche had an extensive intellectual network from which he drew some African American scholars to work in auxiliary roles, as researchers and consultants. It was through these minor auxiliary roles that African American social scientists made important--though largely unrecognized---contributions to *An American Dilemma*.   Bunche's intermediary function was essential, because African American scholars occupied a position of marginality.

It was because of Bunche and Myrdal's close relationship, which developed during their 1939 tour of the Jim Crow South, that Bunche enjoyed more influence on the project than did other African American social scientists. (Jones, 1993) While both men shared a broad range of sentiments, they disagreed about one key intellectual issue: the validity of Marxism in contemporary society.

Bunche at the time was committed to Marxist ideology as a vision for solving the nation's economic and racial problems. Hardly a solitary ideological stance, his optimistic Marxist perspective reflected the idealism of his radical intellectual circle at Howard University which included such talented African American intellectuals as E. Franklin Frazier, Alain Locke, Eric Williams, W. O. Brown, Charles Wesley, Ernest Just, Charles Thompson, Emmet Dorsey, and Abraham Harris. According to Lewis (2000: 320-321), Henry (1990: 52-53), Meier and Rudwick (1986: 102), and G. Franklin Edwards (1980: 109-129), Howard University, in the 1930s and 1940s, was the center of a progressive and energetic social science faculty which made significant contributions to scholarship on the African Americans. The most outstanding members of the faculty were dubbed the "Young Turks" by historian David Levering Lewis (2000).

Myrdal actually found these younger generation African American scholars appealing---not because he shared their Marxist views, but because he admired their dynamic spirit, which he believed stimulated them to fashion new insights into the nation's racial problems. By contrast, except for early conferences with Monroe Nathan Work and W. E. B. DuBois (Jackson 1990: 90), he shunned the older African American social scientists, because he thought they were incapable of innovative thinking.

Myrdal drew contributions from a diverse range of younger African American social scientists: the socialists and Communists Doxey Wilkerson, Lyonel Florant and James E. Jackson; the sociologists E. Franklin Frazier, Ira de Augustine Reid, St. Clair Drake, Charles S. Johnson, Butler A. Jones, and Horace Cayton; and the psychologists Allison Davis and Kenneth B. Clark. Of the second generation African American scholars highlighted in this volume, St. Clair Drake, Butler Jones, and Horace Cayton participated in the Myrdal study.

Despite the broad range of African American scholars who contributed to the study, it is important to reemphasize, they occupied minor roles Stanfield's description of their roles as "field hands" aptly characterizes Myrdal's approach to most their contributions.

Drake, Jones, and Cayton prepared memoranda. However, Cayton's memorandum was never completed because of intellectual and financial disagreements with Myrdal. (Bracey 1994; Stanfield 1985: 164-174). In contrast, Jones' "Negroes in Atlanta" (1940) memorandum and Drake's collaborative monograph with Allison Davis --"Negro Churches and Associations of Chicago" -- (1940) were used by Myrdal.

The participation of African American sociologists in Myrdal's study provided limited recognition for their scholarship which few first-generation scholars ever experienced. While that experience failed to yield major benefits for their academic careers as it did for those of their white counterparts, it gave them some visibility in mainstream sociology, which aided their later professional mobility after the advent of racial integration, in the 1960s and 1970s, as some of these African American sociologists were hired by predominantly white universities. (Winston 1971: 678-719).

Overall, it seems accurate to say, the intellectual promise of the second-generation African American sociologists was stunted by racial segregation, which blocked their access their access to positions in major research universities and professional recognition and rewards through scholarly productivity.

In retrospect, if these African American sociologists had a single major weakness, it was, as we suggested above, their acquiescence to the assimilationist theoretical model. However, it is important to recognize that their training and limited career options provided them few opportunities to pursue alternative theoretical models without jeopardizing their careers. Mainstream white American sociology hardly tolerated challenges to its dominant theoretical models, and challenges from marginalized African American sociologists would have been easily thwarted. As Key puts it, the "dominant group [of sociologists were] not compelled to question or make sense of most of their values. Many [took them] for granted, as normative, and therefore correct (1975:33-37)." African American sociologists lacked the resources to organize an alternative sociological enterprise. Except for occasional "lone rangers" such as Oliver C. Cox, they steered clear of oppositional paradigms.

Organization of this Book

Most of the chapters in this volume focus on the marginality of these second generation African American sociologists, specifically how they adapted to professional segregation and its consequences for their sociological work. As indicated by the names listed earlier, many worthy scholars could have been included in this volume. Those included were selected because they have been the subjects of extensive research over the years by the contributors. As the readers will notice, some chapters presented in this volume were published earlier in professional journals.

The volume is divided into three sections. The first section consists of chapters that address various theoretical issues pertaining to the works of second generation sociologists. While some of the arguments set forth in the chapters disagree, each constitutes an attempt to provide a coherent interpretation and assessment of the works of particular second generation African American sociologists. The first three chapters, for example, consist of a robust debate between Benjamin P. Bowser and Jerry G. Watts about the nature and significance of these sociologists' theoretical contributions. The Bowser-Watts debate, which can be described perhaps most aptly as an " intellectual rumble," sets forth conflicting interpretations of that generation's intellectual legacy. Addressing a different theoretical issue, Alford Young attempts to transform perceptions of Charles S. Johnson and E. Franklin Frazier by arguing that they went beyond prevailing sociological conceptions to create a new vision of African Americans as a under-developed community. However, one may choose to define and assess African American sociology, the works of Charles S. Johnson and E. Franklin Frazier must figure prominently in that process. The last chapter of the theoretical section presents an earlier published article by Wilbur Watson which seeks to provide an analytical conception of African American sociology as a distinct mode of discourse. Written during the period of 1960s racial strife when a new more radical generation of African American sociologists were moving onto the intellectual stage, Watson's chapter reflects the spirit of that new generation's alienation from mainstream sociology as it seeks to articulate the unique characteristics that set African American sociology apart from other modes of sociological discourse. While none of these chapters explains the African American sociologists' preoccupation with race relations, the chapter by Robert Washington, in the conclusion section of the volume, helps to illuminate the history of that preoccupation by focusing on the strategically important influence exerted by liberal integrationist race relations ideology.

The second section consists of chapters that focus on individual African American sociologists of the second generation. While we hardly claim that these individuals are " representative" of the larger group, we do believe many of their personal experiences accurately reflect the difficult -- if not to say peculiar -- adaptations these sociologists were obliged to make, as minority group members, to a racially segregated sociology profession. This section begins with two chapters on St. Clair Drake written by Benjamin P. Bowser. In addition to providing detailed information about Drake's social background and subsequent education, the chapters reveal fascinating insights into the ordeals he confronted during a career that spanned more than one half-century. In the second chapter in this section, Robert Washington provides an overview of Horace Catyon's enigmatic intellectual career as he explains why Cayton's personal and professional frustrations with racism resulted in his failure to fulfill his exceptional promise as sociologist. Charles V. Willie in the following chapter writes about Walter R. Chivers, who was less well known than Drake and Cayton, as an example of a second generation African American sociologist whose creative talents were manifest primarily through his classroom teaching. Similarly, Anthony Blasi's chapter on Charles Henry Parrish, Jr. highlights the career of a second generation African American sociologist whose major contributions derived from something other than scholarly publications. In Parrish's case, those contributions consisted chiefly of his civic activism, which was guided by insights he derived from his sociological training. In the last chapter in this section, Donald Cunnigen discusses the careers of Daniel C. Thompson and Butler A. Jones, two lesser known sociologists who made important contributions through their organizational activity and research work respectively. He places emphasis on their different career trajectories in predominantly white and black colleges.

The third and concluding section of this volume presents a critical historical overview of sociological works by African Americans. In this chapter, Robert Washington raises questions about the continuing relevance of the liberal vision of racial integration that has operated as a major ideological assumption in the works of black sociologists. Washington suggests that liberal ideological assumptions are now obsolete as he proposes a new direction for black sociology.

We should now say a few words about the shortcomings of this volume. Without question, its lack of material on African American female sociologists constitutes its most glaring limitation. This is not the result of an oversight. We made many efforts over the past several years to locate an author to provide a historical overview and analysis of the careers of African American female sociologists without success. We urge that sociologists give this topic serious attention in the near future. Another shortcoming is the lack of articles on such lesser known second generation sociologists as Tilman Cochran, Ira deAugustine Reid, and Joseph Himes. We planned to have a larger number of chapters on second generation African American sociologists, but ran into many obstacles along the way. In some cases, no one could be found to write the chapter we wanted, and in other cases individuals who promised to produce articles could not meet our deadline because of other commitments.

Despite these shortcomings we hope this volume stimulates debates and more studies exploring the roles of African American sociologists.

References
Abbot, Andrew. 1999. *Development and Discipline--Chicago Sociology at One Hundred*. Chicago, IL: University of Chicago.

_____. 1997. "Of Time and Space: The Contemporary Relevance

of the Chicago School." *Social Forces*. 75: 1149-1182.

Banks, William M. 1996. *Black Intellectuals--Race and Responsibility in American Life*. New York: W. W. Norton.

Bernstein, Richard J. 1972. "Critique of Gouldner's *The Coming Crisis of Western Sociology*." *Sociological Inquiry*. 42: 65-76.

Blackwell, James E. and Morris Janowitz. 1974. *Black Sociologists--Historical and Contemporary Perspectives*. Chicago, IL: University of Chicago Press.

Bracey, John H. 1994. "Informal Interview." Association of Black Sociologists, Los Angeles, California.

_____, August Meier, and Elliott Rudwick. 1971. *The Black Sociologists: First Half of the 20th Century*. Belmont, CA: Wadsworth Publishing.

Bulmer, Martin. 1992. "The Growth of Applied Sociology after 1945: The Prewar Establishment of the Postwar Infrastructure." *Sociology and Its Publics--The Forms and Fates of Disciplinary Organization*. Terrence C. Halliday and Morris Janowitz, editors. Chicago, IL: University of Chicago Press.

Bunche, Ralph J. 1973. *The Political Status of the Negro in the Age of FDR*. Dewey W. Grantham, editor. Chicago, IL: University of Chicago Press.

_____ 1940. Letter to Butler A. Jones. May 27. Ralph Bunche Papers. Box 36. Folders 7, 8. The New York Public Library. Schomburg Center for Research in Black Culture. New York, NY.

_____ 1940. Letter to Butler A. Jones. May 7. Ralph Bunche Papers. Box 36. Folders 7, 8. The New York Public Library. Schomburg Center for Research in Black Culture. New York, NY.

_____ 1940. Letter to Butler A. Jones. March 19. Ralph Bunche Papers. Box 36. Folders 7, 8. The New York Public Library. Schomburg Center for Research in Black Culture. New York, NY.

_____ 1940. Letter to Butler A. Jones. February 20. Ralph Bunche Papers. Box 36. Folders 7, 8. The New York Public Library. Schomburg Center for Research in Black Culture. New York, NY.

_____ 1940. Letter to Butler A. Jones. January 27. Ralph Bunche Papers. Box 36. Folders 7, 8. The New York Public Library. Schomburg Center for Research in Black Culture. New York, NY.

_____ 1940. Letter to Butler A. Jones. January 17. Ralph Bunche Papers. Box 36. Folders 7, 8. The New York Public Library. Schomburg Center for Research in Black Culture. New York, NY.

Conyers, James E. 1986. "Who's Who Among Black Doctorates in Sociology." *Sociologi cal Focus*. 19: 77-93.

Davidson, Douglas. 1977. "Black Sociologists: A Critical Analysis. *Contributions to Black Studies*. 1: 44-51.

Doyle, Bertram W. 1933. "Sociology in Negro Schools and Colleges, 1924-32." *The Quarterly Review of Higher Education Among Negroes*. 1: 7-14.

Drake, J. G. St. Clair and Allison Davis. 1940. "The Negro Churches and Associations in Chicago." Unpublished memorandum prepared for the Carnegie-Myrdal Study.

DuBois, W. E. B. 1899 [1967]. *The Philadelphia Negro--A Social Study*. New York: Schocken Books.

Edwards, G. Franklin. 1980. "E. Franklin Frazier--Race, Education, and Community." *Sociological Traditions from Generation to Generation--Glimpses of the American Experience*. Robert K. Merton and Matilda White Riley, editors. Norwood, NJ: Ablex Publishing Corporation.

Eisenstadt, Shmuel Noah. 1976. *The Forms of Sociology Paradigms and Crises*. New York: John Wiley and Sons.

Fine, Gary Alan. 1995. *A Second Chicago School? The Development of a Postwar American Sociology*. Chicago, IL: University of Chicago Press.

Giddings, Franklin H. 1921. *The Principles of Sociology*. New York: The MacMillan Company.

Gouldner, Alvin W. 1970. *The Coming Crisis of Western Sociology*. New York: Equinox Books.

Greene, Harry Washington. 1946. *Holders of Doctorates Among American Negroes, 1876-1943*. Boston, MA: Meador Publishing Company.

Harris, Robert L. 1987. "The Flowering of Afro-American History." *The American Historical Review*. 92: 1150-1161.

Henry, Charles P. 1990. "Civil Rights and National Security: The Case of Ralph Bunche." *Ralph Bunche--The Man and His Times*. Benjamin Rivlin, editor. New York: Holmes and Meier.

Himes, Joseph Sandy. 1949. "Development and Status of Sociology in Negro Colleges." *Journal of Educational Sociology*. 23: 17-32.

Hines, Ralph H. 1967. "The Negro Scholar's Contribution to Pure and Applied Sociology." *Journal of Social and Behavioral Sciences*. 8: 30-35.

Jackson, Daisy W. 1939. Letter to Butler A. Jones. November 15. Ralph Bunche Papers. Box 36. Folders 7, 8. The New York Public Library, Schomburg Center for Research in Black Culture, New York, NY.

Jackson, Jacquelyne Johnson. 1974. "Black Female Sociologists." *Black Sociologists-- Historical and Contemporary Perspectives.* James Blackwell and Morris Janowitz, editors. Chicago, IL: University of Chicago Press.

Jackson, Walter A. 1990. *Gunnar Myrdal and America's Conscience--Social Engineering and Racial Liberalism, 1938-1987.* Chapel Hill, NC: University of North Carolina Press.

Jones, Butler A. 1993. "Informal Interview." American Sociological Association Meetings, Pittsburgh, Pennsylvania.

_____ 1974. "The Tradition of Sociology Teaching in Black Colleges: The Unheralded Professionals." *Black Sociologists--Historical and Contemporary Perspectives*. James Blackwell and Morris Janowitz, editors. Chicago, IL: University of Chicago Press.

_____ 1940. "The Political Status of the Negro." Unpublished research memorandum prepared for Carnegie-Myrdal Study. Ralph Bunche Papers. The New York Public Library. Schomburg Center for Research in Black Culture. New York, NY.

_____ 1940. Letter to Ralph J. Bunche. May 15. Ralph Bunche Papers. Box 36. Folders 7, 8. The New York Public Library. Schomburg Center for Research in Black Culture. New York, NY.

_____ 1940. Letter to Ralph J. Bunche. February 25. Ralph Bunche Papers. Box 36. Folders 7, 8. The New York Public Library. Schomburg Center for Research in Black Culture. New York, NY.

_____ 1940. Letter to Ralph J. Bunche. January 22. Ralph Bunche Papers. Box 36. Folders 7, 8. The New York Public Library. Schomburg Center for Research in Black Culture. New York, NY.

_____ 1940. Letter to Ralph J. Bunche. January 17. Ralph Bunche Papers. Box 36. Folders 7, 8. The New York Public Library. Schomburg

Center for Research in Black Culture. New York, NY.

_____ 1940. Letter to Ralph J. Bunche. January 14. Ralph Bunche Papers. Box 36. Folders 7, 8. The New York Public Library. Schomburg Center for Research in Black Culture. New York, NY.

_____ 1939. Letter to Ralph Bunche. November 11. Ralph Bunche Papers. Box 36. Folders 7, 8. The New York Public Library. Schomburg Center for Research in Black Culture. New York, NY.

Jackson, Daisy W. 1939. Letter to Butler A. Jones. November 15. Ralph Bunche Papers. Box 36. Folders 7, 8. The New York Public Library. Schomburg Center for Research in Black Culture. New York, NY.

Jones, Rhett S. 1992. "Beginning in An-Other Place: Oppugnancy and the Formation of Black Sociology." *The Griot.* 1: 15-26.

Kelley, Robin D. G. 1990. *Hammer and Hoe--Alabama Communists During the Great Depression.* Chapel Hill, NC: University of North Carolina Press.

Key, R. Charles. 1975. "A Critical Analysis of Racism and Socialization in the Sociological Enterprise: The Sociology of Black Sociologists." Doctor of Philosophy Dissertation. University of Missouri--Columbia.

_____. 1978. "Society and Sociology: The Dynamics of Black Sociological Negation." *Phylon.* 39.

Killian, Lewis M. 1994. *Black and White: Reflections of A White Southern Sociologist.* Dix Hills, NY: General Hall.

Lewis, David Levering. 2000. *W. E. B. DuBois—The Fight for Equality and the American Century, 1919-1963.* New York: Henry Holt and Company.

Logan, Rayford W. 1956. *The Negro in the United States: A Brief History.* Princeton, NJ: Van Nostrand.

McMurry, Linda O. 1985. *Recorder of the Black Experience--A Biography of Monroe Nathan Work.* Baton Rouge, LA: Louisiana State University Press.

Maxwell, William J. 1999. *New Negro, Old Left--African-American Writing and Communism Between the Wars.* New York: Columbia University Press.

Meier, August. 1992. *A White Scholar and the Black Community, 1945-1965--Essays and Reflections.* Amherst, MA: University of Massachusetts Press.

_____ and Elliott Rudwick. 1986. *Black History and the Historical*

Profession, 1915-1980. Urbana, IL: University of Illinois Press.

Merton, Robert K. 1972. "Insiders and Outsiders: A Chapter in the Sociology of Knowledge." *American Journal of Sociology*. 78: 9-47.

Morgan, Gordon D. 1994. *Tilman C. Cothran--Second Generation Sociologist*. Bristol, IN: Wyndham Hall Press.

_____. 1973. "First Generation of Black Sociologists and Theories of Social Change." *Journal of Social and Behavioral Scientists*. 19: 106-119.

Myrdal, Gunnar. 1944 [1962]. *An American Dilemma--The Negro Problem and Modern Democracy*. New York: Harper and Row.

Pettigrew, Thomas F. 1980. *The Sociology of Race Relations--Reflection and Reform*. New York: The Free Press.

Platt, Anthony M. 1990. *E. Franklin Frazier Reconsidered.* New Brunswick, NJ: Rutgers University Press.

Platt, Jennifer. 1996. *A History of Sociological Research Methods in America, 1920-1960*. Cambridge: Cambridge University Press.

Rosenthal, Steven J. 1976. "Does Sociology Have Racist Assumptions?" A paper presented at the Massachusetts Sociological Association meetings. Boston, Massachusetts.

Schwendinger, Herman and Julia R. Schwendinger. 1977. *The Sociologists of the Chair--A Radical Analysis of the Formative Years of North American Sociology (1883-1922)*. New York: Basic Books.

Smith, Charles U. and Lewis M. Killian. 1990. "Sociological Foundations of the Civil Rights Movement." *Sociology in America*. Herbert J. Gans, editor. Newbury Park, CA: Sage Publications.

Southern, David W. 1987. *Gunnar Myrdal and Black-White Relations--The Use and Abuse of An American Dilemma 1944-1969*. Baton Rouge, LA: Louisiana State University Press.

Stanfield, John H. 1993. *A History of Race Relations Research--First Generation Recollections*. Newberry Park, CA: Sage.

__ _____. 1985. *Philanthropy and Jim Crow in American Social Science*. Westport, CT: Greenwood Press.

Sumner, William Graham. 1906 [1959]. *Folkways, A Study of the Sociological*

Importance of Usages, Manners, Customs, Mores, and Morals. New York: Dover Publications.

Ward, Jerry W. 1997. *Trouble the Water--250 Years of African-American Poetry*. New York: Mentor Book.

Wilhelm, Sidney M. 1971. "Equality: America's Racist Ideology." *Radical Sociology*. David Colfax and Jack L. Roach, editors. New York: Basic Books.

Winston, Michael R. 1971. "Through the Back Door: Academic Racism and the Negro Scholar in Historical Perspective." *Daedalus*. 100: 678-719.

Young, Alford A. 1993. "The 'Negro Problem' and the Character of the Black Community: Charles S. Johnson, E. Franklin Frazier, and the Constitution of a Black Sociological Tradition, 1920-1935." *National Journal of Sociology*. 7: 95-133.

Endnotes

1.   The attempt at periodization by scholars of an African-American historical tradition has had similar problems. According to Robert L. Harris Jr., the historical periodization of African-American scholars has been influenced by the interests and racial emphasis of scholars. John Hope Franklin provided four generations of historical scholarship which corresponded closely with the sociological periods, i. e., first generation 1882-1915; second generation, 1915-1935; third generation, 1935-1950; and fourth and current generation, 1950 to present. On the other hand, August Meier and Elliott Rudwick began their periodization with 1915. The Meier and Rudwick periods placed emphasis on historians with earned doctorates and significant published works.

Robert L. Harris, Jr., "Review Article--The Flowering of Afro-American History," *The American Historical Review*, 1987, 92: 1150-1161.

PART ONE

Conflicting Conceptions of the Turf: Theoretical Debates on the Social Role of Black Sociologists

Robert E. Washington

The chapters in this section examine theoretical issues pertaining to the work of early black sociologists, with particular emphasis on the implications of their sociological writings on black America, as a distinctive mode of intellectual discourse.

The first chapter by Benjamin P. Bowser, which was published initially in 1981, assesses the role of early black sociologists in mainstream sociology. Bowser begins by asking--did the presence of black sociologists influence the outlook of mainstream American sociology? In response, he argues that, despite the detrimental influence of Robert E. Park and the Chicago School on these black sociologists, they made novel contributions, which mainstream sociology ignored.

In the second essay, published in 1983, Jerry G. Watts launches a robust critique of Bowser's chapter, challenging its interpretation of the social and intellectual history of slavery and subsequent developments in American race relations. Watts also disputes Bowser's assessment of the early black sociologists and provides a more sympathetic reading of both Robert E. Park's views on race relations and E. Franklin Frazier's interpretations of black American culture.

Bowser, in the third chapter--his first opportunity to respond to Watts, submits a rejoinder to Watts' critique. Here, he develops more fully several key arguments that appeared in his first chapter concerning: the social and intellectual history of slavery and American race relations; Park's negative influence on the early black sociologists; and their novel intellectual contributions.

The fourth chapter by Alford A. Young, Jr. raises theoretical issues pertaining to the work of second generation black sociologists from a different angle. Focusing on the works of Charles S. Johnson and E. Franklin Frazier, Young suggests that they made unique contributions which both reified and challenged conceptions of the "Negro Problem." Young contextualizes these contributions within the early 20th century American discourse on race.

Finally, in the last chapter of this theoretical section, Wilbur H. Watson attempts to articulate the defining characteristics of black sociology. Published in 1976 when American society was polarized by racial strife, Watson's article, reflecting widespread sentiments among blacks for black intellectual autonomy, sets forth a normatively oriented typology that differentiates black sociology from other varieties of sociological discourse. Watson argues that unlike the latter, black sociology, as a by-product of the racial caste system, possesses a unique critical role. These issues pertaining to black sociology's meaning and role are also addressed in Part III of this volume by Robert Washington who goes beyond Watson's typology.

Chapter 1

The Contribution of Blacks to Sociological Knowledge: A Problem of Theory and Role to 1950

Benjamin P. Bowser

Introduction

In the late 1960s sociology was a popular major for black undergraduates. There was interest among sociologists in what a generation of black scholars might offer the field since it was clear and of great concern that the social sciences were not bias-free. Methods and interpretations of research were conditioned by the scientist's background, experience, and opinions. If blacks and persons from other diverse backgrounds could enter the field, then all would ideally benefit and sociological research, bias withstanding, would reflect and be able to draw on a greater range of talent and experience than it had in the past.

After a decade there is now a question of whether this accommodation and addition of backgrounds and experiences into sociological research has occurred or was ever desired. Indications are that there has been some reaction against integration. If there had been interest in having more black researchers, there might now be more than the few who have completed doctorates in the 1970s, given the large number of majors in the late 1960s and early 1970s. As interested blacks got beyond the introductory and intermediate courses, many found the methods and theories they were expected to adopt inadequate and alienating. They also may have bee given few opportunities to "do something" constructively and creatively with these ideas and procedures in graduate classrooms and committees. Many left the field bitter. The same experience has reduced the ranks of new black sociologists on their first and second appointments. They are finding little support or interest for their work, and tenure is the final judgment.

The present situation leads one to ask another question. Is there a relation between the social uses or the role sociology plays in society and the presence of blacks within the field? We can look at the role of sociology in society by examining its theories and then the contribution or reactions of the past two generations of black sociologists to these theories. I hope to do four things: 1) show the circumstances under which the social sciences emerged, 2) show that the resulting role the social sciences movement took on in England and later in the United States was anti-black, 3) examine the contribution and potential contribution that the first two generations of black sociologists might have made, and 4) provide a historic context of the embattlement of the present and third generation of black sociologists.

The Social Development of the Social Sciences: The Colonial Factor

African slavery made European economic expansion possible in the eighteenth century. (Williams 1966) Initially royal families profited from colonial ventures but soon the merchant (middle) class began to benefit and grow in size and organization. Stock exchanges started in London and Amsterdam reflected a scale of wealth known only to ancient Venice. (Hayes 1962:. 121; 1943: 210) It was the accumulation of colonial wealth by this long suppressed merchant class that gave birth to the industrial revolution as an attempt to further expand trade and to improve communications and manufacturing. (Sombar 1967: 139)

The cultural leanings of these commercial-minded urbanites were in the intellectual systems of men who represented these historic developments. Francis Bacon (1561-1626) was the model of an urban commercial-minded secularist who developed a philosophical expression of the new sciences. He set the stage for a social science movement with his *The Advancement of Learning*, in which he advocated not more piety but rather experimentation, induction, and more scientific knowledge as a way of improving life. Free from Church dominance (advocated by Thomas Hobbes' *Leviathan* in 1651), sovereigns struggled against each other for colonial control (case in point the Thirty Years War, 1616-1648); but, as one could expect, they soon found themselves in conflict with their influential urban merchants. The transitions in this conflict are exemplified by John Locke's "Of Civil Government" and by Montesquieu's *The Spirit of the Law*. For Locke, one of the major ways that a ruler could practice tyranny was by interfering with commerce, while Montesquieu held that a popular legislature was partly necessary for fair trade regulation. The commercial motive behind this movement toward "popular" government was more forcefully expressed by David Hume in *Essays: Moral, Political and Literary*, in which he singled out specifically foreign trade and taxes as an area which government should not regulate. But he only set the stage for the more sophisticated "laissez-faire" argument of Adam Smith in *An Inquiry into the Nature and Causes of the Wealth of Nations*.

Ironically, the Industrial Revolution and the growth of commercial merchant classes would not have been possible if it were not for the labor of Africans. Blacks were capital-generating property. (Williams: 5, 35-7) What made foreign commerce profitable for both England and France was slave labor; without it there possibly never would have been an Adam Smith, a David Hume, a Louis XIV, or a Francis Bacon. But this is not simply a point of history. The slave-based wealth of England and France also affected intellectual life. Montesquieu's comments on Brazilian cannibals as the lowest form of human existence and David Hume's explanation of an African mathematician as a monkey with a gift for repetition were not uncommon. This was not the doings of brilliant thinkers who were simply prejudiced, but rather that Montesquieu's and Hume's philosophies were racially motivated. To advocate laissez-faire government and unrestricted commerce as the common good and as the basis of national wealth was also to justify continued slavery. Racial inferiority and therefore continued slavery were prime motivations for the growth of the notion of "natural law" which not only justified slavery "scientifically" but also suggested that it was good for Africans since it brought to them the gift of civilization and order.

By the end of the first quarter of the nineteenth century, secular thinkers in England and France began to diverge. St. Simon and August Comte called for a "social physics" --a science, like Newton's physics which could develop a social technology which could transform human society in the same way that physics and other sciences were affecting human material life. A social science was the way to an undreamed-of social utopia as illustrated by their thesis, "plan of the Scientific Operations Necessary for the Reorganization of Society." On the other hand, Herbert Spencer in *First Principles* assumed that "social" laws must be characterized by the persistence and passing of forces as in Physics. (Spencer 1864: 407) Central to Spencer's thesis was the "law of evolution." Societies evolve at different rates from very simple organizations to highly complex divisions of function and labor as in England. These social phenomena were natural laws of society and, because they were natural and in evolution, they were not to be interfered with. An unchanging law was just the opposite of the reform spirit of St. Simon and August Comte. How is it that the English and French differed on this critical point?

There was not coincidence or differing expressions of culture. The French and English variations were rather the outcome of colonial experiences from 1806 which differently affected industrialization in England and France. While England was continuing to expand its empire (after the loss of the thirteen colonies) and to bring in wealth after the pragmatic abolition of slavery in the Empire, the French colonial empire fell apart shortly after that country's revolution. St. Simon and Comte had accurately observed that it was necessary to have a reorganization of metropolitan French society (after almost one hundred years of slave generated colonialism). France's demise was largely due to the successful Haitian revolution (1806) which took away France's most profitable colony. (Nicholas 1974:. 3) Unlike the English, the French could no longer export their discontented to colonies such as South Africa, Australia, Canada, or Louisiana, nor could they stabilize their dislocated rural population by rapid industrialization with cheap foreign resources. On the other hand, the English needed a rationalization for increasing their colonial holdings in order to provide jobs, continue industrial growth at home, and pacify worker discontent. Colonial wealth was vital to England's social stability. (Varga and Mendelson 1940) Thus in France the more attractive social philosophy would have to be concerned with the social reorganization of a France with considerably fewer colonies. In fact, August Comte was critical of the capitalist influences which were having disastrous social impacts in France, (Becker and Barnes 1961, 2:585) while in England (Spencer's) more popular social philosophy provided justification for the existing colonial based society. Both developments reflected the impact of blacks (in Haiti, and by 1840 in Jamaica as well as in South and West Africa) on English and French society and their social thought.

The Emergence of the Social Sciences

By the 1850s, social philosophers were the only ones who could provide believable interpretations and explanations for the effects of the Industrial Revolution. The factory system became the most efficient means of manufacturing and was involving higher proportions of the English and French populations. Though the population was rapidly increasing, the agricultural system was not technically advanced enough to provide a surplus for the rapidly increasing urban labor force. Despite vast wealth in industrial Europe, the poor seemed everywhere and were rapidly increasing, and everyone (even the wealthy) experienced considerable hardship after a crop failure. There were ample defenders of the existing order such as Hume, Smith, Spencer, and Benthan; economic liberalism held that continued capitalism was part of the natural order and therefore good. One of the most significant of liberals was the Reverend Thomas Chalmers, who opposed government taxation and aid to the poor. Chalmers suggested in his *Christian and Civic Economy of Large Towns* (1820-26) that to view the poor uniformly was incorrect and wasteful; each "case" of poverty should be taken singularly and handled according to its circumstance. This was the only way of distinguishing the honest from the dishonest poor.

The social sciences in England and the United States were developed out of the defense of the newly evolving industrial society by Locke, Montesquieu, Hume, Smith and Spencer. By 1850, neither Sociology nor other contemporary social sciences had clearly emerged from the congery of ideals which consisted of utopian socialism, Spencerian evolutionism, economic liberalism, the case work ideal of Chalmers, the political science of Hume, Montesquieu, and Locke, as well as the economics of Adam Smith. (Aron 1968: 13) It seemed as if a distinct "sociology" at this point could have been any of these expressions. But by the second half of the nineteenth century, the more conservative tradition of Spencer and the social Darwinists dominated in England, while the economic liberalism of Chalmers' case study approach survived in social work. It was these two lines of thinking which were exported to the industrial United States and within which the first generation of blacks in American 'sociology' had to work.

The First Generation: Dubois, Haynes, And Daniel

Contrary to popular belief, the first expressions of sociology in the United States did not start with W. G. Summer and Lester F. Ward in the early 1900s. They began with Henry Hughes' *Treatise on Sociology* (1854) and George Fitzhugh's *Sociology of the South:* or *The Failure of Free Society* (1854). Both defended slavery as economic necessities and as part of the natural order. (Frazler 1947: 265-71) Hughes' and Fitzhugh's arguments were precisely those of the English evolutionist (Spencerian) defense of the colonies. One could gather from Hughes and Fitzhugh the growing sense of conflict between the American North's agenda for wealth by industrialization and the Southern view that the nation should continue its basis of wealth through the plantation economy. By 1865 there was no longer an issue; the Southern economic system lay in ruin from the Civil War. The economics of slavery which Hughes and Fitzhugh had sought to defend was no more, and the evolutionist idea of a natural order of superior to inferior man was at the core of sociological thinking and now knew no distinction between North and South. Men quite literally inherited through selected evolution differential mental capacities, civilization, morals, and, of course, physical characteristics. (Curtis 1943) More importantly, this differential inheritance followed racial ancestry and explained the favorable status of some and the misery of most others, especially blacks. (Becker and Harris 1932: 211-16)

The first sociologists of the new Northern economic order were advocates of this Social Darwinism and were direct intellectual descendants of Herbert Spencer. William G. Sumner, Lester F. Ward, and Franklin Giddings had all read Spencer and acknowledged his influence on them. At core there was little difference between their fundamental assumptions of human society -- there were simply differential developments which produced superior and inferior beings. What distinguished one from the other was how much flexibility they saw in this differential development. Sumner saw none. There were fundamental mores which do not change despite human efforts. (Sumner 1906: 53-55) These mores regulate social relations, including the (inferior) place of blacks in American civilization. Evolution was fixed and was not to be tampered with; if so, the consequences would be far worse. (Sumner 1967: 69) Ward, on the other hand, was influenced by not only Spencer but also by Grimplowicz (*Race and State*, 1875). This combination of philosophies made an interesting sociology. Differences in evolution define social place (Spencer), yet social organization is the product of racial and group conflict (Grimplowicz). Spencer's evolutionary differences were to Grimplowicz the products of struggle between groups rather than genetic inheritance. The success of one group over the other points only to more favorable circumstances. In Grimplowicz's notion, it was not only possible but also favorable that one tried to change "evolution." Ward had a flexible evolutionist thesis; what differentially evolved was not necessarily genes but rather the circumstance or life conditions of a race. (Ward 1883:. 82-83) Finally, Franklin Giddings held that differential evolution was not genetic or the circumstances of group (race) conflict. It was rather a psychic evolution. Consciousness of kind or a likeness constituted an attraction and sympathy of minds; the results were manifested physically in forms such as states, empires, cultures, and group solidarity. (Giddings 1896: 328; Hayes 1973: 330-41) Such an evolution occurs in stages and is indicated by the apparent inability of blacks and other races to develop complex civilizations, in contrast to the races of Western Europe.

Obviously, no blacks could be contributors to this intellectual tradition even if there were some who wished to be. There were blacks before and during W. E. B. DuBois' early years who challenged the Social evolutionists. Among these were Alexander Crummel (*The Future of Africa*, 1862), William W. Brown (*The Rising Son*, 1876), George W. Williams (*History of the Negro Race in America from 1619 to 1880, 1882*), and William H. Ferris (*The African Abroad: His Evolution in Western Civilization, 1913*). (Shepperson 1915: xxi) What is remarkable about all these writers was that they held the same notion about human society and behavior. Life and custom were not directly inherited (Spencer and Sumner); they were not products of evolutionary racial struggle (Grimplowicz), nor were they due to psychically evolved common sentiment (Gidding). They were a response to physical and socially perceived circumstances which were products of other men's purposeful behavior. The accuracy and longevity of this notion over the evolutionists' ideas of the Founding Fathers of American sociology would suggest that men named Crummell, Brown, Williams, and Ferris may have been not only the first American black sociologists but their ideas preceded similar ones of Cooley, Mead, Thomas, Boas, and Du Bois by several decades.

While Sumner was writing his first essay, entitled "The Absurd Effort to Make the World Over" (1894), there were serious social problems which needed examination, explanation, and solutions. American cities started to grow rapidly in size and influence over small towns. Large numbers of European immigrants brought to the American mind a consciousness of cultural difference, their own nativism, and the question of whether or not assimilation was desirable, or even possible. The closing of the frontier forced Americans to look at themselves more closely than ever before. Urban life literally redefined and intensified the individual's sense of self, and blacks were moving out of the South.

These rapidly developing conditions were not discussed by the existing academic disciplines. Nor did the imported social philosophy of Herbert Spencer show promise in addressing these issues. In fact, there was no better conservative defense of the new industrialists and their abuses than Spencerian sociology (William Sumner). It was no wonder that sociology was totally inadequate in explaining the developing social conditions or in suggesting ways to improve social problems. Sumner's Ward's, and Giddings' sociology had the same role as Spencer's in England, and in the slave South Hughes and Fitzhugh were laissez_faire defenders of the existing order. But to do nothing and to call it the "natural order," mores of society, or the product of racial struggle was intolerable and not in keeping with the activist American character.

Just as the potential contribution of early black historians (Crummel, Brown, and Williams) to sociology was ignored, so also was that of W. E. B. DuBois. It is ironic that the first "empirical" study of an American community was done by a black man. (Baltzell 1899: ix, xxv-xxvii) *The Philadelphia Negro* (1898) was produced in the very spirit of induction and observation advocated by Francis Bacon more than two centuries before the emancipation of blacks from slavery; it could have served well as a model of community study and as a way of going about finding out precisely the sort of information which was then needed about America's troubled urban communities. But since both DuBois and his study were dismissed as being of no particular importance to the field, his potential for academic leadership was never actualized. (Rudwick) He was the product of three interrelated intellectual traditions which were ignored by the sociology of Sumner, Ward, and Gidding. First, freed black communities had a long tradition of activism which served a vigorous campaign against slavery and the ideas which defended it. (Rousseve 1937) Second, the social work movement which was inherited from England was developing its own theoretical expressions and was in fact closer to actual human problems and life than the academic sociologists were. Ironically, it was the social workers who were at the earliest time receptive to the idea of empirical community studies. (Booth 1902) And finally, the white abolitionist tradition continued to serve as a basis for financial and intellectual support against the racism of the Social Darwinists. In the case of DuBois, the Quaker influenced University of Pennsylvania rather than the University of Chicago under Albion Small, or Columbia (Gidding) or Wisconsin (Ross) supported his social work related study of Philadelphia's Seventh Ward.

To do a community study or to protest slavery never meant that one was devoid of theory. The anti-slavery struggle and the historic research into its origins produced one of the first American conceptions that human achievement or degradation are the results of social and economic behaviors rather than genes, evolution, or the curse of God. Of course, abolitionists, social workers and free black intellectuals were not the only ones to perceive society in this fashion. There were European scholars who objected to the Spencerian evolutionary determinism and who also suggested the independent role of "social" causes. They were theorists such as Emile Durkheim (*Suicide*), Max Weber (*The Methodology of the Social Sciences*), George Simmel (*The Conflict in Modern Culture*), and Gabriel Tarde (*The Laws of Imitation*). Supposedly, these writers were read by the first generation of American sociologists and were reputed to have been influenced by them. (Williams, Jr. 1976) If so, their impact was minimal.

One can only imagine what the early sociology would have been and what impact it might have had on the nation had it taken the social work movement seriously, had it been genuinely influenced by its European counterparts, and had it given Du Bois' *The Philadelphia Negro* the place it deserved. In the more contemporary reviews of the early sociological Fathers, the racist and theoretical closure on race and society (their ideas about the first were not separated from the second) were conveniently forgotten and their alleged appreciation of social and economic causes reassured. (Williams, Jr. 1976) DuBois was not the first nor the last scholar to produce a work of potential but unwanted merit to sociology. *The Philadelphia Negro* was quickly followed by George Haynes' *The Negro at Work in New York City*, Edward Daniel's *In Freedom's Birthplace*, and Mary W. Ovington's *Half a Man*. All of these studies, like DuBois' work, were empirical observational studies of black communities, social welfare sponsored, and produced before the Robert Parks Chicago research tradition.

By the 1920s, the evolutionism of the Founding Fathers began to give way to a variety of intellectual influences from other fields. Franz Boas' rejection of "cultural laws" and particularistic field research method pointed out all of the contradictions of the evolutionist reductionism. (Harris 1968: 254) The biologists, Francis Galton and Karl Pearson demonstrated the distinction between genetic and racial populations. The former population is highly flexible and internally diverse while the latter is only a social conception of little biological significance. but the sociologists who worked after Sumner Gidding, and Ward did not abandon completely the early evolutionist intent.   Their thoughts were either modified to incorporate social causality or their social causality notion advocated that causality was of fixed influences and conditions. (Gossett 1965; Frederickson 1971; Hayes: 332-41)

A good example of a fixed conditionality thesis was that of Howard Odum, a student of the racist Edward Ross. Odum held that although Negroes had the potential to achieve and to be culturally indistinguishable from whites, their moral character was defective and would therefore not provide the motivation to take advantage of their potential for achievement. (Odum 1910) A more interesting rationale was that of James Mark Baldwin's recapitulation thesis. As a child develops into an adult, the youngster's mental development passes through all stages of evolution.   Baldwin 1895) Of course, some groups develop mentally, if not physically, to higher stages. Charles Ellwood, *Sociology and Modern Social Problems* (1910) and, surprisingly, Charles Cooley held the same position.

In Cooley's case, we see a tragic reflection of social influence on a major theorist. Despite his identifying with the Evolutionists, he uniquely defined the individual self as "social" rather than instinctual (William McDougal) or phenomenological (Rene Descartes). The self is an expression of our perception of our appearance to others, perception of their judgment of us and of self--perception (a looking-glass self). (Cooley 1922) Cooley's notion is of timeless analytic merit.   One would think that it would have been deduced easily that the alleged moral, instinctual, or broadly evolutionary defects of Negroes were actually the historic and continued impact of their being negatively perceived by whites and by themselves because of their impotency to make changes in the larger social environment. Instead, Cooley had to twist his own theory and assert that the races have distinct temperaments and capacities and regardless of circumstance would break into caste. In time, mental as well as biological differences had to occur. (Hayes: 337-38; Frazier, p. 266) It was obviously a difficult task for some sociologists to accept a social theory which accounted for dynamic group differences and at the same time accept the prevailing conventional wisdom of inferiority of Negroes. The same ambivalence can be found in W. I. Thomas before his Polish research experience. (Zanieck) He was impressed early in his career with the centrality of instincts disposing differential capacities to manipulate environment.

The result of this seemingly slow acceptance of conditionality (social causation) in social theory was that after Odum, Baldwin Ellwood, and Cooley social theory no longer directly reflected racial opinion, as it did with Sumner, Ward and Gidding. From this point on, social theory appeared "neutral" and one could not know an author's opinion or theoretical application to race unless the writer addressed the topic.   Secondly, while evolutionists held racial categories to be virtually absolute, the new theoretic developments were parallel to evolutionist thought in their acceptance of the idea of there being few worthy exceptions to an otherwise defected race. And finally, since Negroes theoretically could be changed, given the right environment, it was the mission of fair-minded whites to advocate racial reform or accommodation. (Thomas 1896) It was obvious that blacks had no place in formal sociology and that DuBois, Haynes, and Daniels were outsiders.

The Second Generation: Johnson, Frazier, Doyle, Drake, And Reid

The social and professional context as outsiders changed for the second generation of blacks, Johnson, Frazier, Doyle, Drake and Reid, as they entered sociology through the University of Chicago.

While the first generation, DuBois, Haynes and Daniels, were ignored and of necessity independent of the early university centers, Chicago, Wisconsin, and Columbia, the second generation was "sponsored" as graduate students and in research, remarkably enough by W. I. Thomas (after *Polish Peasant*), Albion Small and Robert Park. (Rudwick, Robbins and Edwards) I should point out that this emerging interest in patronizing blacks was not limited to the University of Chicago. It was paralleled by the support whites gave to the Harlem Renaissance of "Negro" arts, letters, and popular entertainment. This was also the period when the Negro theatre came upon increasing economic pressure to be managed and sponsored by white business interests for white audiences. (Mitchell 1967: 53)

There was a great deal of concern for the race problems resulting from increasing numbers of blacks migrating to American cities. Undoubtedly, Robert Park was one of the concerned. Since Park was most directly responsible for the Chicago School of Sociology and for bringing blacks into it, he should be the key to the role blacks (Johnson, Frazier, Doyle, Drake, Cayton) were expected to play. There were two important points: first, Park was closer in thought to Booker T. Washington than to W. E. B. DuBois; and second, Park's ecological thesis was far more revealing of his idea of society than his race relations theory. The ecological thesis was like that of Odum, Ellwood, Baldwin, and the early Thomas; it was a transitional notion bridging social conditionality with social Darwinism. There was a "natural" ecological law by which certain urban conditions emerged. (Park: 24)

In reading Park and the Park inspired Chicago studies one is given social organizational variations in gangs (L. Thrasher, *The Gang*, 1936), delinquency (McKay and Cottrell, *Delinquency Areas*, 1929), dereliction (N. Anderson, *The Hobo*, 1923, suicide (R. Cavan, *Suicide*, 1928), mental illness (Faris and Dunham, *Mental Disorders in Urban Areas*, 1939), drug addiction (B. Dai, *Opium Addiction in Chicago*, 1937) and family instability (E. Mowrer, *Family Disorganization*, 1927). But the explanation for these variations was an overriding ecological order that one can easily take as a "natural law" or first principle. Park apparently did not see variations in social organization and the resulting distribution of social problems as a direct outgrowth of other social facts, in particular, interest-group related behaviors. An objection to an interest-group notion might certainly be one reason why Park had a close relation with Booker T. Washington, who reaffirmed a segregated "natural" order, rather than to W. E. B. DuBois, who by this time was doing his best to change the existing social ecology.

When Charles Johnson entered the University of Chicago he must have had a definite place and role. His role was to be a race scholar and his place was to do research where Park and other whites could not, among blacks. An unintended consequence of the urbanization of blacks was increased race consciousness and the social isolation of blacks from whites. The result was that whites could not observe blacks nor get their cooperation to comment on the race situation. Probably on the agenda for Johnson was the production of some ecological studies of a social problem in the Chicago black community. Apparently he was willing in both role (race scholar) and place (*The Negro in Chicago*, 1919), but did not produce any ecological studies. One reviewer suggests that Johnson may not have finished his degree under Park; instead he went to New York and became editor of *Opportunity* magazine (Robbins: 60) and then went South, where he produced work within the DuBois-Haynes-Ovington-Daniels social work tradition. Charles Johnson's works are to this day classic expressions of social conditionality: *Shadow of the Plantation*, *Patterns of Negro Segregation*, and *Growing Up in the Black Belt*.

E. Franklin Frazier had a different experience from that of Charles Johnson. His thesis and early post-graduate work used the ecological thesis to discuss variations in black family organization, *The Negro Family in Chicago*, and of social class, "Negro Harlem: An Ecological Study." His later work utilized W. I. Thomas' theory of social organization and disorganization. (Edwards: 111) Intellectually, Frazier in comparison with Johnson remained close to Park and Thomas. Ironically, it is Park-Thomas influence which has come under fire in contemporary reviews of Frazier's work on the black family. It was also not insignificant that Frazier rather than Johnson was elected President of the American Sociological Association in 1948. Frazier's election was consistent with the low regard the sociologists of Albion Small gave to the DuBois inspired sociology. The differences between Johnson's and Frazier's work have been overlooked primarily because, by the later 1940s, the segregation of blacks from mainstream sociology paralleled the separation in sociologists' minds of social theory from race relations. What happens in society between the races in as much a part of the social order as any other social event. Race relations should be characterized within general social theory and not separated and discussed with no general social context. Frazier and Johnson also had differing methodological foci. Johnson used interviews and personal histories, and did intensive field work, while Frazier relied more on case histories and census materials. What is important in their approaches was the differing concentrations on field work and primary as opposed to secondary data.

The potential contribution which Charles S. Johnson rather than E. Franklin Frazier could have made at the time to general sociology was not in the defining of a new theory and way of doing research. Johnson's example was of more reliance on participant observation, getting primary information from field work, and giving more attention to historically conditioned behaviors and inductively derived generalizations. In the attention given to historic impact and to social mobility Charles Johnson's work was far more thorough than William L. Warner's. But Johnson's work was relegated (segregated) to race relations not simply because Johnson was black; his work also suggested a theoretic posture (social conditionality) with which many sociologists in the 1920s and early 1930s were still uncomfortable. An appreciation of Johnson's work would have had to place it next to Robert and Helen Lynd's *Middletown* and *Middletown in Transition* and William L. Warner's **Yankee City Series**.

Both the Lynds and Warner were trained as cultural anthropologists rather than as sociologists out of the Sumner-Park tradition. It must be remembered that Franz Boas and his students helped to discredit Social Darwinist sociology. The Boas tradition rejected speculative armchair theorizing as well as the idea of social laws or specifically natural laws. The only way one could learn about communities was through participant observation and induction. (Harris: 261) This approach was almost identical to that of DuBois and Johnson.

St. Clair Drake, Cayton, Reid, and Doyle, who later left sociology altogether, enter the field as Robert Park's Theoretical influence was waning. They obviously had the same role and place as did Johnson and Frazier, but their exposure was not along the ecological lines. Their work reflected the counter-tradition of a Boas-influenced William L. Warner. *Black Metropolis* by Drake and Cayton was in method and sponsorship closer to DuBois and Johnson than was as to Frazier, and uncompromisingly expressed a social conditionality thesis -- one's group life circumstances are the results of another's intent and behavior. Drake and Cayton, like DuBois and Johnson, paid closer attention to historic and mobility backgrounds than did Warner. Their observation, along with that of Oliver Cox, that there are social values and beliefs which vertically divide distinct social classes, is a point of potential use in general sociology. But like their predecessors, Drake and Cayton's *Black Metropolis* and Oliver Cox's *Caste, Class and Race* (1948) were isolated in race relations research. Their work simply did not fit into the needs or interests of white sociologists.

World War II signaled the end of Western political colonialism; indeed, as some whites had feared, the tide of color was rising. This was further complicated by the West's international rivalry with the community and socialist world. (Padmore) Suddenly, the United States racial situation took on a new importance. Segregation, lynchings, and other abuses were now embarrassing to the nation's international image, and blacks had the potential to be both a "colored" enemy within or an ally. It was necessary therefore to assert a national policy on race relations. The need was important enough to warrant the kind of innovative effort which went into the social scientific research on troop morale and management during the second world war. (Stouffer 1949) Instead of being asked to direct the study, Frazier, Johnson, Drake, and others such as Ralph Bunche and Kenneth Clark were commissioned to do field reports. Could a project of such importance be headed by a black? In order to show impartiality and to lend "more credibility" to the project, a Swedish social scientist, Gunnar Myrdal, was invited to head the study. His research associate was another white, the American Arnold Rose, who was a junior in both experience and scholarship to the study's major black contributors. (Edwards: 133) The result was *An American Dilemma* (1944), which turned out to be largely the work of Arnold Rose since Myrdal was absent for a year of the project due to the war.

An American Dilemma's thoroughness of content is to the credit of its contributors. The problem arises with the summary and policy recommendations. The black community was summarized as a pathological expression of American society sustained by segregation. (Myrdal 1944) The solution was an integration (undefined) which would come about due to the moral character of the American people. (Myrdal 1944: 210, 1003-04) What was on the surface a progressive and enlightened viewpoint relative to the segregation of the 1940s was in fact an unintentional throwback to Gidding, Odum, and Ellwood. Blacks as a collectivity were pathological (defective), but some individual blacks were redeemable. The only positive note was that the reason for this defect was not instinct, evolution, or ecology but rather the behavior of others namely whites. If *An American Dilemma* had suggested that the black community is of itself normal but distorted because of discrimination and segregation then it would have been correct. But his was not clearly said and the result was a broad and tragic distortion of the viewpoints and contribution of its contributors. The idea that the white community would resolve the contradiction between its beliefs and its behavior toward blacks because of its moral character results in a characterization of white community life as simply normal and basically moral in contrast to black community life as pathological.

The succeeding years witnessed the reputation of the Boasian tradition of research within sociology and the introduction of an updated evolutionism, Talcott Parsons' *The Social System.* The Parsonian structured-functionalism paralleled Spencer's evolutionism at a time when more aggressive and insightful field work was needed. For Parsons, the status, role place and function of social actors was fluid within a social system which maximizes its own stability and has differing levels of sophistication and division of labor. (Parsons 1951) In fact, Parsons claimed that the American social system was an evolutionary outgrowth of older, less specialized social systems.

Needless to say, after *An American Dilemma* blacks virtually disappeared from sociology. By the early 1960s, with the exception of Drake, the second generation had passed or found their way into other pursuits, and there was no new generation to carry on. the few blacks still in the field were effectively isolated in the South away from mainstream sociology and would not have been allowed to contribute even if they had the circumstance to do so. (Jones, pp. 121-63) The failure of blacks to have an impact on sociology is due to no shortcoming on their part. The loss is that of the science.

References

Aron, Raymond. 1968. *Main Currents in Sociological Thought.* New York.

Baldwin, James M. 1895. *Mental Development in the Child and in the Race.* New York.

Baltzell, E. Digby. 1967 [1899]. "Introduction." *The Philadelphia Negro.* W. E. B. DuBois. New York.

Becker, Howard and Barnes, Harris. 1961. *Social Thought from Lore to Science,* 3 Vols. New York.

Booth, Charles. 1902. *Labour and the Life of the People*, 1889-1891. London: Hull House Papers and Maps.

Cooley, Charles Horton. 1922. *Human Nature and the Social Order.* New York.

Curtis, Curtis. 1943. *The Growth of American Thought.* New York.

Edwards, G. Franklin. 1974. "E. Franklin Frazier." *Black Sociologists.* James E. Blackwell and Morris Janowitz, eds. Chicago.

Frazier, E. Franklin. 1947. "Sociological Theory and Race Relations." *American Sociological Review.* 12 (June): 265-71.

Frederickson, George. 1971. The *Black Image in the White Mind.* New York.

Giddings, Franklin H. 1896. *The Principles of Sociology.* London.

Gordon, Milton. *Social Class in American Society.*

Gossett, Thomas. 1965. *Race.* New York.

Harris, Marvin. 1968. *The Rise of Anthropological Theory.* New York, 1968.

Hayes, Carlton J. et. al. 1962. *History of Western Civilization Since 1500.* New York.

Hayes, James. 1973. "Sociology and Racism," *Phylon.* 34 (December): 330-41.

Fay Karpf, Faye. 1932. *American Social Psychology.* New York.

Mitchell, Loften. 1967. *Black Drama.* New York.

Nicholas, David. 1974. *Economic Dependence and Political Autonomy: The Haitian Experience.* Montreal.

Odum, Howard W. 1910. *Social and Moral Traits of the Negro.* New York.

Robbins, Richard. 1974. "Charles Johnson" *Black Sociologists.* James E. Blackwell and Morris Janowitz, eds. Chicago.

Rousseve, Charles B. 1937. *The Nigro in Louisiana.* New Orleans.

Rudwick, Elliott. 1974. "W. E. B. Du Bois as Sociologist." *Black Sociologists.* James E. Blackwell and Morris Janowitz, eds. Chicago.

Shepperson, George. 1915. "Introduction." W. E. B. Du Bois, *The Negro.* London.

Sombart, Werner. 1967. *The Quintessence of Capitalism.* New York.

Spencer, Herbert. 1864. *First Principles.* New York, 1864., p. 407.

Sumner, William G. 1906. *Folkways.* London.

Thomas, W. I. 1896. "The Scope and Method of Folk Psychology," *American Journal of Sociology.* 1 (January).

Timasheff, Nicholas S. 1967. *Sociological Theory.* New York.

Usher, A. 1943. *The Early History of Deposit Banking in Mediterranean Europe.* Cambridge.

Varga, E . and Mendelson, L. 1940. *New Data for V. I. Lenin's Imperialism* New York.

Ward, Lester F. 1883. *Dynamic Sociology* (New York, 1883), pp. 82_83.

Williams, Eric. 1966. *Capitalism and Slavery.* .New York.

Williams, Robin M. 1976. "Sociology in America." *Social Science Quarterly.* 51 (June 1976): 81

Chapter Two

On Reconsidering Park, Johnson, DuBois, Frazier and Reid: Reply to Benjamin Bowser's "The Contribution of Blacks to Sociological Knowledge."

Jerry G. Watts

The intent of this essay is to redress some of the conceptual and factual errors contained in Benjamin Bowser's essay, "The Contribution of Blacks to Sociological Knowledge: A Problem of Theory and Role to 1950," which was published in *Phylon* (June, 1981). In refuting some of Bowser's contentions I hope to address the issue of Robert Park's relationship with a developing black sociological tradition, the nature of that tradition, the reasons behind the inability presently to analyze that generation and Robert Park, in an honest and analytically nuanced manner.

Phylon committed an error in publishing Bowser's article. Simply put, the article was riddled with errors and misconceptions. Realization that he was attempting to offer a critique of sociology, a discipline in which the founder of *Phylon* labored so audaciously, demands that the conceptual faultiness and rather shoddy scholarship of Bowser's article be corrected.

The first major problem in Bowser's essay stems from his attempt to explain too much in too limited space. Any intellectual exercise which attempts to critique in thirteen pages the evolution of sociological thought from sixteenth century Francis Bacon to the United States in the 1940s must of necessity produce generalizations so tenuous and broad in scope as to render sophisticated analysis impossible.

Bowser (1981: 181) begins by informing us that "African slavery made European economic expansion possible in the eighteenth century." Restating the argument of Eric Williams in *Capitalism and Slavery*, (1944) he tells us that the accumulation of wealth as a result of slave exploitation financed the industrial revolution. As Immanuel Wallerstein (1974: 88) notes, Williams had argued that the per capita profit on slavery was small. As such, slavery could only exist profitably provided the number of those enslaved was large. Because of the absence of a need for technological innovation, slavery was "preeminently a capitalist institution geared to the early pre-industrial stages of a capitalist world economy."

During this time social thought was emerging in Europe which not only advanced secularism but began as well the process of thinking about scientific knowledge as a way of bettering life. Bowser presents Hobbes, Locke and Montesquieu as examples of thinkers who both advanced this secular tradition and offered political theoretical rationalizations which justified the existence of private property. As purveyors of a belief in "popular" government they were but handmaidens for the emergence of the free market (Machperhson 1970).[1] Adam Smith became the most sophisticated exponent of those policies which they had generated.

Bowser runs into difficulty when he attempts to describe too strong a link between slavery and European social thought. He claims that slavery affected European intellectual life in a more direct and concrete fashion than its impact on European industrialization. We are told that the racist/racialist views of Hume and Montesquieu cannot be considered merely prejudiced appendages to their thought but rather as the crux of it. That is, by advocating laissez-faire government and unrestricted commerce, they were in effect justifying slavery. In fact, Bowser claims that laissez-faire government and unrestricted commerce were advocated in order to justify slavery. Furthermore, he contends, the rise of the idea of "natural law" was motivated by desires to continue slavery.[2]

Bowser errs when he implies that the intellectual defense of the free-market arose as an instrumental defense of slavery. In the case of Hume, a defense of slavery was explicitly stated. Though Hume may have felt the need to morally legitimate the slave trade, he did not do so by hiding behind a defense of laissez-faire capitalism but by claiming outright "Negro inferiority" (Popkin   1977-78).

Furthermore, Bowser's linkage between the rise of natural law and slavery is rather problematic. For instance, though defending slavery, Hume was opposed to the idea of natural laws. Certainly natural laws could have been used to defend slavery, but they could serve as the basis for the idea of universal equality (Davis 1966).[3] A belief in natural law influenced Jefferson to include in the Declaration of Independence, "We hold these truths to be self-evident, that all men are created equal, that they are endowed by their creator with certain inalienable rights, among these are life, liberty, and the pursuit of happiness." We should conclude that many eighteenth century thinkers felt a need to legitimate slavery. We cannot conclude a la Bowser that their entire philosophical enterprise centered around such a defense.

In crucial ways Bowser raised a false problem. The issue is not whether a defense of laissez-faire capitalism offered a closet defense of slavery. Eighteenth century Europeans had access to common racist/racialist traditional ideas which could have been used to legitimate slavery. Winthrop Jordon (1971) and David Bryon Davis (1966, 1975) have presented elaborate studies of the way in which slavery as an institution was justified and criticized in Europe during the seventeenth and eighteenth centuries. There was, so to speak, "no need" for pro-slavery advocates to hide behind an economic ideology.

Secondly, laissez-faire capitalism endured long after the ending of the slave trade in England. In some ways one can claim that slavery declined when it became no longer profitable. One cannot however claim as Bowser's argument would suggest that laissez-faire capitalism declined upon the demise of slavery.

Bowser argues that the two traditions dominating European sociological thought during the initial stages of the development of American sociology were the Social Darwinist views of Herbert Spencer and the economic liberalism of the Reverend Thomas Chalmers.[4] In America Spencer's greatest proponent was William Graham Summer. According to Bowser, Chalmer's thought which survived in social work had as its greatest early American proponent W.E.B. DuBois. Ultimately the disciples of Spencer dominated early American sociological thought. It was within a Social Darwinist intellectual milieu that the first generation of black sociologists emerged.

In one sense Bowser is correct in asserting that Social Darwinism and, more precisely, the metaphysical speculation of Herbert Spencer, dominated the intellectual milieu in which the first generation of black sociologists emerged. However, Bowser does not realize that sociology as the academic discipline we know today arose in response to

Spencer's thought. In a review of Spencer's **Principles of Sociology,** Albion Small, the founder of the Chicago school, wrote in 1897, "Yet Mr. Spencer 's sociology is of the past, not of the present. It has a permanent place in the development of sociological thought. Present sociology, however, is neither Spencerianism nor is it dependent upon anything Spencenian."[5]   For Bowser to write as if black sociologists were the primary ones interested in refuting Spencer is clearly incorrect. Sociology was begun in the United States with the mandate of refuting Spencer. The change in orientation which allowed Small to declare Spencerianism of the past was a change away from the search for social laws in behalf of discovering principles upon which social policies could be based (Therborn 1976). Spencerianism was no longer useful because such grand theorizing provided little theory that could be used in "applied sociology." Of course, contrary to Small's pronouncement, Spencer had yet to completely die. Through the works of William Graham Summer and Frank Giddings, Spencerian thought would continue for years to come. However, Small had clearly perceived the wave of the future, a perception that allowed him through the University of Chicago to develop a sociology program that would far outlive the dead end orientations of similar departments at Columbia (Giddens) and Yale (Summer) (Therborn 1976).

Bowser also states that Alexander Crummel, William Wells Brown, George Washington Williams and William H. Ferris were the first blacks to challenge the Social Darwinist claims of the inferiority of blacks. He then argues that because of their anti-Social Darwinist writings these men should be considered among the first black sociologists. Both claims are erroneous. Crummel, Brown, Williams and Ferris may seem to have challenged Social Darwinism by arguing that the life and culture of blacks were conditioned by social circumstance, but this did not make them sociologists. Essentially, they were participants in the centuries old debate over whether blacks were innately equal or inferior. To write that Wells, Washington, Crummel and Ferris offered a sophisticated sociological critique of Social Darwinism is invalid. Social Darwinism was simply one theoretical apparatus used by racist minded intellectuals to argue that blacks were inferior. Wells, Washington, and others directed their responses not specifically at Social Darwinists but at the entire range of thought which proclaimed innate inferiority of blacks (of which Social Darwinism was but one strain). Essentially what these men offered were historically based counter-assertions to the racist assertions of Spencer and his American disciples.[6]

We should not understate, however, the significance of the writings of these black men. They attempted to offer serious challenges to the prevailing racist interpretations of the Afro-American past. Of particular importance in this vein are George Washington Williams' *History of the Negro Race in America from 1619* to *1880* (published 1882) and the work of a man Bowser overlooks, Thomas Fortune's *Black and White, Land and Capital in the* **South** (published 1884).

The appeal of Social Darwinism as a means of justifying the established order, including the established racial order, was premised upon its supposedly scientific basis appropriated from the writings of Thomas Malthus Jean Baptiste Lamarck and Charles Darwin. Yet its greatest exponent, the British philosopher and social scientist, Herbert Spencer, repeatedly vacillated on what he claimed could be explained by this outlook. More importantly, Bowser's claim that Social Darwinism became the dominant strain of social thought in the emerging sociological discipline needs substantiation.

In fact, there is debate over the degree to Which Social Darwinism dominated popular thinking of the time. The claim by Hofstadter and others that it was the prevailing public philosophy at the turn of the century may in fact be a significant overstatement (Hofstadter 1955).[7] Besides the fact that the term *Social Darwinism,* when defined as the "survival of the fittest," lumps together rather disparate strains of thought, Social Darwinism was consistently seriously challenged throughout its heyday. First of all, at the time when Social Darwinism was supposedly the dominant strain of thought, the prevailing ideology among the American masses centered around the myth of the "self made man."[16] The commonly held belief that in America anyone could rise to the top provided the individual possessed a creative idea, sufficient talent and the industriousness necessary for achievement conflicted directly with the Social Darwinist claim that the elite in society would always be a small number and that everyone who should reach the top is at the top. In some sense Herbert Spencer's doctrine which celebrated a certain environmental closeness for the elite appealed to the vanity of some businessmen (i. e., Andrew Carnegie). Yet even Carnegie was too immersed in espousing the rag-to-riches myth of the day to ultimately adhere fully to Spencer's thought.

Another consistent challenge to Social Darwinism was premised upon a religious critique of Spencer's thought.[8] Not only was Spencer attacked because he was secular but also because the world justified in his writing seemed too close to a dog-eat-dog, barbaric struggle. As Robert C. Bannister informs us in his revisionist study, *Social Darwinism: Science and Myth in Anglo-American Social Thought,* the society envisioned by Spencer during the height of his influence was seen then as unduly harsh (Bannister 1979).

In many ways Herbert Spencer's thought must be seen as more philosophical than social scientific. His thought when simplified in America to the doctrine of "the survival of the fittest" and used as an endorsement of the status quo must be considered merely an ideology. Spencer's thought was difficult if not impossible to refute. It lay outside the realm of proof and refutation. It is for this reason that forty years after Small's initial pronouncement of Spencer's death, Parsons could begin the volume that would revolutionize American sociology, *The Structure of Social Action*, by repeating Crane Brinton's question, "Who now needs Spencer?... We must agree with the verdict. Spencer is dead." (Parsons   1937: 3) Parsons argued that "Social Darwinism marked the epitome of that 'anti-intellectualistic' positivism which, in denying the importance of human intentions and activity, made history an 'impersonal process over which [men] have no control.' His targets were both instinct theory (an extreme of hereditarianism) and behaviorism (an extreme of environmentalism)." (Parsons   1937) Though Parsons offers a rather extensive explanation of what it was that "killed" Spencer (the evolution of scientific theory), for my purposes it will suffice simply to state that Spencer's thought was replaced by another dominant paradigm of social scientific discourse. This new method of approaching the study of society, according to Parsons, was best represented in the rise of Pareto, Durkheim and Weber.

Though Parsons could declare Spencer dead in 1938, in the 1890s when *The Philadelphia Negro* was written, Spencer had yet to "die" (contrary to Small's assertions). DuBois, having been exposed to the new social scientific discourse during his study at the University of Berlin (where he attended the lectures of Max Weber) and earlier under the guidance of Albert Bushnell Hart, realized that he was being exposed to a new approach to social science. Years later in *Dusk of Dawn*, he would write about his intellectual attitudes which led him to study blacks in Philadelphia:

> Herbert Spencer finished his ten volumes of Synthetic Philosophy in 1896. The biological analogy, the vast generalizations, were striking, but actual scientific accomplishment lagged. For me an opportunity seemed to present itself... I was determined to put science into sociology through a study of the condition and problem of my own group. I was going to study the facts, any and all facts, concerning the American Negro and his plight, and by measurement and comparison and research, work up to any valid generalization which I could (Baltzell 1969).

It is not surprising that DuBois' criticism of Spencer as someone who has "transgressed the limits of science" resembled Vilfredo Pareto's criticism of Spencer, "Le positivisme de Herbert Spencer est tour simplement une metaphysique."(Parsons 1937: 181) Thus, we can conclude that DuBois viewed his work as offering refutation of Social Darwinism's leading exponent, Herbert Spencer. William Wells Brown, George Washington Williams and their peers were merely engaging in a broader debate much of which occurred outside the specific borders of sociology.

It is therefore somewhat ridiculous to equate, as Bowser does, the oversight of these black historians by mainstream American sociology with the oversight of DuBois' *The Phiadeiphia Negro*. In some ways George Washington Williams, Alexander Crummel and the others were pre-sociology. We must not forget that the American Sociological Association was not founded until 1905. Though the *American Journal of Sociology* had been founded in 1895, the canons of what constituted social facts, proof, etc. would not emerge with a broad level of consensus until many years later. Though we cannot be certain of the extent the rather early entry of DuBois into American sociology played in the oversight of his work, we cannot ignore the fact that DuBois, unlike the later Frazier and Johnson, wrote his sociological classic before American sociology had become an institutionalized professional discipline. Yet, there seems to be little plausible explanation except racism for the fact that the *American Journal of Sociology* chose not to review DuBois' book.

Bowser sees DuBois' work as a realization of the social work tradition. He claims that DuBois' work was "dismissed as being of no particular importance" not only because DuBois was black but also because he was working within an outcast intellectual tradition, i. e., Chalmers' inspired social work. Bowser claims that because of its dismissal of *The Philadelphia Negro,* American sociology missed its opportunity for progressive maturation.

It is true that *The Philadelphia Negro* was commissioned by the University of Pennsylvania's Sociology Department, through the intervention of social reformer Susan P. Wharton. Yet we cannot accurately explain *The Philadelphia Negro* by attributing DuBois' scholarly outlook merely to Chalmers' inspired social work. The reform minded social work tradition is manifested in *The Philadelphia Negro* through DuBois' willingness to study "social problems" and to recommend solutions to the problems he had highlighted. However, the emphasis on fact-gathering and tight empirical research, which dominated the manuscript, must be attributed to DuBois' exposure in Germany to the new approach to sociology, not the social-reform movement tradition. E. Digby Baltzell points out this duality of influences on DuBois in the introduction to the reissued paperback edition: *"The Philadelphia Negro* was a product of the New Social Science and Settlement House movements. ...(Baltzell 1969: xvl)

Secondly, it is simply historically inaccurate to state that American sociology missed its opportunity for progressive maturation by dismissing *The Philadelphia Negro*. The fact is that much of American sociology went in the direction of *The Philadelphia Negro*.[9] It just never gave DuBois credit for helping to pioneer the way. The essence of Robert Park's urban sociology, which later emerged as the dominant strain of sociology at the University of Chicago, was in effect empirically based, a-theoretical sociology. This should not be surprising, for Park had been exposed to the new social scientific paradigm in sociology through his studies in Germany, where he obtained his doctorate.

However, in some crucial sense, Park's approach to sociology was clearly more theoretically oriented than DuBois'. Park initially had been exposed to sociology through his attendance at the lectures of the ultra-theoretical Georg Simmel. He wrote his dissertation under the guidance of one of the leading neo-Kantian philosophers of the day, Wilhelm Windelband. In some ways Park's inability to ever completely break with Spencerian influenced thought testifies to his fondness for philosophical speculation. What becomes problematical to explain is how Park after this German social theoretical

exposure became such a non-theoretical practitioner of empirical sociology (as seen particularly through the dissertations he helped to direct). Park once described the mandate which greeted him upon entering the sociological profession as, "We had in sociology much theory but no working concepts."(Coser 1971: 357)

It is true that Park possessed a lifelong disdain for social reformers. He did not believe that sociology should be practiced for utilitarian purposes. Yet on occasion he would vacillate on this stance. When doing so, he would claim that sociology if practiced correctly (unbiased) would provide the facts upon which intelligent social reform could be devised. Yet a social reform attitude would always be detectable at or near the surface of the Chicago School of Sociology. In many respects this stems from the fact that Albion Small, the founder of the sociology department at Chicago, believed in social reform sociology. Under Small's guidance, the sociology department set up its own settlement house in Parkington in 1894 with a former Hull House resident in charge (Mathews 1977: 94)

Bowser's claim that social-work-influenced sociology was responsible for social-conditionality theses is not true, however, in the case of

Park. Park, though rejecting social-reform-minded sociology, adhered to a belief in the crucial impact of environment and conditioning on individuals and groups, including blacks. Park acquired his social conditionality thesis not through social work, but through the writings of Franz Boas and his interaction with a fellow Chicago sociologist, W. I. Thomas, co-author of the social conditionality premised *The Polish Peasant in Europe and America* (Mathews 1977).

Thus, we can perceive the gross error in Bowser's claim that the emergence of Robert Park and the Chicago School of Sociology became the force which repressed the social-work-inspired, social-conditionality approach of DuBois and his black contemporaries. Though Park was opposed to social-work-inspired sociology, he was clearly an exponent of a social-conditionality thesis. Insofar as Frazier and Johnson emerge as practitioners of social-reform-minded sociology (concerned about the plight of black Americans), we must not only consider them descendants of Park but descendants of DuBois as well.

Community Studies reached its peak influence upon the publication of *Middletown* in (Lynd and Lynd) 1929 and *Middletown in Transition* in (Lynd and Lynd) 1937. The prominence of these volumes immediately upon their publication should offer *prima face* evidence that sociology did not turn away from studies like *The Philadelphia Negro.*

Bowser continues his erroneous interpretation when writing about the "Second Generation" of black sociologists. This second generation consisted of Charles Johnson, E. Franklin Frazier, Bertram Doyle, St. Clair Drake, Horace Cayton and Ira Reid. Bowser states that they "entered sociology through the University of Chicago." This is factually incorrect, for Ira Reid received his doctorate at Columbia University (Bracey, Rudwick and Meier 1971: 5). Curiously, Bowser is silent about the contributions of other black social scientists in a manner similar to that of the white sociologists he criticizes. He simply does not include in his first generation of black sociologists the man who was probably the most prominent black sociologist of his day, Kelly Miller, and who clearly opposed Spencer's thought (Young 1968; Rieff 1968).[10] Furthermore, where in his list of the second generation are Horace Mann Bond, author of the classic study, *The Education of the Negro in Alabama: A Study in* Cotton *and Steel;* Hylan Lewis, author of *Blackways of Kent;* and Allison Davis, co-author of *Deep South* and *Children of Bondage.* Though Davis can be considered an anthropologist because his doctorate was earned in anthropology, his work was clearly central to the sociological enterprise. Like Drake, whose degree is also in anthropology, but who is considered a sociologist by Bowser, Davis was influenced more by W. Lloyd Warner than Robert Park.

In reference to the second generation, Bowser(1981: 192) erroneously wrote, "St. Clair Drake, Cayton, Reid, and Doyle, who later left sociology altogether, entered the field as Robert Park's theoretical influence was waning.... Their work reflected the counter-tradition of a Boas-influenced William L. Warner." The fact is that Reid entered sociology during the height of Robert Park's influence. We should remember that it was he who replaced Charles Johnson in 1928 as director of research for the National Urban League. The reason Reid appears to have been less affected by Park's thought than Frazier or Johnson is rather obvious. They, unlike Reid, had been trained by Park. Also incorrect is Bowser's analyses of Doyle and Cayton. How can Bowser speak about the emergence of Doyle and Cayton during a period of Park's decline when both men were students of Robert Park? In fact Doyle's thesis, which was written under Park's direction, was an attempt to apply the framework of William Graham Sumner to race relations (Doyle 1937). Like Doyle, Cayton also was a student of Park, though he never received his doctorate. Bowser has created a phony argument. In claiming that Warner was influenced by anthropology, Bowser wants us to think that Park and his students and Waner and his students were partners to a substantive intellectual conflict over research methodology. This is utterly false. In fact ***Black Metropolis***, which Bowser claims as the premier black community study in the Warner tradition, is dedicated to: "The Late Professor Robert E. Park of Tuskegee, the University of Chicago, and Fisk; American Scholar and Friend of the Negro People. ..."[11]

It is true, as Bowser notes, that Robert Park was the central figure in the emergence of blacks within the Chicago School of Sociology. Bowser's discussion of Park becomes flawed thereafter. He states that Park was closer in thought to Booker T. Washington than to W.E.B. DuBois. He argues that Park's ecological theory was far more skewed to a defense of the status quo as "natural" than a defense of social conditionality, which Bowser credits to DuBois. Herein Bowser commits three rather blatant errors. First, in claiming that Washington affirmed segregation as the "natural" order, Bowser simplifies the ideas of a very complex and often contradictory man. Washington's public defense of the interracial status quo was a pragmatic tactical act. Washington did not believe that God [read nature] had dictated the existent Southern racial order. One can criticize Washington's vision of the future for black people but one cannot argue that he believed that the oppression of blacks was dictated by a "natural" law. Second, Washington did not authentically endorse the status quo, for he concertedly believed that he was at the forefront of the correct strategy to change the living conditions of black Americans. He just believed that he could effect such a program by using existent political options available in the South during the turn of the century. Third, Bowser not only simplified and distorted Washington's thought, he has distorted the thought of Robert Park as well. One must be careful when claiming too strong a linkage between Robert Park, the sociologist, and Robert Park, the aide and life-long admirer of Booker T. Washington. It is true that Park worked for seven years as a close aide to Washington. In fact, we now know that Park had been at least co-author of Washington's volume *The Man Farthest Down* (Mathews 1977: 66).

As the Tuskegee machine's primary press agent, Park cannot be considered to have been a passive supporter of Washington. Park clearly used his press agent skills in the service of furthering Washington's influence. On one occasion, after having written a celebratory article on Wilberforce University, Park noted, "We are going to have him [the President of Wilberforce] bound hand and feet after the Wilberforce article appears (Mathews 1977: 77).

Park also clearly shared Washington's distaste for DuBois. Park, as noted elsewhere, maintained a clear distaste for social reformers. He viewed them as trying to alter society from "above." In the peculiar instance of DuBois, Park essentially believed that not only was DuBois advocating too quick a racial change but in doing so he was displaying a lack of faith in the black commoners who could not possibly have followed him had they wanted to.

Undoubtedly, Park learned a great deal from Washington about black life and politics. It must have been fascinating for Park to have been able to observe Washington's political "wheeling and dealing" at close hand. Yet can we argue that Park's sociological analysis of black life was dictated by his exposure to Washington? In some ways yes, but mostly no. Insofar as Park believed not in the use of sociology as a platform for inducing social reform, but in rigid "objectivity," one can claim that he adhered lifelong to a belief in the nature of social change similar to Washington's. As one student of Park's social thought observed, "Park believed that political change need not be 'necessarily' slow or evolutionary [in the classic conservative evasion] but that the *mechanism* would not be that of social engineering - rather, it would be largely through the struggle and transformation of the peoples concerned" (Mathews 1977: 185).

Myrdal blatantly misunderstood Park's approach to social change when he claimed in *An American Dilemma* that Park and his students "transmitted a 'naturalistic and therefore, fatalistic philosophy' with the implication that man can and should make no effort to change the "natural" outcome of the specific forces observed. This is the old do-nothing, *laissez-faire* bias of "realistic" social science." The blatancy of Myrdal's misunderstanding is astounding. Johnson and Frazier in practicing Parkian "objective" social science always assumed that they were working behalf of social change by providing the analysis upon which social reforms could be based. Furthermore, it was the absence of a deference towards "objectivity" that had made sociology so racist prior to DuBois' and Park's entry into race-relations research. Myrdal evidently had little knowledge of the social science tradition in the United States. Finally, what is so curious about his dismissal of Park is that much of *An American Dilemma* was conceived and researched by Park's students (i. e., Charles Johnson, E. Franklin Frazier, Louis Wirth, and Horace Cayton).

Furthermore, while Park may have developed his interest in studying blacks during his stay at Tuskeegee, he acquired his training in sociology in Germany. As stated earlier, Park was formally introduced to sociology through the lectures of Georg Simmel, the brilliant German sociologist. Under the direction of the German philosopher Wilhelm Windelband, he wrote his doctoral dissertation on the difference between a crowd and a public. (The actual title of the dissertation was *Masse und Publikum.*) Park's interest in sociology was nurtured previously by his relationship with the American philosopher William James of Harvard University, under whom Park wrote his master's thesis. Incidentally, this was the same William James whom DuBois credited with inspiring his intellectual quest. It is important that we realize that upon his emergence in the sociology department of the University of Chicago, Park was one of the best educated sociologists in the United States. Bowser, in misreading both Washington and Park, perceived a similarity in their endorsement of the status quo when in fact an accurate understanding of both men would have led Bowser to perceive a similarity in the style and substance of their distaste for the racial status quo.

As to Bowser's claim that Park's "ecological" thesis defended the status quo as natural, I can only repeat that Bowser clearly has misunderstood Park. Park's theories, much like European social thought at the time (Marx, Spencer, Durkheim, Weber), were teleological theories. Park believed that human history was directed in a certain meaningful path. The present was merely one stage/step in this process of directed change. In many ways this may sound similar to Social Darwinism since it also is a neo-teleological theory. However, all teleological ideas are not Darwinistic. Does Park defend the status quo as "natural"? In one sense yes, but not in the way that Bowser implies. In a similar vein, one cannot claim that Marx defended the status quo of capitalistic society by asserting that capitalism was a necessary stage on the way to a socialist society. Yet, I suppose a misreading of Marx could lead one to the belief that he endorsed the "status quo" of capitalism by considering it part of a "natural" movement of history. Bowser has confused the "is-ought" problem. Simply because one claims that it is or must be does not indicate that one thinks that it ought to be.

Bowser mistakenly perceives in Park's ecological thesis an endorsement of the racial status quo as "natural." Bowser may have been fooled by use of the concept of equilibrium. As Fred H. Mathews has stated:

> ... Park's model for Society was not one of equilibrium; although states of equilibrium were the theoretical final stages of his patterned sequence of change. Park was perfectly aware that this equilibrium was 'illusory' in the sense that it existed only as a *convenient tool for analysis.* [my emphasis] (Mathews 1977: 134)

The potential for equilibrium was only a logical culmination; in practice some new development always interrupted the process and set in motion another cycle of what Park, borrowing from plant ecology, called *succession* -another period of instability, followed by a cycle of patterned, serial developments, "an irreversible series in which each succeeding event is more or less completely determined by the one that preceded it."(Mathews 1977: 135) In many ways, then, Park's ecological theory, as well as his race-relations cycle theory, were not theories of stability but theories of conflict and change. We should not be surprised by this given the fact that Park was introduced to sociology by the most prominent sociological student of conflict, Georg Simmel.[12]

In the specific instance of Park's ecological theory, he argued merely that he had discovered consistencies in neighborhood spatial changes which would occur as immigrants advanced economically. Immigrant groups first settled in the center of the city, the area of transition. From there they would gradually move toward the periphery of the city, and eventually into the suburban areas. Park believed this movement to be irreversible and claimed that it was accompanied by changes - economic, cultural, and psychological - in the immigrant group (Mathews 1977: 135). How Bowser is able to generate a belief that this ecological thesis was not only an endorsement of the racial status quo (or any status quo) as natural, but a statement in behalf of Booker T. Washington's views as opposed to those of DuBois is baffling.

If one wanted to isolate what could be considered Park's central sociological concern, it would be the interaction [read conflict and adjustment] between ethnic groups in an urban context. Park, for instance, concentrated on the impact of migration on individuals. His idea of the "marginal man" was clearly a concept premised upon social conditionality. He was concerned with analyzing how immigrants would behave when placed in a situation (the city) that forced them to live in a more cosmopolitan manner. Migration to the city forced individuals to live on the "margins" between their culture and the broader community (Park 1928; 1937).

Park entertained racist or quasi-racist beliefs, as well as sexist beliefs. He fluctuated around the belief that races/ethnic groups possessed temperaments. He once wrote:

> Everywhere and always it [the Negro race] has been interested rather in expression than in action; interested in life itself rather than in its reconstruction or reformation. The Negro is, by natural disposition, neither an intellectual nor an idealist, like the Jew; nor a brooding introspective, like the East African, nor a pioneer and frontiersman, like the Anglo-Saxon. He is primarily an artist, loving life for its own sake. His metier is expression rather than action. He is, so to speak, the lady among the races (Park 1950: 280).

To some people Park's statements were racist because he believed in racial temperaments. To others, they were racist because of the substance of the temperament he attributed to blacks.

We cannot dismiss merely as patronizing the fact that Park, more than any other individual, was responsible for bringing blacks into the mainstream of the sociology profession. It cannot be assumed that in Park's absence black sociologists of the quality of Charles Johnson and E. Franklin Frazier would have emerged when they did.

Bowser's discussion of the differences between Johnson and Frazier is as flawed as the rest of the paper. He wants us to believe that Johnson's belief in social conditionality and Frazier's belief in Park's ecological thesis were ultimately responsible for Frazier's greater recognition in academic sociology. Consequently, we are told that it was not accidental that Frazier, not Johnson, became President of the American Sociological Association.

Insofar as I have already shown the fallacy in Bowser's analysis of Park's ecological thesis and the commonplaceness of social conditionality arguments for the emerging sociological discipline, the discussion of the differences in the careers of Johnson and Frazier cannot build upon any insight gained from Bowser's discussion. Certainly we can agree that the somewhat simultaneous emergence of Frazier and Johnson as major figures within the same discipline represented a unique occurrence in Afro-American intellectual life. Yet, Frazier and Johnson were not alone. When we consider that Frazier, Johnson, DuBois, Ira Reid, Bertram Doyle, St. Clair Drake, Horace Mann Bond, Horace Cayton, Oliver Cox, Allison Davis, and Hylan Lewis can be broadly considered as of the same intellectual generation (or at worst, as members of overlapping intellectual generations), it is clear that they represented the high point in the Afro-American presence in American sociology. When these black social scientists are coupled with white social scientists of their generation who studied black life (i. e., John Dollard, Louis Wirth, Hortense Powdermaker, Arthur Raper, Howard Odum, Thomas J. Woofter, Harold Gosnell, W. Lloyd Warner, Guy Johnson, Melville Herskovits, Gordon All-port, Richard Sterner, Burleigh and Mary Gardner, George Mitchell, Will Alexander, Edwin Embree, M. F. Ashley-Montague, W. I. Thomas, Abram Kardiner, Otto Klineberg, B. T. Thompson, Samuel A. Stouffer, Arnold Rose, Everett C. Hughes, Edward Reuter, Everett Stonequist, and those whites who indirectly participated in such studies, e. g., Harry Stack Sullivan, Robert Sutherland, Rupert Vance), the period may well have been the high water mark for the American sociological study of black Americans. But what does this have to do with Frazier's selection as President of the American Sociological Association?

The fact that the emergence of black scholars in sociology was coterminous with the emergence of a large body of white sociologists (many of whom were not racists) interested in the study of blacks meant that Johnson and Frazier, though outstanding, were not as novel as they would have been had race relations become a "black" area of expertise. In many ways the seminal students of race and ethnic relations, both white and black, projected race relations into a dominant area of study within American sociology and the social sciences in general. Bowser is wrong when he suggests that "race relations" was isolated on the periphery of the discipline. That Robert Park, Everett C. Hughes, Edward Reuter, Louis Wirth, Arnold Rose, E. Franklin Frazier, Rupert Vance, Howard Odum, and others would become presidents of the American Sociological Association only testifies to the centrality that race relations had obtained within the sociology profession. Furthermore, all of these individuals advocated various types of social conditionality theses.[13] The failure of the American Sociological Association to select Johnson as its president cannot be attributed to a supposedly novel use of social conditionality as an explanation of black life and culture.

My hunch would be that the reason Johnson was never selected as president may lie more in crude racism, but certainly not in the methodology he used. The sociology profession may not have been able to tolerate bestowing its supreme honor on two black men within such a short span of time. That is, had Johnson been selected president, perhaps Frazier would not have been selected. Who really knows? Bowser, instead of claiming that both men merited the honor, falls into the trap of accepting an either-or situation. Ironically, he fails to mention that the much more conservative Southern Sociological Association selected Johnson as president in 1946 (Jones 1974: 121-63). Furthermore, Johnson was selected as Vice President of the American Sociological Association. Omitted in Bowser's discussion is the ASA's oversight of Ira De A. Reid. Reid was selected as President of the Eastern Sociological Association and Vice President of the national body. He too deserved to be president. It was not merely Johnson who was overlooked! Yet, many qualified white scholars were also overlooked. Harold Gosnell, a student of Park and author of two pathbreaking monographs, *Negro Politicians* (1935) and *Machine Politics* (1937), was never selected as President of the American Political Science Association.

But was Frazier more "acceptable" to white sociologists than Johnson, as Bowser would have us believe? I doubt it. Bowser overlooks the fact that Johnson had to be "acceptable" to influential whites in order to become president of Fisk University. Furthermore, Johnson had been a key participant with Howard Odum, Guy Johnson, and others in the Southern Regional Council, a less than radical organization dedicated to easing racial change in the South. Before becoming President of Fisk, Johnson had been an influential go between for black writers and white publishing firms during the Harlem Renaissance (Lewis 1981). Subsequently, during his days at Fisk, Johnson sat on the board of probably all the major foundations sponsoring research among black Americans. Johnson, to use a colloquial expression, was clearly "plugged in."

Butler A. Jones (1974: 121-63) in his essay, "The Tradition of Sociology Teaching in Black Colleges: The Unheralded Professionals," describes Johnson's rule over the province of black sociology: "He was the new Booker T. Washington, exercising suzerainty over a more limited and specialized territory, but within it possessed of a freedom of action never accorded to Washington." Jones documents the various linkages Johnson held with white foundations that allowed him to severely influence which black sociologists could obtain funding for their research. That this same man, according to Bowser's description, would be seen as too "radical" for the American Sociological Association's presidency is puzzling. (The irony is that though Bowser so forcefully claims Johnson as the hero of social conditionality, it is Johnson, not Frazier, Reid, nor Park who expressed doubts about the innate qualities of blacks.) Johnson once wrote: "The assumption holds, at least tentatively, that the inefficiency of Negro pupils is at least as much a function of a poor educational system and an inferior background, as of an *inferior, inherited mental constitution.*" (Young 1973: 76) [my emphasis]

Though Bowser wants us to believe that Frazier via his appropriation of Park's theories was closer in thought to Booker T. Washington than to DuBois and thus more acceptable to white sociologists than Johnson, Bowser's argument ignores any reference to Johnson's views of Washington. Johns explicitly endorsed a neo-Washington view of social change in several essays, some which appeared in *Opportunity* (i. e., "The Philsophy of Booker T. Washington," Vol. 6, April 1928).

Finally, had Bowser read DuBois' collected letters, he would have seen that DuBois clearly and continually considered Frazier a kindred spirit while expressing doubts about Johnson (Aptheker 1973).[14]

Regardless of how one judges the quality and intent of Frazier's work, one cannot imagine E. Franklin Frazier as president of a black college. His relationship with the black bourgeoisie was far too tenuous. In addition, he never indicated, like Dubois or Johnson, a desire to be an "empire" builder. Furthermore, Frazier served on the editorial board of the Marxist journal, *Science and Society,* and considered himself a neo-Marxist of sorts.[15] How one can consider Frazier more acceptable to white sociologists than Johnson is baffling.

Many current black sociologists are antagonistic to Frazier's writings because of his willingness to explicitly label much of black life and culture pathological.[16] It is clear that Frazier believed that a healthy black community would generally pattern itself after the "white community" (an ideal type), and the farther away blacks were from doing so indicated varying degrees of pathos in the black community. (Charles Johnson adhered to similar beliefs, though unlike Frazier, he was more subdued in conveying them. DuBois also adhered to similar beliefs.) It is because of Frazier's willingness to claim that black pathologies lie at the root of certain black social phenomena that people often want to claim that he is guilty of "blaming the victim."[17] This is an erroneous interpretation. Frazier may have accepted too uncritically the white community as a measuring rod of healthy social adaptation, but his basic premise is not implausible. He believed that the historic oppression of blacks, particularly slavery, left devastating scars on the black community which often manifested themselves in ways that hindered further development of that community. During the present era, when blacks want to claim that blacks endured slavery relatively pathologically free (i. e., the survival of the black family), it is obvious that Frazier would come into disfavor. Yet blacks cannot have it both ways. The claim that slavery was an indescribable horror cannot coincide with the claim that slavery had a miniscule impact upon blacks physically, mentally, and culturally (Elkins 1975). In pointing out that blacks were warped by their historic oppression, Frazier was in effect claiming via social conditionality the innate equality of black people. Today many individuals want to claim that black culture was not warped by the experience of slavery and its aftermath but that blacks are just culturally "different." Frazier, for instance, probably would have seen the current attempt to claim that "black English" is a distinct and valid language form as an attempt to legitimate a manifestation of black oppression (i. e., absence of good schools, etc.). Thus he would also see this as an apology for not providing blacks with better education. Defenders of the "black idiom" would see Frazier as an assimilationist.

This debate would in some crucial aspects resemble the debate between Frazier and Herskovits over the degree to which Africanisms were retained in black culture. It is here that Bowser's claim that Frazier did not adhere to the social conditionality thesis becomes so erroneous as to lead us to wonder if Bowser had in fact read Frazier. He certainly did not understand him. If anything, Frazier should be accused of believing too much in social conditionality. In fact, the entire Frazier-Herskovits debate centers around Frazier's willingness to claim that black Americans were the creati6ns of their American social conditions, beginning with slavery. It is Frazier's thesis that blacks had not been able to retain anything culturally significant from their African cultural heritage. Their culture was the result of their social existence during slavery and its aftermath.

Frazier's famous essay on *The Black Bourgeoisie,* the least scholarly of his monographs, is another example of his use of a social conditionality argument. Frazier argued that the black bourgeoisie entered a world of "make believe" because they were denied access to a complete articulation of their ambitions in white society. He certainly did not believe that blacks innately lived a life of fantasy. Bowser's claim that Frazier's work lay outside of the social work tradition is also erroneous. In fact, Frazier was more closely linked to social work than either Johnson or DuBois. After receiving his master's degree in sociology from Clark University in 1920, Frazier became a research fellow at the New York School of Social Work. It was there that he conducted a study of the longshoremen of New York City. Following a year of study in Denmark, he taught sociology at Morehouse College and directed the Atlanta School of Social Work.

While celebrating social conditionality arguments Bowser overlooks the biases inherent in such analyses. It is social conditionality theses that are unable to perceive any degree of cultural autonomy for black people.

Ralph Ellison provided us with an eloquent critique of social conditionality approaches to the study of black America. In a review of Gunnar Myrdal's *An American Dilemma* published in the collection of essays, *Shadow and Act*, Ellison (1964: 315-16) asks, "But can a people (its faith in an idealized American Creed notwithstanding) live and develop for over three hundred years simply by reacting? Are American Negroes simply the creation of white men or have they at least helped to create themselves out of what they found around them?"

The question, of course, is not a true question but a launching pad for Ellison's discussion of the uniqueness of Afro-American folk culture, music and art. Yet Ellison may be guilty of overlooking some real problems (pathologies) in black life derived from this encounter with America. That is, all "problems" in black life cannot be dismissed or accounted for by cultural relativism.[18]

If Bowser had wanted to explore an authentic difference between Frazier and Johnson, he should have investigated differences in their intellectual ambitions. Johnson believed in pure empirical research while Frazier entertained theoretical ambitions.

The primary problem with Bowser's essay is that he fails to realize the true complexity of the men and the times he writes about. He is not sensitive to the contradictions and unresolved dilemmas in the life and thought of W.E.B. DuBois, Charles Johnson, Robert Park, or E. Franklin Frazier. Therefore, Bowser cannot accurately account for the fluctuations and inconsistencies in the conditions of these men over time. For instance, though Park had worked for Washington and resented the style of DuBois' social reform efforts, he was nevertheless invited by DuBois to participate in DuBois' attempt to establish an *Encyclopedia of the Negro*.[19]   Secondly, though Frazier attacked DuBois' "talented tenth" notion, he nevertheless dedicated the *Negro in the United States* to DuBois (and Park) and credited DuBois with having inspired his work. Frazier, it should be noted, spent time at Fisk working under the direction of Charles S. Johnson but angrily left to go to Howard University (Meier 1977; Jones 1974: 1).   Of the four men, Johnson was second to Park in his admiration of Booker T.

Washington. Yet DuBois would later comment that his conflicts with Washington were not as great over matters of substance as over differences in approach in confronting black America's existence. Needless to say, DuBois never took kindly to Washington's efforts to silence him.

We can claim that the young DuBois of *The Philadelphia Negro* was interested in a reform-minded sociology, but we should not forget the substance of some of the "reforms" endorsed by him. In *The Philadelphia Negro* he argues that black America will better itself once whites give to the black social and economic elite the political power to solve the race's problems. This was but a glimpse of the "Talented Tenth" argument that would arise later. It is E. Franklin Frazier who writes perhaps the most devastating attack on DuBois' elitism and aristocratic political vision as contained in this Talented Tenth idea. Yet Frazier would always pay homage to DuBois' influence on his intellectual development, despite his distaste for DuBois' sporadically articulated disdain for the black masses.

Like Frazier, Johnson believed in social conditionality. Such belief did not require breaking with Robert Park, for Park too believed in social conditionality. Though Frazier, more than Johnson, appropriated Park's theoretical frameworks, Johnson was closer to Park personally. Park, it should be remembered, was brought to Fisk by Johnson after the reformer had retired from the University of Chicago. This can be seen as somewhat of a "pay back" to Park. Park as head of the Urban League in Chicago during the 20s had helped Johnson to obtain his position with the Urban League in New York City. It was at Fisk that Park died. While at Fisk he continued to inspire black students who were studying there (e.g., Hugh Smythe).

Bowser could have written a fair and honest essay, but he did not. In attempting to find simplistic, all-encompassing denouncements and celebrations of complex men, he was simply unable to increase our understanding of these men. Ultimately he exposes one reason why the current generation of social scientists (black social scientists in particular) has been unable to sustain the pioneering efforts of Johnson, Frazier, Park, DuBois and Reid. None of these scholars ever taught in a Ph.D. program. Thus, the most direct means of influencing another generation of sociologists was denied them.

References
Aptheker, Herbert. 1973. *The Correspondence of W. E. B. DuBois, Volume I, 1877-1934*. Amherst, MA: University of Massachusetts Press.

_____. 1976. *The Correspondence of W. E. B. DuBois, Volume II*. Amherst, MA: University of Massachusetts Press.

Baltzell, E. Digby. 1969[1899]. "Introduction." *The Philadelphia Negro*. W. E. B. DuBois. New York: Schocken Books.

Bannister, Robert C. 1979. *Social Darwinism: Science and Myth in Anglo-American Social Thought*. Philadelphia, PA: Temple University Press.

Blackwell, James E. and Morris Janowitz. 1974. *Black Sociologists: Historical and Contemporary Perspectives*. Chicago, IL: University of Chicago Press.

Bracey, John Jr., Elliott Rudwick and August Meier. 1971. *The Black Sociologists: The First Half Century*. Belmont, CA: .

Coser, Lewis. 1956. *The Functions of Social Conflict*. Glencoe, IL: Free Press.

_____. 1971. *Masters of Sociological Thought*. New York: Harcourt Brace Jovanovich.

Davis, David Brion. 1966. *The Problem of Slavery in Western Culture*. Ithaca, NY: Cornell University Press.

_____ 1975. *The Problem of Slavery in the Age of Revolution, 1770-1823*. Ithaca, NY: Cornell University Press.

Doyle, Bertram W. 1937. *Etiquette of Race Relations in the South*. Chicago, IL: University of Chicago Press.

Drake, St. Clair. 1967[1940]. "Introduction." *Negro Youth at the Crossways--Their Personality Development in Middle States*. E. Franklin Frazier. Washington, DC: American Council on Education.

DuBois, W. E. B. 1965[1898]. *The Suppression of the African Slave Trade*. New York: Russell and Russell.

Edwards, G. Franklin. 1980. "E. Franklin Frazier: Race, Education, and Community." *Sociological Traditions from Generation to Generation: Glimpses of the American Experience*. Robert K. Merton and Matilda White Riley, editors. Norwood, NJ: Ablex Publishing Corporation.

Elkins, Stanley. 1975. "The Slavery Debate." *Commentary*. 60, 6.

Ellison, Ralph. 1964. "An American Dilemma: A Review." *Shadow and Act*. New York: Random House.

Ferris, William H. 1913. *The African Abroad: His Evolution in Western Civilization.* New Haven, CT: The Tuttle, Morehouse and Taylor Press.

Hofstadter, Richard. 1955. *Social Darwinism in American Thought.* Boston, MA: Beacon Press.

Jones, Butler A. 1974. "The Tradition of Sociology Teaching in Black Colleges: The Unheralded Professionals." *Black Sociologists: Historical and Contemporary Perspectives.* James E. Blackwell and Morris Janowitz, editors. Chicago, IL: University of Chicago Press.

Jordon, Winthrop D. 1971. *White Over Black: American Attitudes toward the Negro, 1550-1812.* Chapel Hill, NC: University of North Carolina Press.

Lewis, David Levering. 1981. *When Harlem Was in Vogue.* New York: Knopf.

Lynd, Robert S. and Helen Merill Lynd. 1929. *Middletown--A Study in Contemporary American Culture.* New York: Harcourt, Brace and Company.

_____ 1937. *Middletown in Transition--A Study in Cultural Conflicts.* New York: Harcourt, Brace and Company.

Macpherson, C. B. 1970[1979]. *The Political Theory of Possessive Individualism: Hobbs to Locke.* Oxford: Oxford University Press: .

Matthews, Fred H. 1977. *Quest for an American Sociology: Robert E. Park and the Chicago School.* Montreal, Canada: McGill-Queen's University Press.

Meier, August. 1977. Review Essay of *Black Sociologists: Historical and Contemporary Perspectives. Social Forces.* 56.

Moses, Wilson Jeremiah. 1982. *Black Messiahs and Uncle Toms.* University Park, PA: Pennsylvania State University.

Moynihan, Daniel P. 1965. "The Negro Family: The Case for National Action." U. S. Department of Labor.

Park, Robert E. 1928. "Human Migration and the Marginal Man." *American Journal of Sociology* 33, 6.

_____ 1937. "Introduction." *The Marginal Man.* Everett Stonequist. New York: C. Scribner's Sons.

_____ 1950. "Education in the Relations to Culture." *Race and Culture*. Everett Cherrington Hughes, editor. Glencoe, IL: Free Press.

Parson, Talcott. 1937. *The Structure of Social Action*. New York: McGraw-Hill Book Company, Incorporated.

Popkin, Richard H. 1977-78. "Hume's Racism." *The Philosophical Form*. 9, 2-3.

Rief, Phillip. 1968. "Introduction." *Radicals and Conservatives*. Kelly Miller. New York.

Russett, Cynthia. 1976. *Darwin in America: The Intellectual Response, 1865-1912*. San Francisco, CA: W. H. Freeman.

Singal, Daniel Joseph. 1982. *The War Within: From Victorian to Modernist Thought in the South, 1919-1945*. Chapel Hill, NC: University of North Carolina Press.

Smith, Charles U. and Lewis Killian. 1974. "Black Sociologists and Social Protest." *Black Sociogists: Historical and Contemporary Perspectives*. James E. Blackwell and Morris Janowitz, editors. Chicago, IL: University of Chicago Press.

Szwed, John F. 1972. "An American Anthropological Dilemma: The Politics of Afro-American Culture." *Reinventing Anthropology*. Dell Hymes, editor. New York: Pantheon Books.

Therborn, Goran. 1976. *Science, Class and Society: On the Formulation of Sociology and Historical Materialism*. London: NLB.

Toll, William. 1982. *The Resurgence of Race*. Philadelphia, PA: Temple University Press.

Valentine, Charles A. 1968. *Culture and Poverty: Critique and Counter-Proposals*. Chicago, IL: University of Chicago Press.

Wallerstein, Immanuel. 1974. *The Modern World System*. New York: Academic Press.

Williams, Eric. 1944 *Capitalism and Slavery*. Chapel Hill, NC: University of North Carolina Press.

Wolff, Kurt H. and Reinhard Bendix. 1955. *Conflict and Web of Group-Affiliations*. Georg Simmel. New York: Free Press.

Wyllie, Irvin G. 1954. *The Self Made Man: The Myth of Rags to Riches*.

New Brunswick, NJ: Rutgers University Press.

Young, James O. 1973. *Black Writers of the Thirties*. Baton Rouge, LA: Louisiana State University Press.

Endnotes

1. In *The Political Theory of Possessive Individualism: Hobbs to Locke* (New York 1970), C. B. Macpherson argues that the crucial ingredient brought by Locke to the development of the ideology which legitimated capitalist expansion lay within his designation of private property as a natural right and his use of property as a qualifier for political rights, not as Bowser suggests, a belief in popular government.

2. For a definitive study of natural law, see Leo Strauss, *Natural Right and History* (Chicago 1953). For a shorter analysis of the history of natural law and natural rights, see *Political Theory: The Foundation of Twentieth Century Political Thought* by Arnold Brecht (Princeton 1959), pp. 138-46. In these volumes, there is no substantiation for Bowser's claim that "racial inferiority and therefore continued slavery were prime motives for the growth of the notion of "natural law." Insofar as Bowser does not offer a footnote to this assertion, we can only speculate as to the theorists or arguments to which he is referring.

3. David Bryon Davis (*The Problem of Slavery in Western Culture*, 1966) points out the paradoxical and contradictory nature of the relationship between natural law and slavery. While in the case of Thomas Aquinas, slavery was easily reconciled with natural law (and vice versa), natural law arguments also fueled the abolitionists. The contradiction between natural law and slavery is expressed most vividly in John Locke.

4. The mentioning of Chalmers as the founder of a prominent school of thought in the social sciences also demands substantiation, for in none of the books I have read on the history of American sociology is there any mention of him. As Bowser notes, Cahlmers is discussed in the Becker and Barnes volume, *Social Thought From Lore to Science*, but nowhere do they mention him as having had the influence in America attributed to him by Bowser.

5. My entire discussion of Spencer's impact on early American sociology is derived from Goran Therborn's *Science, Class and Society: On the Formulation of Sociology and Historical Materialism* (London 1976), pp. 227-35.

6. For a background on these men, see William Toll's *The Resurgence of Race* (Philadelphia 1979) Chapter 1 and William Moses' *Black Messiahs and Uncle Toms* (University Park, PA 1982). As to Bowser's point that the ideas of these writers preceded those of DuBois, it should be pointed out that William H. Ferris' *The African Abroad: His Evolution in Wester Civilization* was published over a decade after DuBois' *The Suppression of the African Slave Trade.*

7. For an insightful revisionist interpretation of Spencer's thought in America, see *Social Darwinism: Science and Myth inAnglo-American Social Thought* by Robert C. Bannister (Philadelphia 1979).

8. See Cynthia Rusett's *Darwin in America: The Intellectual Response, 1865-1912* (San Francisco 1976), for an excellent discussion of Social Darwinism in America and its critics.

9. Bowser can only make this claim by ignoring the black sociologists who were influenced by DuBois. Of course Bowser, like many others, places black sociologists (i. e., Drake, Cayton, Frazier, Johnson, Reid) *a priori* on the periphery of the discipline and in doing so ironically continues the tradition he claims to be attacking.
Secondly, how many of us realize that twenty years after *The Philadelphia Negro* Howard Odum "repeated" the study? Certainly he knew about *The Philadelphia Negro.* In fact, Odum wrote in 1950 that DuBois, along with Giddings (Columbia) must be seen as the first sociologists in America to attempt to set up centers for applied social research (at Atlanta University).

10. For a discussion of Kelly Miller, see *Black Writers of the Thirties* (Baton Rouge 1973) by James O. Young and Philip Rieff's introduction to Miller's collected essays titled *Radicals and Conservatives* (New York 1968). The volume was originally titled *Race Adjustment.*

11. The rest of the dedication was:
"...who once said: Anthropology, the science of man, has been mainly concerned up to the present with the study of primitive peoples. But civilized man is quite an interesting an object of investigation, and at the same time his life is more open to observation and study. Urban life and culture are more varied, subtle and complicated, but the fundamental motives are in both instances the same."

12. It is, of course, from Simmel's thought that the modern day conflict theorists emerge. See Lewis Coser's *The function of Social Conflict* (New York 1956), and Georg Simmel's two essays published as one volume,

Conflict and the Web of Group-Affiliations, translated by Kurt H. Wolff and Reinhard Bendix (New York 1955).

13. We should note that Bowser's discussion of Howard Odum does not take into account the growth that Odum displayed over time in reference to blacks. It is true that Odum's dissertation at Columbia University argued for the innate mental inferiority of black people. However, by the 1930s the Odum of *Southern Regions* fame had emerged. He saw harmonious relations between whites and blacks as crucial to the development of the South and participated in several organizations (with Charles Johnson) which were intent upon changing the social conditions of black life in the South. For the story of Odum and the development of Southern sociology, see *The War Within: From Victorian to Modernist Thought in the South 1919-1945* by David Joseph Singal (Chapel Hill 1982).

14. In *The Correspondence of W. E. B. DuBois, Volume I, 1877-1934*, edited by Herbert Aptheker (Amherst, MA 1973), see DuBois' letter of January 3, 1934 to economist Abram Harris concerning Harris' proposal for beginning of a black lectureship bureau whose members would tour college campuses proclaiming radical social, political and economic ideas.

15. See, "E. Franklin Frazier: Race, Education, and Community" by G. Franklin Edwards in *Sociological Tradition From Generation to Generation: Glimpses of the American Experience*, edited by Robert K. Merton and Matilda White Riley (Norwood, NJ 1980); and St. Clair Drake's introduction to Schocken Books' 1967 reissued version of Frazier's *Negro Youth at the Crossways*. Oliver Cox perhaps the only explicitly Marxist black sociologists of his time, would interpret Frazier's "neo-Marxism" quite differently. Cox once stated concerning Frazier:

> His professional career had to be contrived on the tight rope set up by the associated establishment. He won many prizes and honors, but the exigencies of winning involved his soul and his manhood. Sometimes *Black Bourgeoisie* is compared to the *Theory of the Leisure Class* and to *White Collar*. It is, in my opinion, nothing of the sort. Had Frazier assumed the position of Veblen or Mills, he would doubtless have been even more completely consigned to outer darkness to endure in silence the agony of his ways. He hardly confronted even tangentially a real power structure. (See "Black Sociologists and Social Protest" by Charles U. Smith and Lewis Killian in Blackwell and Janowitz, op. cit., pp. 202-03.)

While Cox's *ad hominem* attack on Frazier seems to be the utterings of a man embittered by having chosen a path which "consigned him to outer darkness," we should also realize that Cox's reasoning is severely flawed. First, he assumes that Frazier's writings were not the representative products of Frazier's authentic beliefs and values, but the outpourings of a man who sold his "soul and manhood" for purposes of mobility. Second, he never discusses the quality of Frazier's work when mentioning why and how Frazier received honors and prizes.

16. The most prominent monograph which "attacks" this aspect of Frazier's writings is *Culture and Poverty: Critique and Counter Proposals* by Charles A. Valentine (Chicago 1968), in the section titled, "The Pejorative Tradition Established by E. Franklin Frazier." Also see, "An American Anthropological Dilemma: The Politics of Afro-American Culture," by John F. Szwed in *Reinventing Anthropology*, edited by Dell Hymes (New York 1972). A much shallower attempt to critique Frazier but which never succeeds in leaving the level of mere assertions is Smith and Killian, op. cit.
This attack on Frazier reached its peak during the height of protest against the "Moynihan Report," formally titled, "The Negro Family: The Case for National Action." (U. S. Department of Labor, March 1965)

17. Interestingly, in *Blaming the Victim* William Ryanattacks Moynihan's report and offers Frazier*'s The Negro Family in the United States* as a study which contradicted Moynihan's arguments. This somewhat baffling insofar as Moynihan based his proposal on the works of E. Franklin Frazier.

18. The irony of Ellison's and Szwed's analyses is that in their attempt to proclaim a distinct Afro-American cultural tradition they are blinded to actual pathologies which exist in black communities. Their problem stems in large measure from the role which culture (i. e., art, folk traditions, music, etc.) plays in their analyses. In some sense Ellison and Szwed view the denial to attribute distinct cultural artifacts to Afro-Americans as an assault on the validity of Afro-American existence. Yet Frazier when speaking about culture is not concerned with cultural artifacts and expressions. He views culture as a set of beliefs or values which are either functional or dysfunctional to the maintenance and attainment of a viable existence in America. Of course we can claim that Frazier has adopted an upward mobility-middle class, "white" definition of "viable existence." This may be true. Frazier could have called for an alteration in American society in behalf of cultural pluralism and socialism. This would have been the "radical" thing to do. However, insofar as Frazier correctly perceived that the "revolution" in American society would not soon occur (and it still

does not seem to be on the horizon), he was left with the task   of confronting those attributes in the existence of blacks which did not facilitate mobility within the established American social order. For this he is condemned!

19. *The Encyclopedia of the Negro* project would later be called the *Encyclopedia Africana*. However, Carter G. Woodson had begun an encyclopedia project at the same time that DuBois launched his idea of one. Woodson titled his project the **Encyclopedia Africana**, the name which DuBois appropriated for his encyclopedia after Woodson died. Neither Woodson nor DuBois succeeded in completing this task. As for DuBois' interaction with Robert Park on this issue of the *Encyclopedia Africana*, see *The Correspondence of W. E. B. DuBois, Volume II*, edited by Herbert Aptheker (Amherst, MA 1976), pp. 140-41. Within recent years (1999) , Harvard scholars, Anthony Appiah and Henry Louis Gates have completed a one-volume *Encyclopedia Africana* which will be placed on CD-Rom.

Chapter Three

Classical Black Sociologists and Social Theory: Anatomy of A Controversy

Benjamin P. Bowser

I am pleased to have this opportunity to review our essays in retrospect, and tell what I found out when I finally met Jerry Watts. What follows is a review of the main points that both essays addressed. Jerry Watts did not correct my "errors" as much as he provided additional insights and perspective on early Black sociologists and how they worked within a hostile theoretical framework. Both essays provided a sense of some of the issues one has to consider in such an investigation. This review also provides an opportunity to reflect anew on the topic after almost two decades.

Main Assumptions

I worked under the following two assumptions in my 1981 essay. First, the social theory one embraces and produces is heavily influenced by one's social context and identity. Second, the theory early Black sociologists embraced and used in some way reflect their unique social context and identities among sociologists as Black men. Based upon these assumptions, my purpose was to explore the following questions: 1) did the classical Black sociologists produce theory--if so, how, and if not, why not--and 2) how did they use theory to explain the specific experiences of Black people in the United States? I chose to explore these two questions by first looking at the impact slavery and colonialism had on the social context of the most influential classical European and American scholars. I had two working theses: 1) the limits and potential contributes of the early Black sociologists to sociology were largely defined by their expected roles, and 2) theory crafted in the prior century was hostile to their presence in the discipline. It is impossible to fully appreciate the theoretical constraints and potentials of these scholars outside of their societal and professional context.

A Review of Early Influences

Through Eric William's work (1966), I contend the industrial revolution and the commercial merchant class' growth in England and France could not have happened without the labor of enslaved Africans. Citing Wallerstein, Watts attempts to refute my claim by suggesting three points regarding slavery's impact: 1) slavery's impact was most significant during the earlier pre-industrial stages of capitalism; 2) slavery was no longer profitable in later capitalism; and, 3) slavery could not have played a major role in the industrial revolution (that I was in error). What is at stake here is not some minor differences on citation. The fundamental role of African slavery to the development of both capitalism and modern industrial explains the centrality, importance and motivation for European slavery, especially in the English tradition. African enslavement by Europeans set into motion historic circumstances for the inferior position of Africans in the modern world economy. Slavery during Europe's industrial development is also the basis for African peoples' unsettled moral claim against Western Europe. The claim is Blacks were not compensated for creating societies Whites continue to benefit from.

Immanuel Wallerstein does not have the most comprehensive minimization of slavery's centrality to capitalism and industrialism. Other scholars such as Oliver Cox provided views on this topic. In The Foundations of Capitalism (1959) Cox describes the continuous role of colonialism and slavery to Western Europe's enrichment. The best argument against the centrality of slavery in the

North American experience was Robert Fogged and Stanley Engerman's Time On The Cross: The Economics of American Negro Slavery (1974).   Fogged and Engerman argue slavery was not profitable and slave labor was not as important to the southern economy as other historians claim.   Another attempt to minimize slavery was Eugene Genovese's Roll, Jordan, Roll (1974).   To Genovese the psychology of slaves reinforced slavery and played an important role in maintaining Black subordination. That might be because of the thorough critiques by AAA in   BBBBBB regarding Europe, and by Herbert Gutman in Slavery and the Numbers Game: A Critique of Time on The Cross (1975) regarding North America. In the last twenty years, this minimalist view of slavery has been rarely cited and has few champions among historians.

Is it possible for the social philosophies of classical European thinkers to have been influenced by their national experiences with slavery and colonialism? I say they were; Jerry Watts says they were not. Watts and I both cite several prominent European social philosophers who defined slavery in their writing.   Watts thinks those who said little about slavery such as Adam Smith demonstrates the subtly and nuance of classical thought. It is clear to me that Adam Smith and many of his peers did not have to say much about slavery. It was a foregone fact. The rights Adam Smith wished to advance and the markets he wanted freed were not for enslaved Africans. As an example of such nuanced thinking, Watts cites Thomas Jefferson and the Declaration of Independence.   To this day, I am fascinated by Watts' point regarding Jefferson.   First, Jefferson advocated specific social freedoms as written in The Declaration of Independence. Second, Jefferson owned slaves (to maintain his wealth and status) and is alleged to have had a slave family.   Third, Jefferson opposed slavery while owning slaves. According to Watts, these three points are subtle and nuanced with no obvious or compelling connections. I do not think Jefferson's slaves would be impressed by Watts' nuancing of Jefferson. (Jefferson?)   Nor would I expect Leo Strauss, Arnold Brecht, and other mainstream European and American scholars to discuss Jefferson's problem with slavery or to provide evidence of slavery's influence on eighteenth and nineteenth century Western European thinkers--a point I was criticized for making too strongly.

My next grievous error according to Watts was writing about Alexander Crummel (The Future of Africa, 1862), William W. Brown (The Rising Son, 1876), George Williams (History of the Negro Race in America, 1882), and William Ferris (The

African Abroad, 1913). Watts corrected me for not also including T. Thomas Fortune (Black and White, 1884). These writers provide remarkable challenges to the racist social theories of the prior century. Intellectually, they preceded W.E.B. Du Bois' use of social conditionality as a concept explaining variations in the human condition. In this sense, their work is intellectually closer to modern sociology than the first self-conscious sociological writings in the United States which are naturalistic defenses of slavery--Henry Hughes' Treatise on Sociology (1854) and George Fitzhugh's Sociology of the South: The Failure of Free Society (1854). Watts claims Crummel, Brown, Williams, and Ferris did much more than express social conditionality and I erred in labeling them "sociologists" for two reasons: 1) they did not self-identify as such, and 2) the American Sociological Association (ASA) did not begin until 1905. Here, I am baffled. At no point in my 1981 essay do I suggest either these men or the classical European theorists were one-dimensional in their contributions.

Black intellectuals, especially sociologists, have always been interdisciplinary. The emphasis of these volumes speaks to their intellectual diversity as well as shows mainstream influences on their work. Crummel, Brown, Williams, and Ferris wrote before the professionalization of sociology as did William Graham Sumner who began his career as an Episcopalian rector; Lester Frank Ward spent most of his career as a botanist and paleontologist, and Znaniecki turned to sociology from philosophy (Bierstedt 1981: 491). Also, there was the American Social Science Association (ASSA), founded in 1865 and active during the time that Crummel, Brown, Williams, and Ferris wrote. The ASSA had the expressed intent of addressing the new social problem. A number of ASSA founders had been active in the abolitionist movement. They wanted to address the status of Blacks after the Civil War by using the new sociology (Gunther 1974: 22). Instead of dismissing Crummel, Brown, Williams, and Ferris as non-sociologists, they should be embraced as the very first generation. It would be interesting to know what theories they embraced, how did they create their arguments, and if they had any interactions with the ASSA.

The idea that English social thought was heavily influenced by slavery and colonialism was introduced to high light similar influences in the development of American sociology. Thus, I focused on Henry Hughes, George Fitzhugh, and the American Spencerians -- Sumner, Ward, and Giddings as well as Edward Ross, Charles Ellwood, and

Charles Cooley. The necessity to defend slavery and the post-Civil War subordination of Blacks and others in the United States called for notions of innate and natural (meaning permanent) hierarchy. Hughes and Fitzhugh began with a naturalistic defense of slavery that progressed to rigid Social Darwinism under Sumner and Ward; and moderate to conditional Social Darwinism with Ross, Ellwood, and Cooley. Any macro-explanation of society based uncritically on early American social science was by definition demeaning to Blacks, precluded Blacks as sociologists, and could not accurately describe the Black and White experiences in the United States. Nineteenth century White sociologists could not imagine Blacks participating and contributing to the field. The very notions of social hierarchy and differential rates of development among humans within early American sociology justified racial segregation and the belief that Blacks were incapable of intellectual work. This certainly precluded any idea of Blacks advancing theory in sociology. It was no coincidence W.E.B. Du Bois' earliest sociological study, The Philadelphia Negro (1898), was sponsored outside of mainstream sociology. Recent scholarship (Lewis 1996) has suggested greater collegiality between the University of Pennsylvania's Sociology Department and Du Bois than prior reports (Logan 1957: 44). The fact remains his research was sponsored primarily through social work rather than sociology.

Robert Park and the Early Chicago School

It, given what general sociological theory had to say about Blacks, is not clear from our essays why there was interest in recruiting Blacks into Sociology by 1925. An answer to this question is in the perceived social chaos leading to this century. George Holmes wrote to August Commute about the growth of 'revolutionary political speculation and action,' the 'discontent and disturbed state of all populations' as well as 'the decline of religion and moral integrity' (Gunther 1974: 14). Lester Ward wrote the economic growth of the country gave rise to social and economic problems of staggering proportions with growing social divisions and class antagonism (Gunther 1974: 39). As slaves and later sharecroppers, Blacks were thought to be totally dependent, predictable, known, and could be directly watched. In the nation's rapidly growing cities, Blacks and others who had been restrained in the past by tradition and force were free to think as they liked, do as they wanted, and to disappear after work into the isolated social worlds of the ghetto. Despite theoretical views suggesting Blacks generally lacked intellectual capacity, it was now necessary to recruit, train, and sponsor some Blacks to study and interpret the hidden and potentially dangerous new Black world of Black. Andrew Carnegie had already shown the effective of Booker T. Washington in maintaining control of Black aspirations and freedoms in the South. It was no coincidence the Rockefeller Foundation, Rosenwald Fund, Russell Sage Foundation, and Carnegie Corporation funded Black colleges, provided scholarships for Black graduate students, and financed research in African American communities with a similar philosophy of social control. In sociology, Robert Park was undoubtedly the key person linking the successful Washington experience to the specific effort to train and support Blacks in sociology.

I stand corrected by Watts that Albion Small played a much more critical role than Robert Park in starting the Chicago School of Sociology. My focus was not on whom started the Chicago School. It was on whom recruited, sponsored, and supported many of its first and most influential Black students. Scholarship by Matthews (1977) Raushenbush (1979), Young (1993) and Robins (1996) have noted Park's influence on Black scholars. Watts ignores my discussion of pre-Chicago beginnings. He suggests I erred in characterizing Small as a moderate Social Darwinist. As evidence, Watts points out Small claimed "Sociology began in the United States with the mandate of refuting Spencer." Small overlooked Hughes and Fitzhugh. But then Watts goes on to note Small was not free of Spencer's influence as he originally claimed--another puzzling critique that turns to affirmation. My point regarding Park was the theoretical differences between the work of Park and of the second (Chicago) generation of Black sociologists. This point gets to the core of my differences with Watts on the significance of the classical Black sociologists.

If anyone appeared to be subtle and nuanced, it was Robert Park. Like his good friend Booker T. Washington, whose most famous public position on race relations was presented at the 1895 Atlanta Convention, Park's formal theoretical perspective actually provides a rationale for racial inequality. Look at how Robert Park and Ernest Burgess characterize the city in <u>An Introduction to the Science of Sociology</u> (1921). The city is a "natural phenomenon" due to largely uncontrollable forces that generate areas devoted to specific functions--manufacturing, commerce, and residence. Furthermore, people with similar economic, cultural, and (I add) racial traits aggregate together due to these natural forces in specific areas of the city. While Burgess is better known for notions of (natural) ecological areas because of his 1923 essay "The Growth of Cities," Robert Park was no stranger to naturalistic explanation. Explanation based on natural dynamics rather than human conflict is very prominent in Park's work, despite (as Watts points out) Park's study with the father of sociological conflict theory, George Simmel. If Park's naturalistic explanation of the city is not enough, look specifically at Park's race relations cycles. Groups come into contact with one another producing competition, which is eventually adjusted to, by accommodation that in turn ends with assimilation. The stages in this theory may be harmless, but the dynamics behind the process are another matter. According to Park, this is an irreversible and a "natural" process (Race and Culture, 1949). Imagine Charles Johnson giving a naturalistic explanation for "Jim Crow" segregation, or of E. Franklin Frazier explaining the effect of urbanization on Black migrants as a natural and irreversible process? What if Drake and Cayton explained social stratification in Bronzeville as due to differences in natural traits? What power of explanation is gained by Park's declaring White conflict with Blacks will eventually disappear through assimilation? For early Black sociologists to follow Park's theoretical contribution would have meant using (natural) ecological factors to explain "Jim Crow" in the South and racial discrimination in the North. The implications of ecologicalism is that what happens to Black people has nothing to with power, the exercise of power, and how people, Black or White, accommodate themselves to humanly created and planned social structures. Natural ecologicalism is a denial of the notion that human powers exist in and outside of community and shape people's lives. Despite continued dependency during the formative years of their career on Park, Burgess, and other White sponsors who held naturalistic views, it is remarkable that Charles Johnson, Bertram Doyle, St. Claire Drake, and Horace Cayton did not advance the formal theories of their mentors. E. Franklin Frazier is the only exception and only partly so. He appeared to be supportive of Park's race relations cycles (Lyman 1972: 55) and used ecologicalism twice, but not with its naturalist explanation. Such a long-term consensus among a diverse group of scholars would be unheard of today. Here is where some exploration explanation is due into their lives and the work of the second generation.

Explaining the Differences

One of the best ways to gain insight into how Park, Burgess, and others accommodated their theoretical differences with the second generation of Black sociologists is by studying the prefaces and forewords of the second generation's major publications. In Ernest Burgess' Preface to Frazier's The Negro Family in the United States (1939), he acclaims this book as `a natural history of the family' that `epitomizes and telescopes (for Blacks) in one hundred and fifty years the age-long evolution of the human family.' He goes on to point out Frazier and Znaniecki's work looks at `the behavior and forms of the family as they change under the impact of different conditions'; and `this study convincingly indicates that the family is rooted in human nature--in human nature conceived not as a bundle of instincts but as a product of social life' (pp. iii). In Bertram Doyle's preface to The Etiquette of Race Relations in the South: A Study of Social Control (1937), he describes Robert Park's admonishment of attempts to make social changes or to predict race relations because of limits in moral, civil, and natural law. Doyle counters with `we know what can be done in the field of solving problems, (therefore) we can also indicate what should be done and require what must be done' (p. viii). What we learn from Burgess' and Doyle's comments about the study of natural law is social conditions are OUTCOMES of the operations of unexplored laws for Park and Burgess.   This is precisely what Park and Burgess State in An Introduction to the Science of Sociology (1921).

Having social conditions as outcomes of natural laws meant the formal theory used in the prior century to explain Black inferiority coexisted early in this century with attempts to explore and understand the social conditions that Blacks responded to and struggled with. The work of second generation Black sociologists was part of a large experiment to gather data and insight into social conditions to better understand natural law. The difference between Park and Burgess in comparison to Hughes, Sumner, or Gidding is that their natural law theory was held in a scientific and experimental mindset rather than an ideological or race one. In Anthony Platt's very sensitive biography of E. Franklin Frazier, Park is reported to have said he could go to Frazier to get a fight whenever he needed one; and Frazier had profound differences with Park about politics, race relations, and sociology (Platt 1991: 90). Yet, Park was a consistent and reliable sponsor and supporter for Frazier who alienated many others by being so outspoken. Hunter and Abraham (1987) quote Park as impressing upon his students "one's personal status depended on one's ability to gain access to unusual research sites and establish rapport with key respondents" (p. xxxiv). This says a lot about Robert Park. While his formal theoretical views were anachronistic, he knew that to study the world around him required working with a wider spectrum of people and sites.

The early Black sociologists knew natural traits, and irreversible and natural processes have nothing to do with the realities faced by Black people. Where Park, Burgess, and other non-ideological natural law advocates were in agreement with their Black students was on the importance of social conditions as keys to differences in human behavior. The two sides apparently accommodated their differences around exploring social conditions and ignored their differences regarding macro-theory. Watts charges I am in error in asserting there were theoretical differences between Park and the second generation of Black sociologists. He points out Drake and Cayton dedicated Black Metropolis (1945) to Robert Park. My response is Drake and Cayton did not have to follow or agree with Park's theoretical view (as implied by Watts) to dedicate their book to Park. They dedicated the book to Park because Cayton felt acknowledging Park was politically useful. In an interview with Drake, I discovered that Cayton persuaded a reluctant Drake. This point and my 1981 assertion of Park's intellectual sympathy with Booker T. Washington rather than W.E.B. Du Bois have been confirmed in recent scholarship. In Drake's Introduction to The Man Farthest Down (1984), he describes the complex and close relationship between Washington and Park. Drake suggests Park was regarded generally with caution among Black scholars.

Alternatively, there was no accommodation between Robert Park and W.E.B. Du Bois. This was not simply due to differing views of theory. Robert Park was intimately involved in Booker T. Washington's attempt to discredit Du Bois. Furthermore, there is substantial evidence in the Du Bois papers that the classic debate between Washington and Du Bois was not simply a difference of principals (Bowser and Whittle 1996). Booker T. Washington was central to maintaining social control in the Deep South during the rising steel fortune of Andrew Carnegie. Washington did everything he could, nationally, to discredit and professionally destroy Du Bois and everyone associated with him.   The reason is because Du Bois knew about Washington's strategic role with Carnegie. Washington also knew Du Bois was attempting to document the negative impact his compromising leadership regarding Jim Crow was having on Blacks in the South.   Washington's campaign against Du Bois led to Du Bois' closer association with White international race radicals and to the founding of an initially progressive National Association for the Advancement of Colored People (NAACP).   Robert Park was undoubtedly aware of Du Bois disruptive potential for a second generation of 'scientific' Booker T. Washingtons.

My point is: Black scholars were not fooled then as we should not be fooled now over the role of Robert Park in race relations.   It matters little of Watts' point that Robert Park was a close association with Washington, that Park felt that he had become a "Negro" in the South while working with

Washington, of Park's retirement to Fisk University in 1937, and of Charles Johnson's politically astute invitation to have Park retire at Fisk.   Park's social theory does not reflect a close and insightful experience with any Blacks other than Washington.   Not only does Park's theory reflect little insight from years of exposure to Black people,   they are   consistent   with   Washington's   explanation   for Blacks continued   subordination   in   the   disguise   of separate development.   Neither St. Clair Drake, Gunnar Myrdal nor I misread Park.

The Second Generation

E.   Franklin   Frazier   is   correctly   described   by   Watts   as an uncompromising conditionalist.   Yet Frazier is the only member of the second generation of Black sociologists to use Park-Burgess' ecological analysis in The Negro Family in Chicago (1932) and for a commissioned study of Harlem after the 1939 riot.   Given Charles Johnson's "closer" relation to Park, Johnson was the most likely Black scholar to have used ecological theory.   Why did not Drake, Cayton and Doyle also use ecologicalism?   To ask this question from reading their work   is   not   based   on   a   misreading   of   Park   or Frazier. Undoubtedly, there are a number of answers to this question. I suggest in my 1981 essay that one explanation is because of Johnson, Doyle, Frazier, and Drake's own racial experiences and because of their "insider's view" of the Black experience.   For anyone who doubts that there is an insider's view, read Anthony Platt's E. Franklin Frazier Reconsidered (1991) and Horace Cayton's Long Old Road (1965). One does not have to read very far to appreciate how race consciousness and experiences influenced their work as scholars and activists. This is not to say that Frazier was without this perspective. Despite their differences, they knew what Blacks do, even among themselves, is influenced by racial subordination and the human actions that produced and sustained racial subordination, not natural eclogues and theological notions of change.

The question of similarities and differences between early Black sociologists is the most substantial points raised by Watts. It is fascinating that Charles Johnson's administrative work outside of research (Foundation Boards and College President) is properly characterized as conservative. He was a sociological and educational power broker in comparison to Frazier. In my view Johnson's actual research is more deeply grounded in interviews and observations in multiple sites. Frazier did very important work. However, his work might not be regard today as methodologically well grounded as Charles Johnson's Patterns of Negro Segregation (1943). In fact, John Dollar's Caste and Class in a Southern Town (1937) was heavily dependent upon Charles Johnson's fieldwork for Shadows of the Plantation (1934). The key descriptive material of racial segregation in the South and Blacks response to segregation in Gunnar Myrdal's influential An American Dilemma (1944) came from Charles Johnson and staff (Harrison, et al. 1943: XI). Speculations like this got me in particular trouble with Watts, and I concede to him that election to sociological association offices is not an accurate indicator of how Johnson and Frazier were regarded by Whites in the field. My only defense is that my speculation was not meant to stand as definitive canons.

Watts' second major contribution is calling into question whether the work of the early Black sociologists was unique, informed from the Black experience or added to a classical tradition. Watts provides a long list of white students of Black life such as John Dollard, Hortense Powdermaker, Gordon Allport, etc. Here is where Watts clearly states his own thesis and where we find the intellectual reason for his critique of my essay. He holds there are no differences in use of theory and methods between the second generation of Black sociologists and their White peers. The second generation of Black sociologists in fact made no unique contribution to either theory or methods. As Watts states, the social conditionality argument was quite common among all investigators, White and Black. Furthermore, "the emergence of Black scholars in sociology was coterminous with the emergence of a large body of white sociologists interested in the study of Blacks..." In which case, Johnson, Frazier, and other Black social scientists were not novel. Watts' critique has major implications for anyone who considers the first and second generation of Black sociologists to be extraordinary.

The implications of Watts's central thesis are we need to look more specifically at the period and the studies. A reassessment in such a context does not preclude the subtle differences between the second generation and their White peers in the use of theory and methods. Many of these differences could be attributed to racial background. I struggled with this point in my 1981 essay because evidence of differences and influences was not apparent as it was for eighteenth and nineteenth century scholars. I raised the issue and ended my 1981 Phylon essay on this point because an exploration of subtle differences and influences were beyond its scope. My objective was to raise the question so that other scholars might explore it. If indeed the second generation did classical sociology, what was classical about it; what role did they play; and what contribution did they make to sociology and to the study of Black life? What I did not anticipate was that someone (Watts) would close the door on this question and charge that exploration of a unique role for the second generation of classical Black sociologists was erroneous and misguided.

Postscript on Watts

With regard to content, Watt asserts slavery had a minimal impact on industrialization; calls for nuance in defense of classical European theorists and Thomas Jefferson; criticizes then agrees with my read of Albion Small; argues relations between Robert Park and the second generation of Black sociologists were not problematic; and charges the second generation Black sociologist were not unique since they had White peers who also studied Black communities and who used the same theoretical explanations. I consider Watts' points regarding slavery, nuancing, and Albion Small to be reactionary. At the heart of these points, I get the impression it is not what I said so much as the fact I said it. I got a confirmation on this point when I finally meet Watts. We meet several years ago at a National Science Foundation review session. He was surprised to discover that I was Black and a contemporary. He said, "I thought you were some old white dean." He like a number of others was fooled by my first book with Raymond Hunt (now in second edition) The Impacts of Racism on White Americans (1981, 1996), first published when I was an Assistant Graduate Dean at Cornell University. The rough treatment I got in his essay was really about removing what Watts thought was old White competition. It is ironic that Watts' first major work, Heroism and The Black Intellectual: Ralph Ellison, Politics, and Afro-American Intellectual Life (1994), is a very sensitive and excellent treatment of Ralph Ellison, one of my childhood neighbors in New York, whose most famous work, Invisible Man (1947), is a definitive statement on the existence of an African American "insider's view."

Watts made two substantially serious points. The first is regarding Robert Park and the second generation. I have already addressed this point. Watts final point is to question the classical status of the second generation, and is the most important point raised in both of our essays. I want to explore this crucial point briefly in the next two sections.

Contributions to Theory?

Why did not any of the second generation, except Oliver Cox, produce theory? I think a contextualized answer explains this phenomenon among second generation Black sociologists. First, the production of theory would have meant challenging Park, Burgess, and other mentors and sponsors on their intellectual plane. Formal theory production would have provided a contrast to the natural law and ecological views of Park and Burgess. Reid, Johnson, Frazier, Drake, and Cayton did not simply get their degrees, begin careers, and then do their work independent of their sponsors and the foundations, which made their sociological careers possible. To put it bluntly, they did the research and their white sponsors were guardians of what is most important in any science, the theory (Stanfield 1991). Second, "sociological" theory was virtually all macro-level during the second generation of Black Sociologists' student years and careers. Macro-theory production meant not only stepping beyond their ascribed role as race scholars, it would have meant theorizing and acting as authorities on White communities. Third, St. Clair Drake pointed out to me the need to address the problems of Black communities was so urgent and immediate that other professional interests such as writing theory took low priority. Doing theory was another professional interest from race relations and was viewed as a luxury rather than essential to their main line of work.

In the 1920s and 1930s, the most popular alternative to natural law theories (Social Darwinism) and ecologicalism was Marxism. It was embraced by many Black intellectuals (Cruse 1967). In comparison to other intellectuals, Johnson, Frazier, Reid, Drake and Cayton differed by not having an openly Marxist period in their intellectual lives. Personally, I suspect Marxism covertly influenced their work. Openly applying Marxist analysis in their studies would have alienated their sponsors and many opportunities to positively influence social services for the Black community. If my suspicion is correct, it is not Oliver Cox who is the exception, it is the comparatively a theoretical second generation of "leading scholars" who were exceptional during the height of Marxist influence in the United States.

The only member of the second generation of Black sociologists to produce formal sociological theory was Oliver Cox. His contribution was to Marxist theory. At the University of Chicago, Cox left economics in the 1930s partly because of economics' inability to predict The Great Depression. After transferring to sociology, he worked directly with William Ogburn and Samuel Stouffer in statistical methods. Cox's training and specialty were both important and ironic. In the 1920s, there was vigorous debate over the utility and validity of case study, participant observation, and the comparative method. These were the methods that Frazier, Johnson, Doyle, Drake, and Cayton were trained in at Chicago (Bannister 1987: 3). By the 1930s, the more "scientific" and quantitative sociology gained power and influence. It was exemplified by Ogburn at Chicago. While Frazier may have been Park's "most complete" student, Cox was at the center of the new cutting-edge methods with one of its most important leaders. If Cox had gone along with "the program," he may have had an extraordinarily influential career. But he did not and the reason was not simply principled opposition, but also because of his eccentric personality and disability, polio. He chose instead to use the historical and comparative method, and to critically advance Marx's theoretical work on capitalism, its origins, character, and definitive impact on race relations. In doing so, Cox contributed to macro-theory, and he paid for it in relative obscurity.

Another reason why the second generation did not contribute to theory was due to the philosophical underpinnings of American social theory up through Myrdal. Stanford Lyman (1972) points out that virtually all of the theoretical statements applied to Black people through Myrdal were characterized by a "conservative, laissez-faire, and fatalistic bias" starting with William Graham Sumner's Social Darwinism to Lester Ward's meliorative approach through Robert Park (p. 100). Also since Robert Park's race relation cycle was the most prominent race relations theory, a rejection of the possibility of developing a competing sociological theory was seen as a rejection of the possibility of any sociological theory in the field of race relations (p. 174). In which case, the very question of why a second generation of Black sociologists failed to contribute to theory is much more of a reflection on our times. There was a general poverty of dynamic theory in American sociology until after the Second World War. Emile Durkheim, Max Weber, and Karl Marx the theorists rather than the ideologist were not well known until Talcott Parsons introduced them in 1937 (Bierstedt 1981: 498).

Walter Wallace suggests a method to isolate the potential theoretical contributions of sociologists who have extensive written records like the second generation (1974: 301). We should do a careful content analysis of their writing. In doing so, we can focus specifically on the structure of their argument, and to what they attribute specific behaviors, beliefs, and attitudes to. Temporal sequencing, attributions of cause and effects, and specifications of conditions can also be isolated in such an analysis. It is quite possible that there might have been unique arguments among Frazier, Johnson, Reid, Drake, and Cayton in the second generation; Du Bois and Haynes in the first generation; and Crummel, Brown, Williams, Ferris, and Fortune in the forgotten pioneer generation in the eighteen hundreds. Such an analysis would show their theoretical frameworks. We might find then existing frameworks were used, or through fieldwork and experience some of these writers may have been ahead of their times. Such an analysis may very well help to decide whether there is anything unique in the work of the "classical" Black sociologists. Stanford Layman summarized where we were then and now with regard to social theory in the study of race relations. He asserts the sociology of the Black man (as a theoretical enterprise) has not yet begun. Blacks remain a sociological puzzle because American sociological thought has been dominated by a progressively more complex version of Aristotle's view that all things exist and change according to principles of slow, orderly, and continuous motion (1972: 171). The alternatives to this master underlying premise have the potential to produce new perspectives on American race relations that might better explain the African American experience (1972: 177).

A More Central Problem: Culture

There is a major dimension regarding the second generation of Black sociologists that both Watts and I missed. It is how they viewed African American culture. Several books could be written about this issue, focusing on each scholar. The problems and importance of how the second-generation viewed culture is best articulated again by Walter Wallace (1974). The first and second generation of Black sociologists wrote extensively about African American social organization (churches, fraternal groups, extended families, etc.) But they were ambivalent about whether there is an African American culture. Wallace asks how can you have social organization without culture? St. Clair Drake provides some insight on this point. He suggests that Radcliffe-Brown's structure anthropology influenced his and others Chicago School students' works by the 1940s. The new and scientifically sounder approach to field work (which paralleled Marx's influence) was on social structure and not cultural expressions as in Melville Herskovits' work (Drake 1989: 12). For whatever reason the second generation was generally ambivalent about African American culture, any distinct Black social organization was left open to attributions of being pathological rather than "healthy," because the only other acknowledged cultural system was White social organization. Without a clear articulation of Black cultural continuity and discontinuity to account for recurring family practices, etc., the door was left wide open for a Nathan Glazer or a Daniel Patrick Moynihan to exploit the ambiguity. This is precisely what happened with "The Moynihan Report" (1965). This problem also meant the social work basis of much of the second generation's scholarship was directed at eliminating specific Black family, child rearing, etc. practices and organization that sprang from nowhere--a non-existing culture. E. Franklin Frazier was key to this issue and to understanding why the second generation reflected such ambivalence about Black culture.

In writing about Frazier, Anthony Platt (1991) says it is inaccurate to characterize Frazier as having ignored African American culture (p. 5). Frazier was very concerned with the cultural integrity of the African American community. I would agree with Platt. However, I would add Frazier took a short-term view of African American culture. In

Platt's words, he was   "dogmatic and unyielding that slavery had broken the cultural bonds for African Americans of the African past" (p. 5).   This is alleged to also be Robert Park's view, i.e., the African past was severed and that slavery demoralized the Black family (p. 135). Frazier had a particular bias toward African American culture. He is quoted as saying, "I am primarily interested in saving the Negroes self-respect. If the masses of Negroes can save their self-respect and remain free from hate, so much the better for their moral development..."(p. 125). This means Frazier believed Black Americans were a new people sprung from slavery without healthy institutional life. This belief in demoralization colored Frazier's sense that all-contemporary Black behavior and institutions had to be explained within less than one hundred years of behaviors, attitudes, beliefs, and organization since slavery.   This is where Herbert Gutman accurately characterized Frazier as having "used disorganization in a normative sense,   juxtaposed with   civilization;   occasionally   he   used   it (disorganization) synonymously with urbanization. With his continued reference to   the   chaos   and   disorganization   in   urban   black family patterns,   Frazier   seriously   underestimated   the resources, ingenuity, and organization of 'demoralized' families" (p. 138).   Drake believed that Frazier realized the limits of his view after his field works in Brazil (Drake 1989: 18).

Johnson, Reid, Drake, and Cayton are open to the same critiques to the extent that they ignored the African past and agreed with Frazier, i.e., Blacks left slavery de- institutionalized.   While these men were not trained in history, they did reject U.B. Phillip's characterizations of slavery as a benevolent institution as in American Negro Slavery (1918).   They knew slavery was not benevolent. Where Robert Park and the second generation agreed with Phillips was in characterizing the freedman as demoralized and without culture.   The presumption that slavery de moralized and de-cultured Blacks had been challenged in the prior   century   by   George   Williams   (1882);   by   the community historians of the Harlem Renaissance early in this century (see Richard Moore 1969); by W.E.B. Du Bois in The Negro (1915); and by Herbert Aptheker, American Negro Slave Revolts (1943).   Blacks modified African culture in response to slavery.   They created institutions during slavery to survive and resist, and continued to do so after slavery.   Such resistance and responsiveness would be impossible without a cultural basis for resistance.   What modified this problem of interpretation and perspective for Johnson, Reid, Drake, and Cayton was extensive fieldwork. I propose the more time they spent with Black folks in community, the more the presumption of demoralization and de-institutionalization was called into question. What they saw in southern and northern Black communities were not people without healthy institutions and culture. Frazier is more problematic because more of his scholarship was based on secondary sources; he did less fieldwork than Johnson or Drake, and fought with Herkovits about African influences.

W.E.B. Du Bois escaped the same problem of interpretation not only because of Franz Boas, but also because he did off and on more than two decades of extensive field research in the rural South from 1900 through 1930. His work was funded by The U.S. Department of Interior to study sharecropping and race relations in the South. Due to Du Bois' progressive interpretations and increasing reputation as a race radical, his extensive notes and manuscripts (possibly one of his greatest works) were destroyed (Bowser and Whittle 1996: 36). This problem of African American culture--what is it and what are its institutions and effects--was not only a problem for the second generation of Black sociologists, it is still with us today. William Wilson shows the same problem with Black culture in writing about the possibility of an "insider" view some twenty years. He wrote: "In some instances, it is claimed that there is a fundamental causal connection between the skin color of a sociologists and his ability to conduct adequate and meaningful inquiry into the black experience" (1974: 329). "There is no factual evidence to suggest that a sociologist has to be black to adequately describe and explain the experiences of blacks, in the same way there is no evidence that a criminologist must be a criminal to understand criminal behavior" (1974: 326). The debate over "an insider's view" in sociology was not about advancing Wilson's absurd points. There are three issues at stake: 1) is there an African American culture? 2) If so, what role does it play in the sociological view of African Americans? 3) What kind of background, training or perspective does it takes too properly study it? Wilson's comments and subsequent work shows Frazier's ambivalence. For contemporary sociologists, the bigger problem is that Wilson is not alone.

The irony of the cultural question in sociology is not only it still exists, but that it ever existed. While the second generation of sociologists was constrained by ambivalence regarding Black culture, African American creative writers and artists have had a century long celebration of Black culture, Black expression, Black institutional life, and Black values. There is no question here of whether or not there is an "insiders view." It is not a simple one-dimensional view, but a universal view of humanity. Their work suggests that there is definitely an African American culture within American Society that cannot be dismissed as a literary and artistic fiction. bell hooks and Cornel West testify to their "insiders view" and to the significance of African American culture in <u>Breaking Bread: Insurgent Black Intellectual Life</u> (1991). In addition, Black culture is itself the subject of theoretical work. Houston Baker, Jr. explores an inner theory of the blues in <u>Blues, Ideology, and Afro-American Literature: A Vernacular Theory</u> (1989). Henry Louis Gates, Jr. attempts to explore the inner dimensions of Black literature in <u>The Signifying Monkey: A Theory of Afro-American Literary Criticism</u> (1988). During the time of the second generation, Zora Neal Hurston, as illustrated in <u>The Complete Stories</u> (1995) explored the inner dimensions of Black culture as a writer and anthropologist. She like Oliver Cox was marginalized in her time and her work is only now becoming seriously appreciated. Then the Africanisms Frazier claimed do not exist have been explored by the writers in Joseph Holloway's (ed.) <u>Africanisms in American Culture</u> (1991). Finally, one wonders what would be the response of the second generation and of contemporary Black sociologists who are ambivalent about Black culture to Harry Hyatt's <u>Hoodoo, Conjuration, Witchcraft, Rootwork: Beliefs Accepted By Many Negroes and White People</u> (1970). I suspect they would find it too raw and would reject it as indicative of culture. Certainly, it had nothing to say about social structure. In contrast, Zorro Neal Hurst would have loved it.

A Final Word

Some might feel that as in 1981, I have misrepresented the second generation of Black sociologists, and that I now appear to be in agreement with Watts in questioning the uniqueness of these scholars. It is certainly still an open question as to whether or not their work is in any way "classical." I believe the jury is still out. We need to have many more long hard looks at the men, their work, and their lives. It is tragic that book length studies have been done on only two of them-- Oliver Cox and E. Franklin Frazier. A full critical review of Charles Johnson is long overdue. I do have words in defense of Frazier and others whom I have characterized as "ambivalent" about

African American culture. Unlike the writers and artists who were free to create, and who had other Black people as audiences, the sociologists were not free. They were not writing for their students or for the Black community. They were writing for what we now refer to as "public policy." In another words, they were writing then as now to convince powerful White interests to improve conditions for African Americans. Furthermore, the regard those in power would have for their studies was also dependent upon writing within an aspiring scientific framework where personal bias is always suspect. Powerful interest such as Andrew Carnegie and power brooking scientists such as Robert Park could not deal with the idea that African customs and beliefs may have survived slavery and were still around to "pollute" American culture in the assimilation process Park foresaw. So the second generation of Black sociologists as well as contemporary scholars with access to power leave the cultural question alone. It is ironic that William Wilson, who epitomizes the contemporary ambivalence of Black sociologists to African American culture, has joined Cornel West and Henry Louis Gates, Jr. at Harvard. Gates and West are two of the most prominent proponent and students of African American culture outside of sociology.

Finally, we have to consider that the careers, the advocacy within social work, restraint regarding culture and the intellectual politics of the second generation of Black sociologists paid off for subsequent generations of African Americans. Their work led up to and provided the content for Gunnar Myrdal's influential An American Dilemma (1944). It also served as background material for court cases that led up to the successful challenge to racial segregation, Brown vs. Board of Education in 1954. Their work helped set the stage for the advancements of the 1960s. While Black sociologists do not get credit for Brown vs. Board of Education, they provided the volumes and volumes of studies on the effect of racial segregation on Black communities and, especially important were Frazier, Johnson, Warner, et al., and Reid's studies on Black youth.

References
Bannister, Robert (1987). Sociology and Scientism: The American Quest for Objectivity, 1880-1940. Chapel Hill: The University of North Carolina Press.

Bierstedt, Robert (19981). American Sociological Theory: A Critical History. New York: Academic Press.

Bowser, Benjamin and Deborah Whittle (1996). Personal Reflections on W.E.B. Du Bois: The Person, Scholar, and Activist by Herbert and Fay Aptheker. In Rutledge Dennis (ed.). W.E.B. Du Bois: The Scholar as Activist, Vol. 9. (pp. 27-65). Greenwich: JAI Press.

Brandt, Gunther (1974). The Origins of American Sociology: A Study in the Ideology of Social Science, 1865-1895. Dissertation: Princeton University.

Cruse, Harold (1967). The Crisis of the Negro Intellectual. New York: William Morrow and Company.

Drake, St. Clair (1989). Studies of the African Diaspora: The Work and Reflections of St. Clair Drake, Sage Race Relations Abstracts, 14(3): 3_29.

Harrison, Shelby, et al. (1943). Foreword. In Charles S. Johnson. Patterns of Negro Segregation. New York: Harper and Brothers Publishers.

Hunter, Herbert M. and Sameer Abraham (eds.).(1987). Race, Class, and the World System: The Sociology of Oliver C. Cox. New York: Monthly Review Press.

Lewis, David L. (1993). W.E.B. Du Bois: Biography of a Race, 1868_1919. New York: Henry Holt and Company.

Logan, Rayford (1957). The Negro in the United States: A Brief History. Princeton: Van Nostrand.

Lyman, Stanford (1972). The Black American in Sociological Thought: New Perspective on Black America. New York: GP Putnam's Son.

Matthews, Fred H. (1977). Quest for an American Sociology: Robert E. Park and the Chicago School. Montreal: McGill-Queens's University Press.

Moore, Richard (1969). Africa Conscious Harlem. In John Henrik Clarke (ed.). Harlem: A Community in Transition. New York: The Citadel Press.

Platt, Anthony (1991). E. Franklin Frazier Reconsidered. New Brunswick: Rutgers University Press.

Raushenbush, Winifred (1979). Robert E. Park: Biography of a Sociologist. Durham: Drake University Press.

70   *Confronting the American Dilemma of Race*

Robbins, Richard (1996). Sideline Activists: Charles S. Johnson and the Struggle for Civil Rights. Jackson: University Press of Mississippi.

Stanfield, John (1991). Racism in America and Other Race-Centered Nation-States: Synchronic Consideration. International Journal of Comparative Sociology, 32(3-4): 243-261.

Wallace, Walter (1974). Some Elements of Sociological Theory In Studies of Black Americans. In James Blackwell and Morris Janowitz (eds.). Black Sociologists: Historical and Contemporary Perspectives (pp. 299-326). Chicago: The University of Chicago Press.

Williams, Eric (1966). Capitalism and Slavery. New York:

Wilson, William J. (1974). The New Black Sociology: Reflections on the 'Insider' and 'Outsider' Controversy. In James Blackwell and Morris Janowitz (eds.). Black Sociologists: Historical and Contemporary Perspectives (pp. 322-338). Chicago: The University of Chicago Press.

Young, Alford A., Jr. (1993) The 'Negro Problem' and the Character of the Black Community: Charles S. Johnson, E. Franklin Frazier, and the Constitution of a Black Sociological Tradition, 1920-1935. The National Journal of Sociology, Summer, 7(1): 95-133.

Chapter Four

The "Negro Problem" and the Character of the Back Community: Charles S. Johnson, E. Franklin Frazier, and the Constitution of a Black Sociological Tradition, 1920-1935[1]

Alford A. Young, Jr.

---

[1]. A version of this paper was presented at the Annual Meeting of the Association of Black Sociologists, Ft. Lauderdale, Florida, August 10-12, 1993. The author wishes to thank Edgar G. Epps, Carla O'Connor, Thomas Holt, Michael Hanchard and roundtable participants at the ABS Annual Meeting for their guidance and comments on this paper. Direct all correspondence to Alford Young, Jr. Department of Sociology, University of Chicago, 1126 East 591h Street, Chicago, IL 60637.

Abstract

This paper examines how Charles S. Johnson and E. Franklin Frazier framed conceptions of Afro-American social character and how that character shaped the status of Afro-American culture in the early twentieth-century. This inquiry includes an overview of the academic and popular considerations of race and culture in late nineteenth and early twentieth-century America, the initial response of the early Afro-American intellectual community to such a discourse, the changing academic considerations of race and culture in the early twentieth century with particular emphasis on the role played by Robert E. Park and the Chicago School of Sociology, and the contributions of Johnson and Frazier as partial revision and partial support of that school of thought.

It is maintained that Charles Johnson contributed a social-psychological perspective concerning the content of Afro-American social character and culture, while Frazier developed a social organizational perspective. Moreover, both scholars constructed portrayals of Afro-Americans as victims of myriad social ills that crippled their capacity for promoting their own cultural as well as social advancement. The work concludes with an assessment of the role that both scholars played in constructing a revised scholarly focus on the effects of race relations on an oppressed constituency and creating a sociological vision of Afro-Americans as a socially and culturally under-developed constituency with respect to mainstream America.

Throughout the twentieth century, the quest of many Afro-American social scientists has been one of attempting to define the social and cultural character of black America. Charles S. Johnson and E. Franklin Frazier were central figures in the emergence of the black sociological canon--a canon that specifically concerned itself with that attempt. The work of Johnson and Frazier, from the period between 1920 and 1935, spans a period of magnificent change in the ecology and social structure of the black American presence in the United States. This period began with the continued emergence of industrial American society and ended with the rapid formation of the black urban populace. In terms of Afro-American social thought, this was an equally critical period. The era started with the emergence of a black intellectual stratum that took seriously the task of defending and asserting the humanity of black people and ended at a time when social thinkers who focused on issues concerning the black American experience became an institutionalized presence in American academe.

The attempt here is to consider how Charles S. Johnson and E. Franklin Frazier framed their respective notions of the social and cultural life of black America throughout the first third of the twentieth century. More specifically, this work will examine how these scholars defined the "Negro problem" as a presupposition to their vision of the social character of the black American community. The significance of ending this analysis with work completed by 1935 is that the black American and the mainstream American sociological traditions reached a point of convergence in focusing on the impact of the city on social interaction and social organization. The dominant sociological paradigms of the twentieth century for race relations, racial advancement, and racial identity (however flawed they are now considered by contemporary sociologists) then took form in sociological thought. As will be explored, these paradigms provided legitimacy for the notions of the "Negro problem" that shaped the sociological focus on black Americans.

The conception of the social and cultural experiences of black Americans as constituting a social problem is in large part a manifestation of sociology's considerations of the situation of black Americans at the turn of the century (Schwendinger and Schwendinger, 1974). These considerations were as much the attempt of American sociologists to give definition to sociological inquiry as they were a means of affirming the legitimacy of American society as a social and cultural "Melting Pot." It is within this context that black sociologists first engaged in inquiries into the experiences of black Americans. Charles S. Johnson and E. Franklin Frazier both reified and challenged aspects of the "Negro problem" during their careers in sociology. This analysis will carefully examine how these patterns emerged in their early work and what residual effects this had on further sociological analyses of the black American community.

The work of Charles S. Johnson and E. Franklin Frazier cannot be divorced from the social conditions and ideas extant at the time of their activity. Therefore, this analysis will proceed with a number of preliminary inquiries before considering their work. The first will examine the discourse on race in the early twentieth century, as shaped by mainstream scholars and commentators, and how that discourse facilitated, and was then reshaped, by sociological considerations of the black presence in the United States. The second will examine the birth of a black intellectual stratum that attempted to respond to such a discourse, including the contribution made by early black sociologists. Finally, the third inquiry will look at intellectual considerations of the emerging American city and the changing scholarly considerations of race relations in the context of urbanization.

Racialist Thought From Post-Bellum Until 1920

Near the start of the twentieth century, social thought on American race relations were grounded in one of two positions as points of departure. The first consisted of a refined social Darwinism that encouraged the view that blacks lacked three fundamental human characteristics: 1) an intellectual capacity, 2) the ability to cultivate or contribute to civilization, and 3) a moral foundation for their behavior. When placed in the hands of American racialist thinkers, Darwin's work was reconstituted to legitimize these and related viewpoints (Frederickson, 1987: 23033). Darwin, himself, actually made no arguments about racial distinctiveness in human evolution, but this was only one of many misapplications that white racialist thinkers would make in applying pseudo-scientific thought to issues of race throughout the late nineteenth century. As the historian John Hope Franklin stated, "Social Darwinists...declared that if Negroes did not survive it was because they were not 'the fittest' and no law promulgated by the state could change 'the natural order of things'(1965: viii)."

Richard Hofstadter argued that post-belium American society involved rapid economic expansion, exploitative methods in commercial and other business development, and desperate competition (Hofstadter, 1945: 30). Each of these factors helped Darwinist thought to gain credence as an approach for assessing the social circumstances of nineteenth century America, especially with respect to issues concerning black Americans. Reconstruction was only marginally successful in creating socio-economic opportunities that would provide substantial, long-term benefits for the black community (Foner, 1988). The freedmen and women, who had few resources and little experience as free and mobile people in American society, were left to manage a social existence at a time when socio-economic competition and social stratification were increasingly exacerbated by the mood of the industrial era. The overwhelming demands of the Southern populace to control the social opportunities of black Americans were masked by Social Darwinist thought, which questioned the abilities, humanity, and potential of black Americans.

Racialist thought also went beyond the evolutionary emphasis of Social Darwinism in elucidating views on black Americans.[2] The degree to which such thought penetrated popular social commentary on black Americans was immense. Magazines such as Nation, Harper's Weekly, and Atlantic Monthly regularly published articles stressing white supremacy and innate Negro inferiority and hopelessness (Woodward, 1954).

A second brand of racialist thought that flourished during this period also maintained significant ramifications for public sentiment about black Americans. This view was an outgrowth of the paternalistic attitudes about black Americans that developed during slavery. A pivotal document promoting these views was Harriet Beecher Stowe's Uncle Tom's Cabin (1987 [1852]). Her novel presented a depiction of blacks as child-like in their relations to the world. Following this line of thought, some polemicists argued that a gentle manner should be expressed to the freedmen and women so that they would retain the "amiable characteristics" that they cultivated during slavery (Frederickson, 1987: 285-86). In this regard blacks were considered by some whites to possess humble qualities; the "mildest and gentlest of men" who required sensitivity and nurturing in their interaction with the predominantly white world (ibid: 103-106). Although this viewpoint was diametrically opposed to the character portrayals offered by pseudo-scientific thinkers, it was equally as limiting in its depiction of the capabilities of black people.

---

[2]. Some of the views expressed during this period included eugenics (race being the determinant of the size and capacity of the brain, which was used to substantiate notions of black inferiority, criminal behavior and feeblemindedness), ethnology (race as an indicator of physical, moral, and behavioral traits, placing blacks far below whites in terms of abilities), and racialist historiography (which referred to the black American historical experience as one of stagnation, inefficiency, ignorance, sexual license and biologically derived and hereditary savagery). See Frederickson, Cossell (1963), and Newby (1968) for more elaborated accounts of these developments.

The contributions of the racialist scholars, popular writers, and polemicists of the middle and late nineteenth century led to this dichotomy in the construction by white Americans of an image of the social character of Afro-Americans.   Some white Americans (particularly the practitioners of pseudo-social science) regarded blacks as slightly more human than beasts. Others regarded black individuals as emotionally and intellectually immature beings who exemplified passivity, peacefulness, and humility, traits that were perceived to be lacking (at least to an equivalent degree) in the personalities of white Americans. This dichotomy of attitudes set the framework in which early black American scholars began to contemplate the status and possibilities of the black community in America.

The emergence of a black sociological discourse was circumscribed not only by pseudo-scientific and perverse moralistic social thought, but also by developments in an American sociology that was in its embryonic stage in the late nineteenth century. The first sociological treatises published in the United States concerned race relations: Henry Hughes's <u>Treatise</u> <u>on</u> <u>Sociology</u> <u>Theoretical</u> <u>and</u> <u>Practical</u> (1854) and George Fitzhugh's <u>Sociology</u> <u>for</u> <u>the</u> <u>South:</u> <u>or</u> <u>The</u> <u>Failure</u> <u>of</u> <u>Free</u> <u>Society</u> (1854). Both texts regarded slavery as a moralizing and civilizing social process for blacks. Neither of these works, however, had much bearing on later developments in sociology (Frazier, 1947: 265).

In fact, early American sociology spent very little time on issues of black people and race relations. As the sociologist John Stanfield commented, "the prevailing opinion among sociologists was that the innate inferiority of blacks made them irrelevant as subjects of inquiry. 'Why study the obvious? (Stanfield, 1985: 23).'" In any case, the minor attention given to matters of race can be categorized in one of two ways. In the first, Herbert Spencer attempted to frame a paradigm for social science based on scientific causality. This, he hoped, would dismiss the idea that social causes and effects could either be calculated or repaired (Hofstadter, 1945: 29). Spencer's objective was to make sociology the disciplinary grounding for Social Darwinist thought. For sociological enterprises concerning race, then, one half of the discourse was embedded in the attitudes and ideas that emanated from Social Darwinism.

The other strand of early American sociological thought on race was created by individuals such as Charles H. Cooley, Franklin Giddings, and Edward Alsworth. These scholars viewed social life as a process that evolved toward higher forms of cooperation and cohesion

(Frederickson, 1987: 312-13). They explicitly and implicitly asserted that the black experience in America would necessarily have to be an effort to adapt to the normative processes of American life. The mass European immigration that began in the late nineteenth century gave leverage to this domain of thought as issues of assimilation and amalgamation came to the forefront of sociological attention (Stocking, 1968: 50). These scholars, and the portion of the general public who shared their views, argued a range of positions about the potential and possibilities for blacks to adapt to the changing cultural fabric of the country. A shared point of view for these sociologists, however, was that complete adaptation was the only option available for blacks.

At the turn of the century, America consisted of a community of black people still contending with their revolutionary new social status as free people (including managing the ramifications brought about by the effects of the Plessy versus Ferguson Supreme Court case of 1896), a mass influx of immigrants bringing with them new cultural practices and ideas, and technological change that forced most, if not all, Americans to alter their standard ways and/or attitudes about life. When American sociologists considered the first of these circumstances (to a significantly lesser extent than they considered issues of immigration and technological change), their sentiment pointed in two directions. The first was to call attention to the social inadequacies of the black American community (which, as many argued, necessitated policies that instituted some form of social control of blacks). The second was to define a means for increased black American adaptation to the dominant culture of white America. Hence, the legacy of the early discourse on race in early American sociological thought was that it dissolved the distinction between biological and cultural processes in the effort to draw what were believed at the time to be some definitive conclusions on issues of race (ibid: 51-52). Social science took on the language, terminology, and structure of biologically derived scientific thought in investigating and explaining the social phenomenon of race relations and race identity.

The Emergence of an Afro-American Social Science Tradition

An initial Afro-American intellectual stratum emerged during the mid-nineteenth century in response to the assertions being made about the potential for black American capabilities in American society. The early black Church, the abolitionist movement, and the post-Civil War black convention movement each provided a milieu for the growth of a black intellectual community (Meier, 1966: 316). Most black spokesmen from these constituencies were polemically oriented with regard to their interest in the black presence in the United States. Efforts to form a collective of black intellectuals with a primary interest in scholarly objectives, as opposed to political ones, culminated in the founding of the American Negro Academy on March 5; 1897, in Washington, D.C. The objective of the Academy was to organize black scholars, artists, and "those distinguished in other walks 'of life, for the promotion of Letters, Science, and Art (Moss, 1977: 1)."

In essence, the mandate of the American Negro Academy provided a context for black scholarly efforts in the twentieth century. The objective of the group was to offer intellectual definition of the black American situation and to confront the views put forth by the white intellectual community. The historian S.P. Fullinwider stated:

> The first and foremost of the objectives...was to demonstrate the Negro's potential equality with the white man. This task was approached in three ways (Often in the same work): through Scriptures; by historical demonstration of the greatness to which Negroes have at times risen; and, by the argument that culture is a product of environment (1969: 4-5).

These efforts were based upon two premises: first, that Western civilization was unquestionably the most advanced of its time in the sense of what a civilization should be, and second, that blacks had fallen far behind such standards and had to find a means by which to catch up (ibid: 7).[3]

---

[3]. This viewpoint also was shared by many black scholars who were not involved in the American Negro Academy. Subsequently, some of the early black American scholarly work was framed by defensive arguments about potential black abilities in American society. Two such accounts were W.H. Crogman's The Progress of a Race: The Remarkable Advancement of the Afro-American (1902) and William T. Alexander's History of The Colored Race in America (1888), which argued that black Americans courageously persevered in their quest to secure a place for themselves in American society following their tenure in shycry. See Franklin (1965) for further commentary.

It is clear that the first order of business for the black scholarly community was to assert that black Americans could participate in and contribute to society--in essence, the task was to argue for the humanity of black people. Through this effort black scholars could define better what resources black Americans needed to competently and comfortably sustain themselves in American society. A part of this effort meant confronting the fact that, while it was clear that the post-emancipation era was far short of sufficient for black Americans' transition to freedom, it was also clear to black scholars that black Americans differed radically from whites in their cultural and social organization at the turn of the century. Hence, a duality existed for black intellectual thought of that period. The effort of black scholars to assert that blacks could achieve a social existence equivalent to whites, and on the cultural terms of white America, was one half of their intellectual focus. The other was the view that a radical social difference between blacks and whites did exist, and that it was not due to black racial inferiority, but to distinct (and, in some cases, superior) black racial characteristics. The initial establishment of a black sociological discourse prominently displayed both ends of this dichotomy.

The first black sociologists entered the field with passionate concern about the black condition in America. For the early black sociologists the objective for scholarly investigation was quite clear: "Is the Negro to demand full integration and risk losing his racial attributes through assimilation, or is he to accept segregation as the means to develop his particular genius, safely protected from the contaminating mores of American civilization (ibid: 98)?"

William Edward Burghardt DuBois represented the vanguard of black sociological thought, although his identity as a sociologist was but one dimension of his academic career. He maintained the view that sociology could provide an intellectual grounding for the black experience, as well as help facilitate an improvement in American race relations. DuBois set a precedent for later black sociologists who followed him by stressing that through sociology a comprehensive understanding of black life could be achieved, as well as the defeat of prejudice through the accumulation of knowledge (ibid: 50-51, Green and Driver, 1978: 31). In what has been regarded as his seminal sociological contribution, The Philadelphia Negro (1899), DuBois performed a substantive analysis of black life in that city, using survey methodology and demographic techniques (crude by present-day standards, but advanced for his time), in order to consider a range of social issues pertinent to the black experience in Philadelphia. These included the early phase of northern migration for black Americans, the social conditioning processes of urban life, the social institutions and lifestyles that were created there, and the enduring effects of slavery (1976 [1899]). In his effort to formulate a statement on the status of blacks in a municipality, DuBois gave credence to the argument that black Americans could function legitimately in a civilized society. He provided a credible, balanced articulation of how a constituency strove to adapt to as well as reconstitute urban space in the effort to manage their social existence.

DuBois was also a major voice in the early black intellectual community that worked diligently to ascertain the cultural distinctiveness of black America. He assumed that racial differences beyond mere physical characteristics existed and thus committed himself to the task of characterizing the distinctiveness of black people. He stated:

> While race differences have followed mainly physical race lines...no mere physical difference would really define or explain the deeper differences--the cohesiveness and continuity of these groups. The deeper differences are spiritual, psychical differences--undoubtedly based on the physical, but infinitely transcending them (1970: 7686).

For DuBois, the black American had yet to contribute to his or her full capacity in American life. He felt that, because the potential of blacks was presaged in the Egyptian culture of the past, they remained a "great race still waiting to make their full contribution to civilization (Moss, 1977: 68)."

W.E.B. DuBois, then, pioneered the sociological investigation of the black community in two areas. First, he espoused a complex methodological approach for investigating the social processes of the black community. Secondly, he fostered the view that race difference wanscended biology in socially significant ways.

The brief sociological career of DuBois was mirrored by other black sociologists during that period. Kelly Miller (at Howard University) and George Edmund Haynes (at Fisk University) both contributed to the racialist paradigm that contained much of DuBois' work, especially in discussing black American social and cultural manifestations

(Fullinwider: 92-100). These efforts helped to locate a black American discourse in sociology that gave intense consideration to issues of the social character of black Americans. That character was identified by these scholars, in one sense, in the recognition of their cultural lag behind white Americans, and in another by the articulation of the perceived superior caliber of black Americans to affirm the qualities of humility and spirituality as innate aspects of their human condition.

American Sociology and the Emergence of the City

In addition to residual effects of turn-of-the-Century social thought, the sociology of Charles S. Johnson and E. Franklin Frazier emerged out of a social context shaped by rapid change taking place in the first two decades of the twentieth century. Specifically, the influencing factors consisted of the Progressive era and pragmatism, the black urban migration, and the groundwork of Robert Park in the Chicago School of Sociology.

The Progressive Era was an early twentieth-century ideological phenomenon that had a monumental impact on American sociology, particularly with regard to race relations and race theory. This era brought into being a social mood informed by an aggressive search for understanding of the fast-changing social world at the turn of the century. As Nancy Weiss described:

> By the end of the nineteenth century the prevailing perception of the causes of social ills had shifted to an indictment of a hostile economic and social environment rather than individual weakness. This new view...went hand-in-hand with an emerging faith in the power of social reform (1974: 68-72).0

John Dewey's introduction of pragmatism into the social sciences linked popular progressive thought with the intellectual discourse of the early twentieth century. Pragmatist thought was centered on social reform through intricate understandings of personal experience. This concept helped to cripple the promotion of Social Darwinism after the start of the twentieth century (Hofstadter, 1945: 105). The most liberal-minded scholars and social activists extended these new ideas to address the plight of the black community.

The effect of such sentiments and ideas on American race relations must not be overstated. For the most part, the Progressive Era was a period when mainstream scholars were just beginning to look at new ways of considering the black American experience. These ideas would become established in academic discourse no earlier than the second decade of the twentieth century. Part of the reason for this were the pervasive influences of the white intellectual community and popular media in continuing to affirm that blacks were a racially inferior, if not a menacing presence in society (Gossett, 1963: 353-66; Stocking. 1968: 300-301). In the end, however, the impact of the Progressive Era on intellectual considerations of black Americans was substantial. The pragmatists were a significant presence in the aspect of the scholarly community that gave attention to the growth of the American city. At the same time, the city was becoming the locus for contemporary developments in black America. Hence, pragmatist thinkers and black intellectuals found common ground in the early twentieth century.

The major sociological issue with respect to the black community in the early twentieth century was the beginning of its mass migration out of the rural South and into cities. New York, Chicago, Los Angeles Detroit, Philadelphia, St. Louis, and Baltimore each experienced increases (ranging from 59% to 805%) in their population of Afro-American residents between the years of 1910 and 1930 (Bureau of the Census, 1935). During that time, the national urban black American population increased from 2,684,797 to 5,193,913 and the urban to rural distribution of the black population moved closer to parity (ibid).

The movement to city life, and overwhelmingly to northern cities, was the causal factor for a number of other circumstances for black Americans. Social science began to view the black community as a national minority in an urban context instead of a southern problem (Stanfield, 1985: 30). By the 1920s a prominent (and long-lasting) trait of the urban black community was economic distress (Kornweibel, 1976). The growth of a black urban population added new elements to racist thought. The development of overcrowded slums due to poor housing opportunities led to increased crime, poor health, and poor sanitary conditions. Ignoring the explicit role of the predominantly white society in creating black urban ghettoes, certain whites felt that the social ills of the black community proved that blacks were incapable of self-government, acquiring education, or developing their own franchises (Woodward, 1854: 79).

On the other hand, however, American sociology began to focus increasingly on environmental influences as opposed to .hereditary factors in explaining race relations and racial group status in the 1910s and 1920s. While racism and racialist thought remained realities circumscribing investigations of the black experience, sociology attempted to employ scientifically derived empirical research techniques in its exploration of the black experience in America while diminishing the emphasis on uncritical racialist theorizing (Frederickson: 313-316, Hofstader: 144-145). The rise of the city and the subsequent narrowing of social distance between ethnic groups had much to do with these changes in the sociological enterprise (Shils, 1983: 187-205). In addition, major foundations such as the Laura Spelman Rockefeller Memorial, the Julius Rosenwald Fund, and The Phelps-Stokes Fund began funding projects for the sociological investigations of the black community (Stanfield, 1985:61 - 118). These foundations played a central role in how social science formulated an approach to the study of black Americans. This approach was predicated on framing the situation of black Americans as a conglomerate of social dilemmas in need of solvents, instead of a more normative vision of black life that recognized black Americans as contributors to and participants in the varied cultural forms and systems of American life. All of this social activity effected and was affected by the work of Robert Park and the University of Chicago Department of Sociology in restructuring the sociological paradigm for studies of race relations.

Robert Park came to Chicago sociology in 1913 after a career in journalism and administrative work for the Afro-American social activist Booker T. Washington. He became the premier sociologist in the department during the mid-1920s and, from then until 1934 (when he left Chicago for Fisk University), he carefully and astutely cultivated the abilities of his students. In explaining his conception of the role of the sociologist, Park stated, "...he was a kind of super-reporter .... He was to report...the 'Big News'...the long-term trends which recorded what is actually going on rather than what, on the surface of things, merely seems to be going on (Park, 1950a)." Under that rubric, Park made race relations one of his major areas of focus. Subsequently, the University of Chicago became the locus for the training of leading black sociologists throughout the first half of the twentieth century.

Prior to 1935, Park's work resulted in an affirmation the Melting Pot ethic as an appropriate framework for the process of American race relations (Park, 1950b: 283). In relating his work to that ideal Park made at least three lasting contributions to the sociology of race relations: 1) he moved the sociological focus from that of describing supposed racial traits to the examination of changing relations between ethnic groups, 2) he redefined ideas about race by asserting that the concepts used in such discourse in early sociology were problematic, and 3) he identified ethnic prejudice as a function of group and status conflict rather than as a manifestation of natural difference (Matthews, 1977: 157).

Robert Park's race relations cycle was his meta-framework for exploring issues of race and social interaction. Although this heuristic went through a series of revisions during his academic career, Park's general position was that racial or ethnic groups who share social space with other such groups proceed through four stages of interaction--- competition, conflict, accommodation, and assimilation (Persons, 1987: 77-95). The patterns of accommodation and assimilation that take shape depend upon which ethnic or racial group is in the majority status, or more significantly, which groups have greater cultural resources or social power. Ecological, political, economic, and cultural factors help determine the relative status of any group (Park, 1950c: 107). Park stressed that any change in one category for a group will affect the others so that migration, economic advancement, or other social phenomena were interrelated in his framework for the study of race and ethnic groups. The Melting Pot theme is salient to Park's framework in that the final stage of the cycle involved an amalgamation of ethnic or racial groups into one cultural system, based largely on that of the dominant social group.

In essence, the city provided Park with a natural laboratory in which to see his conceptual scheme play itself out. According to Park, groups that have been subjugated or relegated to an inferior status borrow from the culture of their neighbors. Cultural transmission of this sort actually takes place as early as the competition and conflict stages (Park, 1950d: 138-51). In terms of the black American experience, Park looked specifically at the city to observe and interpret how his cycle manifested itself in social interaction. For in Park's view, the city served to reconstitute race relations from territorial affairs to those of domination and subjection within a shared social space (Park, 1950c: 91-104).

Robert Park argued that culture consisted of the resources or shared beliefs that enabled a collective to function in society (Stanfield: 43-46). Included in culture were external and tangible objects (forms of culture) and ideas, norms, and memories (contents of culture). While forms of culture are easily transmitted, content is not. Regardless of the degree of transmissibility, Park believed that racial or ethnic group spatial contact would accelerate the race relations cycle, whereas group isolation would slow it down. Therefore, Park felt that as blacks became acclimated to the city they would gradually abandon the ideas, memories, and norms from prior patterns of social existence, while assuming those of the dominant (white) culture. Park thought it was inevitable that some forms of culture would endure a little longer than others.

The Parkian framework thus suggests that dominant cultural patterns exist. Alternative cultural characteristics were regarded as subordinate. Therefore, Park's framework allowed for a more coherent social scientific definition of pathological or maladjusted behavior with regard to race and ethnicity than had previously existed in scholarly discourse. His views on the cultural aspects of American slavery exemplified his conviction that African cultural manifestations were subordinate in American society. Park believed that blacks retained no African cultural resources. The black Church, black spirituals, and other manifestations of authentic black culture were deemed by Park as definitive products of their American experience (Park, 1950b: 267-281). He believed, however, that black Americans maintained an intangible cultural essence that was distinct from mainstream American experiences. Park stated:

> The Negro is, by natural disposition, neither an intellectual nor an idealist... He is primarily an artist, loving life for its own sake...He is, so to speak, the lady among the races .... The temperament is African, but the tradition is American (1950b: 267-81)."

It is clear from this comment that Park did not break fully with the racialist tradition of the late nineteenth century. The difference in his work is that he grounded aspects of such thought in a more scientific framework for the study of race. His philosophical underpinnings, however, were in many ways a linear development from nineteenth century social thought on black Americans.

Lastly, it is important to note that Park felt that race would become little more than a residual as blacks adapted to American society. Park realized that the significance of race in his era (including racial segregation in housing in the North, and complete segregation in the South) meant that the black American procession through the cycle would be slower than for other ethnic groups (Lyman, 1972: 35-39;

Wacker, 1983: 44). Hence, Park placed emphasis on the unique social status of the black American.

The race relations cycle of Robert Park, and his views on the culture of Afro-Americans and Africans affected the sociological development of his two most prolific black students, Charles S. Johnson and E. Franklin Frazier. Their contributions toward defining the social character of Afro-Americans, and the possibilities for their social advancement, represent methodological and theoretical extensions and revisions of the groundwork laid by Park.

The Social-Psychological Dimensions of the Negro Problem -- The Contributions of Charles S. Johnson

Charles S. Johnson received an undergraduate degree at Virginia Union University prior to acquiring a second baccalaureate from the University of Chicago in 1917. While at Chicago, Robert Park recognized his talents and took him under his wing. In addition to his studies at Chicago, Johnson's scholarship prior to 1935 developed out of his involvement with the Chicago Commission on Race Relations (1919 to 1921), the National Urban League (1919 to 1928), and his position as a faculty member at Fisk University, beginning in the early 1930s. He also edited the National Urban League journal, <u>Opportunity,</u>

In an era when many black scholars sought direct involvement in political movements and activities, Johnson kept distant from polemical circles. He maintained the view that sincere engagement in scholarly endeavors necessitated disengagement from social and political movements (Kirby, 1980: 201-203). Surely, Johnson's conservative stance in regard to such matters had much to do with his strong ties to the philanthropic community throughout most his academic career.

In fact, the difficulty in assessing the scholarship of Charles S. Johnson's views on Afro-Americans lies in the fact that much of his work was directed by the interests of philanthropic entities. As John Startfield II argued, the final product of many of Johnson's ideas were reviewed (and edited) by philanthropic entities that had specific objectives for his work (Stanfield, 1985). Taking Johnson's extensive contact with the philanthropic community into consideration, much can still be learned from his scholarship about his views on race and the social character of the Afro-American community.

Johnson's intellectual posture was that of fact-finder and diagnostician, and he took to heart the Dewey concept of sensitivity to human experience in looking at social circumstances (Bracey, Meier, and Rudwick, 1971: 10; Fullinwider: 114). With such a scholarly lens, Johnson framed his emphasis on the internalization of inferiority that he felt preoccupied much of black life in the early twentieth century (Fullinwider: 108-113). More so than looking at the social organizational aspects of the black community, Johnson was interested in the effect of structure and culture on the condition of the individual. In his view, culture was a product of one's position in the social structure. Therefore, such a position affected the patterns of life, social codes of conduct, and social attitudes of the individual (Johnson, 1934a: 208-12). He stated:

> The organization of life and of values for the Negroes under the regime of slavery was and had to be--as it is true of all cultures--an organization which permitted the most satisfying function of individuals in their setting. Viewed in this light, such meaning and value in the situation as have been given to marriage, the relation of parents to children, divorce, extramarital relations, illegitimacy, behavior in emotional crises involving love, death, religion, take on a new significance (ibid: 212).

Charles Johnson had extensive scholarly exposure to black life in both the South and the North. This allowed him to see the black community as an amalgamation of multiple, varied historical experiences, each shaped by different patterns of social adjustment to its particular ecological structures. He stated:

> American Negroes vary in their cultural development according to the extent of their social and cultural isolation, and according to the character of the cultural patterns to which they are or have been exposed...the variation is as great among these Negro groups, living contemporaneously under different environments, as any of the variations that have existed within the Negro group as a whole at different periods of its history...different planes of culture may be found among different Negro groups within the same community...the extent of the movement--one plane to the next, provides a measure of the cultural development of this group (Johnson, 1934b: 4).

The consistency that Johnson identified in the myriad black experiences (and the basis for his formulation of the "Negro problem" in America) was that they emerged from the same process --the attempt of blacks to adapt to the social, economic, and cultural structure of a specific environment. The different emotional, intellectual, and material resources that blacks possessed in this adaptation process affected the kinds of black communities that emerged in a particular geographic regions. For Johnson, the differential effects of social conditioning were exemplified in one extreme in southern rural communities (Johnson, 1934c: 146), and, in the other, in urban black ghettoes (President's Conference, 1932).

Johnson's approach to the black communities of the rural South was to investigate folk culture, which he deemed an essential arena for social scientific inquiry into the black experience (President's Conference, 1932: 97-98; Wacker: 70-72; Stanfield, 1987: iii). He believed that folk culture provided blacks with a platform for social criticism of American slavery (Johnson, 1936: 97-98). Some critics of his view on folk culture assert, however, that he never clarified whether the emergence of a folk culture was an attempt by blacks to create a normative culture out of a socially disorganized one, or if its existence was the residual effect of social disorganization (Stanfield, 1985: 127). Regardless of any shortcomings that others found in their assessment of Johnson's queries into black folk culture, a persistent point in his thought was that folk culture was a substantive phenomenon that had an instrumental role in the southern rural black community in terms of how black southerners responded to the social conditions affecting their lives.

As for the status of black urban life, Johnson identified social disorganization as the primary result of social conditioning on the black urban community. He believed that black migration -- a gradual emancipation from former social controls affecting black migrants -- resulted in disorganization as a consequence of the relocation of blacks into new environments (President's Conference, 1932: 197). This did not prevent Johnson from affirming that migration was, in many ways, a beneficial experience for blacks. He argued that migration would force blacks to reorganize their "personality(ies) upon new bases of greater control (Johnson, 1934b: 457)." Therefore, their adaptation to hegemonic patterns in American society would be better facilitated. Johnson assertively dismissed the views of scholars like Kelly Miller who regarded vice, disease, crime, and unsanitary living as phenomena affecting blacks because of their lack of a civilizing experience (ibid: 452-58). Instead, Johnson saw these phenomena as consequences of a lack of economic and social resources for better adaptation to the urban environment.

The diversity in the black community was not entirely a celebratory condition for Johnson. He asserted that both positive and negative consequences resulted from this circumstance. In his Preface To Racial Understanding he stated:

> There is no single homogeneous Negro group. Education, experience, and contacts have shaped the circumstances in widely different ways. The largest group may be classified as naive folk whose social information and habits fall dismally short of modern nations...In this group we see preserved folkways and superstitions of Americans of an earlier period .... It is not enough to say merely that they are ignorant or backward or should know better. They must be taught. There is another group just emerging from virtual peasantry and facing new problems of city life. The toll of life among these restless adventurers is tragic and enormous... New standards slowly infiltrate, but with all the waste of the process of learning the ways of the city. There is, hopefully, a new group who have absorbed the new standards and become to a large extent, aware of the accepted values (1936: 52-3).

Implicit in Johnson's argument here is an acknowledgment of Robert Park's race relations cycle. Johnson asserted the importance of assimilation as a means of relieving the trauma created by many of the social circumstances affecting black people. Johnson, however, did not regard value systems as inherent qualities of particular racial groups. He simply regarded value systems as cultural artifacts to be used for normative processes of accommodation, which were available, for the most part, to anyone for the purposes of coping more effectively in American society.

Johnson shared with Robert Park the view that black cultural expression was distinctly American in its manifestations. He held this view about black religious expression, music, and their maintenance of general attitudes (ibid: 92-100). Johnson examined the Marcus Garvey movement, the racial pride that surfaced during the Harlem Renaissance, and the forms of southern black folk culture in the 1920s as possible loci for black cultural expression that reflected strong African influences. In the course of research he concluded that none of these phenomena depicted any African cultural retention by black Americans. He felt that the Marcus Garvey movement was a failure as a mechanism for black American cultural revitalization and that the Harlem Renaissance simply did not enthrall the masses of the black community. Thus, these two developments failed to articulate coherent cultural continuity between Africa and black America. The third development, the emergence of southern black folk culture, was regarded by Johnson as a distinctively American phenomenon (ibid: 549-53). Therefore, the most significant and successful assertions of black American culture in the 1920s were deemed by Johnson as specifically American in their manifestation. While he did not deny that some cultural imponderables derived from Africa could be present in the social and cultural fabric of the black American community, Johnson shared the attitudes of scholars like Robert Park and E. Franklin Frazier in stating that the black experience was a distinctly American one (Johnson, 1934d: 83-88). Moreover, Johnson endorsed Park's view that black Americans had as their only viable option the acculturation into dominant American cultural patterns (Johnson, 1934e: 546-553.

In Charles Johnson's mind, not only did social conditioning play a role in the cultural development of black people, but it also factored in how blacks viewed their possibilities and future options. The general effect of social conditioning was a pervasive feeling of inferiority on the part of black Americans. More than most other black scholars of his time, Charles Johnson concentrated on the internalization of racial inferiority as a major variable in the behavior of blacks. He remarked, "The effect upon the Negro...has developed what psychologists call an oppression psychosis, an inescapable sense of inferiority, an attitude of apology, a sense of guilt over the fact of color (1936: 12)."

Furthermore, Johnson said that blacks suffer an "enforced self-consciousness (that) has developed strange distortions of conduct; it has increased sensitiveness of many Negroes to slights, and prompted the fabrication of compensations for their inferior station (1934f: 233). This, he felt, led to "the process of thought by which opinions are reached and translated into action (which) are, as a result of their isolation, concealed from outsiders (1934f: 233)." Here Johnson places DuBois' notion of the double consciousness in an interactive framework. For Johnson, the double consciousness phenomenon was salient in social interaction in that it facilitated the development of inferiority complexes in black Americans. These complexes then maintained explicit or implicit significance for the varied behavioral expressions of black people. While DuBois introduced the term double consciousness in theoretical language, Johnson delineated its gravity for specific forms of social action.

In further discussion of black American perspectives on inter-racial interaction Johnson said, "The Negro attitude toward the white race has been characterized by a defensive psychology. It is, indeed, doubtful if the racial attitude of a subject group can always be accurately described as prejudice. Prejudice carries with it a suggestion of authority and control (1934g: 535)." Therefore, Johnson concluded that blacks exude a feeling of powerlessness in their interaction with whites, which facilitates the maintenance of inferior self-images.

Aside from black inferiority complexes, Johnson identified the most salient feature of racial group interaction (or, more appropriately, the lack of substantive interaction) as its contribution to the maintenance of white racism. Johnson defined racism as a state of mind, a cluster of attitudes embraced and used by whites to justify the oppression of blacks (Stanfield, 1897: xviii-xliv). "It has been impossible to escape the force of tradition," Johnson stated, "as represented in the customs established under slavery, and adhered to by the white population in their relation to the Negroes, and by the Negroes in relation to themselves (1934c: 208)." For Johnson, the attitudes and beliefs held by white Americans only served to exacerbate the racial attitudes that blacks held about themselves.

The discussion of the racism of white Americans is, perhaps, the only aspect of Johnson's scholarship that could be identified as a form of cultural criticism of American society. Johnson's legacy as a scholar is one of passivity in challenging the cultural and social structure of the American system--he simply desired that blacks have entree into that system (Kirby: 199). In light of that, it is understandable that Johnson saw racial advancement emerging primarily from access to education. He believed that education would provide a means for blacks to better comprehend their status in American society and to begin formulating a social agenda for advancement. In "On The Need Of Realism In Negro Education," Johnson affirmed that, as victims of the American experience, blacks necessitated educational exposure that would allow them to take into account their history and historical condition in order to develop a more profound perspective on their present status (1934h: 376-80). Unlike the tradition encouraged by Miller, Haynes, and others, Johnson felt that blacks needed to realize, through education, the invalidity of emphasizing race as a gauge for measuring human capabilities (1934h: 381). A "character education," he believed, would combat the images of social inadequacy that were prevalent in his view of how black Americans regarded themselves (1934h: 381). Here Johnson exemplified his commitment to a basic mechanism for social advancement in American society -- education -- but he also argued for a revisionist approach in order for education to adequately meet the needs of black Americans.

Johnson benefited intellectually from the work of Robert Park in that he was able to function within and enrich a scholarly framework that had offered legitimacy to the view of Afro-Americans as capable participants in civilization. The impact of Park's work, which became the hegemonic paradigm of the early twentieth century, allowed black sociologists to engage in a fruitful discourse about black social adjustment instead of having to assert the legitimacy of black Americans as functional individuals in society. As indicated in Johnson's work, he was able to move beyond the arena of earlier black sociological discourse to examine issues concerning the difficulties and potential of social adjustment for black Americans.

Moreover, Johnson was also located within the context of Parkian thought by his belief that black social advancement must take place in a manner that "molds" the black American into the cultural fabric of society (Johnson, 1928: 102-15). In Johnson's work, this assimilationist mode of thinking not only resembled the procedural pattern of Park's race relations cycle, but also made a bridge between the scholarly dimensions of Park's model and potential public policy initiatives.

The immense talent of Charles S. Johnson is indicated in the manner in which he carved out his own distinct path outside of the Park tradition. His last published work, Bitter Canaan, reflected his ability to transcend academic boundaries in order to explore more precisely the social phenomena of blackness. Bitter Canaan was a literary work that relied upon certain elements of social scientific investigation to explore the Afro-American domination of Liberian society in the early 1930s. The uniqueness of this work indicates that Johnson was neither hindered by the limitations of disciplinary structures, nor by the objectives of the philanthropic entities that so heavily dominated his career. The irony for Johnson was that, although he considered Bitter Canaan his best work, he could not get it published because of the negative reaction that it elicited from reviewers of the manuscript.[4] In this case, Johnson was ahead of his time. He had written a text that was critical of oppressive Afro-American capitalistic exploits at a time when advancement within such cultural parameters in America was considered the ideal for blacks. This work implied that Afro-Americans

---

[4].   See Stanfield's "Introductory Essay" in Bitter Canaan for more commentary on this aspect of Johnson's life.

possessed the capacity not only to help construct and maintain a societal order much like that of the United States, but to also discriminate against and oppress others as well. Bitter Canaan was eventually published in 1987, 21 years after Johnson's death.

Charles S. Johnson's task was to investigate, characterize, and assert the human condition of the black American within the social structural parameters affecting his/her life. His research question can be framed as "What kind of persons emerge within the varied experience of the Negro in America?" The answer that Johnson provided was that the Negro was psychically impacted by his or her experience in America and was caught in the whirl-wind of adjustment to new forms of functioning within that experience.

As far as the Park race relations cycle was concerned, the diversity of the black experience was exemplified in Johnson's work in that he captured aspects of black life at all stages of the cycle. One of his objectives was to articulate that the reaction of blacks at a given stage depended on the particular structural conditions confronting them at that stage. Johnson stressed that social behavior at any stage reflected, for the most part, rational human reaction in the attempt of blacks to maintain as much stability as possible. Race was a factor only to the extent that whites reacted to black Americans because of their race, and black Americans internalized feelings of inferiority as a response to that.

Of course, this meant that Johnson undoubtedly saw race as a significant factor in the social world. He maintained, however, that race was not a variable for understanding human experience in the manner in which many social thinkers before him had asserted. In other words, a part of his task was to affirm that racial traits were not the causal factors in the social adjustment process of black people. Instead, they served as signifiers for power and subalternity. Moreover, in his look at the Afro-American oppression of Liberians in Bitter Canaan, Johnson proved that he was capable of separating issues of race from those of oppression and dominance (1987). In essence, Johnson argued that a thorough examination of the effects of social conditioning on oppressed people led to some of the most important answers to where such people stood in a social hierarchy, how they behaved in light of that, and how they could positively transform their situation.

In terms of his impact on issues concerning the social character of black Americans, Charles S. Johnson helped to clarify when race was the explanatory variable (for instance, in matters such as inferiority complexes) and when it was not (i.e., behaviors resulting from socio-economic or other structural statuses). This effort helped to diffuse the erroneous view that the behaviors and attitudes emanating from the black community were expressions of inherent racial traits. Lastly, Johnson acknowledged the validity and complexity of distinct cultural practices within the Afro-American community while stressing that such manifestations were distinctly American in their character. Most importantly, he did this without disparaging African cultural traditions or mores. In the end, the work of Charles S. Johnson on the "Negro problem" and the character of the black community prior to 1935 in some ways locates him before, and in others after, the early contributions made to the black sociological canon by E. Franklin Frazier.

The Social-Organizational Dimensions of the Negro Problem -- The Contributions of E. Franklin Frazier

Often regarded as the most prominent of Robert Park's black students, E. Franklin Frazier was a product of Howard University, graduating in 1916 with a B.A., and of Clark University in 1920, graduating with an M.A.. At Howard, Frazier was active in the Intercollegiate Socialist Society, as well as president of the Political Science Club circumstances that would have some bearing on his early sociological thought. He was a student of Park during the early 1920s and worked or taught in New York, Denmark, Atlanta, and at Fisk University (in a sociology department run by Charles S. Johnson) before assuming the chair of the Sociology Department at Howard University in 1934. The years prior to Frazier's association with Howard are the focus of this analysis.

Taken as a whole, Frazier's work spans a number of distinct eras of black scholarly considerations and contributions (Platt, 1991). However, the year of 1935 separates the early Frazier from a later period of his more intense, nationalistic scholarship. An analysis of the early Frazier also permits a more specific focus on his initial contributions to the debates on racial identity and the social predicament of the black community during a time when the contours of these debates were being reconstituted in sociological discourse. During this period Frazier heavily contested certain standard notions of Afro-American social character while vigorously articulating his own.

Frazier precedes Johnson in the development of the black

sociological canon in that he was more specifically committed to Robert Park's race relations cycle as an analytical construct for scholarly investigation of the black experience. Frazier's methodological tools included case histories and census reports, which led to a scholarly viewpoint that was significantly more macro-focused than Johnson's. Frazier's macro-perspective correlated with the race relations cycle of Park, as the cycle was a macro-level analytical construct. The aspect of Frazier's scholarship that places him after Johnson in the black sociological tradition is that Frazier was more specifically focused on black life in the American city, that is, black life in the midst of the twentieth-century rural-to-urban migration.

If Charles Johnson can be considered a more substantive investigator of the manifestations of black identity than were the pioneer black sociologists, Frazier's effort was an outright refutation of the thought of the pioneers. In virtually every one of his published essays in the mid to late 1920s Frazier asserted that African cultural elements in no way survived the Middle Passage to become a part of the Afro-American cultural system (Frazier, 1928: 264; Frazier, 1934: 192-94). In fact, in his contribution to the collection of essays in Race and Culture Contacts, he went as far as to say:

> When one undertakes the study of the Negro he discovers a great poverty of traditions and pattern of behavior that exercise any real influence on the formation on the Negro's personality and conduct. If...the most striking thing about the Chinese is their deep culture, the most conspicuous thing about the Negro is his lack of culture (1934: 194).

Frazier's early attempt to define the Afro-American as a cultural product was to consider him a full-bred American in all but skin color. He considered black religious expression -- at that time considered one of the most authentic cultural practices of Afro-Americans -- to be a distinctively American tradition. He also stressed that the objectives of black education should be to bind the black American to the American experience (Frazier, 1928: 264265). Frazier's logic in arguing that black Americans were foremost products of the American experience was that he considered the history of blacks in America as a series of social shocks. The order of shocks was, first, the enslavement of blacks on the coast of Africa, followed by the Middle Passage, then the slave experience itself, and lastly, a profound social disorganization following emancipation. In Frazier's mind, the residue from all of this was a folk culture in the South that exemplified the expression of a people attempting to reconcile their awkward status in American society (Fullinwider: 105). Hence, Frazier's discourse on the social character of black Americans is clearly and absolutely grounded in it being an American phenomenon.

With such a premise clearly articulated, Frazier explored various aspects of black life before later narrowing his focus to the urban black family. The ontological orientation for his early sociological investigations focused on the black American as a product of the American experience. He stated, "...a group situated as the Negro must avoid the danger of unconsciously assimilating values which have no meaning for him or which the leaders of thought in the world are trying to replace with higher values (Frazier, 1924: 77)." The correct response to this predicament, as he said, was that "the Negro, rather advantageously situated, should be a pioneer in enunciating values that those overwhelmed by their own culture cotrid never attain (1924: 77)."

Frazier's denial of African cultural retention and his commitment to a normative socialization process as an existential necessity for black Americans reflects the bearing that Robert Park's concept of the marginal man had on his thought, especially as his thought pertained to the issue of black identity. Frazier considered blacks to be culturally and socially bounded within the American experience but, as the previous comment makes clear, he assumed that blacks could distance themselves from the mainstream American panorama. Similar to Park's description of the status of the marginal man, Frazier believed that the social distance that blacks were subjected to provided them with a means by which to consider more conducive ways for adapting to American society than had immigrants before them. Moreover, Frazier's prescription for an improved existence for black Americans was for them to increasingly adapt to American life in ways that would inculcate specific values that could either redress the social condition of the black community or highlight whatever social distinctions were extant within that social group. This would allow black Americans to frame their own unique contributions to the advancement of American society. As was the case for most black social thinkers of that era, the educational arena was considered by Frazier as the domain for such endeavors to manifest themselves.

The difficulty in pursuing such educational ends, as Frazier had identified and would explicate in greater detail later in his career, was that the segment of the black community that had the greatest opportunity for smooth assimilation into American culture was unfortunately trapped in a vulgar pursuit of status acquisition and crass socio-economic improvement. He recognized that underprivileged groups should respond to social opportunities in this way. His persistent concern, however, was that the most capable element of the black community for striving for an equal footing with whites was not cultivating "temperamental" development but instead was focused on status gratification and consumption drives (Frazier, 1928: 265~66). Frazier hoped that the unique social position of black people would allow them to identify and adopt the best values and mores in American life (which meant acquiring and maintaining some degree of cultural capital although occupying a marginal status in America), while disregarding the worst values. In essence, this was the emancipatory agenda that E. Franklin Frazier designed for black Americans. His nationalistic tendencies -- a prominent part of the scholarly activities of his later years -- were evident as early as the mid-1920s, as exemplified in the formation of such ideas.

In Frazier's mind, many of those blacks who lacked the means to be a part of an emerging status-seeking black community were locked into the historically "fatalistic" folk culture of the South. In his doctoral dissertation, which was later published in 1932 as "The Negro Family In Chicago," Frazier pointed out that slavery-era and post-emancipation black folk culture was an expression of "surrender" to the white man in terms of attitude and acceptance of life (1932: 79-81). He believed that this resulted in the black community's status as a subaltern caste in American social structure.

Frazier's commitment to the underlying ethos of Park's race relations cycle was exemplified in his view that a totally self-contained black culture and/or community was not viable in America. Frazier viewed American society as a social whole, with most of the black community relegated to the lower caste status (Fullinwider: 103). What is significant here is that, although Frazier considered blacks to be the lower stratum of caste, he did not interpret this phenomenon in racial terms. For him, the conditions affecting the black community were structural in nature and not in any way derived from racial traits. The objective for black people, therefore, was integration at all status levels into the mainstream American society--the fulfillment of the Park race relations cycle.

Frazier saw migration into the city as an opportunity for social and cultural renewal for blacks (Frazier, 1932: 84-85). Race consciousness could develop due to the narrowing of social distance between blacks in the city. Frazier thought that, if developed in the appropriate way, this could help motivate blacks to take advantage of the new social opportunities that would be available to them in the urban sphere (1932: 244). The value that Frazier placed on racial consciousness was another indication of his nascent nationalist tendencies. This emergence, however, should not be interpreted as an encouragement on his part of black cultural autonomy or independence. In fact, Frazier believed that urbanization would destroy any retention of mythical notions of blackness that were cultivated in the past (Frazier, 1928: 248).

Beyond all else, for Frazier, the significance of migration to the city was what it meant for the black family -- the unit of observation for most of his empirical work. Frazier believed that a history of social disorganization, followed by a turbulent effort at reorganization, encapsulated the situation of the black family's attempt to cohere to city life. The hardships of social and economic adjustment, he felt, were the basis for crime, vice, illegitimacy, and delinquency (Frazier, 1931: 204-207). Again, implicit reference to the Park framework was the basis of Frazier's response to this circumstance (i.e., the struggle to assimilate into the mainstream of urban American life).

Frazier's effort was to explain profligate behavior in terms of what it indicated about the gradual civilization process of the black community. He stated:

> The widespread disorganization of Negro family life must be regarded as an aspect of the civilization process in the Negro group. It is not merely a pathological phenomenon....As the Negro is brought into contact with a larger world through increasing communication and mobility, disorganization will depend upon the fund of social tradition which will become the basis for the reorganization of life on a more intelligent and more efficient basis (1932: 252).

Here Frazier implied that the social status of the black community placed it at the early phase of the cycle, and that blacks were responding to that status as would any subaltern group. More significantly, he also alluded to the proposed end-product of the race relations cycle as the ultimate stage of social evolution for black migrants to American cities.

Early in his career, the emergence of a small black middle class was celebrated by Frazier as a realization of the potential of black people to emerge from the race relations cycle on comparable footing with white Americans. The sentiment of his essay, "Durham: Capital of the Black Middle Class," typifies his early thought on social advancement for Afro-Americans. He stressed that blacks had to move from social disorganization and engulfment in a fatalistic southern world to become competitive, hardworking contributors to society. This had to be done without their falling into parochial tendencies of status acquisition that depicted little substantive social progress. In this work Frazier stated the following:

> Durham is the promise of a transformed Negro...Because of the Negro's love of leisure and sensuous enjoyment, men have called him lazy and immoral. Because he lacks calculation, white folks have called him shiftless. But two hundred and fifty years of enforced labor, with no incentive in its just rewards, more than any inherent traits, explain why the Negro has for so long been concerned chiefly with consumption rather than production.... But today, the Negro has his middle class, and with it his middle-class psychology. More and more certain elements of the race are absorbing the typical spirit and push of modern industrialism in America. Through his effort and success, the Negro is becoming an integral part of the business life in America...(1968: 339-340).

The case of Durham, North Carolina in the 1920s exemplified Frazier's view of what remained at the completion of the race relations cycle. Frazier wrote "Durham: Capital of the Black Middle Class" during the time of the Harlem Renaissance, a social phenomenon that Frazier also thought exemplified the potential of black Americans. He felt this way not only because of the plethora of previously unacknowledged artistic capabilities that were promoted during that era, but also because white American interchange with black Americans began to take place in more substantive ways than ever before. This was important in Frazier's thinking because he believed that an isolated and unrecognized black community would suffer a stunted social development, while interaction with whites was a necessity for advancing it (Frazier, 1925: 167). By 1935, then, E. Franklin Frazier was able to identify some potential amidst disparate conditions for the black urban family.

Frazier assertions about the lack of perseverance of African cultural traits helped him to view the black situation in terms of future possibilities -- the most immediate being its complete and permanent stake in American society. Because his methodological tools were specifically suited for macro-level analysis, he was not well-equipped to consider the personal situation of the black individual in society. His objectives, however, did not necessarily concern that perspective. He viewed the black community as a caste constituency in American society. Therefore, his research emphasis was on the black American community as a whole, not its individual members. Moreover, his agenda for social change did not consist of strategies for individual adjustment to mainstream social and cultural patterns in American society. Instead, he attempted to articulate a vision of racial advancement that could evaluate the entire population of black Americans.

Another manifestation of his vision of the black community as a caste within American society was that it facilitated too narrow a consideration of the complex issues concerning the existence and potential utilities of black cultural manifestations. The absence of a contemporary, sophisticated black American civilization following emancipation was an incontestable reality for him, as was the lack of any deeply maintained African cultural traits. The existence of social disorganization as the basis for the behavior of much of the black community was also a given for him. By using quantitative data, as opposed to Charles Johnson's effort to take account of personal histories, Frazier was able to affirm tautological conclusions about the black experience. His early work can be characterized as an almost uniform depiction of where the black community stood culturally and socially in the 1920s and 1930s, what it had to do in order to achieve a more egalitarian social existence in America, and what foibles to avoid in that process. Research questions that pertained to individual variation within the black American community, so much a part of Charles Johnson's agenda, had no place on Frazier's.

Moreover, Frazier's view on the character of black Americans was linked to his vision of the future for black America. He saw some value in race consciousness as a tool for motivation for social advancement. As indicated in his response to assertions about exclusive Afro-American cultural manifestations, however, it can be assumed that, for Frazier, black race consciousness was not to be understood as a shared cognizance of primordially-derived cultural characteristics. Instead, Frazier encouraged the growth of black American racial consciousness solely because of what he felt it could do to motivate a down-trodden constituency in American society to improve its status. Therefore, the significance of fostering race consciousness was not what it did to reify a distinct black culture, but its role as a pragmatic strategy for encouraging social uplift.

Because Frazier's intellectual quests were motivated as much, if not more, by future possibilities than present circumstances, he was inclined to ignore intricate considerations of the present and concentrate more on tautological assertions that pointed toward future possibilities. A final measure of how Frazier followed Charles S. Johnson in the development of the black sociological canon is that, while Johnson was intensely observant of the patterns of black American adjustment to American society, E. Franklin Frazier was driven toward defining the means for improved social progress for black Americans that took seriously their present social, cultural, and economic status as its starting point.

Conclusion: The Negro Problem and the Constitution
of a Black Sociological Tradition

Charles S. Johnson and E. Franklin Frazier were pivotal contributors to the reconstitution of the sociological canon on race studies. To a large extent, under the auspices of Johnson and Frazier, black American social thought moved from a defense of the humanity of the black individual to an articulation of his/her legitimacy as a member of the human community, sharing in the myriad social processes of American life. In sociological discourse in the twentieth century, the case of the black American became firmly entrenched in the latter paradigm. As the sociologist Walter L. Wallace stated, the research tradition that emanated from this paradigm implied three critical questions:

1. Given that distinctly black American social organization obviously exists, does an equally distinctive black American culture exist?

2. Given that distinctly black American social organization and culture exist, in what respect and to what extent are they healthy or pathological, and by what standard?

3. In what ways, and to what degree, are developments in black American social organization and culture autonomous from, or dependent on, developments in white American social organization and culture (1974: 309)?

The legacies of Charles S. Johnson and E. Franklin Frazier can be located in this framework

Charles S. Johnson understood that blacks maintained a diversified, but generally subordinate, status in society. The impact of the social processes contributing to this state of being created varied responses from blacks that depicted different stages of psychological adjustment, acquisition of cultural resources and capital, and attitudinal dispositions concerning in American life. E. Franklin Frazier considered blacks to be a social group that lacked civilization, not because of racial characteristics, but as a consequence of the slave experience. He saw a potential for blacks to acquire civilization, as it was defined in America, from their marginal status in that society. Unlike Johnson, who concentrated on the social psychological ramifications of the black struggle in America, Frazier emphasized the social organizational ramifications.

Johnson and Frazier, then, clearly identified black social organization as a distinct social phenomenon that took shape as blacks reacted and responded to their ever-changing status in American society (Frazier being the more emphatic on this point). In their minds, the culture that emerged in the black community was derived not from any inherent racial characteristics, but from a collective's efforts to create a means for its survival with limited access to societal resources. From this position, Johnson and Frazier helped to further race studies by enhancing methodological and conceptual approaches to the study of black Americans that de-legitimated the racialist paradigm preceding their work. The methodologies included case histories, survey research, census data analysis, the construction of social interaction models, and ethnographic analysis. The result of such applications in the research on black Americans revealed that these subjects were a rich and complex group of people who did not possess an inherent lack of civilizing qualifies based on their race. By rescuing a sense of the humanity of black Americans in an era following one in which their humanity was fervently challenged, Johnson and Frazier helped to facilitate the twentieth century vision of black Americans as a functional, but troubled, constituency. This resultant image comprised the notion of the Negro Problem that social science became preoccupied with when examining the case of black Americans and American race relations.

The notion of the Negro Problem was, perhaps, the primary negative consequence of the legacy of these scholars. Their work helped to constitute a research tradition that objectified black Americans as a marginal community that was, in critical ways, out of step with mainstream American society. Therefore, these subjects were not considered normative referents in social research. The standard for assessing the cultural and social organizational manifestations in the work of Johnson and Frazier was, quite simply, the cultural and organizational apparatus of mainstream American society. Clearly, Johnson and Frazier, as well as their contemporaries, undeniably considered racism to be a pathological response of white Americans toward the black presence in American society. Yet, they did little to critically examine other cultural artifacts of white America in order to explicate what linkages might have existed between them and the social phenomenon extant in black life. For instance, the framing of much of Afro-American culture as under-developed and in need of social reform indicates how white America was legitimated as the normative for the evolution of American cultural and social life. Yet a more intensive examination of folk culture in the black community might have brought about a vision of how resistance to oppressive sites, scenes, and conditions, and how reconstitution of meaning for black Americans might have been facilitated through such cultural forms.

Moreover, the transfer of the black populace to an urban environment speaks to the need to more critically examine alternative ways of managing social space that are not altogether profligate at least contain a blend of profligate and beneficial aspects. Vice, crime, and disease emerged together with the wage-earning matriarchal figure and Be-bop music in early twentieth-century black life in the city. Each of these phenomena, when given appropriate scholarly inquiry, may indicate quite clearly how individual agency and external constraint connected in the production and reproduction of Afro-American urban life that escapes simple depictions made through a lens focused on response patterns emanating from victimization.

Clearly some of these manifestations were very problematic for any constituency in need of social advancement. Yet others exemplified creative patterns of social adjustment that were distinct from the behavior of most white Americans and which spoke to broader possibilities 'for understanding human life. The impact of the early work of Johnson, Frazier and others facilitated the suppression of the vision of black Americans as providers of cultural alternatives that could inform mainstream American life. The suppression of this vision left sociological considerations of the black American narrowly and solely focused on how to make black Americans achieve parity with mainstream America. The issue of how and why their subordination in American society in some ways facilitated their creative capacities both culturally and socially became a marginal issue in sociological inquiry until the late twentieth century.

Today there remains a contentious relationship between some contemporary Afro-American and American social scientists (particularly those equipped with reflexive approaches to sociological inquiry as well as postmodernist perspectives) and mainstream American scholarship (which still too often regards Afro-Americana as external for understanding any basic social dynamics of American life and culture). The activities of the former group of scholars is in many ways an effort to reconstruct the paradigms enhanced by Charles S. Johnson and E. Franklin Frazier. Their reconstruction involves the preservation of an image of blacks as possessors of full human capacities while also debunking the singular focus on the Negro Problem as it was defined in early American sociology. This contemporary pursuit is most appropriately considered a progressive extension of the early contributions of Charles S. Johnson and E. Franklin Frazier to the constitution of a black sociological tradition.

References

Alexander, William T. 1968 [1888]. History of The Colored Race in America. New York: Negro Universities Press.

Bracey, John, August Meier, and Elliott Rudwick. 1971. The Black Sociologist: The First Half   Century. Belmont, CA: Wadsworth Publishing Co.

Bureau of The Census. 1935. Negroes In The United States. Washington, D.C: United States Department of Commerce.

Crogman, W.H. 1969 [1902]. The Progress of a Race: The Remarkable Advancement of the Afro-American. New York: Negro Universities Press.

DuBois, W.E.B. 1970. "The Conservation of The Races." In Herbert Storing (ed.). What Country Have I. New York: St. Martin's Press.

----------. 1976 [1899]. The Philadelphia Negro. New York: Schocken Books.

Fitzhugh, George. 1854. Sociology for the South: or The Failure of Free Society. Richmond, VA.

Foner, Eric. 1988. Reconstruction. New York: Harper and Row.

Franklin, John Hope. 1985. "Introduction." In John Hope Franklin (ed.). Three Negro Classics. New York: Avon Books.

Frazier, E. Franklin. 1924. "A Note on Negro Education." Opportunity, (March): 75-77.

----------. 1925. "Social Equality and The Negro." Opportunity, (June): 165-68.

----------. 1928. "The Mind of The American Negro." Opportunity, (April): 263-66, 284.

----------. 1931. "Family Disorganization Among Negroes." Opportunity, (July): 204-7.

----------. 1932. The Negro Family In Chicago. Chicago: University of Chicago Press.

----------. 1934. "Traditions and Patters of Negro Family Life in The United States." In E. B. Reuter (ed.). Race and Culture Contacts. New York: McGraw-Hill.

----------. 1947. "Sociological Theory and Race Relations." American Sociological Review, (June): 265-71.

----------. 1968. "Durham: Capital of the Black Middle Class." In Alain Locke (ed.). The New Negro. New York: Athenaeum.

Frederickson, George. 1987. The Black Image In The White Mind. Middletown, CT: Wesleyan University Press.

Fullinwider, S .P. 1969. The Mind and Mood of Black America. Homewood, IL: The Dorsey Press.

Gossett, Thomas. 1963. Race, the History of An Idea In America. Dallas: Southern Methodist History Press.

Green, Dan S. and Edwin D. Driver. 1978. "Introduction." In Dan S. Green and Edwin D. Driver (eds.). W.E.B. DuBois: On Sociology and the Black Community. Chicago: University of Chicago Press.

Hofstadter, Richard. 1945. Social Darwinism in American Thought. Philadelphia: University of Pennsylvania Press.

Hughes, Henry. 1968 [1954]. Treatise on Sociology: Theoretical and Practical. New York: Negro Universities Press.

Johnson, Charles S. 1928. "The Social Philosophy of Booker T. Washington." Opportunity, (April): 102-5, 115.

-----------. 1934a. "Negro Personality and Changes in a Souuthern Community." In E. B. Reuter (ed.). Race and Contacts. New York: McGraw-Hill.

-----------. 1934b. "The Cultural Development of the Negro." In Willis D. Weatherford and Charles S. Johnson (eds.). Race Relations. Boston: D.C. Heath and Company.

----------. 1934c. Shadow of the Plantation. Chicago: University of Chicago Press.

----------. 1934d "The African Background of the American 'Negro." In Willis D. Weatherford and Charles S. Johnson (eds.). Race Relations. Boston: D.C. Heath and Company.

----------. 1934e. "Can There Be a Separate Negro Culture." In Willis D. Weatherford and Charles S. Johnson (eds.). Race Relations. Boston: D.C. Heath and Company.

----------. 1934f. "Social Dogmas In Race Relations." In Willis D. Weatherford and Charles S.Johnson (eds.). Race Relations. Boston: D.C. Heath and Company.

----------. 1934g. "The Changing Attitude of the Negro." In Willis D. Weatherford and Charles S. Johnson (eds.). Race Relations. Boston: D.C. Heath and Company.

----------. 1934h. "On The Need of Realism In Negro Education." In Willis D. Weatherford and Charles S. Johnson (eds.). Race Relations. Boston: D.C. Heath and Company.

----------. 1936. A Preface To Racial Understanding. New York: Friendship Press.

----------. 1987. Bitter Canaan. New Brunswick, NJ: Transaction Books.

Kirby, John B. 1980. Black Americans in the Roosevelt Era. Knoxville: University of Tennessee Press.

Kornweibel, Theodore. 1976 "An Economic Profile of Black Life in The Twenties." Journal of Black Studies, (June): 307-20.

Lyman, Stanford. 1972. The Black American in Sociological Thought. New York: G.P. Putnam and Sons.

Matthews, Fred H. 1977. Quest for an American Sociology: Robert Park. Montreal: McGill Queens University Press.

Meier, August. 1966. Negro Thought in America, 1880-1915. Ann Arbor: The University of Michigan Press.

Moss, Alfred A. Jr. 1977. "The American Negro Academy." PH.D. dissertation: University of Chicago.

Newby, I.A. 1968. The Development of Segregationist Thought. Homewood, IL: The Dorsey Press.

Park, Robert E. 1950a. "An Autobiographical Note." In Louis Wirth, Everett C. Hughes, et at.(eds.). Race and Culture: The Collective Papers of Robert Ezra Park. Glencoe, IL: The Free Press.

----------. 1950b. "Education in Its Relation to the Conflict of Fusion of Cultures." In Louis Wirth, Everett C. Hughes, et at. (eds.). Race and Culture: The Collective Papers of Robert Ezra Park. Glencoe, IL: The Free Press.

----------. 1950c. "The Nature of Human Relations." In Louis Wirth, Everett C. Hughes, et al.(eds.). Race and Culture: The Collective Papers of Robert Ezra Park. Glencoe, IL: The Free Press.

----------. 1950d. "Our Racial Frontier On The Pacific." In Louis Wirth, Everett C. Hughes, et al. (eds.). Race and Culture: The Collective Papers of Robert Ezra Park. Glencoe, IL:The Free Press.

Persons, Stow. 1987. Ethnic Studies at Chicago. Urbana, IL: University of Illinois Press.

Platt, Anthony M. 1991. E. Franklin Frazier Reconsidered. New Brunswick, NJ: Rutgers University Press.

President's Conference on Home Building and Home Ownership. 1932. Report of the Committee On Negro Housing. Washington, D.C.

Schwendinger, Julia and Herman Schwendinger. 1974. Sociologists of the

Chair: A Radical Analysis of the Formative Years of North American Sociology (1883-1922). New York:Basic Books.

Shils, Edward A. 1983. "Tradition, Ecology, and Institution in the History of Sociology." In Edward Shils (ed.). The Calling of Sociology and Other Essays. Chicago: University of Chicago Press.

Stanfield, John II. 1985. Philosophy and Jim Crow in American Social Science. Westport, CT: Greenwood Press.

----------. 1987. "Introduction." Bitter Canaan. New Brunswick, NJ: Transaction Books.

Stocking, George Jr. 1968. Race, Culture, and Evolution. Chicago: University of Chicago Press.

Stowe, Harriet Beecher. 1987 [1852]. Uncle Tom's Cabin. Salem, New Hampshire: Ayer Publishers.

Wacker, R. Fred. 1983. Ethnicity, Pluralism, and Race: Race Theory in America Before Myrdal. Westport, CT: Greenwood Press.

Wallace, Walter L. 1974. "Some Elements of Sociological Theory in Studies of Black Americans." In James Blackwell and Morris Janowitz (eds.). Black Sociologists: Historical and Contemporary Perspectives. Chicago: University of Chicago Press.

Weiss, Nancy. 1974. The National Urban League, 1910-1940. New York: Oxford University Press.

Woodward, C. Vann. 1954. The Strange Career of Jim Crow. New York: Oxford University Press.

Chapter Five

The Idea Of Black Sociology: Its Cultural And Political Significance

Wilbur H. Watson

At first impression, the term Black sociology may imply the work done by a Black person trained as a sociologist. It may also imply a certain relation between the racial identity of the sociologist and his/her conduct of inquiry, interpretation of data, and how he/she uses research results. There are certainly race-related variations in the social identities of sociologists. However, whether or not there is a relation between being Black (or White for that matter) and the conduct of inquiry in sociology remains problematic.

This essay presents the results of an exploratory study of the writings of several sociologists and historians who have addressed this issue. My specific objective is to foster conceptual clarification in this area by (1) distinguishing four different meanings of the term Black sociology, each of which is either implicit or explicit in the use of the term in the literature; (2) describing four different types of race-related sociologies generated by an analysis of the interrelations between the elements referred to by the differing meanings of the term "Black sociology"; (3) raising research questions conducive to further inquiry about the bearing of race-related identity on the conduct of inquiry in the sociology of race relations, and (4) identifying implicit distinctions between the ideas of Black and "Mainstream" sociology through successive analyses of the conclusions drawn about the differing types of race-related sociologies.

The primary focus is on writings by authors who pointedly address the social and ideological significance of race-relations research. As we will see, the relation between the racial identity of the sociologist and his stance on race-related social oppression is the focal point. An analysis of ideas expressing varying points of view in some of the literature about Black sociologists will serve as our point of departure.

At first impression, the term Black sociology may imply the work done by a Black person trained as a sociologist. It may also imply a certain relation between the racial identity of the sociologist and his/her conduct of inquiry, interpretation of data, and how he/she uses research results. There are certainly race-related variations in the social identities of sociologists. However, whether or not there is a relation between being Black (or White for that matter) and the conduct of inquiry in sociology remains problematic.

This essay presents the results of an exploratory study of the writings of several sociologists and historians who have addressed this issue. My specific objective is to foster conceptual clarification in this area by (1) distinguishing four different meanings of the term Black sociology, each of which is either implicit or explicit in the use of the term in the literature; (2) describing four different types of race-related sociologies generated by an analysis of the interrelations between the elements referred to by the differing meanings of the term "Black sociology"; (3) raising research questions conducive to further inquiry about the bearing of race-related identity on the conduct of inquiry in the sociology of race relations, and (4) identifying implicit distinctions between the ideas of Black and "Mainstream" sociology through successive analyses of the conclusions drawn about the differing types of race-related sociologies. The primary focus is on writings by authors who pointedly address the social and ideological significance of race-relations research. As we will see, the relation between the racial identity of the sociologist and his stance on race-related social oppression is the focal point. An analysis of ideas expressing varying points of view in some of the literature about Black sociologists will serve as our point of departure.

Defining Black Sociology

The term *Black sociology* is very ambiguous. For example, one suggestion is that Black sociology is the conduct of inquiry by sociologists whose racial identity is socially defined and labeled Black (Roof. 1975: 42).[1]   While this notion draws our attention to racial identity of the sociologist, it leaves inexplicit how racial identity may influence the conduct of inquiry.

In another point of view, with a focus on the subject matter of research, it is suggested that Black sociology is the conduct of race-relations research by Black sociologists (Janowitz, 1974:xvi). This suggests that the Black sociologist is not a generalist in sociology, as implied by the first notion, but a specialist who may work in race-relations research side by side with other specialists who are not Black (Wilson; 1974; 322-338). In large part, the contributions of Black sociologist to the sociology of race-relations was the focus of *The Black Sociologists: The First Half Century* (Bracey at al., 1971). Neither of these perspectives on Black Sociology lends much insight to how racial identity of the sociologist may influence the conduct of inquiry. The following two perspectives, however, are more suggestive.

Turning again to a focus on subject matter, Black sociology can be identified by the extent in which the theoretical frame and substantive issues posed by the sociologist are distinctively matters of interest and concern to Black people (DuBois, 1971; McWorter, 1969). For example, the terms colonization, institutional racism, and Pan-Africanism symbolize persistent themes in the social science literature written by Black social scientists, including sociologists.

Finally, a growing number of Black sociologists are taking the position that Black sociology is identified by the ideological commitment of the sociologist to release of Black people from race-related social oppression (Hare, 1969 and 1974; McWorter, 1969; Staples, 1973; Ladner, 1973; Scott, 1974). On the surface, this implies that race if the sociologist is less important than ideological stance in the identification of Black sociology. However, it does not mean that one is unrelated to the other. In fact, several studies in the history of social theory have shown the national, economic, and racial identities of social scientists have been closely related to the value stance of these scientists on matter of social change in intergroup relations and interpretations of race-relations data (Frazier, 1947; Barnes, 1948; Marx, 1956:41-60; Horwitz, 1972; Scott, 1974;forsythe, 1975). Of course, in a society that favors Whites politically and economically, and treats Blacks and Black sympathizers with odious distinction, it is unreasonable to expect White sociologists-other than marginal members- to show a chief concern with interpretations of race-relations data on the release of Black people from race-related social oppression.

Among White sociologists, "radicals," "Marxists" and some "liberals" have shared the Black's concern with unraveling structures of social oppression. No "leftist" White American sociologists, however, have had as a source of their perspective on society the "Black experience" of physical and mental abuse based on racial membership and/or a sense of social and psychological degradation that may develop through direct and indirect experiences of racially discriminatory treatment. Some may have had similar developmental experiences, e. g., childhood experiences as "poor Whites" may have led these people to perceive American society as unjustifiably harsh and their own mobility as an exception in a society denying economic and political mobility to their peers. Similarly, White females may have suffered cruel treatment, differential opportunities, and male domination. Race-related, socioeconomic, and sex-related dominance, then, can each foster the formulation of critical perspectives by members of suppressed groups which have suffered discriminatory treatment.

Patterns of such discriminatory treatment and oppression which are pervasive throughout our society have been reflected, in microcosm, in the social structure of professional associations and of professional publication, impending some members in their attempt to publish and otherwise gain professional recognition; such discriminations further foster the development of critical social perspectives of both "minority" and "majority" persons. Although the reason may be different, there are White as well as Black sociologists who feel alienated from mainstream" sociology.

Other factors influencing perspectives on race and inter-group (including class) differentiation and relations include funding and research priorities of governmental and private agencies, pressures of civil rights movement, fashions in social thought, etc. A comprehensive and persuasive explanation of the development of differences and similarities in perspectives of Black and mainstream White, and radical and conservative, sociologists will require considerably more research than has thus far been done.

An Ideal Type of Black Sociology

Given the foregoing distinctions between perspectives on Black sociology, let us examine some of the interconnections.

Du Bois stands out among sociologists in general, both nationally and internationally, as a pioneer in studies of the social structure and social organization of race relations. Among Black sociologists in particular, his work is distinguished by his early and extensive combination of the different meanings outlined above as elements in the general framework of his sociology. As a Black sociologist, he concentrated primarily on the social behavior of Black people (DuBois, 1970; 1971), always with a focus on critical analyses of systems of social oppression and a primary interest in the intellectual, political, and economic liberation of Black people (Atlanta University, 1968; Bracey, *et al.*, 1971).

FIGURE I. A THREE FACTOR TYPOLOGY OF
RACE-RELATED SOCIOLOGIES

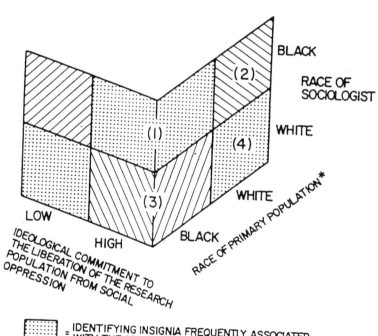

= IDENTIFYING INSIGNIA FREQUENTLY ASSOCIATED WITH THE SOCIOLOGIST

= INSIGNIA INFREQUENTLY ASSOCIATED WITH THE SOCIOLOGIST

* By primary I mean the group whose behavior constitutes the central focus of attention in the research.

When we take DuBois' work as a model in this study, one conception of Black sociology is suggested. Cell No. 1, Figure 1, illustrates the idea. Black sociology means the conduct of inquiry initiated and implemented by a sociologist (1) whose social identity is Black, (2) whose ideological allegiance, as expressed in the formulation of research results, is for the release of Black people from race-related social oppression, and (3) whose primary research population is constituted by Black people. (I must add, parenthetically, that the ideas here represent only my effort to formulate a working definition of Black sociology. No final statement on Black sociology can be formulated before one is completely familiar with the writings of all social scientists who have studied this subject. The three-factor typology of race-related sociologies mentioned above grew out of a probe into the meanings of Black sociology. An exhaustive study guided by this typology must take into account the diversified meanings of these terms. But the major focus of this study is the *idea* of Black sociology, not the variety of race-related sociologies. The discussions of the typology and Figure 1 are included to suggest some possible directions for further study.)

Given the premise that the formulation of research problems and interpretive frameworks are conditioned by the social background of the investigator, especially his value premises about the order of things in human groups (Easton, 1969; Fanon, 1967a; Gouldner, 1970; Horowitz, 1972), it follows that research done by any sociologist will in varying degrees be subject to the risk of value intrusion in the research process. The intrusion of particularistic values can certainly diminish the scientific value of research results. However, since the earliest efforts by Du Bois in the late nineteenth century, Black sociologists – like their White counterparts – have been fully cognizant of these problems and have attempted to minimize the influence of value biases through careful research design (DuBois, 1971; Wallace, 1971).

By their public expression of allegiance to the welfare of Black and other oppressed people, some Black sociologists have chosen to make explicit their value priorities about the order of things in intergroup relations. As suggested by Myrdal (1969:18), although not specifically addressed to Black sociologists, one of the major problems with value biases in the social sciences is not that they are made publicly explicit, but that too many social scientists too often try to conceal their biases from public scrutiny; they often disguise their biases – such as fictions about "White mental superiority"– by labeling them testable beliefs about social and psychological realities.

Within the framework of the ideal type outlined above, Black sociology can be defined as the systematic study of social interaction and social change among Black people and in intergroup relations, from the point of view of Black sociologists. The focus is on the construction of theories of social organization and social change that will contribute to an understanding of Black people's behavior and help point the way to the release of Black people from social oppression. This does not negate the scientific importance of developing empirically grounded social theory that represents underlying uniformities of social behavior. It does mean that social theory and the data brought to bear on it are not independent for the ideology of the scientist (Frazier, 1947; Horowitz, 1972; Gouldner, 1970:29-60). It also means that theoretical propositions about he uniformities underlying social order, and race relations in particular, do not necessarily signify unalterable or unchanging uniformities. For example, it is arguable that the belief embraced by some Whites that being White is "naturally" associated with superior intelligence, in contrast to Blacks, has a greater claim to status in colonial and in folklorist fiction than it does to scientific status as a law of nature. It can be shown that the belief is closely associated with the historical development of institutional racism in the United States and elsewhere, and the need by those Whites who have deliberately and/or unwittingly exploited Black people to use this as a justification for their inhumane conduct in race relations (Frazier, 1963; Jones, 1971; Nkrumah, 1970:17-35). From the point of view of some Black sociologists, there has been an "elitist-like" indifference manifested by some mainstream sociologists when issues are raised about the need for critical analyses of the structural determinants of White people's behavior in race-relations (Frazier, 1947; Forsythe, 1975:10-15; Bryce-Laporte, 1975:353-361). It is, in part, a consequence of this indifference, especially that pertaining to institutional racism, that has led to increasing emphases placed by some Black sociologists on the need for social action by Blacks in the interest of Blacks.

Other Types of Race-Related Sociologies

In Type 2, Figure 1, a Black sociologist initiates the research but focuses his attention on a White research population. Black sociologists and other social scientists who engage in race-relations research sometimes study White or other racial and ethnic groups for comparative purposes (DuBois, 1899). Their attention may be focused on the identification of similarities and differences between Black and White family systems, religious behavior, occupational structures, and other systems of behavior. On the other hand, Black social scientists may study social structures of oppression, in general, to develop insights into the social and psychological factors that underlie intergroup conflict and impede social change in race relations. Included in this area are studies of national and multinational corporations and their quests for cheap sources of raw materials, exploitable labor, and profitable markets (Munford, 1975; Robinson, 1974). Related research may focus on "internal" and external colonization of politically and industrially underdeveloped societies (Fanon, 1967b; Cruse, 1968).

In Type 3 of the race-related sociologies, the focus is on mainstream White sociologists who seek to gain insight to the social behavior of Black people. The products of the research carried out by most of these sociologists are probably best described by Lyman (1972), and Ladner (1973).[2] As suggested in Lyman's discussion (pp. 15-70), mainstream sociologists see Blacks as having little or no cultural identity that is worth preserving. Ladner (p. xx) reached a similar conclusion following her review of several works in the sociology of race relations: she found that mainstream sociologists seemed to think of Black Americans as one more "minority group which would, in time, become part of the 'melting pot' in much the same manner that European ethnic groups have done." Considering this observation and other related aspects of their perspectives, mainstream sociologists are clearly "marginal men" so far as the ideal type of Black sociology is concerned.

Finally, in no sense do the elements in Type 4, Figure 1, fit the requirements of Black sociology. White sociologists' studying White people's behavior without an emphasis on social change represents the typological opposite of Black sociology. We will turn now to a brief discussion of some cultural and political significances of some of the perspectives of some Black sociologists.

Black Social Thought in the Study of Black Culture

In each of two recent volumes, *The Death of White Sociology* by Ladner (1973), and ***Black Sociologists*** by Blackwell and Janowitz (1974), issues are raised about race- and ethnic-related limitations in structures of social theory. For example, it is suggested by several authors in a variety of essays that social thought and sociological theory are fundamentally cultural/historical in substance. In other words, the external structures of social theory are national, class, and ethnic systems of values, beliefs, and rules for behavior. Because of the internalization and development of vested interests in the traditions of a given society, the social scientist will show preferences for research problems and interpretations of behavior that are within the limits of the social structure of that society. As such, some issues and formulations of questions will become taboo as research problems. For example, people who have a vested interest in the structure of race relations in a society, such as the U. S. A., are more likely to choose for research problems and interpretative frameworks those points of view that complement or lead to a reinforcement rather than a negation of the of the values and beliefs of that society. Further study of the literature should show that mainstream sociologists studying race-relations in America, as already suggested by Lyman (1972), Ladner (1973), and others, are more likely to emphasize analyses of the social functions of stratification and the assimilation of the Black to styles of life that members of the mainstream have cultivated and approved for themselves, rather than analytic perspectives emphasizing colonization and the risk that assimilation will lead to the cultural annihilation of the Black

The close or caste-like social relationships that have largely characterized the history of Black relations with White people in the U. S. constitute one of the major background factors and determinants of the distinctive issues in the "cultural knowledge system" of Black people on the one hand and of White people on the other. "Cultural knowledge system" means a socially developed structure of interrelated ideas and sentiments that permits a distinction between ingroup and outgroup members, and provides a framework for articulating a perspective about "the world" or any aspect of it (Richter, 1972:43-44; Durkheim, 1960:325-340).

While there are some clear differences between some of the perspectives of some Black and White sociologists who study race relations in America, a recognition of the differences need not be a source of interpersonal and intergroup hostility. The differences can, instead, be a stimulus to useful social science inquiry.

Written records of Black social thought, including social science theory, can function as a useful source of data in the study of Black culture and culture change. For example, the social theories of Black sociologists can be thought of as a subset of elements in the cultural knowledge system of Black people. Problems of colonization and de-colonization, institutional racism, sexual and economic exploitation, race-roles, and Pan-Africanism symbolize some of the major issues in the history of Black social thought and social theory. In this respect, the writings of Black sociologists and other Black social scientists, along with slave narratives and protest pamphlets; the works of poets, playwrights, musicians, artists, novelists, orators and other Black people are all features of what can be referred to as a cultural "data bank" constituted by symbolic objects that simultaneously represent and contribute to the cultural knowledge system of Black people (Cruse, 1967; Drake, 1975:11). Careful historical description and comparative analyses of these kinds of materials can yield important new insight and perspectives on Black culture and race relations in the U.S.A.

A Note on the Political Significance of Black Sociology

While Black sociology represents perspectives on society with implications and proponents whose thoughts may be unpleasant and unwelcome to some White and some Black sociologists, it nevertheless signifies more than a case of intellectual deviance. Black sociology raises questions about the bearing of (1) inequalities in the distributions of political and economic privilege, (2) social conflict, and (3) race-related social identities on the conduct of sociological inquiry in a society deeply influenced by institutional racism. It also draws attention to race-related differences in perspectives on society and some of the implicit influences that the differences can have on the formulation of social policy. One of the more obvious implications is that social policy – pertaining to intergroup relations – that is based on the thinking of assimilationist social scientists can contribute to the diminution of a people, such as Native and Black Americans, who may embrace the significance of their own cultural heritage and community, but lack the political and economic resources to withstand the intrusions of their oppressors (Watson, 1971).

The formal emergences of Blacks in the social sciences in the U.S.A., beginning with DuBois in 1897, as director of the Atlanta University sociology program, and its annual conferences on urban "Negro" problems (Atlanta, 1968; DuBois, [1899] 1971), followed by various efforts at other universities and by groups of Black professionals such as the Association of Social and Behavioral Scientists in 1935, and the Caucus of Black Sociologists, organized in 1968 (Blackwell, 1974), are partly consequences of the history of Black life in a racially closed or caste society. The organization of special interest groups among Black social scientists also signifies their growing discontent and awareness that many established White social scientists and social science organizations are making too few efforts to develop critical theories of social change in race and intergroup relations. Finally, the growing number of Black social science, behavioral science, and other kinds of professional organizations points to an increasing recognition by Blacks of the importance of collective action as a means of social change.

Summary and Conclusions

In this paper, the ideal type of Black sociology was defined in terms of research (1) initiated by a Black sociologist, (2) with a primary focus on Black social behavior, and (3) with a commitment to the liberation of Black people from social oppression. In the perspectives of these Black sociologists, there are relatively consistent emphases in the following areas when formulating research problems and interpreting research results:

(1) Identifying factors that contribute to an understanding of Black people's behavior including determinants of social oppression, which when eradicated will facilitate the release of Black people from race-related social oppression; (2) racial- and class-based analyses of intergroup relations, especially focusing on social conflict and social change; and (3) critical perspectives in analyses of "established" social institutions with a focus on identifying racist survivals in the structures and social effects of existing organizations.

While this study does not specifically focus on mainstream sociology, some implications about its characteristics are worth noting and may serve as the focus of further inquiry. It is expected that a study of mainstream sociologists will show an emphasis in their perspectives on (1) social control; for example, emphases on gradual change in race relations regulated by existing institutional frameworks; (2) the responsibility of the oppressed for their own suffering, as opposed to the selective effects of color/class patterns and institutional racism, and (3) interpretations of data emphasizing "value free" analysis on questions pertaining to the propriety of change toward, or away from, race-related systems of social oppression.

As humanists, Black sociologists must be sensitive to the broad implications of their work and strive to improve the quality of life for *all* human groups. Although Black sociologists are primarily concerned about the life chances of Black people, the use of comparative methods in race relations and in the study of international stratification will permit them to develop general theories of social change which, in substance, will be conducive to valid generalization beyond the particular circumstances of Black people.

References
Atlanta University. 1968. *Atlanta University Publications, Nos. 1-18, 1896-1914*. New York: Arno Press and The New York Times.

Barnes, Harry Elmer (ed.) 1948. *An Introduction to the History of Sociology.* Chicago: The University of Chicago Press.

Blackwell, James E. 1974. "Role Behavior in a Corporate Structure: Black Sociologists in the A.S.A." *Black Sociologists: Historical and Contemporary Perspectives.* James E. Blackwell and Morris Janowitz (edsChicago: University of Chicago Press. Pp. 341-367

Blackwell, James E. and Morris Janowitz (eds.)1974. *Black Sociologists: Historical and Contemporary Perspectives.* Chicago: University of Chicago Press.

Bracey, John H., Jr., August Meier, and Elliot Rudwick (eds.) 1971. *The Black Sociologists: The First Half Century*. California: Wadsworth.

Bryce Laporte, Roy Simon. 1975. "Review Symposium: Time on the Cross." *Contemporary Sociology: A Journal of Reviews* 4 (July): 353-361.

Cruse, Harold. 1967. *The Crisis of the Negro Intellectual.* New York: William Morrow and Company.

_____. 1968. *Rebellion or Revolution?* New York: William Morrow and Company.

Drake, St. Clair. 1976. "The Black Diaspora in Pan-African Perspective." *The Black Scholar* 7, 1 (September): 2-13.

Du Bois, W. E. B. 1899 [1970]. *The Philadelphia Negro*. New York: Schocken Books.

_____ 1911 [1970]. "The Negro Problems." Speech delivered at the Conference of the Universal Races Congress, University of London, London, England. July, 1911. *W. E. B. Du Bois Speaks: Speeches and Addresses, 1890-1919.* Philip S. Foner (ed.) New York: Pathfinder Press. Pp. 218-225.

_____ 1897 [1971]. "The Study of the Negro Problem." Speech delivered by Du Bois before the American Academy of Political and Social Science, November 19, 1897. *The Seventh Son: The Thought and Writings of W. E. B. Du Bois, Vol. I.* Julius Lester (ed.) New York: Random House. Pp. 229-247.

Durkheim, Emile. 1960. *Essays on Sociology and Philosophy*. New York: Harper Torchbooks.

Easton, H. 1837[1969]. "A treatise on the intellectual character, and the civil and political condition of the colored people of the United States; and the prejudice expressed towards them." *Negro Protest Pamphlets*. Dorothy Porter (ed.) New York: Arno Press and The New York Times. Pp. 1-56.

Fanon, Frantz. 1967a. *Black Skin, White Masks*. New York: Grove Press.

_____ 1968b. *A Dying Colonialism.* New York: Grove Press.

Forsythe, Dennis. 1975. *Black Alienation, Black Rebellion.* Washington, D.C.: College and University Press.

Frazier, E. Franklin. 1947. "Sociological Theory and Race Relations."

American Sociological Review 12 (June): 265-271

_____. 1963. *The Negro Church in America*. New York: Schocken Books.

Gouldner, Alvin W.. 1970. *The Coming Crisis of Western Sociology*. New York: Basic Books.

Hare, Nathan. 1969. "The Challenge of a Black Scholar." *The Black Scholar* 1 (December): 58-63.

_____. 1974. "The Contributions of Black Sociologists to Black Studies." *Black Sociologists: Historical and Contemporary Perspectives*. James E. Blackwell and Morris Janowitz (eds.). Chicago: University of Chicago Press. Pp. 253-266.

Horowitz, Irving Louis. 1971. "The Sociology Textbook: The Treatment of Conflict in American Sociological Literature." *International Social Science Council Information* 11, 1 (February-August): 51-63.

Janowitz, Morris. 1974. "Introduction." *Black Sociologists: Historical and Contemporary Perspectives*. James E. Blackwell and Morris Janowitz (eds.) Chicago: University of Chicago Press. Pp. xi-xxii.

Jones, Rhett S.1970. "The Sociology of Knowledge: Proving Blacks Inferior, 1870-1930." *Black World* 20, 4 (February): 4-19.

Ladner, Joyce A. (ed.) 1972. *The Death of White Sociology*. New York: Random House.

Lyman, Stanford M. 1973. *The Black American in Sociological Thought: A Failure of Perspective*. New York: Capricorn Books.

Marx, Karl. 1956. *Early Writings*. New York: McGraw-Hill

McWorter, Gerald. 1969. "The Ideology of Black Social Science." *The Black Scholar* (December): 28-35.

Munford, Clarence J. 1975. "Imperialism and Third World Economics." *The BlackScholar* 6,7 (April): 15-25.

Myrdal, Gunnar. 1969. *Objectivity in Social Research*. New York: Pantheon Books.

Nkrumah, Kwame. 1970. *Class Struggle in Africa*. New York: International Publishers.

Richter, Maurice N. Jr. 1972. *Science as a Cultural Process.* Cambridge, MA: Schenkman

Robinson, Randall. 1974. "Gulf Oil's Strategy to Appease and Oppress." *The Black Scholar* 5 (December-January): 51-55.

Roof, Wade Clark. 1975. *"The Death of White Sociology:* A Review." *Contemporary Sociology* 4 (January): 42-43.

Scott, Nolvert P. Jr. 1974. *"The Death of White Sociology:* A Review." *The Journal of Marriage and the Family* 36 (May): 423-426.

Staples, Robert. 1973. "What is Black Sociology? Toward a Sociology of Black Liberation." *Death of White Sociology.* Joyce A. Ladner (ed.) New York: Random House.

_____ 1976. *Introduction to Black Sociology.* New York: McGraw-Hill.

Wallace, Walter L. 1971. *The Logic of Science in Sociology.* Chicago: Aldine.

Watson, Wilbur H. 1971. "Aging and Race." *Social Action* 38 (November): 20-30.

Wilson, William J. 1974. "The New Black Sociology: Reflections on the 'Insiders and Outsiders' Controversy." *Black Sociologists: Historical and Contemporary Perspectives*, James E. Blackwell and Morris Janowitz (eds.). Chicago: University of Chicago Press. Pp. 327-338.

Endnotes

1.   Other socially ascribed labels that are widely used to refer to Black Americans including Black social scientists, are "Negro," Afro-American, and African.

2.   For a more recent and extensive review b y a Black sociologist focusing on White and Black perspectives in the sociology of race relations, see Staples (1976: 1-24). Unfortunately, his book was published after my completion of this paper. But even though we had worked independently, he and I have drawn many of the same conclusions about the bearing of race-related social identities on perspectives in the sociology of race relations.

PART TWO

Outside the Spotlight: Case Studies of Lesser Known Black Sociological Careers

Donald Cunnigen

The second-generation Black sociologists came from a wide range of backgrounds. And as noted earlier in the introduction chapter, their life experiences were shaped in a racially segregated world that severely restricted educational and occupational opportunities for Blacks. Despite the obstacles imposed by the racial caste system, they made significant academic achievements, which were influenced, in part, by support they received from their families. Most were southerners who came from families committed to an ethic of hard work and education which was evidenced by the fact that many had parents or siblings who had attended college.

Although most of the second-generation African American sociologists received their undergraduate education in the South, at such historically Black institutions as Fisk University, Howard University, Virginia Union University, Tuskegee Institute, and Hampton Institute, most did their graduate work at one of several northern white universities: the University of Chicago, Columbia University, Washington State

University, and Ohio State University. The northern universities, which included some of the nation's leading graduate sociology departments, shaped not only their intellectual orientations but also their conceptions of their professional role.

Those graduate departments were hardly alone in shaping their conception of their professional role. Also influential were the larger social forces that affected their generation, particularly the Great Depression, World War Two, and the gradually rising post war tide of black civil rights protests. So in a very real sense, their careers unfolded during a transitional era. As the nation shifted from a conservative laissez faire value system to a liberal social democratic value system, most of these second generation sociologists sought to advance that liberal value system in race relations, through their professional work. They expressed those views in books, scholarly journals (e.g. *Phylon, Journal of Negro Education*, and *Southern Workman*) and journalistic publications (e.g. *Pittsburgh Courier, The Chicago Defender* and *Opportunity*) .

The articles in this section examine the careers of a select group of second generation Black sociologists. Each of the six individuals featured here -- St. Clair Drake, Horace Cayton, Butler Jones, Daniel Thompson, Charles Parrish, and Walter Chivers -- can be classified in one of three categories: 1) nationally recognized research scholar; 2) lesser known research scholar; and 3) influential teacher/community activist.

Benjamin Bowser's chapter, which is based on a series of in-depth interviews of St. Clair Drake initially published in **Sage**, reveals surprising insights into Drake's social background and educational experiences, including his leftist political involvement during the 1930s. Though Drake earned his Ph.D. in anthropology, his role in co-authoring **Black Metropolis** as well as his subsequent scholarly writings on African Americans and race relations justify including him among the second generation African American sociologists. This chapter makes an important contribution to our understanding of one of the second generation most recognized and productive scholars. Similarly, his retrospective on Drake offers a coda to the great man's life and work.

Charles V. Willie's chapter on Walter R. Chivers appeared initially in **Phylon**. Chronicling Chivers' work at Morehouse College, Willie provides a glimpse of African American academic life behind the veil of southern racial segregation. Willie particularly highlights Chivers' creative classroom teaching and his role in mentoring young African American students, who subsequently went on to make significant professional achievements. As revealed in this chapter, Chivers constitutes an outstanding example of a lesser known second generation African

American sociologist who, despite the constraints of the segregated American racial system, exerted profound influence as a teacher.

Robert Washington's chapter explores the very unusual life experiences of Horace Cayton, co-author of **Black Metropolis** and one of the most talented second generation sociologists, who abandoned his sociological career while in the prime of his life. Washington suggests Cayton's failure to find a critical theoretical paradigm in sociology that resonated his feelings of racial alienation led him away from sociology in search of a more reflexive intellectual profession. Cayton represents an example of a recognized second generation African American sociologist whose scholarly career was derailed by racial frustrations.

Highlighting a very different type of career, Anthony Blasi's chapter on Charles Henry Parrish, Jr. explores the contributions of a pragmatic civil rights activist. Blasi suggests that the intellectual influences of the Chicago School, particularly the symbolic interactionist ideas of George Herbert Mead and Herbert Blumer, which Parrish absorbed as a graduate student at Chicago, shaped his pragmatic perspective on race relations and made him especially effective in his work as a community activist. Parrish, like Chivers, represents an example of a lesser known second generation African American sociologist whose primary contributions derived from non scholarly work.

In the last chapter in this section, Donald Cunnigen presents a comparative analysis of the careers of Daniel C. Thompson and Butler A. Jones, two African American sociologists whose careers were based in small liberal arts colleges which emphasized teaching. Thompson had a more productive scholarly career which continued even after he became a college administrator. Jones, in contrast, was involved extensively in professional sociological organizations, specifically the SSSP, ABS, and ASA, and work as a social activist. In addition to illuminating the constraints that confronted African American sociologists who worked in small black colleges, this chapter illustrates the changing career trajectories of the second generation sociologists after the 1960s civil rights reform.

Chapter Six

Studies of the African Diaspora: The Work and Reflections of St. Clair Drake

Benjamin P. Bowser

Biographical Introduction

My seventy-eight years can be divided into three periods which have shaped my scholarly interests. The first were my adolescent years of early manhood spent in a racially segregated South (though my very early years were spent in Pittsburgh). My experiences as a student at Hampton University in Virginia and contact there with Professor Allison Davis moved me to want to study, understand, and change the odd world of Jim Crow. This desire led me during my post-Hampton years to the Quaker Graduate Center, Pendle Hill, for a year, and then later to fieldwork with Davis in Mississippi helping to gather data for the book *Deep South* (1941). After that I went on to the University of Chicago for graduate work in Sociology and Anthropology. It was there that Horace Cayton and I gathered the data which resulted in *Black Metropolis* (1945).

The second period began with the end of the Second World War. There was the excitement and promise of a new world free from Fascism and racism. The war had shown that deep and rapid change in America's race relations was possible. But this promise and possibility was frustrated by Cold War politics at home and neocolonialism abroad. This is the period when my interest in race relations as an international and diasporic experience developed. In 1951, I published "The International Implications of Race and Race Relations". In 1954, I went to Africa for a year of teaching and research in Liberia and Ghana. In 1958, I returned to Ghana for two years at the national university and then helped to train four teams of Peace Corps teachers for the country. I went back again to the University of Ghana in 1965. After the coup of 1966, I shifted the focus of my field research to the Commonwealth Caribbean. One of the results of these experiences was a book (not yet published) *Africa and the Black Diaspora: Impact of Africa on the New World* (1970).

The third and current period began for me when I was 58 years old in 1969. Black students' reactions to the traditional humanities and social science curriculum in American colleges resulted in some very provocative questions being asked about the respective roles that Europe and Africa have played in the history of western civilization. For the most part, black scholars of the older generation, with a few exceptions (a significant one was Carter G. Woodson), wrote with white readers in mind. Now there were a significant number of black readers who had a deep personal interest in race, culture and the African Diaspora. It also became apparent that there were serious flaws in the portrayals and assessments of the roles which Africans have played in the new and old worlds. A number of black scholars have been quick to address these issues and this is where my current work focuses with the series *Black Folks Here and There* (1987), Vol. 1.

This essay goes into the background of these three periods. My intent is to outline the underlying contexts which have influenced my work and that of other black scholars since 1935. An understanding of "context" is important in determining how current and future scholars will interpret mid-twentieth-century scholarship on race relations and ethnic cultures. The importance of seeing black scholarship in context is that it has set the stage for the development of a comparative scholarship on the African Diaspora that is new and exciting.

The Pre-War Years

The Formative Years

My early years were spent first in Pittsburgh, Pennsylvania, and then in Staunton, Virginia, where Jim Crow was moderate relative to the deep South. My earliest attitudes towards racist practices were formed in communities in the North and upper South, but my knowledge about

Africa and the variety of cultures within the black world was developed earlier by my father. He was from Barbados in the British West Indies, a Baptist preacher who left the ministry temporarily to become International Organizer for Marcus Garvey's Universal Negro Improvement Association (UNIA). I spent one year in the West Indies with my father's family. A then famous black minister, William H. Shepperd, would periodically visit our church and home; he had been a missionary among the Bakuba in West Africa, where he had attacked the colonial policies of the Belgians and was jailed for being outspoken. He and my father's other missionary friends talked often of events and experiences in Africa. Thus, I had to deal with the cultural similarities and differences between Africa, the West Indies and the United States as a youth.

Africa was not an uncommon topic in black homes before the Second World War and the coming of television. All of the black religious denominations had missionaries working in the "ancestral continent. Black newspapers and opinion magazines like DuBois' *Crisis* were the major sources of information in black communities about African affairs and prominent personalities. They kept Africa very much before us. This point is documented in my chapter, "Negro American and the Africa Interest," in John P. Davis (ed.) *The American Negro Reference Book* (1966).

During the 1920s and 1930s, young black students could walk right by a big white high school to reach their under-financed segregated school, as I did, and not give much thought, if any, to segregation. Our classes were lively. Basketball was exciting and the annual Negro History Week inspirational. However, I could not use the city library. I was told that I could have access to books if one of the white students at the college where my grandmother was a maid checked them out for me. My first publication was a letter to the editor of the Staunton daily newspaper protesting their practice of calling black women in their newspaper articles by their first name rather than by "Miss" or "Mrs". To my and everyone else's surprise they actually changed. This taste of victory spurred me on to become a habitual protestor. We were segregated, but it was not with the same harshness of the deep South--Mississippi, Alabama or Louisiana. Later, I read C. Vann Woodward's discussion about the gradual growth of segregation in *The Strange Career of Jim* Crow (1966).

Hampton Institute

In 1927 I graduated from the Booker T. Washington High School and

went to Hampton Institute (now University), the school that produced Booker T. Washington. I did not know what I was in for. The students at Hampton were in revolt during my first month in college. The 1960s was not the first time black students rebelled, marched and protested. Hampton had a largely white faculty and administration. The presence and influence of the old post-Civil War, New England school-mistresses was still very strong. They believed they were on a "civilizing mission" and saw as a part of their role the curbing of their black students' "natural passions" and of maintaining proper decorum. Dancing was taboo and semi-military discipline was imposed on the men.

Initial conflict began over whether the lights were to be left on in the back of Ogden Hall where movies were shown. Only seniors could "escort" girls to these film shows; 'When lights were kept on in their section of the hall, these young men felt that this newly adopted policy was insulting to "Negro Womanhood". They began chanting, "Lights Out, Lights Out". The protest spread to the dormitories. A decision to strike was taken, kicked off by a refusal to sing spirituals at Sunday night services. There is an excellent history of this period at Hampton in Enoc Water's *American Diary* (1987). But Hampton was not the only black school with protests at the time. There was a general mood of protest, Impatience with segregation and willingness to change outdated practices all across the South. An analysis of the strikes in black schools can be found in Raymond Wolters *The New Negro on Campus* (1975).

There was a close relation between Hampton Institute and Tuskegee Institute. Thus, I came to know of the historic conflict between Dr DuBois and Booker T. Washington over a desirable policy for educating ex-slaves. But it was not until I visited Tuskegee as a representative of Hampton Institute's student council in 1931 that I first experienced the deep South's segregation which impacted on Booker T. Washington. White and black guests stayed at different guest houses on campus Our visit came when racial tension was high in Alabama and Mississippi. Sharecroppers were restless. The Scottsboro case had gripped the attention of the entire world. International pressure generated by the involvement of the Communist Party saved them from being lynched or executed. The mobs that smashed the windows of the United states Embassy in Hamburg, Germany, in protest at the treatment of the Scottsboro Boys seemed a long way from the rural Alabama I saw that spring. But consciousness of Africa was not.

Booker T. Washington had been competing over thirty years with W. E. B. DuBois for influence in Africa. Instead of the conferences of intellectuals that DuBois sponsored, Washington was proud to have sent teams of agricultural experts to Togo as early as 1900. Another team was sent to the Anglo-Egyptian Sudan in 1906. King Leopold had invited Washington to set up little Tuskegees in Africa from the Atlantic to the Pacific Ocean. The king wanted to whitewash his brutal rule of the Congo and reputation as an oppressor; Fortunately, Robert Ezra Park, who was Secretary of the Congo Reform Association, saved Washington from being used. Later, he became Washington's assistant at Tuskegee for seven years. Then he went on to the University of Chicago and became one of the country's leading sociologists. In my introduction to *The Man Farthest Down* by Booker T. Washington and Robert Park (1984), I have discussed the interaction between the black educator and sociologist. I did not know of this close relation until the 1960s.

While I was at Hampton, I read W. E. B. DuBois' column in *Crisis*. I was a biology and education major with Dr. Thomas W. Turner as a mentor. Dr. Turner had been a colleague of Ernest Just. He was also a founder of the Catholic Interracial Association and his feisty fighting influenced me. But the person who most influenced me was Allison Davis who was then a young English instructor. This black scholar had taken a master's degree in English literature from Harvard. Despite being near the top of his class, Harvard could not help him find work teaching at a white institution. This was just not done in those days. Sterling Brown, Davis' black contemporary in English at Harvard, went on to Virginia Theological Seminary. Then, later, Brown went to black Howard University for the same reason that the most talented black scholars ended up at black institutions and, in particular, at Howard. The segregation of American university faculties was the main reason. Here was an illustrious group: sociologist E. Franklin Frazier, political scientist Ralph Bunche, Doxey Wilkerson in education, Eric Williams in history and Alain Locke in philosophy. Allison Davis addressed the question of academic elitism in "The Negro Deserts His People", *Plain Talk Magazine* (1929), and called for dedication to the needs of the South. In 1931, the year I graduated from Hampton, Davis wished to become more relevant to Afro-American needs. He left English and Hampton and went back to Harvard to begin studies in Social Anthropology. He worked with W. Lloyd Warner at Harvard and spent a year in London with Malinowski. His shift in academic interests influenced my decision to move from biology to the social sciences.

Pendle Hill and the Quakers

During my senior year at Hampton, Allison Davis was invited to teach at the Quaker school, Pendle Hill, in Wallingford, Pennsylvania, outside Philadelphia. But he was "retooling" as an anthropologist He recommended me instead. I was offered a scholarship in exchange for working with the Joint Committee on Race Relations of the Society of Friends. I gave speeches and par l icipated in a variety of peace and anti-racism organizational activities. On one project, the Peace Caravans, a friend of mine and I went down South as far as Tuskegee collecting signatures along the way to be sent to thc First World Disarmament Conference in Geneva in 1932--that was a risky venture. It was at Pendle Hill that I first heard Reinhold Niebuhr speak. This is when I read his important *Moral Man and Immoral Society*, with a chapter suggesting non-violent civil disobedience for Negro Americans.

There was great interest in the Gandhi movement at Pendle Hill, for Gandhi had been in London during 1931 and had sent one of his followers to lecture to us. It was the head of Pendle Hill who founded the Fellowship of Reconciliation out of which the Congress of Racial Equality (CORE) eventually emerged. When you look closely at the history of peace and anti-racism activities in this country Gandhi's influence on us predated his influence on Dr. Martin Luther King. In fact, an Indian student is now doing research that suggests that Afro-Americans through their press were well aware of Gandhi and the non-violent movement and tactics decades before King's adoption of Gandhism. I also read Reinhold Niebuhr's *Reflections on the End of an* Era (1934) during this period and was greatly impressed by his call for fundamental structural reforms of American society.

After my year at Pendle Hill I taught science at the Quaker-run Christianburg Normal Industrial Institute in the mountains of Virginia. The western part of Virginia could not afford to run segregated schools in each county. Black children were simply told to go to white schools for their elementary education. For high school, several counties contracted with the Quakers to run a boarding high school for blacks. As a consequence, the black students were getting a private boarding-school education at the state's expense -another irony of segregation. The first irony was Quaker support for such a solution to keep schools segregated. But even under those circumstances my experience with racial segregation, no matter how mild, was to me a daily affront and was barely tolerable. I welcomed a letter from Allison Davis who was then in England. He was about to return to the United States to begin anthropological fieldwork in

Mississippi and asked me to assist in various ways. This was my initial entry into the field of social anthropology.

Deep South

In 1935 Allison Davis joined the faculty at Dillard University in New Orleans as a base *from* which he could conduct research in Mississippi. It was Davis' objective to use anthropological techniques to find out the facts--how is Jim Crow organized and what motivates it? Then, as he said, 'We shall destroy the system", Davis' motives and objectives were very different *from* those of his mentor, William Lloyd Warner, This is a point which is not discussed in Warner's "Methodological Note" to *Black Metropolis* (1945). The "Deep South" project was conceptualized several years earlier than the northern study by Warner while he was working on his Yankee City series. Warner wanted to study an American community by using the same participant observational techniques one would use to study a non-literate society. Warner's theoretical focus was similar to that of Radcliffe-Brown with emphasis on social structure rather than the traditional anthropological focus on cultural practices, institutions and artifacts. Warner was interested in how you could chart people's movements across class lines. Well into the writing of his second volume he realized that no one had really conceptualized the southern racial situation with structural concepts. So the idea of *Deep South* was born.

Warner observed that Southerners were primarily concerned with blacks as an endogamous group, insisting that each race be separated from the other in family and associational relations. Warner felt that this was consistent with a minimal definition of caste, where all institutional expectations and interpersonal interactions were organized by a "colour line". What was intrinsically American about each caste was that each caste was subdivided by social class. The sanctions were secular rather than religious, as in India. This caste analysis was the theoretical perspective within which Allison Davis and I were identified as fieldworkers. In order to conduct the research even the black and white researchers were not able to associate with each other.

In fact, Davis had briefly worked with Warner in Newburyport, Massachusetts (Yankee City), in the small black section of town. Davis' manuscript, which should have been a part of the Yankee City series, was never published. There were others interested in the social class aspect of research on black communities. E. Franklin Frazier, for instance, had such a study in mind when he wrote *Black Bourgeoisie* (1937).

The research for *Deep South* was done by having a white couple (Burleigh Gardner and his wife) live in the white community and a black couple (Allison Davis and his wife) live in the black community. Their objective was to learn how people in each community defined their position in relation to others--who was "higher" and "lower" than they and why? By doing "evaluative participation" at the top and bottom of a society , you could find out where the collective understanding of social boundaries was. It was these divisions within a community which Warner called "social classes". Furthermore, the lines between groups were marked by "symbolic placement--each group identified themselves by their automobiles, dress, speech and so on (see the first volume of the Yankee City series for Warner's methodological discussion, *The Social Life of a Modern Community* [1941]). Warner was also concerned with how indigenous class and caste lines were maintained. By the third year of the project, Allison Davis and his wife were identified with the black upper class in town and, therefore, did not have access to the black lower class. It was my job to move Into the black lower class community and do that part of the ethnography on the bars, juke-houses, shouting churches and general lower-class areas. This gave me an experience in dealing with the bottom strata of society that stayed with me in research for *Black Metropolis,* and in British race relations.

The *Deep South* research was not begun simply because William Lloyd Warner was interested in doing it. His attention and that of others were called to the South by the Scottsboro Case and the Communist involvement generally in the South: There was general acknowledgment that little was really known in the North about the deep South and the potential for other Scottsboro cases. The Deep South research was funded by the Rosenwald Fund and the Harvard Graduate School of Business Administration which was interested in how costly it was to maintain segregation. There was another research team from Yale in the same area under John Dollard whose efforts resulted in *Caste and Class in a Southern Town* (1937) and Hortense Powermaker's *After Freedom* (1939).

It is clear that the location and timing of these projects were no coincidence. The Communists were very active throughout the South. Concepts of "class" and theories of the role of the economic factor in social change were being widely discussed. These researchers made it clear that the social class they were discussing was different from the economic solidarity espoused by Marxists. When I went to the University of Chicago I found William Ogburn insisting that there was no resemblance between his culture lag theory and Marxian observations about changes in the social superstructure which were responding to changes in the base. Professor Warner points out in one of the Yankee City volumes that the idea of social class having any relation to the means of production is irrelevant in the United States!

Black Metropolis

When the *Deep South* project ended, it was my intent to go and work for the Southern Tenant Fanners' Union as an organizer. Their interracial co-operative cotton farm in Mississippi had impressed me greatly. But Allison Davis persuaded me to apply for another Rosenward Fellowship, this time to Study Anthropology at the University of Chicago. Davis also wanted me to continue working with him in analyzing the *Deep South* notes. It was 1937 in the middle of the Great Depression. Roosevelt's New Deal made it possible for William Lloyd Warner to get a WP A grant to support graduate students' fieldwor1 for Yankee City. When he moved his base to Chicago, his students with WPA aid worked with Horace Cayton to build a data bank.

I joined the project and conducted research on a subject of interest to me. I prepared a monograph, mimeographed, of which about 500 copies were circulated: *Churches and Volunteer Associations among Negroes in Chicago* (1941). This monograph has a number of hand-coloured maps since WPA rules would not authorize printing them, and now sells as a collectors' item. A number of pH dissertations were produced from the data bank. Initially, there was no intention of using the material for any major publications. Later we decided to write *Black Metropolis*.

The WPA grant paid salaries but not rent for the research project. Cayton managed to get rent money from local numbers racketeers, referred to in *Black Metropolis* (1945) as "shadies". Cayton developed strong rapport with them. My participant-observation specialty was with the "lower class". At first, the numbers syndicate on the Southside of Chicago was composed of ten blacks and one Italian. Later an Italian group took it away from the blacks. Cayton estimated that during the Depression the numbers business had the largest payroll in Bronzeville. The running of the research project is described in detail in Cayton's autobiography, *Long Old Road* (1972). Working on this project was an important contribution to my graduate training in social anthropology at Chicago. This experience further confirmed my belief in the possibility of rapid change in American race relations.

In the late 1930s it was not odd for me to live in the ghetto participating in the life of the lower-class segment of the community. My not-too-well-educated associates felt that they were helping an upwardly mobile "brother" trying to save money. In 1939, eleven people were writing theses and dissertations from the data bank. At this point, Warner and Cayton decided that a book should come from the project. They both asked me to apply for another Rosenwajd Fellowship in order to write the first draft. At first, I was more interested in finishing the work for my degree, but I postponed that goal. My focus had been on the black churches and on the lower class, and Cayton's on the Shadies and upper strata of Chicago.

You will find a methodological note in *Black Metropolis* by Professor Warner, where he describes the research on *Black Metropolis* as a continuation of *Deep South*. To Warner, both the North and South met the requirements for a minimal definition of a caste-ranked social stratum with endogamy as a cardinal rule. Louis Wirth disagreed, as did Horace Cayton, with the idea of calling the interracial situation in the North as "caste". To them the North is characterized by the social structure of an urban setting, fluid, not fixed.

Also we could not use Warner's techniques of evaluative participation strategy in stratifying individuals in Chicago. The population was too large. Also "Bronzeville" was far too complex to understand as a whole through participation. This was only possible in small towns such as Natchez, Mississippi or Newburyport, Massachusetts. So we focused in Chicago on using club and church memberships, studying a sample of them to determine class dividing lines, with census categories as a check. What some sociologists call "status inconsistency" was apparent. Social status was not dependent on either occupation or income. What determined status and participation was, lifestyle, with occupation *and* education determining the limits. Education was more important than these two criteria. in relation to lifestyles.

Meanwhile, Robert Redfield was becoming a major influence on my work in a department that had been dominated by Radcliffe-Brown's functionalist theory. However, the influence of Radcliffe-Brown's variety of British social anthropology is apparent in *Black Metropolis*. The emphasis was on social structure, not on culture- -much to Melville Herskovits' dismay. I was very much interested in black church rituals and sermons' style and content. There are stock phrases and common elements in prayers. Very little of this sort of behaviour was used in *Black Metropolis*. You will find more interesting analyses of sermons in Joseph Washington's *Black Religion* (1984). Nor is there discussion in *Black*

Metropolis of black folklore, the blues or gospel music (which, incidentally, started in Chicago at Rev. Dorsey's Pilgrim Baptist Church shortly before I began doing research). *Black Metropolis* has other shortcomings. Our selection of material for presentation is biased towards the middle class. There was nothing in the book that took note of and assessed the "disrespectable" behaviour within the middle class--for instance, the "blue movies" of the male subculture of clubs and fraternities. The sexual activities of the lower classes are not handled with "kid gloves". Another major weakness is that *Black Metropolis* lacks adequate statistical sampling procedures such as those in Helen and Robert Lynd's *Middletown* (1929). For instance, the representativeness of many of the generalizations might legitimately be called into question. Our only defense is that our own participant observation; forty years ago, made *Black Metropolis,* to some extent, an "inside view".

An American Dilemma and the Left

Like *Deep South, Black Metropolis* was not written simply out of academic interest in the black community. There was a great deal of general concern about the black condition during the Depression and the early years of the Second World War. Marxists were using Jim Crow in the South and the condition of the ghettos in the North as very effective propaganda against the United States both at home and abroad. During the war years, the potential for black disloyalty and disruption .was a very real threat. The foundations and the New Deal government sponsored research in the hope that it would help in decision making. At the same time that Cayton and I were at work on *Black Metropolis,* the important Gunnar Myrdal project was "under way which resulted in *An American Dilemma* (1944). The Carnegie Foundation had hoped to lend credibility to the research it sponsored, and to actually minimize bias by having it directed by a Swedish social scientist, Professor Gunnar Myrdal.

E. Franklin Frazier was passed over as director because of his newly found emphasis on the global implications of race relations and because of his conflict with Melville Herskovits over the African survivals question. It was decided that the way to utilize black scholars was to ask each to do a working paper. I did one on black voluntary associations and churches in the North with Allison Davis preparing one on the South. Oliver Cromwell Cox would have no part of the project. Ralph Bunche did one on black political leadership. When Gunnar Myrdal had to leave the country because of the war I Arnold Rose took over the project, but

Ralph Bunche did some of the most important tasks in preparing two volumes for the press. Ironically, Myrdal did not publish Bunche's paper. It has been thought by some that his *World View of Race* (1937) had made him a project liability, since he concluded that pamphlet with the statement that racial conflict would only end after a "great class war" breaks out around the world.

The great concern about race in the United States would not have occurred had not the Left made race relations a key part of their critique of American institutions. After the Scottsboro Case, race relations in the United States ceased being an isolated domestic issue and became an international embarrassment It was defined as a flaw in the United S identity as a progressive democracy. The need to counter this image was partly expressed by the willingness of foundations to fund research into domestic race relations. As mentioned previously, the Rosenwald Fund supported *Deep South* and *Black Metropolis*. The Carnegie Foundation supported *An American Dilemma*. The American Council on Education supported Allison Davis and John Dollard's *Children of Bondage* (1940) as well as E. Franklin Frazier's *Negro Youth at the Crossways* (1967); Charles Johnson's *Growing up in the Black Belt* (1941); Ira De A. Reid's *In a Minor Key* (1940) and William L. Warner and Buford Junker's *Color and Human Nature* (1941). The American Council on Education funded a series of studies on white youth as well.

There were other reasons, too, why the 1930s was so productive of books and articles about Afro-Americans. There was an informal coalition between major black leader, many union leaders, and the Communist Party USA, which was protected by the New Deal. For example, John L. Lewis, who was a Republican, depended on the Communists to organize where management was particularly recalcitrant about recognizing unions. But as soon as the Congress of Industrial Organizations (CIO) was well established, Lewis expelled twelve unions because of their alleged Communist leadership.

A number of conservative black college presidents quietly protected black radicals on their faculties. Mordecai Johnson, for instance, the President of Howard University, managed to fend off white federal legislators, who controlled Howard's budget, from engaging in a witch hunt on his campus. Howard's faculty was a virtual centre of activity for black Left intellectuals during the Depression years. John Hope invited W. E .B. DuBois, the most prominent of black radicals, to be on his faculty at Atlanta University after the National Association for the Advancement of Colored People (NAACP) became dissatisfied with him. He was fully aware of the opposition this would cause among trustees and donors at a time when the University was hard pressed for financial support, but he was loyal to DuBois. The president of a little black college in Texas once said to a radical faculty member "I hear you are publishing articles and poems in a magazine up there in New York run by people called 'Trotskyites'. You keep publishing up there, but not down here. These crackers ain't never heard of a Trotskyite." In a previous period, covert support which made it possible for the NAACP and other organizations to successfully investigate lynchings in the deep South came from none other than Booker T. Washington. This protection of radicals, left-wing and other, became a part of the academic tradition, breached only when severe pressure came from Southern legislators.

The white Left on college campuses who played such a crucial role in internationalizing domestic race relations did not have white conservatives as administrators to run interference for them. An example is the case of Bernhard J. Stem. the assistant editor of *The Encyclopedia of the Social Sciences* Stem wrote a book on Lewis Morgan. the anthropologist whose work on the family was used by Frederick Engels to write *The Origin of the Family, Private Property and the State*. Despite Stem's distinguished scholarship. he was a virtual non-person at Columbia University, "frozen" at the lecturer level. Randolph Bourne. who was important in the early days of *The New Republic*. was fired from Columbia. Gene Weltfish, a less prestigious colleague who coauthored *Races of Mankind* (1959) with Ruth Benedict was the object of a federal witch hunt when their pamphlet on race was used in the army during the Second World War to combat racism. She was fired. The white Left gave important support to the Southern Negro Youth Congress and the National Negro Congress (NNC) led by A. Philip Randolph. It is forgotten that E. Franklin Frazier and Ralph Bunche played important roles in the National Negro Congress movement when A. Philip Randolph was president.

The role which the Left played in making race an important issue and in supporting black organizations needs to be reassessed. The older view is questionable that Afro-Americans were cynically "used" by West Indian and white Communists to advance their own cause and agendas. There was a lot more to the relation that each side was trying to "use" the other. Harold Cruse popularized the view of left-wing perfidy in *Crisis of the Negro Intellectual* (1967). A more accurate appraisal is apparent in Nell Painter's *The Narrative of Hosea Hudson: His life as a Negro Communist in the South* (1979) and in Mark Naison's *Communists in Harlem during the Depression* (1983). The close working relation between the Left and black intellectuals unraveled rapidly in 1941. The Communist Party USA initially refused to take sides in the Second World War due to the Soviet agreement with the Nazi leaders that neither would attack the other. The United States was clearly committed to aiding Britain and the European nations. A. Philip Randolph of the National Negro Congress (NNC), who was not a Communist, resigned as president of the "United Front" organization. NNC executive board member, Ralph Bunche, proceeded to draft the Republican Party's statement on the Negro for the 1940 elections.

The period of the holistic studies of community was over as well. Evaluating and monitoring change became' more important to social scientists than understanding the internal structure of community.

The Postwar Promise and Focus on Culture
The Promise

The Depression years showed us that profound change in American race relations was possible. Anthropologist William Lloyd Warner was impressed, however, by the extent to which rigid caste in the Southern boundaries was maintained. Allison Davis and I, on the other hand, were impressed by just the opposite -the extent to which whites and blacks ignored caste codes --in unions and in some churches. For examples of how the codes were often violated see Charles Johnson's ***Patterns of Negro Segregation*** (1943). Change was even more pronounced in Chicago where the CIO was organizing the packing houses and steel mills. Some of the most popular labour leaders who, were effective in mobilizing Italian and Polish workers were black! 'There were daily events which were at variance with scholars' traditional view that Sumner's gradualism was the most appropriate form of social change -"slow change in the folk- ways".

Robert E. Park's theory of "a race relations cycle" was questioned and Marx's idea that workers of the world could unite seemed justified. While Allison Davis and Warner had been instrumental in starting me on an academic career in Anthropology, sociologists Louis Wirth and Everett Hughes had a greater influence on me during this period. They were taking activist positions in the Chicago struggles against racial discrimination. Amidst the excitement surrounding interracial co-operation, I remember a warning from an old and uneducated black preacher in the South. He told me "wait until the white brothers get the wrinkles out of their bellies, young man", After the war ended, the euphoria diminished, disappearing even in the CIO unions. The radicalism of the 1930s and the internationalization of racial politics of the 1940s led a number of scholars, including myself, to greater interest in the subordinate condition and circumstances of black people internationally. The prospects of postwar national independence in Africa reinforced this interest in Africa and the Diaspora, especially in Latin America and the Caribbean.

It was very clear to us by the end of the war that, if the Federal government in the USA stood firmly behind the social objective of equality for Negroes, fundamental change could be brought about. During the war many of us saw ordinary whites in the South for the first time acting outside their "normal" caste context. It was particularly striking to see southern whites interacting with blacks as peers in non-union situations. What made the difference was the weight of the government and military situations. However, protest was necessary to keep up the momentum.

But then, in 1943, I was given choices -be drafted to fight in a war which I opposed, go to jail or volunteer for the Maritime Service to serve abroad on its only integrated ship. I volunteered and here is where I saw change at first hand: We were assigned bunks alphabetically and not by race. The fact that we all had to depend on one another in order to survive at sea made black and white crew members peers regardless of race. We saw that racial barriers did not have to be a permanent part of the nation's social mores, changed only by time and social evolution. Racial barriers were situational and could be changed purposefully and directly. The idea that purposeful change was possible and that change would occur went deep into black postwar expectations. In a way, the expectations which served as a backdrop for activism and massive support for the Civil Rights movement in Montgomery in 1954 came out of the war years. McCarthyism and the Cold War only delayed this activism and eliminated what might have been well-organized support from the Left for the movement.

After doing my Ph.D. research in the British Isles and teaching in Liberia between 1945 and 1954, I became involved with the Southwest Hyde Park (Chicago} Association. By then, I was less inclined to study race relations in the abstract or race relations in which I was directly involved. We were struggling against the University of Chicago's efforts to control and maintain racial segregation in the community. This experience taught me a lot about institutional racism and denial. "Denial" was an important part of the strategy to maintain segregation in Hyde Park. Ironically, the argument in the 1950s was that race was of declining significance. It is also ironic that the current chair of the University's Sociology Department is William Wilson, author of *The Declining Significance of Race* (1979)--the most recent articulation of denial. The chair in the 1950s was Philip Hauser and the Department's emphasis on demographics was very useful in "saving" the neighbourhood for the University. There is a chapter on this community struggle in Peter Rossi and Robert Dentler's *Politics of Urban Renewal* (1961). In 1958 I left for Ghana.

The Comparative Study of Black Cultures

Africa and the Black Diaspora: I was in Ghana as chair and Professor of Sociology at the University of Ghana from September 1958 to February 1961. While I was in Africa, the classic Frazier-Herskovits debate was put into perspective for me. I would now agree with Melville Herskovits that there has been a conditional maintenance at Africanisms in the New World. Initially, Herskovits did not see this. Not until he had returned from Surinam in the early 1920s did he see African retentions in the US as well. He held that there were reinterpretations, a few synchronisms and retentions. He also believed that each major cultural group had a focus. For New World Africans their cultural focus was around religion and was most readily expressed through music and dance. Herskovits claimed that Cayton and I had suppressed evidence of Africanisms in Chicago church behaviours and that Pentecostal behaviour was an "obvious" case of an African retention. It was in this emphasis on "focus" that Herskovits was led astray. By the time he wrote *The Myths of the Negro Past* (1941) he was sensitive to the more subtle and significant manifestations of Africanisms such as body movement, worldview and family traditions rather than to specific concrete cultural forms.

In contrast to the Herskovits position, E. Franklin Frazier and I initially believed that rural Southern folkways had replaced Africanisms. We argued that in social class and rural isolation, blacks were culturally no different from whites. After Frazier had spent time in Brazil he modified his view and acknowledged that there were still Africanisms among blacks in the United States. What the overseas experience had shown us both was that the basic structure of African societies was not organized around the conjugal unit. The centre of family life was the lineage usually of one parent only. In these cases, the African extended families were worship units for ancestor veneration and the maintenance of ancestor shrines. The destruction of African family ties in slavery weakened the basic religious unit and substituted elements of Christianity. Men having multiple conjugal relations was a reinterpretation, especially in the Latin countries; there was the practice of marriage "in the church" and then there was marriage "in the community". In black communities in both North and South America, there have not been clear sanctions against extramarital relations. See Frazier's "The Negro Family in Bahia", *American Sociological Review,* Vol. 7, No.4, August 1942, pp. 465-78.

The reason why Africanisms are more tenuous in North America is because of the thoroughness of Protestant insistence on eliminating all evidence of what they called "heathenism". Also Africans were a smaller proportion of the population than in a country like Brazil or on Caribbean islands. Blacks in colonial North America had more exposure to European culture. In the Catholic Latin countries slaves were encouraged to maintain some elements of their culture and to reinterpret religious and family traditions. For example, in Brazil, urban slaves were not only allowed but encouraged to set up voluntary associations under the auspices of a specific saint. Anthropologist Roger Bastide has given us a magnificent analysis in his book *The African Religions of Brazil* (1978).

One value of comparative studies is the insight they give us of the different way in which race is defined in Brazil. Brazilian scholars describe race relations in the United States as "the prejudice of blood". Regardless of social status, skin colour or anything else, you are "black" if one of your parents or grandparents is so classified. In contrast, Latin race relations are based on "prejudice of mark". Colour rather than "blood" is the basis of ascribed racial status. Some Brazilians insist that if you are wealthy or highly educated, you can enjoy the privilege of white status. But, in reality, even money does not completely "whiten". All of the Latin countries, including Brazil, draw distinctions at the extreme top and bottom of society --whites and blacks. What Stanford's Carl Degler calls the "mulatto escape hatch" is the key to understanding what it means to say education or money "whitens". Mixed blood individuals, not blacks, can reach the "top", (Carl Degler, *Neither Black Nor White*, 1970).

Latins are willing to call variations of racial mixtures "white", whereas this is not the case in North America. The larger numbers of Africans brought into Latin America and the inability to maintain rigid control over them were important reasons. For example, there were 40,000 Africans in Mexico City at the same time Jamestown (the first North American settlement) was founded. The result in the Latin countries is a tripartite system of race relations. Whites are at the top, mixed bloods (mestizos and mulattos) are in the middle and blacks are at the bottom of society. This is certainly the case in Brazil. It is also true, in some non-Latin Caribbean islands: thus, in Jamaica where coloured intermediaries between blacks and whites are referred to as "brown", or as Jamaicans phrase it, "red". "Shade of colour" is highly relevant. Haiti is the only exception to the Caribbean tripartite system. The French whites were driven out so mulattos and blacks have fought for power. An important student of Caribbean societies suggests that in time there will be racial homogeneity: see H. Hoetink's *Caribbean Race Relations: Two Variants* (1967). But what stands in the way of this eventual homogeneity are social class differences where whites and coloureds are slowing the pace of miscegenation. For the long run, Hoetink is probably correct. There are many poverty-stricken whites in the slums of Sao Paulo and Rio living right next to blacks. They are being "Africanized" and have little reason to defend the racial status quo.

Some significant work has been done on African culture in the Caribbean. Franklin Knight wrote *Slave Society in Cuba during the Nineteenth Century* (1970) followed by *The African Dimensions of Latin American Societies* (1974). In Cuba, slavery was ended in 1885, but by then 70 percent of slaves were free. Many of these were mulattos. Ibos and Yorubas were being brought into the country as late as 1885. This meant that African culture in Cuba was vigorous just two generations ago. The Trinidadian musicologist, Jacob Elder, did work on the preservation of African social structure, *Song Games from Trinidad and Tobago* (1962) and *From Congo Drum to Steelband* (1969). Michael G. Smith, a Yale anthropologist, studied the Hausa in Africa and the continuation of African (Ibo and Yoruba) cultural forms in the New World, and *Culture, Race and Class in the Commonwealth Caribbean* (1984) was the result. He also wrote *Black Puritan* about a cult leader in Grenada who drew on Africanisms within the population.

George Simpson of Oberlin wrote about Jamaican religious movements. Much of his work appeared in the journal, *Social and Economic Studies*, published out of Jamaica. John Rickford at Stanford is doing important work on Africanisms in language: see *Social Contact and Linguistic Diffusion* (1986). Several French scholars have studied the diaspora. Their collected work can be found in *Les Afro-Americains, Memoires de l'Institut Francais d'Afrique Noire* (IFAN), No.27 (Dakar, Senegal, 1952), pp. 11-101. Then there is Joseph Harris' edited volume, *Global Dimensions of the Diaspora* (1982), which contains a number of significant papers. You will notice that there are relatively few anthropological studies on West Indian cultures carried out by West

Indians. Until very recently West Indian scholars focused on economic and political studies, a priority in developing nations. Governments and economies needed to be established, while local cultures were primarily associated with poverty and backwardness--a class bias. There is now a growing appreciation for the complexity and richness of local Caribbean cultures. These studies of African peoples spread across the New World have shown the variability of African retentions. The work done to date gives us only a glimpse of what exists. Several more generations of scholars have more than enough work waiting for them in uncovering additional reinterpretations, synchronisms and retentions of African cultural elements in the Diaspora. When we look back on the Frazier and Herskovits' debate and consider what we have learned since then, there is an Afro-American culture. But in comparison to other African-American cultures in Latin America and the Caribbean, Africanisms in the Afro-American culture are far more attenuated. Also in comparison to other core cultures in the New World, the North American culture has been influenced the least by Africanisms. The impact of Africanisms on the larger American culture is another area which is largely unexamined except in music. Herskovits had a rating scale on Africanisms with the Bush Negroes of South America at the top and urban blacks in North America at the bottom: see Herskovits (ed.) *New World Negroes* (1966). He was correct in having United States Afro-American culture at the bottom and the urban United States at the very bottom. Overall, the cultural differences between Afro-Americans and white ethnic Americans is much less than the differences between white ethnics and Japanese-Americans, Chinese-Americans or Jewish Americans.

The Current Period: Race and Culture in Comparative History

It has been a long struggle within anthropology to move away from physical and biological classifications of race. In the 1940s most anthropologists began to insist that what were considered racial differences were really cultural. Some anthropologists suggested that we simply drop race as a concept, substituting ethnicity as a more useful one; see Ashley Montagu's *The Myth of Race* (1974).

Until very recently there were anthropologists who believed in the existence of a "Hamitic" race in Africa. They held that the Hamites were a cattle breeding, light-skinned people who conquered ancient African Negroes and brought a higher civilization to the African continent. I challenged this view in 1958 with "Destroy the Hamitic Myth" in

Presence Africaine. A person who did pioneer work to destroy this myth was Joseph Greenberg, then at Columbia, now at Stanford. He demonstrated in the *Southwestern Journal of Anthropology* that there never was a Hamitic language. If there was no language. there was no people.

But the Hamitic myth was only an introduction to the work which is now under way. Until 1970 the issues of race and culture were largely the province of scholars. The 1930s was the last time there was popular interest in race and culture. due then to racist theories emanating from Hitler's Germany. But the Black Studies movement changed that. Black students became new readers. They asked serious questions and were motivated by personal interests in identity. At the same time, some black scholars had declared the beginning of a new era--see Joyce Ladner's *The Death of White Sociology* (1973). The critiques of traditional scholarship and the university curriculum as Eurocentric were particularly pointed. There was a new interest and openness to understanding the African experience outside the US and an understandable exasperation at not knowing just what Afro-American culture was like Herskovits' initial enthusiasm. I was one of the very few scholars of my generation to head an Afro-American Studies programme (at Stanford) in the early and stormy years of the formation of Black Studies. I had to rethink my work and direction.

A New Direction

Amidst the new interest in the African Diaspora, I had just finished a still unpublished book, *Africa and the Black Diaspora: Impact of Africa on the New World* (1970). At the same time, Cheikh Anta Diop's *The African Origin of Civilization* (1974) was emerging as a central challenge to the western view of the role of Africa in world history. Diop's research challenged the view that the ancient Egyptians were a mixed race and that the Egyptian high civilization came out of the Middle East. Diop's thesis is that the early Egyptians were indigenous Africans--a "Negro" people--and that their high civilization was a refinement of existing African cultures, not a European or Middle Eastern importation. Diop insisted that his thesis could be proven if the Egyptian government would allow the testing of mummies in the Egyptian museums for amounts of melanin in the skin. However, Arab scholars have resisted Diop's work because by implication it makes them invaders of Egypt. Diop's work also follows after the very popular work of Howard University Professor Chancellor Williams, *The Destruction of Black*

Civilization (1971). Williams' work gives us a sense of the gravity of what a West Indian professor, George James, called *Stolen Legacy* (1954) and British classicist Martin Bemal reveals in his book, *Black Athena* (1987).

The emerging studies of the African Diaspora and the corrective of ancient Egyptian history represents a formidable challenge to current American and European views. An important western misconception was reflected in Carl Degler's *Neither Black Nor White: Slavery and Race Relations in Brazil and the US* (1971). This excellent study is marred by Degler's contention that racial prejudice is natural and that it was normal for light-skinned people to look down on dark-skinned peoples. Degler has also privately criticized Frank Snowden's claim in *Blacks in Antiquity* (1970) that the ancient Greeks were not prejudiced against Ethiopians. Degler believed that Snowden should have known better. Degler's view is not simply his own. It is affirmed at length by social psychologist Kenneth Gergen in his essay "The Significance of Skin Color in Human Relations", *Daedalus* (Spring 1967). This view of the superiority of light skin over dark skin runs through much current European and British scholarship on virtually all aspects of European contact and relations with the African world from ancient Egypt through the modem African Diaspora. Sometimes it is a subtle assumption; occasionally it is explicit. It seemed to me that the view articulated by Degler and Gergen was an appropriate point from which to begin critical comparative studies. The question of the universality of prejudice against dark-skinned people should be examined in this fashion.

I began such critical comparative studies right after finishing *Africa and the Black Diaspora* (1970). The trail of enquiry led from the New World back through the old. Bastide had pointed out some very significant developments in Brazil where poor whites participated in ceremonies of syncretized African and Catholic worship. In this sense, there was a declining significance of colour and race but not of Africanity. In this context the question arises as to how African cultural elements as well as "blackness" (phenotype) function in different places in the New World. This called for basic conceptual clarification: racism, colour prejudice and slavery are three very different elements in human experience. Slavery is the oldest and does not necessarily have any reference to colour. At some points in history many different racial groups have been slaves and slavers. In contrast, racism is relatively recent, if wc defined racism as a system of belief avowing that a group of people are thought to be either superior or inferior based on heredity J sometimes symbolized by a distinctive phenotype. Specifically, a racist system assumes that all people in positions of power should be drawn from the superior group with those who are inferior being excluded from consideration.

If racism is recent, then racial slavery is also recent, where the distinction between the master and the slave is based on race. The Aryan myth is one such form of racism. The Nazis' distinction between themselves and Jews has as its counterpart the Hamitic myth --wherever you find light-skinned people in Africa with features of Caucasian people, they are superior to Negroes. I contend that these racist myths are recent, having developed since the eighteenth century .What has been difficult about the attempt to trace the origins of racism is its constant confusion with colour prejudice which has a much older history distinct from racism. I asked the question, "Have sub-Saharan Africans been viewed universally as inferior in the realms of aesthetics, status allocation, erotic appeal, and mystical/religious attributes?" By exploring this question I found that societies prior to the eighteenth century, including those in Europe, reveal all sorts of inconsistencies. Colour prejudice certainly existed in the Old World in various degrees, but it did not in itself fix a group's position in relation to power. *Othello* is a good example. Colour prejudice towards Othello was expressed, yet he was recognized as having high status. Here is where I would be critical of Frank Snowden's recent book, *Before Color Prejudice* (1983). He did not draw a distinction between colour prejudice and racism. A more appropriate sub-title for his book would be "Before Racism". He discusses attitudes towards black people in antiquity; and there was some colour prejudice.

Racism is Recent

There are many examples of colour prejudice in the Old World, but it is in the New World after the sixteenth century that colour prejudice, slavery and racism become intertwined. It is in the African Diaspora that colour prejudice begins to be used to justify slavery. Racism as a systematic justification and belief develops later (eighteenth century) to justify both colour prejudice and slavery. In Europe from at least the eleventh through the fifteenth centuries, blacks held high status in the religious symbol system until the expansion overseas began. Evidence would include almost three hundred Black Madonnas in France, and the veneration of St. Maurice. Four towns in the Alps are named St. Moritz after the black military saint who was marlyred in Roman times. Henri Baudet states in his *Paradise on Earth: Images of the Non-European World* (1965) that blacks were virtually canonized prior to the sixteenth century. In contrast, this respect and veneration was not carried into the New World where slavery had to be justified. The only black saint venerated in the Americas is Martin de Porres of Peru, the saint of the poor and dogs. His counterpart in Europe, St Benedict the Moor, became the head of his monastery in Sicily. Nothing like this happened to Martin de Porres. St Benedict could be tolerated. He gave up his high position for the kitchen.

Charles Verlinden's studies, *Beginnings of Modern Colonization* (1970), are very important in verifying the recent origins of racial slavery. Prior to 1500, white slaves from the Black Sea area were held in slavery throughout southern Europe and on Crete and Cyprus. When Constantinople was taken by the Turks in 1453, the European Mediterranean nations began to look elsewhere for slaves. Prisoners of war from North Africa were replaced gradually by blacks from below the Sahara desert. The sugar complex--including African slaves -was brought to the Americas by Spanish and Portuguese settlers. Even after African slavery had been an established fact for over 100 years, racism had not clearly come into existence. In fact, theories of racism developed in the seventeenth and eighteenth centuries as adjuncts to nationalist European conflicts: see Theophile Simar, *Etude Critique sur la Fondation de la Doctrine des Races au 18e et Son Expansion au 19e Siecle* (Brussels, 1922). Racism (the doctrine of ascribed superiority and inferiority) was first applied by the French upper class to the peasantry, and later by the English aristocrats to the English urban lower class. Eventually, European nations were thought of as "races". The initial rationale for European racism began as a defence of nationalist and class superiority. These ideas embedded in European cultures were not applied to blacks until African slavery had to be defended against early abolitionist attacks in the eighteenth and nineteenth centuries.

The racism applied to blacks was at a religious defence (sons of Ham whom Noah cursed) which evolved into a pseudo- scientific defence (defective genes). What was being defended was the basis of class privilege and who would hold wealth and social control. Here is when history, back to the Egyptians, had to be rewritten to justify current and future superiority--the evidence is quite clear: see George Fredrickson's *Black Images in the White Mind* (1971). An example is furnished by the authors of an early classic in "scientific" racism, the founders of the American School of Ethnology. They were very pleased that their book was selling well in the slave South. That book was *Types of Mankind* (1855) by Josiah C. Nott and George R. Gliddon. But the most vicious attacks against blacks did not come from writers such as George Fitzhugh, who wrote *Sociology for a South* (1854). They came, rather, from Northerners defending the position of new European immigrants who were competing with increasing numbers of former slaves and their children for jobs and housing.

Abraham Lincoln told a group of abolitionists that if he freed the slaves, he would lose all of his (white) troops. Four million freed slaves would go North and fight the Irish far more than those who had come by way of the Underground Railroad. After the riots of New York Irish workers against blacks in 1863, the policy of recruiting black soldiers was accelerated (see James McPherson, *Marching toward Freedom: Blacks in the Civil War*, 1968). Fredrickson reminds us that along with the emancipation of slaves in the District of Columbia, Congress passed a bill to fund emigration of freed Negroes to Haiti, Nicaragua and the Congo.

After the Civil War and general emancipation, blacks and abolitionists were no longer a threat to upper-class white privilege in the South. Instead freed blacks were a threat to two other groups who kept racism going--the new unions in the North defending petit bourgeois white immigrant privileges and upwardly mobile poor whites in the South. C. Vann Woodward presents the career of Tom Watson, the politician and populist leader, as a good example. He was initially an anti-racist and defended blacks from lynching, but once he began to perceive blacks as a threat to upwardly mobile poor whites, he became violently anti- black.

For the past century and a half racism was applied to blacks at first as a defence of slavery , later as justification for continued black subordination, and then to give white labour a competitive advantage for privilege and status. Racism is purposeful--it eliminates competition. Racism was first employed by the French upper class, continues to be class-bound and was not used until the latter stages of slavery in the United States against blacks. Thus, racism is not an expected and natural event across all peoples and times. We might conclude that racism can be eliminated in the future.

Future Challenges

Racism across all times and peoples is based on myths that include the Aryan myth and the Hamitic myth. A number of scholars are in the process of exposing it. Martin Bernal's *Black Athena: The Afroasiatic Roots of Classical Civilization*, Vol. 1 (1987) is an important contribution showing, as it does, how classical history was rewritten and distorted in the past century in order to justify continued derogation of blacks. Once we can get beyond racism and its denial, the task will be before the scholarly community of correcting the omissions and distortions about black societies in the New and Old Worlds--ancient, recent and contemporary. This will be an exciting task and challenge. My current project is just such a beginning, *Black Folks Here and There*, **Vol. 1** (1987). In the first chapter on the Nile Valley civilizations, there is a challenge to other investigators to critically examine the counter-racist theses. Also Chancellor Williams' miscegenation thesis about Egypt's fall needs to be further studied. Diop's characterizations of African and European civilizations need modifying and Yosef Ben-Jachannan's work in religion needs critical analysis. These authors are for the most part factually accurate, but are their interpretations of these historic periods accurate?

We have to take care that we do not read back the present into the past and continue distorting the human record. Based on the three periods of work reflected in my journey as a scholar I there are a series of research (paper and thesis) topics which I hope will be pursued. They are in addition to points already discussed in this review.

1.   An analysis of the new type of social system that is replacing caste in the American South.

2.   To what extent have Southern whites been acculturated into black (Afro-American) culture? Such work would have to be done institution-by-institution   and   be   sensitive   to   cultural   and situational factors. Investigators might begin in sports and music. What are the implications of white acculturation of black culture?

3.   There is need for a comparative study of race relations using samples from three settings: integrated high schools in the South, integrated southern colleges (private and public) and integration in historically black colleges in the South. What are the impacts of stereotyping in each situation on the black and white students' sense of self and cultural identity?

4.   A re-examination of the "culture of poverty" theory with reference to current urban Afro-American communities and the so-called "urban underclass". This will require renewed study of the internal dynamics and cultures of communities.

5.   A comparison of black and white racial and cultural relations in a

sample of small towns selected by region. This information is needed to contrast with generalizations about black-white relations based on large urban settings.

6. A comparative study of inner city riots in the United States with riots in London and Liverpool. Were the objectives of American and British rioters different? Were the dynamics leading up to the riots the same? Were the reactions of the authorities any different?

7. A comparative analysis of changes in values, leadership and group formation and cohesiveness among Afro-Americans during and after, roughly, 1974. Our current circumstances reflect a very different era than the historic periods prior to the mid-1970s. What were the forces which produced and now sustain these changes?

8. What has been the impact of the increasing number of Asians in the population on black-white relations in the United States and in the western states particularly?

9. There is a need for a re-examination of Melville Herskovits' "intensity scale" of African retentions, reinterpretations and syncretisms.

10. There is a great need for "Middletown" type studies of Caribbean and Brazil peasant communities. We need to know for fact the range and types of Africanisms still existing and what impact (if any) modernism has had on African indigenous cultures and community in the New World.

11. A comparison of differential values and patterns of interaction between blacks and East Indians in four locations: Trinidad, the Cooperative Republic of Guyana, the Natal province of South Africa and Kenya.

12. The role of Ghana in southern African liberation struggles during the Nkrumah regime.

13. A critical examination of the implications of the "Negritude" concept for social action in Africa and the Diaspora. This concept is still strong in West Africa and is used as a counter to Communism.

14. An analysis of the United States Joint Committee of Recovery in the 1930s Depression and the subsequent careers of its members.

This group was largely responsible for implementing programmes which headed off major conflict.

15. An objective assessment of the period of collaboration between Afro-American leaders and the Communist Party USA during the 1930s. Most recent information suggests that a reassessment of this relation is due.

16. A translation of *Al-Jahiz: Boast of the Blacks* from Arabic is needed along with a critical review of western responses to this work. Some individual work has been done on issues related to the topics above, but each topic deserves more focused attention. Throughout, my work has been motivated by curiosity and indignation rather than anger and harsh experiences. My career has been atypical partially due to coming from a bicultural family. Also I never saw a ghetto until I was twenty-one. In a way I have been an outsider from the upper South looking into the deep South and northern ghettos. Mississippi was more of a culture shock for me than West Africa. See "Reflections on Anthropology and the Black Experience", in *Anthropology and Education Quarterly*, Vol. 9, No.2, Summer 1978, pp. 85-102.

Finally, my contributions have not been in mainstream Anthropology, but rather in area studies and peripheral theoretical questions. Oliver Cox and C. L. R. James were the only black social scientists of my generation who dealt with "mainline" problems such as the overall impact of capitalism on all whom it had touched, and on sociological theory. Black scholars such as myself have been more empirical--concerned with documenting our specific conditions and the circumstances of our oppression. But our struggle against racism and its distortion of the African and European past and present has brought us to a crucial point. In order to eliminate racism and better understand ourselves we will have to deal with and correct the "mainline" scholarship which has been produced in the past two centuries.

References
Bastide, Roger. 1978. *The African Religions of Brazil*.

Baudet, Henri. 1965. *Paradise on Earth: Images of the Non European World*.

Benedict, Ruth and Gene Weltfish. 1959. *Races of Mankind*.

Bernal, Martin. 1987. *Black Athena: The Afroasiatic Roots of Classical Civilization, Volume I.*

Bunche, Ralph. 1937. *World View of Race.*

Cayton, Horace. 1972. *Long Old Road.*

Cruse, Harold. 1967. *Crisis of the Negro Intellectual.*

Davis, Allison. 1929. "The Negro Deserts His People." *Plain Talk Magazine.*

_____ and John Dollard. 1940. *Children of Bondage.*

Davis, John P. 1966. *The American Negro Reference Book.*

Degler, Carl. 1970. *Neither Black Nor White: Slavery and Race Relations in Brazil and the US.*

Diop, Cheikh Anta. 1974. *The African Origins of Civilization.*

Dollard, John. 1937. *Caste and Class in a Southern Town.*

Drake, St. Clair. 1941. *Deep South.*

_____ 1958. "Destroy the Hamitic Myth." *Presence Africaine.*

_____ 1966. "The Negro American and the Africa Interest." *The American Negro Reference Book.* John P. Davis, editor.

_____ 1987. *Black Folks Here and There, Volume I.*

_____ 1970. *Africa and the Black Diaspora: Impact of Africa on the New World.*

_____ and Horace Cayton. 1945. *Black Metropolis.*

_____ . 1941. *Churches and Volunteer Associations among Negroes in Chicago.*

Elder, Jacob. 1962. *Song Games from Trinidad and Tobago.*

_____ 1969. *From Congo Drums to Steelband.*

Engels, Frederick.   . *The Origin of the Family, Private Property and the State.*

Fitzhugh, George. 1854. *Sociology of the South.*

Frazier, E. Franklin. 1937. *Black Bourgeoisie.*

_____ 1942. "The Negro Family in Bahia." *American Sociological Review.* 7, 4: 465-78.

_____ 1967. *Negro Youth at the Crossways.*

Fredrickson, George. 1971. *Black Images in the White Mind.*

Gergen, Kenneth. 1967. "The Significance of Skin Color in Human Relations." *Daedalus.*

Harris, Joseph. 1982. *Global Dimensions of the Diaspora.*

Herskovits, Melville. 1966. *New World Negroes.*

_____ 1941. *The Myths of the Negro Past.*

Hoetnik, H. 1967. *Caribbean Race Relations: Two Variants.*

James, George. 1954. *Stolen Legacy.*

Johnson, Charles S. 1943. *Patterns of Negro Segregation.*

_____ 1941. *Growing Up in the Black Belt.*

Knight, Franklin. 1974. *The African Dimensions of Latin American Societies.*

_____ 1970. *Slave Society in Cuba during the Nineteenth Century.*

Ladner, Joyce A. 1973. *The Death of White Sociology.*

Les Afro-Americains, Memoires de l'Institut Francais d'Afrique Noire. 1952.

Lynd, Robert and Helen. 1929. *Middletown.*

Macpherson, James. 1968. *Marching Toward Freedom: Blacks in the Civil War.*

Montagu, Ashley. 1974. *The Myth of Race.*

Myrdal, Gunnar. 1944. *An American Dilemma.*

Naison, Mark. 1983. *Communists in Harlem during the Depression.*

Niebuhr, Reinhold. 1932. *Moral Man and Immoral Society.*

_____ 1934. *Reflections on the End of an Era.*

Nott, Josiah C. and George R. Gliddon. 1855. *Types of Mankind.*

Painter, Nell. 1979. *The Narrative of Hosea Hudson.*

Powdermaker, Hortense. 1939. *After Freedom.*

Reid, Ira de Augustine. 1940. *In a Minor Key.*

Rickford, John. 1986. *Social Contact and Linguistic Diffusion.*

Rossi, Peter and Robert Dentler. 1961. *Politics of Urban Renewal.*

Shakespeare, William.   . *Othello.*

Simar, Theophile. 1922. *Etude Critique sur la Fondation de la Doctrine des Races au 18e et Son Expansion au 19e Siecle.*

Smith, Michael G. *Culture, Race and Class in Commonwealth Caribbean.*

_____   . *Black Puritan.*

Snowden, Frank. 1970. *Blacks in Antiquity.*

_____ 1983. *Before Color Prejudice.*

Stern, Bernhard J.   . *The Encyclopedia of the Social Sciences.*

Verlinden, Charles. 1970. *Beginnings of Modern Colonization.*

Warner, W. Lloyd. 1941. *The Social Life of a Modern Community.*

_____ and Buford Juncker. 1941. *Color and Human Nature.*

Washington, Booker T. and Robert E. Park. 1984[   ]. *The Man Farthest*

Down.

Washington, Joseph. 1984. *Black Religion.*
Waters, Enoc. 1987. *American Diary.*

Williams, Chancellor. 1971. *The Destruction of Black Civilization.*
Wilson, William Julius. 1979. *The Declining Significance of Race.*

Wolters, Raymond. 1975. *New Negro on Campus.*

Woodward, C. Vann. 1966. *The Strange Career of Jim Crow.*

Endnote

1. St. Clair Drake was the co-author with Horace Cayton, of *Black Metropolis* (1944). This work is still the major study *of* black urban life in the United States. Professor Drake was an Anthropologist at Stanford University. This essay was drafted by Benjamin Bowser based on a series of taped interviews with St. Clair Drake.

Chapter Seven

Retrospective on St. Clair Drake

Benjamin P. Bowser

The prior interview with the late St. Clair Drake was written in the spring of 1989 based on almost ten hours of tape recorded conversation. I provided him with a detailed list of questions for an interview lasting two half days. Once we started, his reflections and recollections flowed. I ended up spending a week with him exploring aspects of his life and work. As we worked through the questions, new ones arose and became part of the subsequent day's discussion. After Professor Drake's passing, there was a retrospective panel on St. Clair Drake at the 1993 meetings of The Association of Black Sociologists and The Society for the Study of Social Problems in Florida. At that meeting, John Bracey, who was a student of Drake at Roosevelt University in Chicago, provided personal testimony, additional insight, and an assessment of Drake's work. This retrospective is based on a second review of the 1989 interview tapes and John Bracey's reflections. Both provide additional insight on Drake, and the second generation of Black sociologists.

Retrospective on Black Metropolis

Black Metropolis (1945) was not initially planned as a book. Drake came to Chicago in 1937 after money for the Deep South field project ran out and was looking for work. His initial plan was to return to the South to work for the Southern Tenant Farmers Union. Allison Davis and William Lloyd Warner, whom he had work with on the Deep South project, convinced him to apply for a Rosenwald Scholarship to do graduate work at the University of Chicago. Drake applied out of his high regard for Allison Davis, who had been his faculty mentor at Hampton, and who "went out of his way" to praise Drake for his field work in the preface to *Deep South* (1941). When the list of recipients was published in *The New York Times*, Drake was listed as going to Fisk College and to The University of Chicago with his $2,500 grant. Charles S. Johnson chaired the Rosenwald selection committee and wanted Drake to come to Fisk to work under him. Drake quoted E. Franklin Frazier as saying that Johnson was the gatekeeper for the Rosenwald scholarships and used all his graduate students and faculty for his own books. Frazier left Fisk because he was not going to contribute to "Massa Johnson's plantation."

The Rosenwald scholarship was not enough money to attend the University and live in Chicago, so Drake also worked as a graduate student on Davis and Warner's Work Program Administration (WPA) grant to build a data base on the Black community in Chicago. Drake stated that the real purpose of the WPA grants was to keep writers, artists, and intellectuals from going Communist in the 1930s. The Communist Party was a very attractive political alternative to laissez-faire, pro-capitalism of the major political parties at the height of the Great Depression. There were close to 300 other people on this project under Horace Cayton's direction. Drake worked on the Chicago Southside with the Chicago Baptist Institute's training program. The purpose of the Institute was to train Baptist storefront preachers in general literacy, the history of Chicago, and how to preach. Based on this placement, Drake wrote "Churches and Voluntary Associations in Chicago" (19   ).

It was not until 1938-39 that Cayton and Warner began discussing the potential of the field project as a book. Drake was not aware of their planning until they turned to him, while was still a graduate student, to "plan a book comparable to *Deep South*." Drake spoke of the intellectuals' influences on him at that time that helped shape what *Black Metropolis* (1945). Robert Park, Ernest Burgess, and even William Lloyd Warner were not the major influences on him. Everett Hughes in Sociology was the person Drake worked most closely with along with Robert Redfield in Anthropology. The then dominant intellectual influence in Anthropology in the Department of Anthropology and on Drake as a student in that department was the Englishman, Radcliffe Brown, who did British Social Anthropology.

This was a popular subdiscipline of Anthropology, very similar to Rural Sociology. Drake defined British Social Anthropology as the "sociology" of non-literate people with the objective of looking at their social organization rather than more broadly at their culture. Brown was the major intellectual source of William Lloyd Warner's work as well.

It was Drake's social anthropological focus on social organization rather than culture that explains *Black Metropolis'* dual emphasis on class structure and intra-community strata -- the church related, secular related, and "shadies." A 1969 criticism of *Black Metropolis* by Hylan Lewis is that it missed variations in lower class cultural behaviors and beliefs that became central to the perception of Blacks in later public policy statements such *as The Moynihan Report* (1965) and now in William Julius Wilson's work. Drake pointed out that Black church gospel music emerged right there in Chicago during his field work and he missed it because of the emphasis on social structure rather than culture. Drake was very much aware of his orientation. In an interview with Melville Herskovits for an Africa travel grant, he had to defend his approach. Herskovits ended up calling Drake "one of those University of Chicago sociologists who calls himself an anthropologist." Despite his structural emphasis, Drake did note Black cultural patterns. He did extensive unpublished work on Black church rituals and sermons which have common themes and stock phrases used by Black preachers. Joseph Washington later learned this from Drake and did extensive work on it.

In the methodological introduction to *Black Metropolis*, William Lloyd Warner states that *Black Metropolis* is a continuation of *Deep South*. He states that both studies are descriptions of a minimalist caste system as a basis of social stratification in the United States. While writing, Horace Cayton decided that *Black Metropolis* was NOT going to use the caste approach. Other than in Warner's introduction, there is almost no mention of caste in *Black Metropolis*--another ironic difference between what is said by a sponsor and what is actually done. The reason Drake and Cayton did not advance the caste approach is because they felt that the Black communities in Chicago had a much more fluid social systems than did Natchez, Mississippi, the site of the Deep South study. He and Cayton felt that, in Chicago of the 1930s, there were varying degrees to which people were racially integrated--this was not the case in Mississippi at the same time. Not all Blacks or Whites were at the same level of social or cultural integration. Therefore, a caste approach was not the most appropriate. Ironically, variations in integration and their effects are still an open question today, especially when one had such examples of a culturally disaffiliated Black Supreme Court Justice and new "'Buppy' middle class" on one hand, and a deeply isolated and embattled underclass on the other.

Drake did defend the methodological approach used in *Deep South* and *Black Metropolis*. This approach is best illustrated in William Lloyd Warner and P.S. Lunt's *The Status System of a Modern Community* (1942) which was an application of Radcliffe Brown's theoretical work. As one would do in a "pre-literate" nonwestern society, Horace Cayton "moved in" to develop social affiliations with the Black upper strata, and Drake did the same with the Black lower class in both Natchez, Mississippi, for *Deep South* study and on the Southside for *Black Metropolis*. Allison Davis first recruited Drake to the Deep South study when Davis realized that he could not also develop social affiliations with the lower class and maintain his relationships with the Black upper strata. This was a very different method from Robert Park and Ernest Burgess' ecological approach. In Chicago, Drake lived with a murderer and thief, nick named "Slick," under the correct pretense of being a student and used his proximity to study the lower class bars, juke houses, churches, social clubs, and street life. Based on regular meetings between four differentially placed teams, placed in both the white and black upper and lower strata, each team would work their way through their social affiliations at the top and bottom to the middle of the social system. As they moved from one friendship and social network to the next, they noted continuities and breaks in relationships. These continuities and breaks were the bases of the "social" class lines Warner's teams found in the Yankee City and Deep South studies, and of the social structures Drake and Cayton reported in *Black Metropolis*.

While Oliver Cox critiqued Warner's notion of American race relations as a caste phenomenon, Drake pointed out that Myrdal's critique of Warner's social class concept had a more immediate long term impact. Myrdal suggested that American social classes do not really exist except in the minds of Warner and others who did such studies. This critique plus the post-war shift of American society from small towns and rural communities to large towns and cities ended the period of macro-community studies. Hylan Lewis' *Blackways of Kent* (1954) was the last of the Black community macro-studies. The Warner approach worked best for small towns with very stable social relations such as in the Deep South of the 1930s. Drake noted that he and Cayton had to revise their field method for *Black Metropolis* because of the greater complexity and fluidity of social relations in Chicago of the 1930s. They had to work through social clubs and voluntary associations as indicators of differential social affiliations rather than through social networks. Because of the size of the new urban communities, Drake also felt that *Black Metropolis* could have benefited from the relatively new statistical methods actually used in Warner's Yankee Studies series. What the statistical methods could have brought to *Black Metropolis* was the possibility of determining the extent to which their observations were or were not representative of the community.

In the mid-1960s Drake taught in the winters and springs months at Roosevelt University in Chicago and living in Palo Alto, California, the rest of the year with his family. While in Chicago, he returned to the Southside and used this as an opportunity to reflect on how things had changed since his field work in the 1930s. With a black family and church as his points of entry, he was struck by the complexity of black families regarding social class status and culture. He gave examples. There was a hairdresser who would cut up her husband during marital fights (clearly lower class behavior) and the rest of the family was equally riotous, yet her son was a brilliant college bound mathematician with a great deal of support from the family and community. Other families were clearly middle class, but had family members in jail and did not hide the fact as they would have in the 1930s. The church was a sanctuary of respectability, yet prominent and not so prominent members had well known sexual affairs. A church member who was a homosexual was counseled by the minister to confine his sexual activity to other men in the church because it was dangerous for him to be a homosexuals out side of the church. These are all point which were either inconsistent or not taken into account in Drake and Cayton's social class typology in *Black Metropolis*. By the 1960s Drake felt so many people cut around former symbolic and behavioral cues that we really need to rethink what is social class and what it means for Black people. Take any individual or their family and you will find Warner defined lower, middle, and work class behaviors as well as "respectable", "church", and "shady" intra-class orientations. How do you classify supposedly Black middle class college educated sorority women who play the numbers and have "shady" boyfriends? These inconsistencies existed in the 1930s but not nearly to the extent that Drake observed in the mid-1960s.

In reflecting on *Black Metropolis* Drake provided us with two important reminded. First, his work along with Cayton and Davis, and that of Charles Johnson, E. Franklin Frazier, Ira De Reid, were products of the times. They worked within existing theoretical and methodological frameworks. When the theories and methods changed after the War so did the long term significance of the work of second generation Black sociologists. Second, there has been a major shift in American sociology and anthropology since World War II from macro-community studies to attempts to generate representative information about attitudes, beliefs and behaviors. The mainstream of Post War sociological studies have purposely avoided the complexity of single urban community. Studies using statistical analytic techniques are much more practical for generating representative information across multiple communities and for higher levels of aggregation--races, classes, genders, cities, states, and national states. But there is yet another and even more important reason for the shift in the times.

Why The Interest in Black Communities in the 1930s

After re-listening to the interview tapes, I realize that Drake said a lot about why the 1930s was so important to the study of Black communities. Until the 1930s racial segregation in the South had gone largely unchallenged outside of the South and lynchings were daily traumas and reminders of the powerlessness of Black people. Drake is very clear about the prominence of the Communist Party in challenging "Jim Crow" in the early 1930s. The Communists' brought national and international attention to Jim Crow segregation in the South through their defense of the Scottsboro Boys. This was the first time the South was on the defensive since the Civil War. The international condemnation of Jim Crow suggested to Drake's generation that racial segregation could be challenged. From this hopefulness, Drake went to work as a community organizer for the Quakers after graduating from Hampton in 1931; and Allison Davis, Drakes mentor in English at Hampton, went back to school to study anthropology so he could "get the facts to smash the system"; and a number of Drake's peers joined the Communist Party.

In the early 1930s one of the largest public event in the United States was the celebration of the world Communist May Day. The Communists were a growing force to reckon with during the Great Depression. An indication of the times is in the extraordinary progressive legislation passed in the 1930s creating Social Security, Widows Benefits (later AFDC), The National Labor Relations Acts,

Workmen's Compensation, Public Housing, The Work Program Administration, and huge public works programs such as the Tennessee Valley Authority. Drake explained that what made the 1930s so productive with such progressive legislation was a working relation between the Community Party, the labor unions, and major Black leadership. For example, John L. Lewis was the head of the CIO and a strong Republican, but he depended on the Communist to organ new union affiliates where opposition to unions was particularly strong. A. Philip Randolph's union and National Negro Congress worked closely with the Communist Party to get white support for their organizing in the South, for bring more Blacks into the union movement, and against racial segregation in the North. Until this coalition collapsed at the beginning of World War II, both the Federal government and business made major concessions to labor and to their Black allies.

Drake explained: because the Communist took the plight of the "Negro" as one of their central issues in the early 1930s, there was growing concern in government and private foundations about the communists' explanations of the plight of "the Negro" by 1935. To Drake, this is what moved the Rosenwald Fund, Carnegie Corporation, etc. to became particularly active in sponsoring research on Black youth and communities, in offering scholarships to Black graduate students, and for supporting Black schools. Their concern created and then sponsored the work of the second generation of Black sociologists, and then led to what Drake described as "the book to end all work on the Negro"--Gunnar Myrdal's *An American Dilemma* (1944). By the late 1930s, it was well known that the foundations wanted an "objective view." Drake described what this really meant on two levels. First, there were the personality disputes. Melville Herskovits wanted to run the Myrdal study, but there was the problem of his unwanted heavy emphasis on Africa and of his ongoing dispute with Frazier over Africanisms. Myrdal's strategy to minimize disputes was to put everyone who had done studies on Blacks on the payroll, and to have them write papers.

The second reason foundations wanted an "objective view" was because so many who had studied "The Negro" were either on the left or in the Communist Party. Ralph Bunche had concluded in his *World View of Race* (1937) that "a great class war" would break out around the world. Bunche had also been a member of the Communist Party and worked closely with A. Philip Randolph's Negro National Congress. Frazier was not a card carrying member of the Party, but he kept his name prominent on the masthead of the leftist magazine

"Science and Society." Du Bois was out of the question because of his long affiliation with left radical scholars and activists. Other than Charles Johnson, Myrdal did not have any other prominent Black scholars who were not in some way identified with the left. Frazier, Davis, Du Bois and other Black scholars would have not supported Johnson in the lead role with Mrydal, and Drake was still a graduate student. The sentiments of White scholars who had sympathetically studied Black people and communities during the 1930s were also close to the left. *An American Dilemma* was intended to be a definitive mainstream statement of what needed to be said about "the Negro" and to end what was viewed at the time as potentially left influenced studies of Blacks. It is no coincident that major foundation support for the macro-community studies ended after *An American Dilemma* was published and these studies disappeared as major statements about race in the United States.

A Shift Away From U.S. Race Relations

By 1945 Drake had served in the U.S. Maritime Service during the War, completed *Black Metropolis* with Horace Cayton and contributed to *An American Dilemma*. Drake characterized this point in his career in the following way, "from 1935 to 1945, my attention was focused on trying to understand patterns of racial segregation in the United States and the dynamics of changing this segregation. After the War, I decided to view race relations in the United States in a comparative context." From 1947 to 1953, he completed field work and wrote a doctoral dissertation on value systems, social structure, and race relations in Great Britain. From 1954 to 1965, Drake went back and forth between West Africa and Chicago. In 1954 he taught in Liberia and spent nine months in The Gold Coast as it became a politically independent Ghana; from 1958 to 1961 he was professor and head of the Sociology Department at University College of Ghana; he returned to Ghana in 1965.

His decision to do comparative studies was not simply an intellectual one. He was an activist in Chicago, and was involved in the largely unsuccessful struggle against the University of Chicago's efforts to gentrify Hide Park. This struggle showed him a new side of racism-- where power and money was used in a more calculated and covert fashion than in Jim Crow. In his own words, "The struggle embittered me and is partly why I left for Ghana. This made me less interested in studying race relations, especially institutional racism where there was such denial." Here there was a temporary split in Drake's life and career between the activist and the scholar. With regard to his experiences in Chicago, Drake went on to say "I was not writing about race relations during this period. I would rather act, be unscientific, and unscholarly." There was in Drake a heightened sense of impatience, disgust, alienation and self-imposed isolation from race relations in the United States. After his experiences during the Depression and World War II, it was clear to him that change in race relations was not only possible but long over due. Drake spoke of accumulating all sorts of evidence of the possibilities of change during his graduate years in the 1930s. One surprises was that Blacks were the most effective union organizers among the Irish and Italians in Chicago--the most racist of the working class--and that the labor movement in those years was largely interracial. This was all before the War when the possibilities were even greater. So the experiences of racial segregation and inequality in the 1950s was much less tolerable. In this sense, Drake reflected the mood of African Americans who sparked the Civil Rights movement.

For those who knew Drake, this impatience with the pace of change is not surprising. In fact, Drake's academic career was more like to diverging from his activism. He was a student leader at Hampton right after the Black student strikes in 1927. After graduating in 1931, he went to the Quaker school and activist community, Pendle Hill, and went into the Deep South on a Peace Caravan to get signatures for the First World Disarmament Conference. Then he spent three years teaching at a Quaker high school in western Virginia. During the Deep South project he had a faculty appointment at the newly started Dilliard College in New Orleans (Horace Mann Bond was Dean). He and the historian, Benjamin Quarles, were chastised by the college President for raising money for students arrested after challenging racial segregation on the city's buses. Shortly afterward, Drake was fired. After The Deep South project, he wanted to go back into the South to work for The Southern Tenant Farmers Union. So his activist experience in Chicago in the 1950s and 1960s was simply a continuation of his life long effects. The only scholarly work Drake did on race relations from 1954 to 1965 was due to an invitation. His mentor, Everett Hughes, asked him to write a chapter for the 1965 *Daedalus* issue, "The Negro American." That chapter was "The Social and Economic Status of the Negro in the United States." With regard to Africa, Drake was differ. He was collecting extensive materials on race and culture in West Africa and the Caribbean, and began work on the still unpublished *Africa and The Black Diaspora*. This is where his new intellectual focus was.

Comparative Studies of the African Diaspora

Nineteen sixty-nine was Drake's first year at Stanford University. The administration wanted him to take leadership in addressing race at the University. White students needed to understand the new and conflict filled world of race that was emerging all around them. The Stanford President, Lyman, told Drake that if they were going to train Black students, they wanted them to be the next Thurgood Marshalls and Barbara Jordans, not ghetto leaders. The public focal point for addressing race was a large introductory class where about fifteen Black students had demanded a separate discussion section the prior year. That discussion section was led prior to Drake's arrival by a Black psychiatrist. Here is where Drake reports a major shift occurred in his thinking. From working with these Black students and others in subsequent years he stated: "I was forced to rethink whom was I writing for. Virtually all of my writing and that of my generation was directed at explaining the Black condition to Whites." Blacks asked different questions and had different informational and educational needs apart from the mainstream disciplines and professional training. The profound implications in this statement was articulated by Bracey, Meier, and Rudwick in Joyce Ladner's (ed.) *The Death of White Sociology* (1973). They state that from Du Bois' *The Philadelphia Negro* through *Black Metropolis* sociology had been written for Whites on the problem of Blacks. This period was over. Now it was time to write for Blacks and Black students who were in their identity quest. So much of the truth about Black people in history and of the Black potential in the contemporary world was obscured by Whites and White control of knowledge.

Drake and his wife had just finished *Africa and The Black Diaspora*- -three volumes and over 3,000 pages. Drake put this two decade project aside when he realized that it like *Black Metropolis* had been written for Whites. Only one chapter was published on "Ethiopianism." What was attractive about this chapter is that it referred to the high status of Ethiopians in the ancient world. Vincent Harding of the Institute of the Black World and Haki Madhubuti of Third World Press asked Drake if they could reprint this chapter. Without consulting Drake they put in new subtitles and renamed it "Black Religions and the Redemption of Africa" (1971). In the back of

Drake's retitled work, Robert Hill put in some very serious discussion questions about what Drake wrote.   Hill questioned Drake's earlier analysis that Africanisms were more strongly maintained in the Caribbean and Brazil, and much less so among African Americans. Drake said "They questioned whether Brother Drake, who is of the older generation, was telling it correctly." This is when Drake realized that he had to write something for the younger generation that put into perspective their quest for identity and accurately reflected African Americans' place in the Diaspora.   At the same time, Drake had his encounter with Carl Degler when he had to defend Frank Snowden's *Blacks In Antiquity* (1970)--see prior interview essay for details.

By 1970, Drake felt compelled to respond to three closely related problems.   First, there was the Degler/Gergen's effort to look back in time at international and comparative race relations in terms of current racial ideology--light skinned people have always been dominant throughout the world. Second, there was the quest of Black students to learn about their identity and place in history and contemporary society. The answers to this concern would also have to be drawn from comparative studies.   The final problem was on the accuracy and validity of the new vindicationist Black studies literature. Drake was concerned that vindicationist Black scholars may have been writing into the past contemporary biases and views toward race.   Drake was faced with how far he would go to build up "the mystic of Blackness."

He was sympathetic with the objective of the Black Studies movement to get the big ideas and belief systems to energize Black people.   But even with his activist background, Drake was not comfortable with this charge any more than he was with the Degler/Gergen view. He pointed out that it is the role of intellectuals to question any movement's ideology, even Black Studies. Also it the role of intellectuals to address the accuracy of claims driven by ideology. Drake pointed out that we needed to look very carefully at the work of Chancellor Williams, Chiop Anta Diop, Ivan Van Sertima and others. We needed to turn a critical eye toward these works.   It was especially important to look at William's *The Destruction of Black Civilizations* (1971) because it was the most widely used book in Black Studies. Williams' central thesis is that there was a deliberate attempt on the part of Arab and European peoples to destroy Black civilizations, and one of the devices they used effectively was miscegenation. Drake suspected that Williams was reading back into the ancient world what happened to us since the 16th century. Drake's response to all of these concerns was to begin work on *Black Folks*

Here and There (1987).

Sociology and The Comparative Approach

Drake recognized that the Black Studies movement as well as White scholars such as Degler and Gergen were fundamentally flawed in their explanations of race in contemporary society and in history by their lack of a comparative perspective. Drake believed that the cultural and social complexity, and diversity within the African Diaspora in itself was evidence of the conditionality and variability of race as a factor in society and culture. Modern sociologists lack this perspective as well and cannot see history or other societies outside of their own ideological and experiential frameworks. Drake pointed out that there is an African American subculture which can be studied and described in comparative perspective. Otherwise, you get a sociology like that of E. Franklin Frazier who believed that African culture was replaced by southern folkways which were not complementary to urban life. To Drake there were parallels between West African cultures and African American family lineage. The difference is that the African American lineage have weaker conjugal ties. In West Africa, family lineage is strong enough to also be the religious unit and the basis of ancestor worship, while this has all been lost in North America. These are important and subtle points that require a comparative approach to fully understand. Drake believed that Frazier came to appreciate Africanisms among African Americans after his year in Bahia. Comparatively, there is a much higher level of African retention in Brazil than in the United States which confirmed Frazier's view, but there are still retention in the United States nevertheless--a point that Frazier missed for most of his career.

To Drake, Herskovits was closer to the mark in that African retentions were lowest in the urban United States and highest in rural Haiti and Bahia. The rest of Caribbean and Latin American African communities were somewhere in between. Drake attended several conferences in the 1980s on African influences in the Caribbean and in Latin America. But Herskovits like Frazier was unnecessarily inflexible in his view. He looked for specific and intact Africanism in the United States, and later came to realize that Black experiences in the New World modified and transformed the original African cultural scripts. He needed to look more broadly at culture as he did in *The Myth of the African Past* (1941). But in some cases such as Yorubaism in Bahia, the original script changed more in Africa than it did in the New World. A lack of comparative perspective in Sociology leads one to de-center and exaggerate differences in one hand and miss them on the other. Based on Drake's comparative work and experiences, he believed there was greater social distance between Virginia and Mississippi in the 1930s than between America and West Africa, or between Japanese or Chinese and White Americans than between White Americans and African Americans. Drake stated that he experienced greater culture shock in the Deep South during the 1930s than on his first trip to West Africa.

Lack of a comparative perspective affects American Black sociologists in other ways. When one can only see one's immediate ethnic community, then this is all one can feel responsible for and, therefore, there is a strong tendency to do polemical and vindicationist writing, and insist that others do the same. This difference can be seen between major African American and African Caribbean scholars. The African Caribbean scholars have their primary experiences in Afrocentric island communities and then take their higher education abroad. They become more aware of the comparative differences between peoples of African ancestry. So their perspective is broader than their island cultural origins. They believe that they can fulfill their ethnic responsibility and also contribute to the bigger picture--the world beyond their immediate ethnic experiences. In fact, when you realize that your world is only an island within a larger world community, you know that by also positively affecting this large world, you contribute to the improvement of your our sub-community.

There are examples of scholars with this broader and comparative perspective. C.L.R. James wrote *Black Jacobians* (1938) as an important chapter in the African overseas history, but he also wrote *The History of the Russian Revolution* (19) because he felt that Stalin was making major mistakes due to a misreading of his own revolution. James was highly regarded in the Caribbean as well as in Great Britain. Most West Indian scholars did not hold it against him for also being an expert on world socialism and an activist in Europe. Sir Author Lewis was the first person of African descent to get a Nobel Prize in economics for something other than peace. He is from the Caribbean, teaches at Princeton, taught at the University of Manchester, and occasionally goes on leave to teach and consult in the Caribbean and West Africa. African Americans have trouble with this sort of duality. Drake quotes Oliver Cox, the only African Caribbean in the second generation of classic Black sociologists, as saying to him "why don't you get your nose up out of the Negro churches in Chicago and look at the big problems ..." Drake believed that Cox was correct, and pointed out that William Julius Wilson is regarded as one of the top Black sociologists today, but Wilson does not look at the big picture. There are no Black sociologists today on the same level as Parsons, Merton, or Durkheim because we lack a broader world perspective. African Americans scholars are distracted from such achievements. Clearly, not all Caribbean scholars are masters of their immediate and outer worlds, and not all African American sociologists lack a broader perspective. But Drake's point is well taken because he is describe the central tendency, the limits of perspective on most African Americans in the discipline.

Retrospective on St. Clair Drake

Drake was able to make the connections between the limit of perspective that in turn limit the scholarship of Black sociologists for a number of reasons. First, he was not simply a member of the second generation of classic Black sociologists who did extraordinary work in the 1930s. He was younger than Frazier, Johnson, or Reid, and was able to work and reflect on the "classical" period, the evidence that created the period, and its personalities well into the 1980s.. He bridged the community studies of the 1930s with comparative studies of race and culture during the 1950s and 1960s, and then with the Black Studies movement of the 1970s. Second, he was an activist as much as he was a scholar, and therefore, never fully identified as a scholar. He said in the interview: "I did not have a scholarly career." Third, Drake was a marginal man and described himself as such. He grew up in a bicultural family. His father was from Barbados and his mother was African American--unusual for the 1920s. As a child, he spent a year in Barbados and learned about Africa through missionary friends of his father. He never saw a ghetto until he was 21 years old. While he worked with Warner, Davis and others, he was too junior to be a peer and really had no contemporaries. Fourth, he pointed out that the institutions he worked in made a difference for him intellectually. Every one of them was just starting or was experimental. Hampton shifted from a trade school to a college in his first year; his first teaching job was in an experimental school; Dilliard College was in its first year when he was briefly on the faculty; Roosevelt University in Chicago was in its first year when he began teaching there; and the university he taught at in Ghana was in transition to becoming an independent institution. Finally, he was the only member of his generation to director a Black studies program.

I would add that St. Clair Drake is the only African American scholars in the classic generation to do extensive research in the United States and in Africa. Most see Drake as a member of the second generation of Black sociologists (while he was formally trained in Anthropology), and mark his major work as *Black Metropolis*. Drake had a different assessment:

At 77 years old, I have spent the past forty years doing research, writing, and teaching on two basic themes--comparative race relations and relations between West Africans and African peoples in the Western Diaspora. These two themes merged when I began to study sub-Saharan Africans and other Diaspora after the fifteenth century. Urban sociology and anthropology were secondary and incidental. It is embarrassing to say that my emphasis is not in what I am most recognized for. There are people who say that I am one of the pioneers in the field of urban sociology or anthropology, when my major attention and work has not been in either. Since there were so few Black anthropologists before the 1950s, they can go ahead and make me some sort of symbol, but beware of my limited contributions.

Drake's comments about himself are quite modest. He, more so than Frazier, Johnson, or Reid, provides us with a challenge for the work that needs to be done (See his extensive list of potential studies in the interview essay). We need to renewed community studies; do assessments of how African Americans have used culture to survive and thrive in the past and present; assess the impact of African American culture on American society; and look carefully at the work of our scholars who have provide insight about us as a people. This is important work which Black sociologists must engage in. St. Clair Drake has shown the way with what may be his greatest contribution to this post-vindicationist perspective, the two volumes of *Black Folk Here and There* (1987). This is a comparative and critical work bridging sociology, anthropology, and comparative history, written with Black students in mind. I suspect that Drake has an even greater and more immediate contribution, and that is the three volumes of the unpublished *Africa and The Black Diaspora*. In both of these works, sociologists may find the beginnings of that comparative perspective that Drake felt would move us to make vastly more substantial contributions to our community's self understanding and well-being, and bring us into what Oliver Cox called "the bigger picture."

Chapter Eight

Horace Cayton :
Reflections On An Unfulfilled Sociological Career

Robert E. Washington

Introduction

In *The Structure of Scientific Revolutions* Thomas Kuhn argues that normal science depends on the existence of a dominant paradigm (Kuhn 1970). One important implication of this argument is that a scientist must be oriented to an established paradigm to achieve a productive and successful professional career. This is relevant to sociology and other social sciences, even though they --as Kuhn and others point out --are characterized by multiple established paradigms rather than a single dominant paradigm (Kuhn 1970; Mullins 1973). The sociologist must adhere to one of these established paradigms, because they are linked to employment, publication in major journals and research grants, the means to professional success.

Going beyond this issue of paradigm functions, Alvin Gouldner (1970: 495) in his *Coming Crisis of Western Sociology* draws attention to the importance of "reflexivity" in sociological work; the sociologist's adherence to a paradigm that resonates his/her personal experiences and values. In stressing the importance of reflexivity, Gouldner not only rejects the notion of value-free sociology as hypocritical posturing, he also criticizes the theoretical paradigms that prevailed in American sociology prior to the *1960s* because they ideologically supported a conservative American social order. In effect, Gouldner argues, those paradigms intellectually stifled the work of many sociologists. Elaborating, he notes:

> The sociological enterprise, like others, becomes edged with a
> tragic sense when men suspect that they have wasted their lives. In
> confining work to the requirements of a demanding and unfulfilling
> paradigm, sociologists are not using themselves up in their work and
> are, indeed, sacrificing, leaving unexpressed, certain parts of
> themselves –(Gouldner 1970: 495)

This tragic sense (or rather, from the standpoint of the individual involved, the personal tragedy) to which Gouldner refers can result not only from the sociologist obediently producing scholarly work within the constraints of an unfulfilling paradigm for reasons of career expediency, but also, and perhaps most significantly, from the sociologist's failure to produce scholarly work for reasons of disillusionment, the experience of arrested productivity, the frustrations of wasted potential.

In fact, this latter situation, I argue in this paper, describes the predicament that confronted Horace Cayton. Despite his initial intellectual achievements, which included co-authoring what many regard as the best sociological study of an urban black community yet produced, Cayton never realized his outstanding scholarly potential. Because of the narrow career options open to black sociologists in the late 19405 and his inability to locate a critical theoretical paradigm through which he could resonate his feelings of racial alienation, Horace Cayton departed from sociology in the early part of his scholarly career in search of a more reflexively grounded professional calling, an alternative intellectual career.

Over the past several decades increased attention has been focused on the history of black sociologists, as evidenced by discussions of their works in recent books and articles (Conyers 1958: 209-23; Rudwick 1969: 303-6; Bracey, Rudwick and Meier 1971; Hunter 1983: 249-61; Hunter and Abraham 1987). But those discussions have tended primarily to chronicle the career patterns and to commemorate the publications of earlier black sociologists rather than to analyze the effects of the constraints under which they worked. As a consequence, those discussions of earlier black sociologists have neglected to ask perhaps the most problematic question: namely, why so few had productive scholarly careers?[1] This is of course a complex question and we can not hope to fully answer it here. Rather our present aims are more limited. Taking a critical sociology of knowledge perspective, this paper focuses on the constraints mainstream sociology imposed on the careers of black sociologists during the pre-1960s era in order to explain why Horace Cayton failed to sustain his productive scholarly career.

In pursuit of this objective, the following discussion is organized in four sections: first, a brief narrative of Cayton's social background and life experiences before he became a sociologist; second, an account of his sociological career; third, an explanation of his departure from sociology; fourth, and finally, an explanation of what became of his quest for an alternative intellectual career.

Early Years and A Comfortable Middle Class Childhood

Horace Cayton came into sociology from a very unusual background of family and personal experiences --which began with his birth in 1903 in Seattle, Washington. Both of his parents had graduated from black colleges in the South and migrated to Seattle. His maternal grandfather, Hiram Revels of Mississippi, was the first black American elected to the United States Senate during the reconstruction era; and later, after leaving political office, became the president of a southern black college. His father, who had been born a slave in the South, transcended the disadvantages of his social background through education and relocation to Seattle, where he became a successful newspaper publisher. An ambitious man strongly committed to mainstream American middle class values, the elder Cayton earned a good income and maintained the family in affluence and comfort, as was evidenced by their home in a wealthy white neighborhood and their employment of a full-time Japanese servant. The elder Cayton was also active in politics and associated with national black political leaders; for instance, Horace Cayton recalled that during his childhood Booker T. Washington was among the politically prominent black guests who stayed at their home. Though his parents adhered to an upper middle class life style, they also participated in social service activities aimed at uplifting poor and uneducated blacks in Seattle, activities in the tradition of ethnically based social services in the urban black communities. However, like many middle class blacks of the era, the Caytons' efforts to help lower class blacks were oriented to mainstream white American values, uplift through assimilation, rather than identification with black American culture. For the social milieu of Cayton's early childhood, situated in an affluent white neighborhood and characterized by such activities as violin lessons, attendance at operas, symphony concerts and Shakespearean plays, was isolated from the cultural world of poor blacks. And this had significant effects on the formation of Horace Cayton's character; he always felt marginal in relationship to black ethnic culture

A Disturbed Adolescence

Horace Cayton's early childhood reflected the storybook quality of the American Dream; but this life of upper middle class privilege was not to last. Primarily as a result of white reaction to the increasing black migration during the World War One period, Seattle's racial climate changed. Tensions and antagonisms between blacks and whites increased. The elder Cayton's newspaper lost many of its white subscribers; and though he tried to reorient the paper to the expanding black community, he failed to attract readers among the recent black migrants, a group comprised mostly of poor and uneducated agricultural workers from the South. Consequently, the paper soon folded; and the economic fortunes of the Cayton family declined. As financial hardships set in, the elder Cayton was obliged to take a job as a janitor; and the family moved to a more modest, working class Italian neighborhood. Further compounding these difficulties of downward social mobility, with the onset of these drastic changes in life style, the quality of their family relations deteriorated.

Thus in sharp contrast to Horace Cayton's almost idyllic early childhood, his adolescence was plagued by emotional strains and conflicts. Following his worsening family situation and the increased racial tensions in Seattle, Cayton went through a period of rebellion. This was initially manifested in his resistance to racism as he staged-a one man protest and was arrested for refusing to leave the 'white' section of a recently segregated Seattle movie theatre. Following that experience, he gradually submerged into a life style of aimless drifting. He dropped out of high school and began hanging out in the local pool hall. A short time later, he took a job as a mess-man on a ship to Alaska where he was abandoned by the ship; and for several months had to earn his room and board by working as a houseboy in a brothel. Finally, not long after returning to Seattle, he was arrested for participation in a robbery and sentenced to a state reformatory for juvenile delinquents. "For the first time," he noted in reflecting on that experience many years later, "I was made aware of the might and power of the authority of organized society ."(Cayton 1965) He spent almost six months in the reformatory .Following his release and brief stints working as a steward on a steam ship and as a strike-breaking longshoreman (for which he almost lost his life), Horace Cayton came to a sobering realization: his life had reached a dead end. Repelled by the degrading jobs open to blacks and what he perceived as the frivolous life styles of his fellow black workers, he decided to change the direction of his life, to escape the bleak reality of black working class life and to resume his education. Encouraged by his father, who had been distressed by his aimless drifting, Cayton returned to high school; and after graduating, entered the University of Washington. Being one of only three black students at the university , Cayton found the racial atmosphere uncomfortable. His adjustment to university life was also aggravated by financial hardships. But this did not deter him. With assistance from one of his father's old political associates, he got a job as a deputy sheriff, becoming the first black employed as a policeman in Seattle. On the salary from that job, he managed to finance his college education. But even more significant, aside from providing him with a badly needed income, police work influenced the direction of Cayton's intellectual aspirations, by arousing his interests in social influences on human behavior and teaching him observational and interviewing skills, interests and skills that, would later resurface in his work as an ethnographic researcher. In a very real sense, his experiences while working as a deputy sheriff marked the beginning of his sociological training. Though he found police work enormously interesting, he soon realized that he disliked exercising power over other people, that he lacked the ideological and emotional disposition to be a policeman.

During this period, Cayton had vague career objectives of teaching and doing sociological research in the South. However, those plans were soon altered. As a result of his marriage to a white female undergraduate at the university, Cayton's life suddenly changed, exposing him to new and harsher realities of race relations. Though he was no stranger to white racial prejudice, none of his earlier experiences prepared him for the white racism he encountered after his marriage. His wife was fired when the supervisor of the social service agency where she worked discovered she was married to a black man. Cayton did not lose his job but he encountered problems with his white supervisor and fellow police officers when they learned of his interracial marriage, a situation that compounded his feelings of frustration because he dared not express his anger and risk being fired. For the most part, during this period following his marriage, he and his wife were socially ostracized, living in relative isolation from both the black and white communities. That experience not only intensified Cayton's sense of outrage about racial intolerance in Seattle; it prompted his decision to leave. It was through R. E. McKenzie, one of his sociology professors who was a former student of Robert Park and Ernest Burgess, that Cayton learned about the University of Chicago and gained entry to its sociology department as a first year graduate student. Though often frustrating and stressful, his youthful experiences shaped and reinforced his commitment to a middle class life style and a professional intellectual career. But even more important, by exposing him to a rich and bewildering variety of social worlds, by opening his eyes to the influence of group mores on individual behavior, and by teaching him the value of detached observation, those experiences prepared him to become one of the most talented ethnographic researchers of his generation.

Cayton's Sociological Career

Upon his arrival in Chicago, Cayton began the approximately fifteen year span of his sociological career. The city of Chicago was in the depth of the depression and he witnessed first hand the hardships and struggles of the black community .However, being married interracially, he felt out of place in the black belt and spent most of his time around the university. His initial involvement in the black community resulted from a research job. He was hired to interview black policemen as a part of a study on black politicians in Chicago conducted by Herbert Gosnell, a University of Chicago political scientist. Though Cayton's contributions were not cited in *Black Politicians* (Gosnell 1935), the much acclaimed book Gosnell wrote based on the study, he gained invaluable knowledge through that field research, knowledge about the Chicago underworld and the corrupt activities of police and politicians in the black community , which he would later elaborate and refine in *Black Metropolis* (Drake and Cayton 1945).

During this period in American academic life, aspiring black sociologists faced many constraints on their career options. The only academic positions available to them were in black colleges and most of these were located in the South. As already noted, Cayton had vaguely assumed that he would teach and do research in the South. But his interracial marriage complicated his career options. Cayton realized he was being groomed to fit into the mainstream black sociological career pattern, to teach sociology and do research on blacks within the theoretical tradition of the Chicago school. Thus he was not surprised when Robert Park arranged a summer job for him at Tuskegee Institute. "You may not like what you see," Cayton recalled Park saying as they talked in the latter's office, "and I doubt that it will be possible for your wife to go with you. But you'd better have a look around down there if you can possibly manage it. " (Cayton 1965: 190)

Not only was this Cayton's first contact with Southern racial discrimination, which he found repulsive; it was also his first exposure to a black college faculty which, it would hardly be an exaggeration to say, he found disappointing. Most had only bachelor degrees and lacked the intellectual sophistication of his associates at the University of Chicago. He made few friends among the Tuskegee faculty. Further aggravating his discontent, the administration had assigned him to put out a weekly news bulletin rather than to do sociological research. Observing the racially subservient attitude of the Tuskegee administration toward the surrounding white community, Cayton soon concluded that black colleges such as Tuskegee were hopelessly irrelevant to the central problems of black Americans. As he later recalled:

> The Institute was merely mouthing the worn out generalities and formulae that the whites wanted to hear. ..All in all, I felt I had seen as much as I needed or wanted to see.(Cayton 1965: 203)

He requested permission to return to Chicago before the summer was over and his request was granted. Significantly, the only positive thing Cayton felt he gained from that experience were insights into why Southern blacks migrated North, insights he would later articulate in **Black Metropolis,** where he discussed the development of the Chicago black community during World War One.

Cayton returned to Chicago where he resumed his sociological work. Through Charles S. Johnson of Fisk University, a protege of Robert Park and the most prominent black sociologist of the era, he gained his first major research position. He was hired along with George Mitchell of Columbia University by the Secretary of Interior to study the effects of New Deal legislation on black workers. Now no longer enrolled in the university, he moved to New York city, the place where the project was located, and along with George Mitchell completed and published the study in 1939 under the title, **Black Workers and the New Unions** with an introduction by Charles S. Johnson (Cayton and Mitchell 1939).

But despite this promising beginning of his sociological career, Cayton's personal problems and his feelings of alienation from the racial situation in the United States worsened; in part as a result of tensions surrounding his marriage. (He and his wife were eventually divorced.) It had cut him off from the black community in Chicago while causing him to feel he could live a normal life in the United States only if he accepted his designated place, the position of a second class citizen. This he refused to do.

Under the pressure of those tensions, he accepted the offer of a Swedish friend to accompany him on a trip to Europe in the late 1930s. Cayton was now thinking seriously about the possibility of settling in Europe and that trip constituted a major formative experience in his life. Not only did that trip broaden his perspective on race relations; it also increased his feelings of estrangement from American society. As he traveled around Europe, he was especially struck by the difference in his relations with white women, the absence of racial tension in encounters between blacks and whites of the opposite sex. In his words, "for the first time I had an unusual emotion. I realized with a start that I could compete for any of these women on equal terms with any other man, not just for the white French girls but those of any color or culture. The fear surrounding white women, to which I had been subject even though I had known many in the United States, had suddenly disappeared and with it some of their attractiveness, for now they were no longer forbidden to me." (Cayton 1965: 220) His bitterness toward the United States became even more pronounced after he met a black French prostitute who seemed to lack any semblance of racial consciousness or feelings of being an outsider in French society. He later recalled:

> ...France had made this girl, though she was perhaps only a prostitute, feel at home, feel that she belonged. Why stay in a country that did not want me, where I was a stranger? To hell with the United States, I thought. But I couldn't quite mean it.(Cayton 1965: 225)

Europe was on the verge of the Second World War. Hence, despite his disdain for the racial situation in the United States, Cayton returned to Chicago and the beginning of the most active phase of his sociological career. Still he had not completed his doctoral degree. But his Chicago mentors encouraged him to continue in sociology. He was offered a job at Fisk where Charles S. Johnson was chairman of the sociology department and Robert Park was now located as a scholar in residence. This was Cayton's last effort to adapt to a mainstream black sociological career pattern. As he recalled, "it would give me an opportunity to see what I could expect if I continued my work in sociology, as teaching positions for Negroes were available only in Negro institutions. " But he soon found the middle south no more appealing than the Deep South. "...I finally made up my mind that I could never live in the South no matter how important a job might be offered me." (Cayton 1965: 233) This marked a crucial watershed in Cayton's career; he was rejecting the only mainstream career option open to black sociologists. Significantly, this preceded the research for *Black Metropolis*. Though it was not then obvious to his sociological colleagues, the direction of Cayton's aspirations were already being influenced by his relationship to Richard Wright, the famous black novelist, which I will say more about later.

Cayton's return to Chicago from Fisk marked the beginning of his most productive period as a sociologist. He had married again --this time to a black graduate student he met at Fisk --and felt securely based in the Chicago black community. Quite unexpectedly, as a consequence of going over to the university one day to look for a job, he had a stroke of good luck. He learned of a job possibility from Lloyd Warner, the anthropologist, who had submitted a research proposal to the federal government for a large scale study of the Chicago black community .The federal government approved the grant; and Cayton was appointed to administer the project, which -- because the government intended it to provide jobs --employed a large number of people. Cayton was later joined by Sinclair Drake, then a graduate student in the anthropology department, as the project's co-director. The book that resulted from that research was *Black Metropolis*. Published in 1945, *Black Metropolis* received the Anisfield-Wolf Award and widespread acclaim. As an ethnographic analysis of urban black life, that study constituted a major achievement, providing the most detailed and comprehensive delineation of an urban black American community ever undertaken. *Black Metropolis* established Cayton's reputation as one of the leading black sociologists of his generation. Yet oddly, after completing that study at the relatively young age of forty-two, Cayton departed from sociology .He took a job as director of a community center on the south side of Chicago. Marking the end of a very promising scholarly career, he never again worked as a sociologist.

Explanation of Cayton's Withdrawal from Sociology

This brings us to the critical question: why was the productive phase of Cayton's career so short? Why, after the success of *Black Metropolis*, did he not finish his degree and settle into the mainstream sociological career pattern as had Charles S. Johnson and E. Franklin Frazier? A set of interrelated factors were involved in Cayton's failure to continue his scholarly career. First and foremost, as noted earlier, was his inability to find a critical theoretical perspective in mainstream sociology, a perspective focused on white racism, through which he could express his feelings of racial alienation. I will have more to say about this later in reference to Cayton's paradoxical attitude toward the Chicago school perspective, the unresolved contradictions in his pronouncements about race relations. Second, also noted above, was his contempt for the South and southern black colleges. He felt repelled by the prospect of not only living amidst white southern racism, but also of being confmed to exist within a segregated black community. Third, and closely related, was his desire for a cosmopolitan life style, which included a high profile professional career and interracial friendship networks. This, he realized, would have been impossible if he accepted an academic appointment at a southern black college. Finally, a fact perhaps not well known about Cayton, was his aspiration to become a literary artist, his hope to find a more existentially resonant intellectual profession in creative writing.

While living in Chicago, outside of his activities as a sociologist, he established friendships with a number of black writers and performing artists, including luminaries such as Langston Hughes, Arna Bontemps, Paul Robeson, and Richard Wright. But it was Wright, the famous young black novelist, who most impressed him. As Cayton later said, "the person who most influenced my life during this period was Richard Wright "(Cayton 1965: 247)

Aside from their shared feelings of dislocation, the frustration of living in Chicago as a young black intellectual, what apparently lay behind Wright's influence on Cayton was the protest orientation exemplified by Wright's work. Wright functioned outside constraints that confronted professional black sociologists. Through his celebrated novel, *Native Son* and his other literary works, Wright projected indignation and anger about white American racism, emotions that Cayton felt but was unable to articulate within the mainstream sociological perspectives on race relations. Equally significant was the life style associated with Wright's career pattern. A free lance literary career which did not necessitate being located in a southern black college, Wright's professional role offered the prospect of a cosmopolitan life style and intellectual freedom, the possibility of existential fulfillment. Through intellectual work that was reflexive, critical and consequential for racial change, Wright had gained an international reputation, setting a standard of black intellectual achievement Cayton very badly wanted to emulate.

Cayton and Wright had met as young men in Chicago during the depth of the depression through Mary Wirth, the wife of the University of Chicago professor Louis Wirth. Mary Wirth, then employed as a social worker at a protestant welfare agency, had been assigned to assist the Wright family, a household composed of Wright, his mother, younger brother and aunt, living on Chicago's south side in desperate poverty. In an effort to help Richard Wright, then an unemployed youth with the responsibility of supporting his family, Mary Wirth sent him over to the university to see if her husband could assist him in finding a job. Horace Cayton was working as a graduate student research assistant in the office where Wright turned up looking for Louis Wirth. (Mary Writh Interview 1971) Cayton later recalled:

> One day there came a tapping on the door of (the) office. I opened the door and there was a short brown-skinned Negro, and I said, "Hello. What do you want?" He looked like an undergraduate, so I was perhaps condescending in a polite fashion, and, of course, he was also colored. He said, "My name is Richard Wright. Mrs. Writh made an appointment for me to see Dr. Writh." That made me a little more respectful. I told him to come in. "Mrs. Writh said that her husband might help me. I want to be a writer."
>
> Well, I thought that was a little pretentious, a brown-skinned *boy* coming into the University and saying he wanted to be a writer. Who didn't want to be a writer? But who could write? I began showing him the files in the office --I would not say that we were totally statistically oriented at the University at the time, but we were very empirical. We were going *out* studying every facet of the city. We were discovering the Italian district, the Polish district, the Irish district, the Negro community .We were studying the vast complex of human beings who make up that monster of Chicago, and Dick said, "You've got all of your facts pointed, pinned to the wall like a collector would pin butterflies." I looked at him. He was a poetic little Negro.(Hill, Cayton Bontemps and Redding 1966)

Their association began with that encounter. Later, after Wright moved to New York and achieved literary fame, he would stay at Cayton's home as a house guest when visiting Chicago; and Cayton, in turn, would stay at his home when visiting New York. Without question, Wright's influence on Cayton's perception of his own intellectual career began with the publication of *Native Son*, a book that provoked a storm of controversy. Cayton, it also should be noted, influenced Richard Wright. By exposing him to the Chicago school's perspective on black culture and social disorganization, a perspective Wright would incorporate into a more radical outlook on race relations, Cayton helped to transform him into the most sociologically astute black writer of the era. In fact, the seventeen page introduction Wright wrote for *Black Metropolis* bears perhaps the strongest testimony of his influence. Noting the linkages between his writings and that study, Wright pointed out:

> If, in reading my novel, *Native Son*, you doubted the reality of Bigger Thomas, then examine the delinquency rates cited in this book; if, in reading my autobiography, *Black Boy*, you doubted the picture of family life shown there. then study the figures on family disorganization given here. *Black Metropolis* describes the processes that mold Negro life as we know it today.(Drake and Cayton 1945: xx)

Cayton and Wright remained closely associated for approximately twelve years --until Wright expatriated to Paris in the late 1940s.

Evidence of Cayton's attraction to a literary career can be seen in several places. First, while visiting Europe in the late 1930s, he attended a writer's conference in Paris where, through the efforts of Mike Gold, a white American Marxist writer, he was designated an official delegate. Having no reputation as a writer, Cayton was reluctant to accept the offer. But Gold --a man not noted for deferring to protocol --had insisted, by reassuring him that, "the conference needed an American Negro."(Cayton 1965: 212) As it turned out, Cayton very much enjoyed that experience of interacting with Andre Malraux, Nancy Cunard, Gold and other leftist literary intellectuals. Second, after the publication of *Black Metropolis* in 1945, he applied for and received a fellowship to attend a writer's colony in Saratoga, New York. It is noteworthy that at this point he was trying to transcend his racial identity, as were other black literary artists of the time, referring to himself as a writer first and a Negro second. Third, he and Wright planned to collaborate in publishing a magazine on the racial problem in the United States. They had even gotten a pledge of financial support from a wealthy donor but for some unexplained reason the donor backed out. And finally during the early 1950s, after he moved to New York City, Cayton enrolled in a creative writing course at the New School for Social Research. This conclusion about Cayton's attraction to a literary career like that of Richard Wright was also supported by comments made by Mary Wirth. "Horace seemed never to take much pride in his achievements as a sociologist, " she said, recollecting Cayton's relationship to Richard Wright "He seemed to think more of Dick's achievements. He really admired Dick and never felt his own work measured up to Dick's writing. But I think he was terribly unfair to himself." (Mary Wirth Interview 1971) What Mary Wirth failed to perceive were Cayton's feelings of anger and racial alienation, his desire to ventilate his outrage about white racism, which caused him to admire Wright's literary achievements more than he did his own sociological accomplishments. Cayton apparently kept his feelings of racial alienation hidden from his University of Chicago associates.

Unfortunately, little became of Cayton's literary aspirations. Except for his autobiography **Long Old Road**, Cayton authored no book after **Black Metropolis**. Though innovative, indeed a unique and invaluable chronicle of the pre-1960s life experience of a black sociologist, his autobiography fell far short of being a major literary-existential work on the level of Wright's **Native Son**, James Baldwin's **Notes of a Native Son, The Autobiogaphy of Malcolm X**, Eldridge Cleaver's **Soul on Ice**, or Franz Fanon's **Wretched of the Earth** (Wright 1940; Baldwin 1968; Little 1965; Cleaver 1968; Fanon 1963). These works, in addition to achieving major influence, projected critical-reflexive social perspectives that resonated their authors' feelings of alienation and anger about race relations. For reasons I will explain shortly, Cayton never located such an intellectual perspective, a radical perspective on race, through which he could express his discontents.

About as close as Cayton came to realizing his aspirations to become a writer was the weekly column he wrote as a journalist for the **Pittsburgh Courier**, the black American newspaper; an activity he performed for approximately thirty years. Marking the high point of this part-time journalistic career during the 1950s while he was living in New York, Cayton got that newspaper to appoint him as its United Nations (UN) correspondent.   As the only black American correspondent at the U.N. during the volatile period of debate and controversy surrounding the struggles of African and other third world nations to achieve liberation from colonialism, he reveled in the excitement of attending conferences and socializing with diplomats. But this job with the *Courier* was no consequence for his becoming a creative writer. Moreover, the *Courier* paid very little and he was eventually obliged to seek other sources of income.

In fact, Cayton's life throughout much of the second, unproductive phase of his intellectual career, following the publication of *Black Metropolis*, was characterized by mounting personal crises which were reflected in his periodic unemployment and psychological deterioration. His increased cynicism toward the moderate liberal approach to the race relations was evident as can be seen in his recollections of the disillusionment he had felt with his job as director of the community center .

> I hated my job for I had come to feel that the community center was a
> sop thrown to the Negro community by wealthy and middle class whites,
> who felt virtuous by supporting it but who would resist with all their
> strength any move on the part of Negroes for better jobs, housing in
> white areas, for the free exercise of civil rights. Indeed, I began to look at
> myself and my work at the center as part of the machinery by which the
> subjugation of Negroes was perpetuated rather than as an instrument for
> easing caste bonds.

He then went on to state his predicament candidly.

> I wanted to quit and find a job where I was not controlled by white
> philanthropy. ...But what could I do? For in my impatience to get into
> public life I had neglected to complete my doctorate, which would
> certainly hamper me now in obtaining a good teaching or research
> position. (Cayton 1965: 310)

Cayton eventually quit the job at the community center in the late 1940s. However, he apparently never seriously considered the possibly of returning to the University of Chicago and completing his graduate work. His second marriage had by now broken up and he moved around in a small interracial circle of bohemian friends. "We were all relatively successful and lived in expensive apartments," he noted, "but we were all lost, alienated from both the Negro and white communities. Each of us had reached a position where we could no longer trust our emotions and establish meaningful relations except among ourselves.

We simply fed each other's neuroses. " (Cayton 1965: 312)

It was during this period, Cayton's emotional problems became so intense he turned to psycho-analysis, under the pretense of wanting to enter a training program for social scientists set up by the Institute of Psychoanalysis. But he later admitted, "I fooled no one, including myself. I was desperately unhappy and in need of help, no matter what I called the process." Cayton entered psychoanalysis --choosing a female analyst who had a deformed arm because, he reasoned, "if she could accept her own physical handicap so well she would be likely to have some understanding of my social handicap." (Cayton 1965: 257)

Through this slow (it lasted five years) and painful process of psychoanalysis he discovered that his psychological problems were racial. Though aware of his misgivings about many whites, he had not realized the extent to which his anger about the racial situation in the United States had become deeply rooted in his personality.

> My friends were liberals, and I believed in and was committed to the democratic ideal. ..I had spoken and written to the effect that America could solve its race problem if only the white man was not so timid. That I might have feelings of hatted toward white people had never occurred to me, for some of my most meaningful relationships were with whites. But my dreams and my associations, those unconscious revelations of truth, startled me.

One day his analyst put the question to him bluntly. "Could it be hatred?" And Cayton recalled:

> A great revelation came to me, and I sat bolt upright on the couch. "Yes --I hate white people. Not all of them, but the idea of white people as a group. I hate them for what they have done to me, to my parents, to my people. I do hate them but I never realized it before.(Cayton 1965: 260-61)

A short time later, he experienced a nervous breakdown. Afterwards, though not fully recovered, Cayton moved to New York where, cut off from most of his friends and suffering from feelings of racial persecution, he hit the bottom of his life. During part of the period while living in New York, he was unemployed --and residing in a cheap apartment in lower Manhattan. He also had a drinking problem. In fact, after depleting his savings, he was so desperate for money he was reduced to selling blood to get funds to eat. Eventually he began to recover his mental health and located a job in the research department of the American Jewish Committee; but it did not work out Finally, with the assistance of friends, he found a job with the National Council of Churches in New York which he held until the late *1950s*- when he decided to move to the West Coast. It was there he landed a teaching job at the Extension of the University of California and wrote his autobiography, which was his last book.

Cayton's Failure to Find a Successful Alternative Intellectual Career

While Cayton's experience of racial alienation caused him to withdraw from sociology; it did not cause his failure to find a more reflexive world view that would have launched him into a successful alternative intellectual career. That failure was caused by his identity ambivalence, the unresolved contradictions of his class and racial identity, which paralyzed his intellectual development, his ability to channel his anger into a new and more resonant sociological perspective on American race relations. Perhaps the most glaring manifestation of that ambivalence was evidenced in the discrepancy between the disdain he expressed toward the moderate liberal approach to race relations and the respectful --indeed almost reverential --attitude he continued to express toward the Chicago school of sociology .Even though he viewed the white liberal perspective on race relations as hypocritical, Cayton seemed oddly incapable of attacking the Chicago school. In fact, nowhere in his published writings does he criticize or even express reservations about the Chicago sociology .As can be seen from his admiring testimonial –

> My work in the Social Science Division was exciting, especially the sociology department, which was using the city as a laboratory to study urban life. As a result of its many studies more became known about the sprawling metropolis of Chicago --how it was run, how it loved, stole, helped, gave, cheated, and even killed -- than perhaps any city in the world. In no other place had social scientists studies a locality so intensively –(Cayton 1965:183)

There is not a hint of any inadequacy or flaw in the Chicago school's perspective on race relations. Nor, for that matter, did Cayton express any misgivings about his mentor, Robert E. Park, the leading Chicago theorist on race relations, a former secretary to Booker T. Washington and the author of some controversial opinions about blacks. Cayton's attitude toward Park remained deferential. In recalling his compliance with Park's suggestion that he spend the summer at Tuskegee, Cayton noted .."Dr. Park was perhaps the most important voice in American sociology, so one listened to it." (Cayton 1965: 190) Even when it was urging him to accept a career pattern and intellectual outlook that he found alienating? Apparently, the answer was yes. Accepting the Chicago school's rhetorical rationale, the view that it constituted an "impersonal science," Cayton never questioned its apolitical, accommodationist approach to racial practices in American society. Based on the naturalistic assumptions of the ecological tradition, the Chicago school propagated the politically dubious conceptions of racially segregated neighborhood as "natural areas" and of racial conflicts as the outcomes of natural processes, conceptions which Cayton, despite his abhorrence of white racism, never challenged.(Park and Burgess 1969) Nor did he challenge the Chicago school's lack of a macro-sociological perspective on the role of capitalist political and economic interests in maintaining the American racial system, the white elite's interests that exploited and benefited from the racial subjugation of blacks.

How then does one explain this discrepancy between Cayton's disdain for the white liberal approach to race relations and his respectful pronouncements about the Chicago school perspective? At the simpler and more cynical level, one might argue that Cayton deliberately suppressed his misgivings about the latter. Which is to say his silence about its flaws resulted from his feelings of loyalty to the Chicago sociological establishment for the patronage he received; for after all his reputation was linked to the Chicago school's prestige. Criticism would have amounted to biting the hand that fed him. But this seems an implausible explanation; there is no evidence Cayton was actually aware of this discrepancy. Alternatively, at a more complex and less cynical level, a different explanation seems warranted. Namely, that discrepancy appears to have been due to Cayton's emotional attachment to the Chicago school which blinded his perceptions of its flaws. Simply put, Chicago sociology remained an essential part of his identity, an identity embodying unresolved contradictions, that prevented him from embracing a more radical sociological perspective.

Which brings us to consideration of the only two prevailing alternative orientations in which Cayton might have found a more critical and reflexive perspective on race relations.

Marxism, the first of these alternative perspectives, never attracted Cayton's interests. He saw it only in terms of the communist party which --given the historical period --is understandable. While living in Chicago, Cayton had a number of bad experiences with communists, beginning with the party's control over the WPA union which organized the workers on the *Black Metropolis* research project. As he recalled, "though there were few real communists on the project, these few caused me much grief, until I began to learn how to manipulate them." (Cayton 1965: 337) Cayton was also aware of the difficulties Richard Wright encountered as a party member, after publication of *Native Son*, which the party attacked as a distoned representation of black American social reality. Also, in the early 1940s, he and Wright had gotten into a feud with the party over its willingness to accommodate segregationist practices in the United States as a result of Stalin's popular front strategy, following Germany's invasion of Russia. In a complete reversal of its earlier anti-war stance, the party now urged blacks to support the war effort and donate blood to the Red Cross, even though the latter maintained racially segregated blood supplies. This manifest communist hypocrisy enraged Wright; and Cayton allowed him to use his column in the *Pittsburgh Courier* to attack Ben Davis (the black communist leader) and the party. Cayton subsequently became an object of the patty's scorn. As he later recollected, "I had attacked communists in my column from time to time but this ended any casual association I had had with them on a United Front basis. I became head man in the groups they labeled "Negro misleaders." (Cayton 1965: 253)

Conspicuously absent from Cayton's account, however, was any mention of the group of black intellectuals around the NAACP, including prominent figures such as Abraham Harris, Ira De A. Reid, Ralph Bunche and Charles Houston who --during the depression -- attempted to shift the Association to a more radical critique of American capitalism and racial relations. (Record 1964: Fullinwider 1969) Cayton was never inclined toward a radical class analysis of American race relations. At least in part, his early work experiences in Seattle had shaped his attitude toward class politics. As he recalled, "the fundamental fact was that the Negroes simply did not trust the white working class and its discriminatory labor unions. And they did not trust them for good reason, for the white working class had traditionally been the Negroes' enemy and in this there had been no fundamental change."(Cayton 1966: 47)

But aside from his unpleasant experiences with the party and white labor unions, the other reason Cayton found Marxism unappealing was his strong identification with a middle class life style. In fact, the attraction of middle class black Americans to the communist party puzzled him, as indicated by his reflections on Ben Davis who he had met some years earlier on a visit to Atlanta during the summer he spent at Tuskegee. Noting that Davis was the son of a prosperous Atlanta family, Cayton observed:

> Davis had just graduated from Harvard, where he studied law, and to my great envy he was smoking a Dunhill pipe. We gossiped about the city and Tuskegee and then parted. I did not see or hear from him again until he had become a leading figure in the communist party *.I've often wondered what encouraged him to break with his comfortable past and become a communist.* (emphasis added) Eventually he landed in prison for his beliefs.(Cayton 1965: 201)

Having worked at menial jobs as a black laborer, Cayton was hardly inclined to identify with the black working class. As noted earlier, he felt repelled by the life styles of his fellow black workers. Equally important, it should be noted, Cayton knew that Marxism would not lead him to a successful and rewarded intellectual career. The career of Oliver Cox, the Chicago trained black sociologist who had embraced a Marxist perspective, bore testimony to that fact. Virtually ostracized by mainstream sociology, Cox not only experienced intellectual isolation, working in obscure southern black colleges, and rejection by foundations of his requests for research support. But also, and perhaps most frustrating, he encountered much difficulty getting his work published and recognized by the profession. (Hunter and Abraham 1987: xvii-xvix) Thus, even though it constituted a radical perspective through which Cayton might have resonated his feelings of alienation, Marxism comported with neither his class identity nor his professional ambitions. These factors caused him to ignore the importance of class dynamics for race relations.

Black nationalism offered the other possibility of a more critical and reflexive perspective on American race relations. But Cayton, like Richard Wright, thought the political sentiments of Black Nationalism were misdirected and delusional. As can be seen from his comments about the Garvey movement.

I remember vividly when Marcus Garvey had come to Seattle, though I was only a young boy. ..It was a ludicrous spectacle, but the dignity and pride of the participants had raised that demonstration out of the absurd and kindled fear or admiration in the watchers. The Garvey movement. ..was the only real mass movement among Negroes in this country. It was laughable, certainly, but it fulfilled a deep hunger in the hearts of more than a million American Negroes. That hunger still exists and, in the thirty or thirty-five years since Garvey, it has deepened, grown more acute. If America doesn't soon allow the Negro to take pride in himself as an American, he'll inevitably seek acceptance as a black man.(Cayton 1965: 387-8)

In short, Cayton viewed the Garvey movement not as a force for the cultural and political liberation of the black community but as a reaction formation generated by the frustrations of racial outcast. Similar, though somewhat more ambivalent, were his views of the Black Muslims, who were emerging as a formidable political force during the period he was writing his autobiography. In response to a friend's question about whether he could ally himself with the Black Muslims, Cayton replied:

Their goals are as foolish as   Garvey's. ..but they are appealing. As to whether I'd join them, I wouldn't. I still have hope --and forgive me if I seem more naive --for the fulfillment of the American Dream. I haven't given that up yet. But, yes, ..there is a little of the Black Muslim in every Negro.(Cayton 1965: 388)

Like most other black intellectuals of his generation, Cayton accepted the Frazier side of the Frazier-Herskovits debate about the origins of black American culture. He rejected the notion that black Americans possessed African cultural traits. In a conversation about this matter with an African diplomat at the U.N., he stated his position unequivocally.

I'm not taken in by any spurious notions of my African heritage. American Negroes are really just dark skinned Americans. We are not held together by any idea of a common African background, history , or culture but rather by the opposition of white Americans. As a group we don't even resemble Africans. Culturally we are wholly American. (Cayton 1965: 371)

We can see E. Franklin Frazier's influence when, several years later in writing about the issue of black American's cultural heritage, Cayton cited Frazier as his point of reference.

> E. Franklin Frazier in his last book, *The Negro Church* , describes the
> slow growth of cohesiveness in the Negro community. The cruelty of the
> plantation system did not even permit the development of a stable family
> group. It was the Negro church that first brought some cohesion to the
> Negro. It was many years before the Negroes as a group could even
> envision a free world. (Cayton 1966: 40)

This view of African American culture has been of course superseded
by more recent scholarship that presents a far different account of the
black American slavery experience, particularly the early history of the
black American family life. (Gutman 1976) Nevertheless, Cayton --as
the product of the pre- 1960s era --failed to comprehend the resilience
of the black family structure that emerged out of slavery .But even
more important, at least from the standpoint of his social identity, he
felt no attraction to either African culture or black American culture.

The core of Cayton's identity confusion derived from his
simultaneous feelings of attachment and hostility toward the white
American social world. Recall his statement in reflecting on the Garvey
movement "If America doesn't soon allow the Negro to take pride in
himself as an American, he'll inevitably seek acceptance as a black
man." Aside from its ostensive effort to explain Garvey's appeal to
many blacks, this statement indicates Cayton's negative conception of
black identity, the notion that it exists only as a reaction formation to
white American rejection rather than as the product of a distinctive
communal and cultural life. What's especially revealing about Cayton's
dichotomous conception of identity --acceptance by whites or pride in
blackness -- is that he possessed neither. Yet, because of his attraction
to the white American social world, he remained preoccupied with his
feelings of resentment resulting from white exclusion. As a
consequence, the problem of race relations became for him a matter not
of trying to explain the social structural forces --the political, economic
and cultural dynamics --of racial oppression. Rather it became a matter
of trying to explain the causes and effects of racial rejection in
interpersonal relations. And this led him to embrace a Freudian oriented
psychoanalytic perspective on race relations. Though he failed to fully
develop that perspective, I think it is useful to quote at length a passage
from one of his published articles in order to indicate this new direction
of his thinking. Beginning with the qualifications of his opening

statement, we can see Cayton's ambivalence --"although I am for human dignity and would fight for whites if they were abused, humiliated and spat upon, there is a residue of hate in my heart as I think there is in most Negroes living in the United States. "

He then proceeds to say that he has developed a theory to explain this residue of hatred:

> I am convinced that at the core of the Negroes mentality there is a fear-hate complex. My assumption is that all men in Western European civilization have unconscious guilt and fear of punishment for this guilt. In the case of the dominant group this guilt is to a large extent irrational. It can be shown to be false, a figment of the imagination, a holdover from early childhood experiences. Guilt can more easily be resolved by psychiatric treatment or even by rational cogitation.

However, notes Cayton, this is not applicable to black Americans. The situation is different.

> In the Negro the psychological problem is ever intensified. For him, the punishment in the actual environment is ever present: violence, psychological and physical, leaps at him from every side. The personality is brutalized by an unfriendly environment. This reinforces and intensifies the normal insecurity he feels as a person living in our highly complex society. Such attacks on his personality lead to resentment and hatred of the white man. However, the certain knowledge that he will be punished if his hate emotions are discovered only compound his fear. This is the Negro reaction to his own brutalization, subordination and hurt.

Thus Cayton suggests the black American, confronted by this dilemma, succumbs to what might be termed "the trapped rat syndrome. "

> It is this vicious cycle in which the American Negro is caught and in which his personality is pulverized by an ever-mounting self- propelling rocket of emotional conflict. The Negro has been hurt; he knows it. He wants to strike back, but he must not --there is evidence everywhere that to do so would lead to his destruction. (Cayton 1966: 42-43)

To get at the actual meaning of this passage, it is instructive and revealing to replace Cayton's usage of third person references with the first person references. Thus transformed, we see a far more coherent and disturbing statement.

revealing to replace Cayton's usage of third person references with the first person references. Thus transformed, we see a far more coherent and disturbing statement.

It is this vicious cycle in which I am caught and in which my personality is pulverized by an ever-mounting self-propelling rocket of emotional conflict. I have been hurt; I know it I want to strike back, but I must not --there is evidence everywhere that to do so would lead to my destruction.

Though clearly reflexive and critical, as the above translation reveals, Cayton's new perspective constituted little more than a thinly disguised expression of his personal psychological predicament. Not only did it lack sociological imagination, in C. Wright Mill's sense of the term, the ability to link personal troubles of milieu to public issues of social structure. It also ignored the supportive roles of black community and black culture. What James Baldwin wrote in criticizing the conception of blacks in Richard Wright's protest novels could be said also of Cayton's conception of black American personality .It suggested, in Baldwin's words, "that in Negro life there exists no tradition, no field of manners, no possibility of ritual or intercourse, such as may for example, sustain the Jew even after he has left his father's house." (Baldwin 1968: 28) Not surprisingly, given his attraction to the white American social world, Cayton perceived black American personality as existing in a void of brutalization, outside the context of family, community life and spiritual beliefs, a situation that described quite well his life but not that of most black Americans. Ironically, the rich ethnographic depiction of black American community life in *Black Metropolis* stood as one of the most important refutations of Cayton's later conception of black personality.

But most important, as an outcome of its atrophied sociological imagination, Cayton's new perspective reinforced his intellectual confusion by deluding him into believing that the problem of black racial oppression could be understood and resolved at the level of interpersonal relations. This was hardly a compelling formulation. Anguished, derivative and simplistic, his psychoanalytical perspective not only lacked the insightfulness of his earlier sociological work; it failed to comprehend the root causes of his difficulties, the systematic forces of racism, the perils of assimilation and the abyss of self-hatred, that resulted in his tragically unfulfilled intellectual potential.

References

Baldwin, James. 1968. *Notes of a Native Son*. New York: Bantam Press.

Bracey, John, August Meier and Elliott Rudwick. 1971. *The Black Sociologists: The First Half Century*. Belmont, CA: Wadsworth Publishing Company.

Cayton, Horace. 1966. "Ideological Forces in the Work of Negro Writers." *Anger and Beyond*. Herbert Hill, Arna Bontemps and Eds.

_____ 1965. *Long Old Road*. New York: Trident Press.

Cayton, Horace and George Mitchell. 1939. *Black Workers and the New Unions*. Chapel Hill: University of North Carolina Press.

Cleaver, Eldridge. 1968. *Soul on Ice*. New York: McGraw-Hill.

Conyers, James E. 1958. "Negro Doctorates in Sociology in America: A Social Portrait." *Phylon* 29: 209-23.

Drake, St. Clair and Horace Cayton. 1945. *Black Metropolis*. New York: Harcourt, Brace and Company.

Fanon, Frantz. 1963. *The Wretched of the Earth*. New York: Grove.

Fullinwider, S. P. 1969. *The Mind and Mood of Black America*. Homewood, IL: Dorsey Press.

Gosnell, Herbert. 1935. *Negro Politicians: The Rise of Negro Politics in Chicago*. Chicago: University of Chicago Press.

Gouldner, Alvin. 1970. *The Coming Crisis of Western Sociology*. New York: Basic Books.

Gutman, Herbert. 1976. *The Black Family in Slavery and Freedom, 1750-1925*. New York: Vintage.

Hill, Herbert, Horace Cayton, Arna Bontemps and Saunders Redding. 1966. "Reflections on Richard Wright: A Symposium on an Exiled Native Son." *Anger and Beyond*. Herbert Hill, editor. New York: Harper and Row.

Hunter, Herbert M. 1983. "Oliver Cox: A Biographic Sketch of His Life and Works." *Phylon* 44: 249-61.

_____ and Sameer Abraham, eds. 1987. *Race, Class and the World System: The Sociology of Oliver Cox*. New York: Monthly Review Press.

Interview with Mary Wirth. Author February 1971.

Kuhn, Thomas. 1970 2nd ed. *The Structure of Scientific Revolutions*. Chicago: University of Chicago Press.

Little, Malcolm. 1965. *The Autobiography of Malcolm X*. New York: Grove Press.
Mullins, Nicholas. 1973. *Theories and Theory Groups in Contemporary American Sociology*. New York: Harper and Row, Inc.

Park, Robert and Ernest Burgess. 1969. *Introduction to the Science of Sociology*. Chicago: University of Chicago Press.

Record, Wilson. 1964. *Race and Individualism*. Ithaca, NY: Cornell University Press.

Rudwick, Elliot. 1969. "Notes on a Forgotten Black Sociologist: W. E. B. DuBois and the Sociological Profession." *The American Sociologist*.

Wright, Richard. 1940. *Native Son*. New York: Harper.

Endnotes

[1]1. Discussion of the problem encountered by Oliver Cox are among the few notable exceptions. See Hunter, 1983 and Hunter and Abraham, 1987.

Chapter Nine

Walter R. Chivers--An Advocate of Situation Sociology

Charles V. Willie

Walter Richard Chivers was my mentor and friend. He was born in 1896 and died in 1969. As a sociologist, he is less well-known than E. Franklin Frazier, W. E. B. DuBois, Ira Reid, and Hylan Lewis, his sometime colleagues at Morehouse College and in other Atlanta University Center schools during the second quarter of the twentieth century. Despite his relative professional invisibility in sociology nationally, Butler Jones said that "it is doubtful that any black sociologist has had a more seminal influence upon the development of [other] black sociologists (B. A. Jones 1974: 148).

Jones and I studied under Walter Chivers. Several of his other students who have made significant contributions to the discipline of sociology are Charles Lawrence, John Reid, James Conyers, and Richard Hope.

In 1925, Chivers joined the faculty of Morehouse College. He continued as professor in the institution which also was his alma mater until retirement in 1968. In the language of that period, DuBois described Morehouse as "a colored institution with a colored faculty where their sons are getting sympathetic attention and first-class training..." (E. Jones 1967). Part of that brigade of scholars who provided a sympathetic and first-class education, Chivers, born in Montgomery, Alabama, began his teaching career following graduate studies in New York. Chivers earned a master's degree from the New York School of Social Work in 1924 and later completed study for a doctoral degree in sociology (which he never received) under Henry Pratt Fairchild at New York University. In recognition of his outstanding career in higher education, and his many civic and professional contributions, Chivers was awarded an honorary doctorate by the University of Arkansas at Pine Bluff when he retired. During an academic career that extended over forty-three years, he "sent a steady stream of young blacks to the centers of graduate sociology study" in this nation (B. A. Jones 1974: 148-49).

A review of the life and times of Walter Chivers could focus on his sense of humor and pathos, his low-keyed, rambling teaching style, his tutorial relationship with his students, his newspaper reading addiction, his involvement in community affairs, his courageous investigations of lynchings, or the racial and other difficulties that he encountered in his graduate education. As a former student and friend who majored in sociology at Morehouse College from 1944 to 1948, and who later served as his research assistant (while studying for a master's degree at Atlanta University), I could testify about Chivers' various professional activities such as his connection with the National Planned Parenthood Federation, his founding of the Institute on Marriage and Family Relations at Morehouse College, and his work with Arthur Raper investigating racial injustices in the South. I prefer to limit this analysis to his unacknowledged contributions to sociology as a discipline and particularly his contribution to social theory.

A Kind and Courageous Mentor

Walter Chivers, the man, was gregarious. He would rather talk than write. This probably is why he is known by only a few sociologists. He authored a half-dozen or so articles that were published between 1939 and 1943 in such journals as *Phylon, Journal of Negro Education, Social Forces*, and *Southern Frontier,* but never wrote a book.   Chivers also was a loner who had experienced many disappointments, ranging from the dissolution of his first marriage to failure to complete all requirements for the Ph.D. degree. He was a friendly and warm person, deeply devoted to his daughter, who prepared for a medical career, and invested himself unstintingly in helping others. Personally, however, he seemed not to be fulfilled until toward the end of his life when he remarried. Perhaps this is why he was so concerned with the accomplishments of his students: their achievements, vicariously, were his own.

It is possible, also, that Chivers was such a wonderful tutor because of his early training as a social worker. He used his wide network of professional contacts which he cultivated at national professional association meetings to place his students in programs of graduate study in the major research universities of this nation. My matriculations for graduate study both at Atlanta University and Syracuse University were due, in part, to the intercessory activity of Professor Chivers.

He was a courageous man, and when necessary he could be contentious. He was not afraid to go against the grain. Frazier described W. I Thomas as among the first social scientists to be critical of biological determinism as an explanation of social adaptation; he praised Thomas as one who "assumed that race prejudice could be destroyed" (Rudwick 1974: 52). Chivers, however, was critical of Thomas for not always spelling Negro with a capital N in his book on *Primitive Behavior* and for illustrating aberrations in kinship behavior with "a disproportionate number of anthropological cases [of] ... African Negroes," and not indicating at the same time that such aberrations are not peculiar to blacks (Chivers 1943: 358). Chivers particularly was incensed about a passage in Thomas' book that described Hottentot society as one in which a man could have sexual relations with both his wife and his wife's sister, as if this was a generalized form of behavior among Hottentots, and also a form of behavior found only among African blacks. Chivers was not reluctant to criticize his contemporaries or the leading social scientists of the past.

The Sociology of Personal Experience

His sociological method involved the derivation of theoretical generalizations from direct or vicarious personal experiences. He was an inveterate reader of daily newspapers and taught his students to read them too as sources of the original stuff of sociology. Other sources of information were his personal involvement's in crisis situations.

According to Jones, "in the years 1925 and 1936, when lynching was still a fairly frequent occurrence in the South, Chivers was often the black investigator dispatched by the Commission on Interracial Cooperation to the black community to study and report on the aftermath of the event... In this way he came to have an almost boundless storehouse of knowledge of the overall conditions of life among the rural and urban blacks in Alabama, Mississippi, and Georgia" (B. A. Jones 1974: 151-52).

He combined the information obtained from investigating these tragic events in the South with experiences of urban blacks in the North that he gained while a social worker and graduate student. These complementary sources of knowledge enriched his understanding of human social organization, including that of whites as well as blacks, rural and city dwellers, and Northern and Southern populations. It is appropriate to describe Chivers as a cosmopolitan sociologist in tune with his time who understood the social relations of a range of social types.

A Concerned and Understanding Teacher

Chivers measured the value of sociological knowledge in terms of whether or not it helped or harmed his students. He believed that knowledge and action should be linked and kept his eye on the outcome, as a criterion of what might be an appropriate input. He was critical of the negative illustrations about blacks that some white authors included in their textbooks, not only because they failed to mention the fact that majority-group members exhibit similar behavior, but because such illustrations provided white people with justifications for denying full human status to blacks in general and to his students in particular. Anything that might harm his students he opposed.

Walter Chivers' gentleness and sensitivity were demonstrated by the way he communicated with students. He discovered that psychoanalytic concepts that were part of his social work training were difficult to comprehend by some of the young students in mid-adolescence who had been admitted to Morehouse College to replace older students drafted into the armed forces in the early 1940s. Chivers recognized that these concepts also disturbed some of these younger college students because of their age and the strict religious tradition in which they had been socialized. In discussing planned population growth, Chivers said that he often talked of "family regulation" rather than "birth control." The former phrase was less threatening to his students and was one way, he said, he could outwit the preacher and not deliberately generate conflict between science and the environment from which his students came. If necessary, Chivers would modify his teaching technique to accommodate the feelings and personalities of his students. His belief was that "the extent to which a student is able to assimilate knowledge gained is the test of its value..." (Chivers 1943: 358)

Among the stream of scholars from Morehouse College who were influenced by Professor Walter R. Chivers and who became professional sociologists and made major contributions to the field are the following: Charles R. Lawrence, II, who received a Ph.D. degree from Columbia University and served as Chairperson of the Department of Sociology at Brooklyn College of the City University of New York; John Reid who received a Ph.D. degree from the University of Chicago specialized in demography, consulted with the Population Research Bureau, and served as a professor in the Department of Sociology at Howard University; Richard O. Hope who received a Ph.D. degree from Syracuse University and served as Chairperson of Departments of Sociology at Morgan State University and Indiana University at Indianapolis, Visiting Professor, Department of Sociology, Princeton University, and Vice President of the Woodrow Wilson National Fellowship Foundation; Jomills Henry Braddock II, an eminent researcher, who received a Ph.D. degree from Florida State University, has conducted large scale longitudinal studies on equality of opportunity in education, employment, and sports and has served as Chairperson of the Department of Sociology at the University of Miami; James E. Conyers who received a Ph.D. degree from Washington State University, has served as Professor in the Department of Sociology at Indiana State University, as President of the Association of Social and Behavioral Scientists and as National Chairperson of the Caucus of Black Sociologists in America (now the Association of Black Sociologists), and who is recipient of the Distinguished Career Award of the Association of Black Sociologists; Curtis T. Langley, who received a Ph.D. degree from the University of Washington, has research interests in crime, housing, and quality of life issues, has served as professor, Department of Sociology and Assistant Dean of the School of Social Sciences and Director of the Urban Affairs Graduate Program, Norfolk State University. Other Morehouse College graduates mentored by Walter Chivers who have made significant contributions to higher education are Doctors Andre D. Hammonds, a professor at Indiana State University, MacArthur Steward, Dean of University College, Ohio State University, Charles F. Lyles, a professor at the Baruch College of the City University, and Butler Jones, a professor at Cleveland State University, who held several important positions in the Society for the Study of Social

Problems.

Walter Chivers specialized as an applied sociologist and attracted several students as concentrators in sociology because of this orientation. Probably, the most famous Morehouse College graduate who majored in sociology but who made his greatest contribution beyond this field was Dr. Martin Luther King, Jr. When he graduated in 1948, the Sociology Department was under the guidance of Professor Chivers.

Another outstanding scholar who was mentored by Walter Chivers and who made his mark in applied sociology is Arthur L. Johnson, who retired from Wayne State University in Detroit as Vice President for University Relations and Professor of Educational Sociology.

Johnson, a sociology major at Morehouse, served as Executive Secretary of the Detroit Branch of the National Association for the Advancement of Colored People immediately after receiving his Master of Arts degree in sociology from Atlanta University. He was the Chief Executive Officer of the Detroit Branch fourteen years and made it into one of the most successful and stable branches of the NAACP. Later, he became Deputy Director of the Michigan Civil Rights Commission and Deputy Superintendent of the Detroit Public Schools before his appointment to the central administration of Wayne State.

Johnson's career was a manifestation of the leadership vision that Chivers gave to all of his students. Eventually, Johnson served as president of the Detroit NAACP, President of the University Cultural Center Association, Chairman of the Detroit Board of Police Commissioners, and Vice Chairman of the Board of Trustees of the Detroit Public Television Station.

All of Walter Chivers' protegees have been ceaselessly involved in public affairs. Curtis Langley for example, has directed the Graduate Program in Urban Affairs at Norfolk and has done research on pregnancy prevention among teenagers. James Conyers has studied the problems of youth in urban areas and leadership in the black community. Jomills Braddock has published in scores of professional journals on school desegregation, employment opportunities, and other educational issues such as tracking. Richard Hope gave leadership as Executive Director of the Quality Education for Minorities Project sponsored by the Massachusetts Institute of Technology and the Carnegie Corporation, was Director of Research and Evaluation for the U.S. Defense Department's Equal Opportunity Management Institute and conducted research on the educational system in Harlem with Kenneth Clark's Metropolitan Applied Research Center.

Another characteristic of Walter Chivers' protegees is the leadership responsibility they have assumed for the various organizations and associations in which they have participated. Among the selected group mentioned in this essay, there are a goodly number of Chairpersons of departments, deans and assistant deans, directors of programs and presidents and vice presidents of organizations.

Considering the geographic range of universities from which the students of Walter Chivers receive doctoral degrees, their areas of specialization, and their extensive publications record, one must conclude that during the generations that he presided over the Department of Sociology at Morehouse College a cosmopolitan and daring group of scholars were developed, sent forth, and commissioned to effect the field of Sociology in a positive way. This they did according to their talents. I, for example, who also was coached by Professor Chivers, have served as president of the Eastern Sociological Society, vice president of the American Sociologist Association, and Chairperson of the Syracuse University Department of Sociology. Professor Chivers taught all of us that professional associations have educative functions, that we should participate in them and learn from these experiences, and, if possible, give direction to their mission. By and large his students followed his advice and had an impact.

Another outstanding scholar who was mentored by Walter Chivers and who made his mark in public affairs and applied sociology is Arthur L. Johnson, who retired from Wayne State University in Detroit as Vice President for University Relations and Professor of Educational Sociology.

Johnson, a sociology major at Morehouse, served as Executive Secretary of the Detroit Branch of the National Association for the Advancement of Colored People immediately after receiving his Master of Arts degree in sociology from Atlanta University. He was the Chief Executive Officer of the Detroit Branch fourteen years and made it into one of the most successful and stable branches of the NAACP. Later, he became Deputy Director of the Michigan Civil Rights Commission and Deputy Superintendent of the Detroit Public Schools before his appointment to the central administration of Wayne State.

Johnson's career was a manifestation of the leadership vision that Chivers gave to all of his students. Eventually, Johnson served as president of the Detroit NAACP, President of the University Cultural Center Association, Chairman of the Detroit Board of Police Commissioners, and Vice Chairman of the Board of Trustees of the Detroit Public Television Station.

An Advocate of Situation Sociology

Chivers was an advocate of situation sociology. He described a number of social problems such as criminality, rioting, daily gambling on numbers, mental illness, and mortality among blacks as situationally determined. Not only the behavior, but the manner of computing rates, he said, was situational. He argued, for example, that the higher rate of criminality reported for blacks compared with whites was in part a function of the decision of some white judges to deny the designation of juvenile delinquency to black youthful offenders.

Chivers also said that there was a situational basis for the lower hospitalized rate of mental illness reported for blacks earlier in the twentieth century. Despite the stress that blacks endured, Chivers said they had a hospitalized rate for schizophrenia that was lower than the hospitalized rate for whites with the same disorder in the United States in the 1920s. He explained the difference in rates between the races as due to the residential location of most blacks in the South at that time.

Few mental hospitals were available to blacks in the South during the age of segregation. In the North where blacks had access to this kind of hospital, Chivers said their hospitalized rate for schizophrenia was the same as that of whites or even higher. In Illinois, for example, the rate of blacks hospitalized for schizophrenia was nearly four times higher than the rate for such white patients in the 1920s. However, the hospitalized rate for white patients suffering with this mental disorder in the North was the same as the rate for similar whites in the South. In all regions of the country, whites had access to mental hospitals. Variability in the mental illness rate for blacks then was, in part, a function of the situation in which blacks lived and the facilities available to them.

Chivers analyzed riots as spontaneous situational phenomena - not planned events. He described them as outbursts in response to situations of deprivation in which the urban blacks found themselves (Chivers 1939: 42).

Situational Determinants of Leadership

Unlike DuBois, who hypothesized that blacks in America would be saved by their leaders of thought and culture, the teachers of teachers, or the talented tenth, (DuBois 1903[1970]: 226-28) Chivers had a theory that leadership was a response to crisis situations, and that morality was the essential component of leadership.

Moral leaders, according to Chivers, are ethical and honest (Chivers 1942). He saw intelligence as an asset to morality but not the basis of it.

He explained that many black parents send their children to college not to become leaders but to protect them from having to earn a living from menial tasks such as they had to perform, and possibly to enable them to outwit the white folk (Chivers 1943b). Chivers realized that educated people may become leaders but that not all leaders are educated people.

When Southern blacks were largely rural dwellers, Chivers said the black agricultural agents exhibited real leadership mettle. They fashioned techniques that enabled tenant farmers, farm laborers, and black land owners to survive. He said the agents had courage, intelligence, restraint, and the ability to develop flexible strategies. It was in the racially explosive Black Belt farm area where these black political-agricultural leaders evolved. Some were field agents of the federal government. Others were connected with agricultural and technical schools. Chivers observed that these agents were ethical and religious people who understood black people in the situations where they worked and were accepted by them. It was the ingenuity and political sophistication of these folk leaders that enabled them to prevent lynchings and other challenges to the tolerable existence of rural blacks (Chivers 1942).

These experiences led Chivers to formulate a theory that "effective leadership in society arises out of conflicts and crises" (Chivers 1943a). Out of such situations emerge leaders. His theory of leadership did not deny the value of education and training; but these were not essential in the development of situational leadership. Chivers probably avoided an elitist concept of leadership because of his understanding of and respect for black preachers. He said they are not as a whole well-educated but they speak the language of their clientele, appreciate their limitations, and probably know the great masses of blacks better than any other American (Chivers 1943a).

Racial Symbiosis

Identifying the source of conflict and crisis in the South during the first half of the twentieth century, Chivers said it came from the refusal by whites to implement their responsibility as dominant members in the power structure to correct the wrongs. In his carefully researched article on "Northward Migration and the Health of Negroes," Chivers concludes with this statement: "The fact that Negroes are more susceptible to certain diseases than white people is not as important as the fact that the matter of [their] health is not important in the minds of those people who are in a position to do something about it.   White people who control the mechanics necessary for health improvement have shown an alarming indifference to the health of [America's black people]" (Chivers 1939: 43).

While Chivers did not subscribe to an elitist theory of leadership, neither did he embrace a Booker T. Washington concept of self-reliance. Chivers saw blacks and whites connected in a symbiotic power relationship in which the more powerful had to act in a particular way if the less powerful was to be delivered from misery and misfortune. Chivers believed that it was incumbent on whites to make the first move to overcome the social pathologies of racial oppression. In Chivers' world-view, blacks and whites were all caught up together, as Langston Hughes might say, "in the sweet flypaper of life" where the less powerful ultimately are dependent on the more powerful to change their way of life.   This is an interesting theory and deserves examination. It, of course, is not comprehensive and this is one of its limitations. It does not recognize the veto role of minorities in the power structure and the initiatives that they must make. The decision to cease cooperating in one's own oppression is decisive and is an action of subdominant people of power that probably triggers the decision by the dominant people of power to cease their oppression and to assume their appropriate responsibilities.   Ultimately, it was Chivers' conclusion, neither whites nor blacks could go it alone.

Centuries ago, Francis Bacon advised learned people to live in the eye of other people, and not withdraw to pursue a private life of contemplation "untaxed with sensuality and sloth and free from indignity." Further he said that those who teach duties but do not also practice them "contend sometimes too far to bring things to perfection" (Bacon 1973: 16-18).   Walter Chivers fulfilled the calling of the learned person described by Bacon. He was ceaselessly involved in social affairs and remained in the eye of others. He would not settle for society as it was but neither did he insist on perfection. He wanted a society that is fair. In all of its imperfections, however, he believed that the leaders of society should be moral, and that moral leaders are ethical and honest people who prevent disaster even if they cannot create utopia.

References

Bacon, Francis. 1973. *The Advancement of Learning*. London.

Chivers, Walter R. 1939. "Northward Migration and the Health of Negroes." *Journal of Negro Education*. 8.

_____ 1942. "Negro Agricultural Leadership." *Southern Frontier*. 3.

_____ 1943a. "Negro Church Leadership." *Southern Frontier*. 4.

_____ 1943b. "Teaching Social Anthropology in a Negro College." *Phylon*. 4.

DuBois, W. E. B. 1903[1970]. "The Talented Tenth." *The Black American*. Leslie H. Fishel, Jr. and Benjamin Quarles, editors. Glenview, IL.

Jones, Butler A. 1974. "The Tradition of Sociology Teaching in Black Colleges: Unheralded Professionals." *Black Sociologists: Historical and Contemporary Perspectives*. James E. Blackwell and Morris Janowitz, editors. Chicago: University of Chicago Press.

Jones, Edward A. 1967. *A Candle in the Dark*. Valley Forge, PA: The Judson Press.

Rudwick, Elliott. "W. E. B. DuBois as Sociologist." *Black Sociologists: Historical and Contemporary Perspectives*. James E. Blackwell and Morris Janowitz, editors. Chicago: University of Chicago Press.

Chapter Ten

Using Pragmatist Sociology for Praxis: The Career of Charles H. Parrish, Jr.

Anthony J. Blasi

Introduction

The name, C.H. Parrish, is not generally known by people who did not make his acquaintance; he was a modest man who probed much and published little, who served the Civil Rights movement as a remarkable facilitator and shrewd observer but who avoided the limelight. On occasion he saw fit to author blunt arguments, often in letters to newspaper editors, but in most instances he brought local people together for action in numerous towns and cities in the American South, forming teams of grass roots leaders rather than thrusting himself into the forefront. He was invariably thoughtful and deliberate, and fashioned his analyses in the manner of the pragmatist social scientist that he was.

Charles Henry Parrish, Jr., was born in Louisville, Kentucky, in 1899. His father, Rev. Charles Henry Parrish, Sr., was a noted African American clergyman and educator who had been born to former slaves. His mother, Mary Cook Parrish, was an educator of African American and native American ancestry. C.H. himself graduated from Central High School in Louisville in 1916. In an undated statement, he says he held his basic beliefs since childhood and attributes them to his parents. However, "As the son of a Baptist minister, I have often wondered why my religious beliefs were not more strictly orthodox. Undoubtedly it was the sort of person my father was rather than what he said in sermons or pamphlets that influenced me most. My father's private secretary was Catholic. It never seemed incongruous to me that he should bring back to her a crucifix that had been blessed by Pope Pius X, or that a large picture of the Pope hung in the front hall of our home."[1] In addition to this rather cosmopolitan openness, he knew a humanitarian morality from his childhood home: "Nearly always, as I remember, there were non-paying guests in our house. Uncomplainingly, my mother would do the necessary things to make them comfortable."[2] And notably, after observing that they enjoyed a moderate prosperity despite such generosity, "*It has thus become a part of me to believe that in the long run I could never lose anything by helping other people.*"[3] He goes on to mention that his father fought, without bitterness, against racial intolerance.

In 1920 Parrish earned an A.B. in mathematics from Howard University; he never mentioned in my presence any experiences from his college years. Unsure of where his interests lay, he proceeded to earn the M.A. in sociology at Columbia University (1921), though he never mentioned in later years any significant experiences at Columbia. His thesis was a community study of the organizations--business, cultural, social--of the African American population of a town in New Jersey. He visited the town on weekends, consulting census and archival information but principally interviewing leaders and ordinary people. He cited no literature apart from data sources but kept the focus of the manuscript on the formal organizations of the community. He was careful not to over-manipulate the quantitative data that he reported in tables, given its limitations. The manuscript is notable for its economical reporting of every entity among the African American population--churches, clubs, music groups, businesses, etc. The reader is given an immediate grasp of the vibrancy or lack thereof of each one of them. Here is a typical example:

The eldest of these orders now existing is the order of Good Samaritans which had its beginning over fifty years ago. It has a financial membership of thirty, all but three of whom are women. Though the Methodists are in the majority, there are a considerable number of Baptists (a few of them Southerners), who constitute an almost equal portion. The organization's influence in the community is on the wane. Some of the members pay their dues religiously, but rarely trouble themselves to attend meetings and in consequence lose the effect of the social intercourse which the meetings promote.

He notes the control of the three churches over most of the African American organizations, and underlines the lack of organizations for young people. A few people are the life of several organizations at a time.[4] His ability to generate shrewd assessments is remarkable at such an early age; it would be a skill that he would use time and again in the future.

From 1921 to 1930 he taught mathematics and sociology at Simmons University in Louisville; in a letter from 1950, when the prospect of a change in employment seemed imminent, he says of this period only that he also taught in the Men's Bible Class of Calvary Baptist Church and served as an unofficial consultant to the Louisville City Zoning and Planning Commission.[5]

Parrish's *curriculum vitae* indicates that he taught sociology and education in the Louisville Municipal College for Negroes, which was affiliated with the University of Louisville, from 1931 to 1951. Because he wrote a midterm paper for the Advanced Social Psychology course offered by George H. Mead at the University of Chicago in the winter of 1931, when Mead died and Herbert Blumer took over the conduct of the course, we can surmise that Parrish was for at least one semester in 1931 a full-time graduate student at Chicago.[6] His intellectual focus seems to have coalesced from the nineteen thirties; he often spoke in later years of his Chicago professors, and his manuscripts, dealing with social science and with the situation of African Americans in the United States, date from 1931 and later. As will be seen below, his guiding perspective during his involvement in the Civil Rights movement reflected the "Chicago school" approach. He spoke to me with regard to his years with Louisville Municipal College, saying that he had to teach both psychology and sociology, and that he coached the basketball team as well. The Chicago figures who turn up in his papers are E. Franklin Frazier, Louis Wirth, and Herbert Blumer, though in his later years he often used to speak principally of Robert Park and Herbert Blumer.

Before earning the Ph.D. in sociology from Chicago (1944), he served as state director for the Works Progress Administration project, "Study of Negro White Collar Workers" (1936) and received an appointment from E. Franklin Frazier to supervise the collection of life histories from African American children and youths in Louisville (1936_38). Frazier used the materials, together with a similar set from Washington, D.C., for a book on African American youth.[7] Parrish used a carbon copy of the interview transcripts and notes made during the interviews, for his dissertation on the role of skin color shade in the concepts of self and others among African American children and

216   *Confronting the American Dilemma of Race*

youth.[8] Meanwhile, he had charge of some food distribution during a 1937 flood, conducted a survey of local businesses operated by African Americans (1942), and adapted a Chicago manual on police work with minorities for the Louisville police department (1950). In addition, "During the war I was Co-Chairman of Emergency Recreation and member of a panel of the War Manpower Commission. Briefly, I was on the Executive Committee of the Mayor's Committee on Race Relations."[9] He also mentions serving on a committee on the police school and a judge's advisory committee to the juvenile court.

The municipal college was to be closed in 1951, with the University of Louisville being integrated racially. The move would give the university a progressive image, but the plan called for the dismissal of all of the municipal college's (African American) faculty. Under the threat of litigation, the university offered financial settlements and one position to the college's faculty. The faculty members drew straws to determine who it would be who would integrate the university faculty, and it was to be C.H. Parrish. Almost immediately, Parrish became an example in the controversial "experiment" of racially integrated education. He would spend much of the next two decades in a heavy schedule of race relations workshops, leadership formation sessions, meetings, and speaking engagements throughout the South--all worked in around his schedule of university duties (professor of sociology, 1951-69; department chair 1959-64). He became a Civil Rights movement organizer throughout the South and Border States, largely under the auspices of the Southern Regional Council.

The Pragmatist Perspective and the Status of African Americans

The first evidence of the pragmatist perspective in the thoughts and deeds of C.H. Parrish is the midterm paper he wrote in 1931 for the Advanced Social Psychology course offered by George H. Mead. At the advice of Robert Park, Parrish wrote to explain the course to himself.[10] The paper corresponds well with the first two sections of Mead's posthumous book that was based on the course lectures.[11] On the final page, Parrish presents the "main points" in eight brief statements. I will present them one at a time, offering some comments on their relevance to Parrish's study of race relations.

"Self" and "other" appear together and are inseparable in consciousness. This dialectical view of the self, which Mead developed on the basis of the psychology of William James, would have the individual's sense of self emerging in the context of its emerging as an object to others of races other than one's own as well as one's own.

1. "Self" and "other" and consciousness are all products of a preexisting social order. This is phrased in more deterministic language than Mead would have used, and given Parrish's general approach more deterministic than he probably meant. It goes beyond the first statement by affirming the necessity of understanding a given individual's consciousness in the context of a relevant social order. Of course, a racial or an ethnic consciousness does not exist in a vacuum but needs be seen in its context of social relations.

2. These social relations are possible only by means of some system of communication. Consequently, any attempt to bring about changes in consciousness should be directed at the communication system in which the consciousness emerges. If cross racial awareness is an aspect of one's consciousness of self, cross racial communication is an important instrument.

3. Cries and bodily movements (collectively called gestures) are the 'material' condition of human interaction. It is important to make observations of material factors that are used by people to define themselves and others.

4. Sub-human gestures are without meaning to the interacting forms. The importance of making observations of material factors is not to identify anything intrinsically connected to them but the meanings that people attribute to them.

5. A gesture is significant only when the participants involved react or tend to react to it in the same way. Thus it is important not only to identify the meanings an individual attributes to material factors but also to identify which other people the individual has interacted with in the process of creating or acquiring the meanings.

6. An important implication is that objects and meanings along with consciousness of "self" and "other" arise simultaneously in the individual's experience. Objects and meanings are the matters of import in communication; they emerge with the consciousness of the parties to the communication--self and other. The objects that one recognizes and to which one pays attention, as well as the meanings with which one thinks, are understandable with any adequacy only in the context of the social relations in which these emerge. If the relations are multiracial, it would be a distortion to withdraw into the imagined culture of only a part of the society.

7. The *act*, of which the gesture is an element, seems to be a valid object of study for social psychology. Deeds in the society are the adequate units of analysis. One cannot record "attitudes" on

race apart from deeds without substituting the part for the whole. For research, it becomes necessary to engage in on-sight inspection rather than hide behind questionnaires and other formal instruments. Parrish's subsequent "engaged" research on race relations was not the product of a personal predilection for activism but a logical element of social science as he conceived of it.[12]

The kind of sociology that had been inspired by pragmatist philosophy involved the researcher becoming acquainted with both the more or less spontaneous statements of individuals in social settings and the facts of the settings in which such statements come to be articulated. Thus the Chicago sociologists, much in the manner of Thomas and Znaniecki's monumental study of Polish peasants and migrants to America, collected both subjective materials such as life histories and letters as well as objective observations and official records.[13] Not only were members of the general public interviewed, with observations made of their physical and cultural situations, but statements of intellectuals and influential persons as well. As early as 1931 Parrish had begun to collect materials on the situation of African Americans in this manner. One 1931 paper collects excerpts, mostly from African American intellectuals, in order "to give a not untrue picture of the attitudes of the so-called 'new' Negro."[14]

A particularly interesting paper on the effects of subordination on African Americans also dates from 1931.[15] It takes the form of a review of the literature on the subject, and therefore consists of strategically selected excerpts from other authors, with a minimum of commentary. The selections dwell on the theme of the emergence of a collective inferiority complex that takes the form of an artificial racial solidarity, with such correlates as self-pity, collective representation, a tendency to glorify race achievements, the development of a sense of mission, a feeling of moral superiority, sensitiveness to insult, and a sentimental solidarity with other oppressed races. Not all these correlates (some of which could be viewed as weaknesses and some as resources) appear in each member of the subordinated group, but vary by such factors as literacy, urbanization, and the experience of disagreeable interracial contacts. "The mass of individuals comprising a group probably accept the situation, and make the best of it. They are 'accommodated.' Others may acquiesce under stress of circumstances. Only a few will be able to detach themselves sufficiently from the situation to adopt the objective viewpoint in their judgments."[16] The theme that is common to the excerpts included in the paper is the emergence of a set of attitudes that are not objective in nature but need be understood as social psychological embodiments of subordination and hence correlates of a repressed individual self-concept and compensatory group-level self-concept.

By 1936 Parrish was collecting his thoughts for his doctoral dissertation. An unfinished paper from that point in time addresses the topic of stereotypes of African Americans in the popular culture at large and in the history of the social sciences.[17] It points out that many social scientists who authored widely-used textbooks were slow to realize that the studies by Charles Horton Cooley and Franz Boas required not only the abandonment of biological explanations of psychological traits but of stereotypes as well. "The significance of this early textbook support of popular prejudices cannot be overestimated. The spectacle of sincere and well-meaning social scientists, after an apparently careful consideration of all available factual material, being forced reluctantly to concede that the case of the Negro was hopeless gave impressive confirmation" of the popular prejudices.[18] It was in the tradition of what we now vaguely term the Chicago tradition of sociology that Parrish found promise. "The few notable exceptions like Cooley, and later, W.I. Thomas, Robert E. Park, and others consistently emphasized status as a cause rather than an effect of 'racial' traits, but their emphasis has received general recognition only in the last fifteen years."[19] The paper goes on to document the acceptance by many African Americans of the negative stereotypes. One result of the stereotypes is the temptation to de-emphasize physical traits of the race though cosmetic techniques or to evaluate them negatively; this was the entry into the particular topic of Parrish's dissertation on the role of shades of skin color in African Americans' concepts of self and other.

E. Franklin Frazier appointed Parrish director in Louisville of a study of African American youth in 1936. Parrish was responsible for collecting life histories from children and youths, often in public parks, and establishing a file of the resultant interview transcripts. Topics in the interviews included home life situations, attitudes about the standing of African Americans in society, and whatever else the respondents chose to talk about.[20] For purposes of his own dissertation, Parrish, using a numerical shade scale, included notations of the skin colors of his respondents and of people to whom they made reference in the interviews. He especially asked about stereotypes and made notations on how popular or respected the respondents were in the settings in which he encountered them. The guiding concept Parrish used in approaching the data once it had been collected was *self-concept*: "...there would logically occur some sort of self feeling when the child becomes aware of its own color."[21] His findings led him to consider the situations of the extreme color types--the very light and very dark African American children. "As I see it both the attitudes about extreme color types and the overt acts directed against them constitute the social environment to which these types are exposed."[22] In the concluding chapter to the dissertation, the contradictory evaluation schemes found in the African American experience are highlighted--the prestige of Caucasian traits and racial solidarity. "Light skin-color has positive value for the *individual*, whereas dark skin-color has positive value for the *'race'*. The unconscious attempt to resolve this conflict of color values has resulted in the compromise acceptance of brown as a happy medium."[23] However, "The ever-present fear that color might become a public issue has conferred upon its discussion all of the characteristics of a taboo."[24] This kind of observation requires an awareness of the attitude/context dialectic for the self-concept that is characteristic of the pragmatist approach.

In his advice to Parrish, Herbert Blumer, who was directing the dissertation, made typically pragmatist kinds of suggestions. He wrote of pointing to "how color has tended to symbolize race differences between whites and Negroes, and how accordingly it has been made into a crucial item in Negro self consciousness. The point is that color has become loaded with all sorts of meaning, in general, for Negroes since more than anything else it marks their difference, their social position and their general grievance."[25] The relationship between public symbol and self-concept is thematic to all this, and it would seem to reinforce the approach used for many years already by Parrish himself.

The Pragmatist Perspective and Civil Rights Activism

Even though the involvement of perceptions of skin shade in children's and youths' self-concepts may seem to be a quaint topic today, it was playing a role in court cases over school integration at mid-century. C.H. Parrish was keenly interested in the integration process, and upon integrating the faculty of the University of Louisville himself in 1951 he found himself to be an "activist" by default. Over the next two decades he would participate in studies of school integration in the Louisville metropolitan area and the integration policies of the public and private institutions of higher education in the Commonwealth of Kentucky. He would also be writing descriptive accounts of the school integration process in the

American South and numerous letters to newspaper editors on these topics.[26] However, his activities went well beyond these formal observations. Parrish participated in an April 16-18, 1952, conference at Howard University, "The Courts and Racial Integration in Education." Most of the conference focused on a question of N.A.A.C.P. legal tactics-- whether to challenge segregation in public education on constitutional grounds, irrespective of any inequality of funding and the like. Keeping in mind the importance pragmatist thought places on the direct, face-to-face interaction among persons in the development of shared perspectives, it is instructive to see how Parrish himself described the event: "The conference was notable because it brought together face to face so many persons of high prestige in the Negro group who held widely divergent views of racial policy. The sharpest disagreement was over a technical problem of NAACP legal strategy. Under attack was the new NAACP policy, evident in recent cases, of testing the constitutionality of segregation per se, whether or not there was inequality involved. When the conference ended the new, direct approach had strong support from nearly everyone there."[27] His own presentation at the conference described his experience of integrating the University of Louisville faculty and observing African American students attending that formerly white institution. Most tellingly, he observed ambivalence over the prospect of integration itself. "Although it was tacitly assumed that all of the people at the meeting were in favor of racial integration, it soon became clear that some had deep misgivings over the prospect. In the event of complete integration what would become of the Negro colleges? Where else would there be an outlet for Negro scholarship? Would not the elimination of the 'Negro' college deprive many Negro high school graduates of the opportunity of going to college? Can the Negro student on a 'white' campus participate fully in college life?"

In pragmatist thought, much is made of the difference between people on the one hand who take nearby others as their "reference group" and think matters through by imagining a discourse with them, and on the other hand people who take a wider, more cosmopolitan circle of others as their "reference group" and think matters through by imagining a discourse that could be meaningful to anyone in that wider social circle. Sometimes this has been called the difference between locals and cosmopolitans. George H. Mead associated the ability to think more objectively and to develop a more universal ethical perspective with mentally engaging oneself with the wider social circle. Parrish seemed to use this local/cosmopolitan dichotomy in understanding the difference between African Americans who opposed and those who favored the integration of educational facilities. "Long preoccupation with the 'Negro Problem' has fostered among Negroes a racial isolationism that is just as deadly and self-defeating as isolationism on the national level. The very efforts to break down segregation by law have served to promote segregation by free choice. Negroes tend to be 'on edge' in the presence of white people; it is only when they are back behind the ghetto walls that they are completely comfortable. There is a strong sentimental attachment to what are popularly known as 'our own institutions.' A racial orthodoxy has developed...to which all good 'race' members must adhere...."[28] He went on to speak not only of the African Americans who held power in segregated institutions, but ironically of leaders in civil rights organizations whose power and prestige depends on the existence of a system of segregation in place to be fought against.

In February and March, 1954, anticipating a favorable decision on public school integration from the United States Supreme Court, the Southern Regional Council secured the services of Parrish to travel throughout Alabama to draw together local discussion groups on the schools and the courts. The following summer the SRC sent him elsewhere in the South to "sound out opinion, and particularly Negro opinion, as to the needs of the state for organized work in the field of race relations, and as to the leadership and financial resources available."[29] In explaining the appointment, SRC Executive Director George S. Mitchell described Parrish as a sound fellow, a judicious observer.[30] Mitchell had sent Parrish to Alabama with only a vague idea of what needed to be done, but Parrish proved to be so valuable that Mitchell was prepared to send him elsewhere in the months immediately after the Supreme Court decision had been announced. In late January, 1954, Parrish described his initial mission for the SRC this way:

I am leaving town today to spend a month in Alabama under the auspices of the Southern Regional Council. As yet, the exact nature of my job for them is obscure, but it would seem to involve making contacts with influential people in several Alabama communities in order to ascertain their attitudes about the impending Supreme Court decisions on segregation in the public schools. It is hoped that these people will be stimulated to raise the questions "What will happen in this community if there is a decision outlawing segregation? What can I do to delay misgivings and prevent disorder in the event of such a decision?" I will meet many of these leaders in Montgomery next Thursday, February 4, where a statewide conference is being held.[31]

It needs be recalled that the pragmatist research paradigm in which Parrish received his formal sociological training postpones the formulation of formal propositions and calls for the gathering of informal, spontaneous materials from their originary context, from which propositions could be drawn. It specifically called for observing verbal and other symbolic texts within the framework of ongoing activity. This preparation seemed to be well-suited to what Parrish was about. He was going into the midst of action--the negotiation of impending racial integration. He would be getting people talking so that he, together with local leaders, could develop an understanding of the situation.

As you will see from the enclosed map, I have seen quite a bit of Alabama since I left Louisville. If I can manage to digest and report what I have seen and heard there will be an interesting story to tell. The state is full of surprises and contradictions and one can never guess from one day to the next what will turn up. I am getting a liberal education.

I have had to define my job and redefine it day after day. Briefly put, I am going from town to town trying to find a few people, Negro and white, who will be willing to talk objectively about the desegregation of the public schools. I am urging upon them the importance of seeking the facts about the schools in their own community. I suggest to them that now is the time to assess their local resources for meeting the impact of a possible Supreme Court decision that would knock the legal props out from under the whole segregation system.[32]

Anyone familiar with Chicago-school sociology will think of the "definition of the situation" when noting Parrish writing of defining and redefining his job from day to day. The definition of the situation is the process in which people engage in intensive interaction, in the to-and-fro of discourse, whereby the perceived natures of circumstances emerge. Parrish was not merely observing the process as an outsider and reporting what he saw to the Southern Regional Council for action; he was participating in the defining process himself. He wrote a colleague of posing these questions and points to the people he met in Alabama: "What are the problems involved in adjustment? I point out that such a change does not mean the end of the world. And that confusion and disorder will result only if the people permit themselves to be stampeded into rash and emotionally dominated behavior by the falsehoods and distortions of the selfish few who are concerned only for the perpetuation of themselves in power."[33] He went on to speak of encounters with many who altogether rejected what he had to say; he said he was like a salesman in many instances, having to get his foot in the door and talk fast to keep from being thrown out.

Parrish's involvement in furthering integration led him directly to the dialectic between meaning systems and social contexts--the basic pragmatist theoretical concern. He took up the matter in a letter to Kenneth Clark, following a 1955 conference in Nashville on strategies. "I share with you a distrust of programs based upon a gradualist, 'cart-before-the-horse' philosophy that people must somehow be persuaded to change their attitudes as a preliminary step toward desegregation. It is unrealistic to hope that people will relinquish their prejudices as a result of propaganda alone as long as they are continuing to function in a situation which supports these prejudices."[34] In writing to Clark, Parrish seemed to have prejudiced whites in mind. However, he was aware of a similar need to begin with situations rather than propaganda alone when it came to African Americans and otherwise sympathetic whites who were comfortable in the segregated situation; his greatest problem seemed to arise in trying to persuade them to cooperate with the organizational apparatus the Southern Regional Council was setting up throughout the South. "The most persistent problem of reorganization was the difficulty of achieving a new perspective in light of the desegregation decree of the Supreme Court. Many of the people who had been connected with the Southern Regional Council and even earlier with the old Committee on Interracial Cooperation were more or less committed to a continuation of segregation and were concerned primarily with bettering the lot of Negroes within the segregation pattern."[35]

Importance of the Research Process

In a memorandum to Harold Fleming of the Southern Regional Council, Parrish proposed that the process of African American and white researchers studying community problems in various localities, in contrast to African American intellectuals acting as "special pleaders," would subtly but effectively undermine the status system upon which segregation rested.[36] He particularly advocated unmasking the class-based inequalities that are frequently disguised as racial inequalities. In much of his later work, Parrish would pursue this and similar research agendas.

Beginning in 1957, Parrish participated in an interdisciplinary faculty group at the University of Louisville that investigated what kind of research would be most useful to the local school systems in effecting integration. The major problem in the community seemed to be the widespread belief that African American students were poorer students and that the schools would have to lower standards to accommodate them. Parrish and his colleagues showed that environmental factors, not the students exposed to varying environments, explained educational outcomes. Ecological comparisons of majority group students in the elementary schools of different parts of the metropolitan area became an important research stratagem.[37] They were also thinking of comparing pre-integration and post-integration data to see the effects in educational outcomes of integration breaking down the cultural isolation of African American students--this well before the massive federally funded study known as the "Coleman Report." Unlike much educational outcomes research, the analyses were not to rely on statistics alone. "Wherever possible behavior will be described as it occurs in its natural setting by participant observers."[38] For the pre-integration setting, guided interviews were to be used. As the various studies carried out as a part of the project were completed, Parrish became increasingly convinced of the primacy of economic, as opposed to racial, factors in affecting educational outcomes.[39]

Parrish did not limit his concern with "action research" to processes such as school integration. In the mid-nineteen seventies he began to think about the personal formation of activists. He wondered, for example, whether members of the Southern Regional Council would be willing to undergo a critical self-examination.[40] By the summer of 1976, after consulting widely, he proposed such a study formally. His focus was not unlike the skin-color perception research he had done nearly forty years earlier.

Although it is generally conceded that stereotypes have major importance in determining the nature and quality of intergroup relations, the study of the acquisition and disappearance of stereotypes has been largely neglected. It seems probable that stereotypes are learned in much the same way that superstitions are learned. They are generally arrived at early in life....

...It has occurred to some of us that this is an area of research to which the Southern Regional Council could make a major contribution.

...It is the collective experience, the early memories that can be recaptured, the belief systems council members might be persuaded to reexamine....

The particular concern of the inquiry are the early memories of interracial contacts and experiences. Also an effort would be made to get interviewees to reexamine their belief systems in this area and to recall the circumstances under which these belief systems were acquired.[41]

A series of open-ended questions accompanied this descriptive memorandum that he sent to the Southern Regional Council members. A copy of the proposal also went to Herbert Blumer, who responded favorably and recommended a further inquiry of "situations which invited or called for their (the SRC members') action in terms of their stereotypes, but in which they did not so act."42

Finally, it should be noted that Parrish participated in an extended campus discussion at the University of Louisville over the creation of a black studies program. His various memoranda indicate a concern that social science research figure prominently in the plans.

Conclusion

C.H. Parrish lived an interesting life in interesting times. However, because well into adulthood he acquired the flexible pragmatist social scientific perspective ("Chicago school" of sociology) he was able to interpret events in which he played a mature, responsible role with a first rate intellectual formation fresh in mind. The demands of his various commitments prevented him from extensively writing and publishing research reports in the usual manner of academicians--his letters and memoranda often apologize for delays occasioned by his work--and his unassuming personality prevented him from thrusting himself to the forefront as a public persona. Nevertheless, there is enough of his work in unpublished materials to enable us to appreciate the way that he used his intellectual perspective in social activism, and to appreciate the advantages such a perspective afforded him. He was a shrewd, even unsettling observer.

References

Blumer, Herbert. 1976. Letter to C. H. Parrish. August 10.

Frazier, E. Franklin.   1940.   *Negro Youth at the Crossways–Their Personality Development in the Middle States*. Washington, DC: American Council on Education.

Joas, Hans. 1985.   *G. H. Mead: A Contemporary Re-examination of his Thought*. Cambridge, MA: MIT Press.

Mead, George H. 1934.   *Mind, Self, and Society*. Chicago: University of

Chicago Press.

Mitchell, George S. 1954. Memorandum to Southern Regional Council Board of Directors. July 20.

Parrish, Charles H. 1921. "Social Organization among the Negroes of a New Jersey Town." Master of Arts Thesis. Columbia University.

_____ Undated. Memorandum to Dr. Herbert Blumer. Re: Chapter VII.

_____ Undated. Memorandum to Harold Fleming.

_____ Undated. Memorandum to John Hope, III.

_____ Undated. Memorandum on Thesis Project.

_____ 1931. "The Effects of Subordination upon the Negro." Unpublished Paper.

_____ 1931. "What the Negro Wants: The New Negro." Unpublished Paper.

_____ 1936. "Emergence of Traditional Negro Traits." Unpublished Paper.

_____ 1946. "Color Names and Color Notions." *Journal of Negro Education.* 15: 13-20.

_____ 1946. "Negro Higher and Professional Education in Kentucky." *Journal of Negro Education.* 15: 289-295.

_____ 1947. "The Education of Negroes in Kentucky." *Journal of Negro Education.* 16: 354-360.

_____ 1952. Memorandum to Philip G. Davidson. May 8.

_____ 1953. Letter to P. L. Prattis. July 1.

_____ 1954. Letter to Herbert Blumer. January 29.

_____ 1954. Letter to Robert I. Kutak. February 21.

_____ 1955. "Desegregation in Public Education." *Journal of Negro Education.* 24: 382-387.

_____ 1955. Letter to David Riesman. January 24.

_____ 1955. Letter to Kenneth B. Clark. March 9.

_____ 1958. "Desegregated Higher Education in Kentucky." *Journal of Negro Education.* 27: 260-268.

_____ 1958. "Studies of Desegregation in Process." Paper presented at American Association for Public Opinion Research, Chicago, IL.

_____ 1976. Memorandum on "Rationale and Procedure for an In-Depth Study of SRC Members." July 14.

Thomas, William I. and Florian Zaniecki. 1918. *The Polish Peasant in Europe and America, Volumes 1 and 2.* Chicago: University of Chicago Press.

_____ 1919-1920. *The Polish Peasant in Europe and America, Volumes 3-5.* Boston: Badger Press.

Endnotes

1. C.H. Parrish, "This I Believe...." Unpublished paper, undated. I had come into the possession of many of the Parrish papers before and after his death, and have turned them over to the University of Louisville archives to be added to their substantial collection on C.H. Parrish.

2. Ibid.

3. Ibid., italics in the original.

4. C.H. Parrish, Jr., *Social Organization Among the Negroes of a New Jersey Town.* Unpublished M.A. Thesis, May 1921, Department of Political Science, Columbia University.

5. C.H. Parrish,letter to Wilson W. Wyatt, October 29, 1950.

6. C.H. Parrish, "The Emergence of Social Psychology..." Midterm Paper, 'Advanced Social Psychology', Professor Mead. "This paper is an attempt at an introduction to Professor Mead's theory, and lecture materials are used freely." There are also a few extant class notes from a winter, 1934, course from Louis Wirth.

7..E. Franklin Frazier, *Negro Youth at the Crossways. Their Personality*

Development in the Middle States (Washington: American Council on Education, 1940). Frazier's acknowledgments (p. xi) include the following: "A word of appreciation is due first to Charles H. Parrish, instructor in sociology at the Louisville Municipal College for Negroes, who supervised the field work in Louisville and organized the materials on the Negro community." According to a list of staff at the back of the volume, Parrish had two interviewers, Mrs. Thelma L. Coleman, A.B., and D. Gardner Kean, A.M., to help him in the project.

8..It should be remembered that these kinds of concern would become important in court cases pertaining to the integration of schools.

9. C.H. Parrish, letter to Wilson W. Wyatt, October 29, 1950.

10. C.H. Parrish said this to me on a number of occasions.

11..George H. Mead, *Mind, Self, and Society* (Chicago: University of Chicago Press, 1934).

12. C.H. Parrish, "The Emergence of Social Psychology," p. 12 of typescript copy. Parrish also knew about the classical experimental model of science, as is evidenced by a 1950s memorandum, "A Memorandum on the Nature of Experiment," suggested, according to Parrish's introductory note, "in class discussions under the direction of Mortimer J. Adler at the University of Chicago _ Spring 1931." The presence of a conservative thinker as Adler in the philosophy department greatly upset Mead; see Hans Joas, *G. H. Mead. A Contemporary Reexamination of his Thought* (Cambridge, Massachusetts: MIT Press, 1985), p. 28. Parrish had been exposed to an alternative, but seems to have favored the pragmatist approach.

13. William I. Thomas and Florian Znaniecki, *The Polish Peasant in Europe and America* (Volumes 1 and 2, Chicago: University of Chicago Press, 1918; Volumes 3_5, Boston: Badger Press, 1919-1920).

14. C.H. Parrish, "What the Negro Wants: The New Negro." Paper, 1931, p. 1.

15. C.H. Parrish, "The Effects of Subordination Upon the Negro." Paper, 1931.

16. Ibid., p. 6.

17. C.H. Parrish, "Emergence of Traditional Negro traits." Paper, 1936. A note on the typescript indicates that Parrish wrote the essay as a rough draft of a chapter for his dissertation, but that it was never used.

18. Ibid., p. 8.

19. Ibid., p. 8.

20. See note 7, above.

21. C.H. Parrish, "Memorandum on Thesis Project." Undated typescript, p. 2.

22. C.H. Parrish, "Memorandum to Dr. Herbert Blumer. Re: Chapter VII." Undated, but internal evidence points to some time during the U.S. involvement in World War II.

23. C.H. Parrish, "Chapter IX. Summary of Findings and an Interpretive Comment." Dissertation draft chapter, p. 10.

24. Ibid. The study was published in article form; Charles H. Parrish, "Color Names and Color Notions." *Journal of Negro Education* 15 (1946): 13_20.

25. Herbert Blumer, hand written comments on a draft of the Ph.D. dissertation of C.H. Parrish, in the Parrish papers, University of Louisville archives.

26. C.H. Parrish, "The Education of Negroes in Kentucky," *Journal of Negro Education* 16 (1947): 354_360; "Negro Higher and Professional Education in Kentucky,," *Journal of Negro Education* 15 (1946): 289_295; "Desegregation in Public Education," *Journal of Negro Education* 24 (1955): 382_387; "Desegregated Higher Education in Kentucky," *Journal of Negro Education* 27 (1958): 260_268.

27. C.H. Parrish, memorandum to Philip G. Davidson (president, University of Louisville), May 8, 1952.

28. C.H. Parrish, letter to P.L. Prattis (executive editor, Pittsburgh *Courier*), July 1, 1953.

29. George S. Mitchell, memorandum to Southern Regional Council Board of Directors, July 20, 1954, p. 2.

30. Ibid.

31. C.H. Parrish, letter to Herbert Blumer, January 29, 1954.

32. C.H. Parrish, letter to Robert I. Kutak (Department of Sociology, University of Louisville), February 21, 1954.

33. Ibid.

34. C.H. Parrish, letter to Kenneth B. Clark (Department of Psychology, City University of New York), March 9, 1955.

35. C.H. Parrish, memorandum to John Hope III (Southern Regional Council projector director, professor at Fisk University), undated.

36. C.H. Parrish, memorandum to Harold Fleming (Southern Regional Council), undated.

37. C.H. Parrish, "Studies of Desegregation in Process." Paper presented at the meeting of the American Association for Public Opinion Research, Chicago, 1958, pp. 4_5.

38. Ibid., p. 7.

39. C.H. Parrish, letter to David Riesman (Professor of Social Sciences, Harvard University), January 24, 1975.

40. Ibid.

41. C.H. Parrish, memorandum on "Rationale and Procedure for an In-Depth Study of SRC Members," to SRC members, July 14, 1976.

42. Herbert Blumer, letter to C.H. Parrish, August 10, 1976, University of Louisville archives, Parrish papers.

Chapter Eleven

Daniel C. Thompson And Butler A. Jones: A Comparison Of Interdisciplinary Approaches To Sociology[1]

Donald Cunnigen

Within the last thirty years, the study of African-Americans' contributions to sociology has developed from a relatively obscure area of inquiry which focused on the intellectual activities of a select group of individuals such as Charles S. Johnson (b. 1893, d. 1956), E. Franklin Frazier (b. 1894, d. 1962), and W. E. B. DuBois (b. 1868, d. 1963) to a broader area of inquiry which offered important information to scholars on the sociology of knowledge and historical sociology. The expansive new inquiries into the lives and contributions of African-American sociologists have focused on the intellectual context and influence of their work. The study of their unique contributions has led to the investigation of a wide range of issues related to their participation in the discipline including the development of a methodological and theoretical paradigm for African-American sociological thought; a review of institutional and departmental characteristics of the African-American participation in the discipline; the intersection of an African-American sociological tradition with other approaches such as phenomenology; and a critique of the scholarship produced by African-American sociologists.[2]

John Bracey (b. 1941), August Meier (b. 1923), and Elliott Rudwick (b. 1927) suggested the half century from the appearance of DuBois's *The Philadelphia Negro* in 1899 to the publication of St. Clair Drake (b. 1911, d. 1990) and Horace Cayton's (b. 1903, d. 1970) *Black Metropolis* in 1945 was the "Golden Age" in the sociology of African-Americans.[3] While one may question the Bracey, Meier and Rudwick periodization of African-American participation in the sociological enterprise, it does clearly place Daniel C. Thompson's (b. 1912, d. 1988) and Butler A. Jones' (b. 1916) work in a different historical perspective than some of those individuals who may be considered the "first generation" African-American sociologists as suggested by Jacquelyne Jackson, Butler A. Jones, Charles Key, and Gordon Morgan.[4]   Key described this as a period of African-American exclusion and segregation from the sociological profession.   He described Thompson and Jones as second generation sociologists.   The second generation was noted for its accommodation and assimilationist orientation.   The careers of Thompson and Jones reflected some elements of the Key categorization.   Yet, a close examination of the social context, disciplinary characteristics, and the life experiences of these sociologists shows individuals who defined themselves and their scholarship in a very complex manner which belies the Key attempt at simple categorization.

The Early Socialization of Daniel C. Thompson
and Butler A. Jones

The comparisons between Jones and Thompson may be made on many levels. Jones and Thompson were southerners who received their undergraduate education from institutions in Georgia, i.e., Morehouse College (Morehouse) and Clark College and a master's degree from Atlanta University (AU). They went North to New York state where their Ph.D.'s in sociology were taken from New York University (NYU) and Columbia University (Columbia), respectively. In addition to their sociological study, they studied in other disciplines. Thompson received a master's degree in divinity from Gammon Theological Seminary. Jones completed the first year at the Webster School of Law. Initially, they taught exclusively at historically African-American institutions such as the Atlanta University Laboratory School (Laboratory School), Howard University (Howard), Dillard University (Dillard), Barber-Scotia College (Barber-Scotia), and Talladega College (Talladega).

Not surprisingly, Jones and Thompson attended African-American colleges at the very time which William M. Banks claimed they served as a breeding ground for African-American intellectuals. Despite their many inadequacies, they provided fertile soil for the growth of a new generation of thinkers, especially the "better" institutions like Fisk University (Fisk), Morehouse, and Howard.[5]   Similarly, their enrollment in African-American graduate programs for their first advanced degree was a common pattern of academic advancement during the period. According to Henry E. Cobb, the African-American graduate schools had a unique purpose and function. Cobb said:

> [African-American] graduate schools provide[d] an avenue of cultural mobility for those people who...had constrictive experiences of success in the traditional educational systems of the country. ...These institutions, however, accepted this condition as a point of departure; they fashioned programs, developed materials, and assigned faculty to transform their students, or an astonishingly large percentage of them, into creditable graduates. ...The mission of the [African-American] graduate schools [was] closely related to the [African-American] community.[6]

Their doctorates were taken from two of the four leading white institutional producers of graduates from African-American colleges.[7] Thus, Jones and Thompson pursued higher education in institutional settings designed specifically for the production and advancement of segregated African-American scholars.   Subsequently, they acquired doctorates from the select group of white graduate programs which recognized and accepted African-American college graduates.

Jones Grows Up in the African-American Professional Community of the New South

Butler Alfonso Jones was born in Birmingham, Alabama.   He was the grandson of slaves.   His paternal grandparents, former field hands, lived in rural Macon County (Alabama).   His maternal grandparents, former skilled artisans, lived in the small town of Dothan, Alabama. His immediate family consisted of young "New South" African-American professionals.   His mother was a school teacher.   As a Tuskegee Institute (Tuskegee) graduate, his father began his career as a school teacher. After the death of his wife, he received a degree in 1928 from Howard Law School. He briefly practiced law in Marion, Indiana.   The high professional achievement of Jones' parents, especially his father, was indicative of a pattern which James E. Conyers reported in his 1968 survey of African-American sociologists. Conyers' study reported 26% of their fathers had a college degree or some college training.[8]

Jones and his only sister grew up in the home of his maternal grandparents after his father's untimely death.[9] The Butler family was a prosperous part of Dothan's African-American society.   In the 1890's, they were the proprietors of the Butler Hotel near the Dothan City Hall.   In addition, the family rented space to   local businesses. He acquired a strong sense of accomplishment from his family which helped to shape his personality in later years.[10]

As a youngster, he attended Dothan's segregated public elementary school.   He received his secondary educational training from the Southeast Alabama High School, a private parent-supported school.   It was established by African-American members of religious congregations due to the lack of a public high school for their children. The small school had approximately one hundred students and seven to eight teachers.   He graduated as co-valedictorian in his senior class of fourteen students.[11]

From Southeast Alabama High School, he went to Morehouse. Although his sister was an AU alumnae and his father was a Tuskegee alumnus, the choice of Morehouse over Tuskegee was attributable to a familial attachment, i. e., several uncles were "Morehouse Men." According to Jones, "the axis between Dothan and Atlanta was a natural [one] because my grandmother often went to visit her sons [who lived in Atlanta].   When you thought of going to school in Atlanta, you thought of Morehouse, not Clark [College]."[12]

During the "Great Depression," the Morehouse of Jones' years was a school operating under financial strain.   Unlike its sister school, Spelman College, it was not well endowed.   At Morehouse, he had a major in history and political science and a minor in sociology and economics.   As an undergraduate, he was inspired by two social scientists on the Morehouse faculty, Walter Chivers (b. 1896, d. 1969), sociologist and Thomas Curry, historian.[13]

Chivers provided exposure to sociological research methods through field projects in rural Georgia and Alabama.   According to Jones, Chivers' field projects made sociology come alive for his students.   In addition, he sponsored a "Family Institute" on the Morehouse campus which provided students with additional exposure to social issues.   He maintained close contacts with leading white liberal Southern race relations scholars and leaders such as Arthur F. Raper (b. 1899), Agnes

Scott College sociologist, and Will W. Alexander (b. 1884, d. 1956), Commission on Interracial Cooperation leader. His ties with prominent Southern whites provided limited access to some of the major funding sources and allowed him an opportunity to be creative in the classroom.[14]

Thomas Curry provided Jones with the incentive to study history through his first hand contact with the discipline. As a student in Curry's International Law course, Jones prepared a "long" term paper on the "Doctrine of Continuous Voyage." This exercise made him very excited about the study of law. Although Curry was not an impressive lecturer, students admired his great knowledge.[15]

After his 1937 Morehouse graduation, he entered the AU Graduate School. In 1938, he took a master's degree in history. The decision to enroll in graduate school was made after he was offered a choice between an eighty dollars a month graduate scholarship and an eighty dollars a month salaried teaching position in the Atlanta (Georgia) Public School System. While the monetary incentive for graduate study was attractive, Jones felt the intellectual pursuits were most exciting. He was impressed extremely by AU scholars such as DuBois and Rayford Logan (b. 1897, d. 1982). Logan was a noted African-American historian with a wide sphere of social contacts which included involvement in the Paris Peace Conference and the Pan-African Congress. The DuBois-Logan contact gave Jones the unusual opportunity to observe productive and highly regarded African-American intellectuals.[16]

Jones' acquisition of the master's degree led him into a professional life as a dedicated teacher and scholar. He began his teaching career on the secondary level. He was appointed as a social studies instructor at the Laboratory School. The Laboratory School was one of the few accredited Southern high schools for African-Americans. It was better equipped than many public schools. Its faculty was better trained than most Southern African-American schools. In addition, the faculty/student ratio was excellent. Jones' employment in the Laboratory School was a consequence of several fortuitous events. Logan recommended him for the job when a vacancy occurred as a result of an instructor returning to graduate school. Consequently, employment in the school was a coveted professional honor for the young scholar. During his tenure (1938-1942) at the Laboratory School, Martin Luther King Jr. (b. 1929, d. 1968) was his student. With his exacting standards, Jones provided King's only failing report in eighth grade social studies.[17]

After the Laboratory School closed in 1942, he assumed the position of administrative assistant to the president of Barber Scotia Junior College. He served in this capacity for only one year. His departure from Barber Scotia resulted from ideological differences with the school's chief administrator. The school was a women's college under the auspices of the Presbyterian Church. Despite its unique role in the educational processes of African-American women, the administration displayed a condescension toward women which Jones felt was sexist. In an unprecedented action, he presented a speech during the mandatory Vesper Service which highlighted his disagreements with the administration.[18]

After leaving Barber Scotia, he was appointed an assistant professor of social sciences at Talladega. Talladega was one of the premiere colleges among the segregated African-American institutions of higher learning. In 1943, the college was approved by the Association of American Universities as being one of the top 15% of the nation's schools. Talladega's unique characteristics were described in a study as follows:

> Talladega became an unusually successful educational institution because of the quality of its organizational components. The faculty members were well-trained and committed to their tasks. Their training was superior to that of the faculty of many other historically [African-American] colleges because of the requirements of the American Missionary Association. The student body was equally talented. Talladega was serving the needs of students of serious purpose. The College was most selective in its admissions policy and became a home to many [African-American] high school salutatorians and valedictorians.[19]

According to Jones, Talladega's high admissions standards contributed to its attraction for the children of the intellectual and social elites within the African-American community around the country, especially urban centers of Chicago, New York, and Charleston. Although many Talladega students struggled with college finances during the depression years, the college's well-to-do students reflected the description which David Lewis offered of Fisk students, a sister American Missionary Association sponsored institution, i.e., [a student body] dancing off a pinhead of privilege, the sons and daughters of affluent Afro-America...[who] set the tone and defined the institutional character.[20]

Jones found Talladega an engaging work environment during the presidential administrations of Buell Gallagher (b. 1904) and James

Cater (d. 1958).[21] Gallagher instituted a progressive administrative style which included building a new library, offering survey courses, and establishing a College Council composed of administrative officers, faculty, and students. Cater, a former dean, served as interim president following Gallagher's resignation in 1943. Jones remained at Talladega from 1943 through 1952.[22]

After the Gallagher and Cater administrations, Jones had a difficult time on campus with the new administration. Much of his difficulty related to America's changing political climate having an impact on all American colleges, including small African-American liberal arts colleges. The "McCarthyism" of the 1940's and 1950's created problems for radical European refugee scholars on African-American college faculties. A popular economics and German professor, Fritz Pappenheim (b. 1902, d. 1964) became a victim of the anti-Communist sentiments of "McCarthyism." Pappenheim was denied tenure as a result of a specious charge regarding the college's changing academic focus. Suspicious Talladega students rallied to Pappenheim's defense. They responded by locking the board of trustees in a campus building during a sweltering summer day's board meeting. The board of trustees was forced to concede to their demand for the resignation of the college president, Adam Daniel Beittel. Pappenheim and several sympathetic professors resigned from the faculty. Although Jones counted himself as a supporter of the group, his departure was prompted by greater professional opportunities.[23]

In 1947, he entered the NYU Graduate School. His doctoral graduate study was financed through a Rosenwald Fellowship and General Education Board Fellowship, the primary educational benefactors for African-Americans during the period. He studied with Wellman Warner (b. 1897), Henry Meyer (b. 1913), Robert Bierstedt (b. 1913), E. Adamson Hoebel (b. 1906), and Paul Tappan (b. 1911). As a Southern racial discrimination victim, he developed intellectual interests in law and social issues. His exposure to Hoebel and contact with Tappan helped to refine his intellectual interests.[24]

His NYU graduate school days were difficult because he was the only African-American sociology graduate student. African-Americans were not welcomed on NYU's campus. Jones felt distinctions were made between African-Americans who attended white schools and African-American schools. He had limited contact with other African-American graduate students such as Charles Lawrence (b. 1915, d. 1986), a fellow Morehouse Man, who was studying sociology at Columbia.[25]

In 1952, he made the transition from "all African-American" Talladega to "all white" Ohio Wesleyan University (OWU). From

1952 through 1954, he served as a visiting associate professor of sociology at OWU. The initial invitation was extended by OWU's president, Arthur Fleming. Fleming had been active in national civil rights circles. He served on the Fair Employment Practices Committee. Fleming's invitation was a part of behind the scenes activism centering around the personality of Branch Rickey (b. 1881, d. 1965), an OWU board member. Rickey had played an influential role in the integration of professional baseball. He believed the time was due for American white colleges to take an active role in societal integration through their admission of African-American students and hiring of African-American faculty members.[26]

While working at OWU, Jones completed his doctorate in American Civilization and sociology at NYU in 1955. After receiving his degree, he advanced to full professor in 1956. He had a distinguished career at OWU, including service as departmental chairperson from 1960 through 1968.[27] He moved from OWU to Cleveland State University (CSU) in 1968. In 1969, he became departmental chairperson. After relinquishing the chairmanship in 1975, he remained at CSU until his retirement in 1982. Through his various appointments, Jones honed his teaching skills. He became known by his colleagues as a teacher-activist.

Jones as Teacher-Activist

Since Jones was considered more of a teacher-activist than a traditional scholar, an examination of his teaching style and relationship with students offers important information regarding the second generation sociologists' pedagogical influences. Unlike Chivers, Jones' teaching style was not remembered for his non-traditionalism.

As a teacher, he attracted students with an engaging lecture style. A former Talladega student, Edgar Epps (b. 1929), highlighted his "knowledge and erudition" as a unique asset among the college's faculty.[28] Epps gained knowledge of Jones from a freshman honors course which featured reading original sociological texts such as *An American Dilemma* and *Caste, Class, and Race.*[29] Jones' critical perspective regarding the American public's ignorance made a lasting impression on his students. As a young member of the academy, he attempted to perfect a lecture style and classroom demeanor which reflected the strengths of his Morehouse and NYU mentors, i.e., Logan, Chivers, Curry, Hoebel, and Tappan. Their strengths were their ability to keep students intellectually engaged via the introduction of provocative ideas.

In a small liberal arts college with a faculty having a variety of teaching skills, including a significant number of European emigres who had some difficulty speaking fluent English, Jones' ability to enliven lectures made him a memorable instructor. In addition, his inclusion of personal experiences in lectures and discussions gave his classes a rich focus. His approach to teaching was highlighted in an unpublished paper on the function of social science in African-American colleges. He suggested African-American college instructors should have as their "controlling assumption...that democracy as a political mechanism and a way of social organization afford...the most effective means for the achievement of the ultimate good."[30] In addition, Jones provided six general propositions important to understanding social science teaching. They were (1) the individual human being is of surpassing worth; (2) the earth and human culture belong to all men; (3) men can and should rule themselves; (4) the human mind can be trusted and should be set free; (5) the method of peace is superior to war; and (6) racial, cultural and political minorities should be respected and valued.[31] With these propositions as the basis, he provided two overall functions of social science teaching (1) the assembly and distribution of such pertinent factual data as will make for a fuller comprehension of the nature of the contemporary social order, its historical evolution and its identifiable trends and tendencies; and (2) the transmission of ideational patterns that will provide the basis for the continuous examination and re-examination of the motivating factors in the contemporary social order.[32] He believed African-American colleges had a special role in providing students with a sound social scientific training. According to Jones, the African-American college teacher's role was as follows:

. Social science teaching in Negro colleges must be directed toward the end that the individual understands and is able to critically evaluate the influence of racial proscription upon his personality development. ...Above all, social science teaching in the Negro college must so imbue Negro youth with faith in the humanity of man and a belief in his innate dignity and worth as a human being that he will have the necessary psychological weapons to face the modern world with its irrational prejudices. This does not and should not be taken to mean a superficial pride in oneself or in one's group, spring from an essentially false set of values. It means instead that the individual must believe so deeply in the spirit of liberalism that, though he recognizes the imperfections of men and circumstance, he subscribes still to the ideal of the perfectibility of man.[33]

It was his universal concept of mankind based in the liberalism of the New Deal which he attempted to offer his Talladega students. During his Talladega years, he taught Introduction to Social Sciences, Race Relations, and Social Problems. Although he occasionally taught other courses, his regular teaching load consisted of two large lecture classes in the social studies curriculum. The Introduction to Social Sciences course was a large general lecture presented to approximately one hundred students. The lectures focused on "special areas."[34] The large lecture classes were divided into three or four smaller tutorial sections which he also led as half of a two person department. His course was required by the college. According to Jones, "I had every [Talladega] student at one time."[35]

In addition to providing students with a competitive classroom experience, he offered students enriching extracurricular activities such as field trips. His Laboratory School students were taken on a tour of the local police force. He has kept a photograph of a young Martin Luther King Jr. as a Laboratory School student visiting the police force and wearing a pin saying, "I am somebody."[36]

In 1948, the Talladega administration through its board of trustees established an Off-Campus Contacts Program (OCCP) with $1200.[37] The modest funding of the OCCP provided Talladega faculty and students an opportunity to travel and participate in a wide range of intellectual and cultural activities. Jones took Talladega students on a trip to an academic conference in Washington, DC. Similarly, he escorted OWU students on a trip to a conference in New York. Jones viewed the field trips as opportunities to expand students' horizons. While the limited resources of Talladega and the Laboratory School restricted his ability to provide student travel experiences, he attempted to advantageously utilize the schools' limited resources.

Through his work as a teacher, he served as a scholarly role model for students. Some of his students became influential student leaders such as James W. Kelsaw, editor of the *Talladega Student*, the student newspaper. Kelsaw's leftist editorials caused a campus sensation during his college years. In a controversial editorial, he "belittled the NAACP, denounced Walter White and A. Philip Randolph (b. 1889) as appointees of the 'Great White Father,' and quoted Paul Robeson." (b. 1898, d. 1976)[38] Kelsaw and Epps followed in his footsteps as sociologists. They received their doctorates from Washington State University.[39] After his former students received their degrees, his relationship shifted into a new realm. By this time, he had received his doctorate and become the first African-American faculty member at OWU. His contacts and exposure to white sociological colleagues were expanded through professional organizations. According to Epps, "[W]hen I became reacquainted with him, it was generally more a colleague kind of relations with Butler serving as the older scholar-mentor; and generally telling me and other younger scholars what we needed to do to be successful as sociologists."[40]

Jones' Relationship with Other Second Generation Sociologists

Although his OWU years provided new insights on professional expectations, his years in African-American institutions afforded contact with other second generation African-American sociologists. These encounters allowed him to discuss the discipline as well as his opinions regarding the leading sociologists in the country. In Alabama, he developed close relationships with Lewis Jones (b. 1910), Oliver Cromwell Cox (b. 1901, d. 1974), and Charles Goode Gomillion (b. 1900, d. 1995), Tuskegee faculty members. Lewis Jones provided him within an "insiders" perspective on Robert Ezra Park (b. 1864, d. 1944). Lewis Jones served as Park's chauffeur while he conducted research projects.[41] During those trips, he heard Park's personal comments regarding various ethnic groups, including many anti-Semitic comments.[42] Since Park had a strong influence on many leading second generation African-American sociologists, the "insider" knowledge regarding his personal attitudes on race and ethnicity gave the young group of Alabama African-American sociologists an unusual perspective on the "white liberal" voices within their discipline.[43]

Although his most famous political action, i.e., *Gomillion v. Lightfoot*, 364 U. S. 339 (1960),[44] took place after Jones left Alabama, his friendship with Gomillion was influenced by Gomillion's involvement in the Tuskegee Civic Association (TCA). Gomillion was the consummate political activist. According to Jackson, Gomillion's role in the TCA from 1941-1971 made him "the prototype...black sociologist in higher education."[45] Since some of his political activism took place during Jones' Talladega years, Gomillion offered an example of a colleague who was a scholar-activist.

In addition to acquiring an understanding of the complicated dimensions of the discipline's African-American/white relationships, he acquired a clear understanding of the socio-political dynamics of African-American colleges. If his personal Barber-Scotia experience had not provided a sufficient demonstration of the idiosyncratic nature of African-American colleges, the difficulties of his Tuskegee colleague, Oliver Cromwell Cox, provided an excellent example of the administrative vagaries common to African-American institutions. Cox received a higher salary at Tuskegee than many of his colleagues in smaller and less prestigious segregated institutions. Despite the claims of Herbert Hunter and Sameer Y. Abraham, Jones believed Cox was released from his Tuskegee position at the height of his career because his neo-Marxist political views were "a source of concern."[46]

Although he was known in intellectual circles as a Marxist by the publication of *Caste, Class, and Race*, Hunter and Abraham claimed his departure from his lucrative Tuskegee position was attributable to the school's inadequate support for the social sciences and his critical commentary on its founder, Booker T. Washington (b. 1856, d. 1915). In a paper presented at the Association of Social Science Teachers (now the Association of Social and Behavioral Scientists--ASBS), he described Washington as an individual who "was not a leader of the masses...because he was in reality sent [by whites] with a mission to subdue the spirit of protest in the masses." His negative Washington comments resulted in Cox's defense of his ideas in a public campus forum. Similarly, he felt compelled to write a letter to the institute's president, Frederick Patterson, regarding his political beliefs.[47] The Cox experience and insider knowledge on Park were indicative of the delicate balance which second generation African-American sociologists maintained in the racially charged professional world of segregated America.

Thompson's Transition from Provincial to Cosmopolitan

Like Jones, Daniel Calbert Thompson was born in a small rural Southern community, Farmington, Georgia. Thompson described Farmington's race relations as follows, " When I grew up in Georgia, segregation was a cultural way of life."[48] His family lived on a 300 acre farm. The farm was purchased by the family before 1901. His family consisted of twelve siblings, mother, and father. He described his mother as having physical features of an Octoroon who could pass for white. On the other hand, his father was darker-complected.[49]

Within the Farmington community, his extended family included 63 first cousins. He described the family as the only African-American family to acquire any education in the community. His mother's oldest sister was in the first Spelman Seminary graduation class. He claimed his father taught Martin Luther King Sr. (b. 1897, d. 1984) to

read and write.[50] His mother taught local church members to read in her home. His family had a tradition of reading and study.[51]
He received his early education in a rural school. According to one account, he traveled to Atlanta with only a dollar in his pocket to pursue secondary training. When he arrived in Atlanta, he met with Charles DuBois Hubert who served as Acting Morehouse College President from 1937 until 1940.[52] Hubert was a member of a prominent African-American family and a friend of the Thompson family. Due to Thompson's exceptional intellectual abilities, Hubert arranged for his advancement by examination to the twelfth grade despite his completion of the seventh grade in Farmington. He graduated as the class salutatorian.[53]

In 1941, he received a bachelor of arts degree from Clark College. Within three years, he received a bachelor of divinity degree from Gammon Theological Seminary; and a master of arts degree in sociology from Atlanta University. At Gammon, he was influenced by Bishop Willis J. King. According to Thompson, King was the first African-American to receive a Ph.D. in Old Testament studies from Boston University. King's fluency in several languages such as Hebrew, Greek, and Latin, had a great impact on young Thompson.[54]

Thompson's Atlanta years were influenced by the great intellects of the community. He was a student of DuBois at AU. It has been suggested by a colleague that Thompson shared DuBois' penchant for elegant dress and style. In addition, he admired his scholarship.[55]
After receiving his first graduate degrees, he taught for one year at Clark. In 1945, he was hired as an instructor of sociology at Dillard University where he remained for the balance of his career with exception of one year as chairman of the sociology department at Howard University in 1962-1963.[56]

In 1950, he received a master of arts degree in social relations from Harvard University. At Harvard, he worked with Robert K. Merton (b. 1910) and Pitirim A. Sorokin (b. 1889, d. 1969). While taking pride in his exposure to Harvard scholars, it is not clear whether the healthy and often critical intellectual exchanges between Merton, Sorokin, and Talcott Parsons were important in Thompson's development of a worldview.[57] In Thompson's only recorded interview about his Harvard years, he offered very little information about his experiences as an African-American scholar.[58] Within recent years, Martin Kilson (b. 1931) has described in detail the 1950's African-American Harvard experience. Kilson suggested the 1950's student population was large enough in size to "constitute a critical mass."[59] He defined the character of the Harvard African-American community as being split between "competing establishment-pretenders" and "small-towners," i. e., individuals who were "less given to fashion and more circumspect toward establishment-pretenders."[60] According to Kilson, there were two groups of establishment-pretenders: (1) mainstream and (2) secondary. Each group had distinct characteristics. Most notably, the mainstream establishment-pretenders consisted heavily of WASP's and "careerist-minded high-achieving white ethnics."[61] They viewed the Harvard experience as the mechanism for acquiring knowledge for their future positions of power. The secondary establishment-pretenders consisted of first generation white ethnic students and upper middle-class urban African-Americans who were usually light-complected and members of African-American fraternities and sororities.[62] The small-towners, like Kilson, were not a part of either group. Consequently, they formed small networks based on intellectual interests.

From Thompson's discussion of his Harvard years, he had a similar small-towner experience. As a product of a rural Georgia experience, he was beyond the pale of Boston's well-defined "elite colored" social circles in the 1940's and 1950's.[63] He could not make a claim to being a secondary establishment-pretender such as Gail Jones, the daughter of Lena Horne.[64]

After Harvard, Thompson followed Merton to Columbia University. Years after leaving Columbia, he held fond memories of the stimulating lectures by Merton. Merton's ability to mesmerize students through an engaging lecture style has become legend among students of the '50s.[65] While studying at Columbia, he worked with C. Wright Mills. (b. 1916, d. 1962) He acquired a doctorate in sociology from Columbia in 1956. Merton was his dissertation advisor.[66]

In the 1950's, Columbia's role in sociology was "at its peak."[67] According to James S. Coleman (b. 1926), the Columbia department was ruled by a triumvirate of Robert K. Merton, Paul Lazarsfeld (b. 1901, d. 1976), and Robert S. Lynd (b. 1892). Merton and Lazarsfeld were the dominant personalities in the triumvirate. The graduate students vied for their attention.[68] Thus, it was not surprising to find Thompson highlighting his connection with Merton in later years.

While Coleman's reminiscences of his sojourn at Columbia contain extensive references to the period's white sociology graduate students, he does not mention Thompson or any other African-American graduate students such as John A. Morsell (1950, Ph.D.), Charles Lawrence (1952, Ph.D.), and Lewis Wade Jones (1955, Ph.D.). The world of African-Americans and "less significant students" in Columbia was described by Coleman in the following comment: "There were a number of others, but in the peculiar social system of Columbia sociology they seemed to matter little, or matter only to those who themselves seemed to matter little."[69] In the opinion of Coleman and his white contemporaries, Columbia was the center of American sociological scholarship. He described this centrality in the following passage:

> Graduate students were not encouraged to read the professional journals; no self-respecting graduate student at Columbia entertained the thought of journal publication as a goal. ...[T]he world of sociology was confined to Columbia. Graduate students followed suit, with no interest other than having a paper read by Merton or Lazarsfeld. Once *that* had occurred, there was little interest in having it read by others. ...For us, there was no sociology east of Morningside Drive nor west of Broadway.[70]

The absence of African-American scholars from the social world of white graduate students such as Coleman at Columbia may have been more attributable to their research emphasis than racial attitudes. Nevertheless, it highlighted the racial isolation of African-American graduate students of the period. Although Thompson cherished his exposure to the "great" sociological thinkers of his time, his graduate school experiences reflected the institutional racism of the period.[71] In addition to his Columbia work, he studied a year at the Union Theological Seminary under Reinhold Niebuhr (b. 1892, d. 1971) and Liston Pope (b. 1909). This study was a continuation of his interest in religious studies which began in Atlanta. His educational training was an important aspect of his teaching career in African-American universities.

Since Thompson's career was based primarily in a single institution, it lacked the colorful detail of Jones' career because he managed to reach a happy median with the difficult challenges faced by scholars in an institution with limited financial resources. In fact, he advanced into the upper ranks of Dillard's administration, i.e., vice president for academic affairs. This afforded him greater opportunity to explore his scholarly interests.[72]

While some sociological studies have suggested the career trajectories of African-American sociologists were limited by their employment in African-American institutions of higher learning, an examination of the intellectual productivity and professional growth of Thompson's and Jones' careers provides interesting clues on the impact of racial segregation on their professional growth and development.

Black School vs. White School:
The Different Career Trajectories of Thompson and Jones

The professional careers of Thompson and Jones followed similar paths up to a point. While most of Thompson's career was based at Dillard and the bulk of Jones' early career was spent at Talladega, their long-term career paths were quite dissimilar. Jones' move from Talladega to OWU dramatically altered his professional experiences. Although personality characteristics played a significant role in their professional activity, the professional growth of both scholars was circumscribed by the discipline's restraints on African-American participation.

In the early histories of white professional social science organizations such as the American Sociological Association (ASA), the presence of African-Americans in the white organizational structures provided their white leadership and constituents with a twofold purpose: (1) it offered white sociologists the satisfaction of having token minority participation which suggested their organizations were non-discriminatory and (2) served as a mechanism for filtering the professional participation of minorities, especially African-Americans. Similarly, the active participation of African-Americans provided a twofold purpose: (1) it offered the satisfaction of knowing their educational training and scholarship were not banished completely behind the veil of segregation and (2) provided exposure to liberal whites who would extend professional favors which advanced their careers.

According to Robert Washington, the relationship of African-American intellectuals with white sponsors was characterized by co-optation and hegemonic dependency. White sponsors not only influenced their participation in scholarly organizations but they influenced their degree of theoretical creativity. Washington believes the white scholars' lack of theoretical creativity regarding African-American life had a profound impact on African-American sociologists. The scholarly organizations provided the forum for the exposition of white scholars ideas. Thus, disciplinary activism had an influence on African-American sociologists, especially those involved in scholarly organizations.

Meier has suggested disciplinary activism was best represented in the personality of Charles S. Johnson. Johnson was described as the

African-American sociological philanthropy "czar" who played as influential role as Booker T. Washington in the African-American community.[73] Despite the personality clashes between Johnson, Frazier, Cox and other second generation sociologists, each of these individuals maintained healthy ties to certain whites within the sociological profession. Recently, Anthony Platt has suggested that Frazier's scholarship was promoted through his contacts with white sociologists.[74] Many of those contacts were formed in professional associations.

The use of white professional organizations and white liberal sociologists for self-promotion was no more exploitative for African-Americans than the exclusion of African-Americans and women by white sociologists. Recently, William H. Sewell (b. 1940) has suggested that exclusion may have been inadvertent. According to Sewell, "the poor showing" of the ASA in the participation of women and minorities from 1905 through 1970 was related to "the control of an all-white male power structure that informally set 'universalistic' professional standards for office holding that were very difficult for women and minority sociologists to meet, given the conditions existing in the universities and colleges in which they were employed [and] outright discrimination and indifference in [the] professional organization to the merits of women and minority sociologists."[75] Sewell's explanation of universalistic professional standards as limiting minority access to "mainstream" professional groups minimized the significance of institutional racism in the adoption of the discipline's standards. To many young African-American sociologists, the so-called universality of the discipline mirrored the racist beliefs and actions which permeated American academia.

The exclusion of African-Americans from professional organizations such as ASA led to the development of African-American professional organizations. African-American professional associations played a role in networking for employment. According to Jackson, the annual ASBS meetings played a pivotal role in the employment prospects of many African-Americans.[76] As white associations became more inclusive of African-Americans and white institutions hired more African-Americans, older African-American associations became less and less important to African-American sociological employment opportunities.

In the case of accomplished and well published African-American sociologists such as DuBois, Reid, Frazier and Johnson, their activities in white and African-American professional organizations and the small benefits derived from their participation were merely complementary aspects of their careers. For African-American sociologists with limited publication and grant records, the white and African-American professional organizations provided the only opportunity to participate in the profession as a colleague. Thus, the white and African-American professional organizations played a critical role in the formation of their identities as sociologists. By the late 1960's, this pattern of professional activism became considerably less appealing to a younger and more aggressive group of African-American sociologists.

In 1968, a new minority professional organization developed in academia. The Association of Black Sociologists (ABS) was the outgrowth of the Caucus of Black Sociologists (CBS). The CBS consisted of young African-American sociologists who presented a challenge to the ASA's exclusivity.[77] The changing role of African-Americans in white and African-American sociological organizations was important to Thompson and Jones. They maintained active membership in many organizations, including the ABS.

Jones as the Organizational Man--Finding a Niche in the White Male Scholarly Club

During Jones' years in African-American institutions, his professional affiliations were limited to a few organizations. He was active in the Eastern Sociological Society (ESS) and the Association for the Study of Negro Life and History (ASNLH). He became a member of the ESS during his graduate school days at NYU. He continued to pay his ESS membership dues at Talladega. Similarly, his ASNLH membership was as a dues contributor.[78] Jones' greatest professional activity occurred after leaving Talladega. According to Jones, the African-American colleges' limited budgets were often used by their administrators to prohibit participation and financial support for travel to professional meetings.[79]

Beginning in 1958, Jones played an active role in the ASA. He organized his first ASA session on the sociology of law. Throughout the next three decades, he organized various sessions at ASA meetings. His most outstanding ASA contribution was provided through participation on various committees. His ASA committee memberships included such diverse committees as the Committee on the Visiting Scientists Program for Sociology, Committee on Regional Affairs, DuBois-Johnson-Frazier Award Selection Committee, Minority Fellowship Committee, and the Executive Committee. His active participation in ASA programs gave him unusual exposure to the inner workings of the organization.

This vantage point made his involvement in the CBS quite influential. He served as a referee for its short-lived journal, *The Black Sociologist*. In 1990, the CBS's successor, the Association of Black Sociologists (ABS) recognized his contributions with the Founders Award. Similarly, he received the W. E. B. DuBois Award, the highest honor bestowed on a scholar by the ASBS.

Upon moving to OWU, he became an active member of the North Central Sociological Association (NCSA), formerly the Ohio Valley Sociological Society. He served in various official capacities in the NCSA. In 1963-1964, he served as its president. His involvement in the NCSA included serving as a referee for *Sociological Focus*. In 1982, he was given the NCSA Distinguished Professional Service Award for outstanding creative and sustained service to the advancement of the sociological profession in the region. The NCSA recognized his contribution by establishing the Butler A. Jones Minority Scholarship. Although Ohio had two African-American universities, Jones' activity in the NCSA was significant because of his unique position as an African-American faculty member at a white school.

In 1956, he became an active participant in the Society for the Study of Social Problems (SSSP) by serving on its Program Committee. Jones maintained an active role in the organization for more than thirty years. He served on various committees such as the C. Wright Mills Award Committee, Budget Committee, Intergroup Relations Committee, Executive Committee, and Committee on Permanent Organization. He was an editor of the SSSP Newsletter and *Social Problems*. He served as parliamentarian, secretary, vice president, and as a board of directors member. In 1985, he was given the Lee Founders Award in recognition of his service to the organization.

According to his SSSP colleague, Herbert Aurbach, Jones "was very active in the early founding of the organization."[80] His early SSSP involvement resulted from a close working relationship with Alfred McClung Lee (b. 1906) on the famous *Brown v. Board of Education, Topeka* case, 98, F. Supp. 797 (1951), 347 U. S. 483 (1954). Lee spearheaded the SSSP's development. Jones had very "strong relationships with people [and] a number of the leaders of SSSP."[81]

Although Jones faithfully served the organization from its earliest years, he was never elected as SSSP president. Other African-Americans have been elected as president such as James E. Blackwell (1979-80) and Doris Y. Wilkinson (1986-87). Despite the recent election of African-American SSSP presidents, Aurbach highlighted the glaring inequity of the organization's failure to elect a dedicated member such as Jones. He said, "[A] lot of people over the years who became president...never were active in the organization...before or after [serving as president]."[82] Aurbach's explanation for their election was their recognition as "outstanding scholars" who "had written important books" and "published a great deal, often in [SSSP's] *Social Problems*."[83] In the extreme case, an inactive SSSP president never attended more than two meetings subsequent to serving in office.

Jones' election as vice president followed an SSSP tradition of recognizing a member's "contribution to the organization."[84] His special contribution to SSSP was trying "to involve other African-Americans in the organization."[85] According to Aurbach, "with very few exceptions [Jones] didn't seem...to have a great deal of influence [on the SSSP membership's racial composition] until quite a bit later when he began to get active in the Association [of Black Sociologists]."[86]

The irony of the situation was Jones felt comfortable in SSSP because of its commitment to integration. Yet, the organization did little to support its most vocal African-American proponent's early efforts to attract African-Americans. His lack of influence reflected his social marginality as an African-American intellectual and as an SSSP member. This status of social marginality was defined by Jerry G. Watts as, "the condition of being simultaneously denied access to the mainstream intellectual resources and critical audiences while being a member of an ethnic group that did not have the resources and/or educational attainment sufficient to sustain *serious traditional* [italics mine] intellectual activity."[87] Jones' social marginality as an African-American intellectual persisted despite his appointment at a white school. His social marginalization did not deter his activism.

For Jones, active participation in the ASA and other predominantly white professional organizations provided an important connection to "mainstream" sociologists. Each organization played a different role in the sociological community. Consequently, Jones' participation in each group gave him exposure to a diverse range of white constituencies. They facilitated his progress as a sociologist. Although his publishing productivity was limited in earlier years, his professional participation in the discourse of sociological issues was heightened by his work in those organizations. They gave him a professional identification with his white peers as well as professional exposure. Similarly, his involvement in ABS sustained him as a member of the community of African-American sociologists. As an early member of the CBS, Jones was privy to the key issues which shaped the group's identity. Thus, his professional ties to white and African-American sociological organizations formed an important part of his development of a sociological perspective.

In addition to the activism in sociological organizations, he was very active in the American Association of University Professor (AAUP). Jones' AAUP activities dated back to his Talladega days. During the very contentious period of the Pappenheim controversy, the college was the center of internal political bickering between Beittel and the faculty/students regarding a number of other issues.[88] Jones spoke out as an AAUP official. He said, "So long as it [Beittel's hostility toward the faculty] is maintained I believe it will become increasingly difficult to find a rational basis upon which the local AAUP and the chief administrator of the college can cooperate in building a better Talladega."[89] While his comments reflected the gravity of the situation, some Talladega board members were not impressed by his outspokenness. Jones' perspective as an AAUP leader became clear to the board in subsequent years. In 1952, the political situation was so bad at Talladega that nearly one-third of the staff did not return to the college.[90] His involvement in AAUP continued after his departure from Talladega. He served on the national AAUP board. He also organized the OWU chapter and served as the Cleveland State University chapter's president. His AAUP participation centered around issues of academic freedom rather than labor disputes. Academic freedom was the early emphasis of the AAUP. Jones became less active in the AAUP after it became a union organization.

In Jones' own words, "We changed the original [university] culture of the usual expressions of academic freedom. You had no more influence than what you could get from the institution in respect to academic freedom. ...[M]any of the people who were involved in it through the years I was, were much more concerned about academic freedom. Our censure list was very effective, particularly in major universities and in those smaller institutions that wanted status as first-rate institutions. Our report on violations of academic freedom carried an awful lot of weight. ...We specifically rejected the labor unions because you had your only weapon, that was at the end when we struck."[91] He believed the shift from an organization which supported academic freedom to a labor union resulted from the influence of junior colleges who were more interested in economic matters rather than topical issues or academic freedom.

His work in scholarly organizations was complemented by involvement in race relations work such as the Anti-Defamation League

(ADL). Aurbach described Jones as a "very, very strong advocate of relationships between African-Americans and Jews."[92] In the ADL, he worked very closely with its executive officer, Oscar Cohen. He attended "strategy meetings that ADL had in New York in efforts to bring the Jewish and Black community together on issues, particularly those that involved civil rights."[93] His ADL activities supported his deep belief in an integrated society as well as his commitment to social activism. His social activism led him to community involvement in interracial groups such as the Delaware (Ohio) Civil Rights Committee. These organizations focused on local race relations issues.[94]

Thompson as the Institutional Man--Surviving the African-American College World

Like Jones, Thompson was a person who was very active in professional organizations. Thus, it was not surprising that he was also chosen as a leader in his profession. It is surprising that his leadership roles were so ephemeral to the central power of white authority within the profession. According to Ida Simpson, Thompson was a part of a generation of younger African-Americans "who served the [Southern Sociological] Society with distinction."[95] As a Dillard faculty member, his ascension to the vice presidency of the Southern Sociological Society (SSS) signaled a departure from the institutional power base of the Fisk University, Atlanta University, and Tuskegee Institute triumvirate which provided the lion's share of the SSS African-American leaders.[96] This was particularly significant because SSS African-American membership has always been small.[97]

Although Thompson was ranked in Conyers' 1968 top ten list of living African-American contributors to sociology, he was conspicuously absent from his 1986 list of "top" African-American sociologists. This may be a clear indication of his minor presence in the field.[98] However, it may be a greater corroboration of Simpson's and Key's point that African-American colleges and their faculty have had a declining role in "mainstream" sociological organizations. While African-Americans have held ten percent of elected positions in the SSS, with four presidents--Charles S. Johnson in 1946, Joseph Himes in 1966, Charles U. Smith in 1975, and John Moland in 1995, there have been very few SSS African-American executive committee members, the key decision-making group.[99]

African-American presidents of the SSS served in other capacities prior to election. While Johnson served as first vice president, Himes and Smith served as second vice president. It is interesting to note that Thompson was unable to use his vice presidential position as a stepping stone for greater recognition in the SSS. According to Simpson, second vice president was "seldom a rung on a ladder to the presidency." The SSS second vice presidency has been described as the "token" minority office with African-Americans seven times as likely to be elected to the position. The Executive Committee has been described as the "training ground for [SSS] presidents."[100]

According to Simpson, racial desegregation resulted in African-Americans becoming less visible within the SSS. She believed visibility was linked to external constraints reminding white members of the need for racial representation. There may be other reasons for Thompson's and African-Americans' failure to make lasting inroads in the SSS and professional sociological organizations. The presence and influence of predominantly African-American professional organizations may have played a role in Thompson's inability to rise beyond a certain level within the SSS.

Thompson's relative lack of visibility beyond the SSS and the South was due to the following: (1) his unique personality and (2) his involvement in the African-American college network. According to one of his colleagues,[101] Thompson exhibited an idiosyncratic manner which distinguished him from many of his contemporaries. Thus, Thompson was not noted for the type of organizational involvement that characterized Jones' career. The financial constraints of working in a small African-American liberal arts college exacerbated the idiosyncratic nature of Thompson's personality regarding professional activity. Since Dillard had few resources, Thompson's participation in professional organizations was an expense covered through personal funds from a low salary. As a participant, he had to pay for travel, lodging, and dues in organizations that may or may not have valued his presence and participation. While he was an active member of SSS and ABS, he was not a prominent member of ASBS. Consequently, his affiliations were chosen very carefully.

A major consideration in the selection of a professional affiliation was the benefits related to career advancement in the African-American college network. Like their white counterparts, African-American colleges and universities maintained a complex social structure. Tobe Johnson suggested the African-American colleges in which Thompson and Jones worked might be examined through their internal processes as part of a "system involving several subsystems or components which interact to produce an output."[102] He believed the internal processes of the African-American college were understood best by examining "the nature of the interrelationships between the colleges and the supersystem."[103]   The supersystem consisted of individuals and institutions who controlled the colleges' survival resources.[104]   He suggested the African-American college had adapted to the supersystem's restrictions on African-American higher education.   The adaptation was an enduring part of the institutional character which became an inherent element of its conditioning and survival process.[105]

While Johnson's systems theory approach to the African-American college may be questioned regarding the validity of its application to the diverse range of African-American colleges and universities, it does provide an understanding of an academic world of scholars and students operating under the constraints of a racially segregated educational community.

When Dillard was formed from the merger of New Orleans University, a Methodist college, and Straight University, a Congregationalist college, the institutional supersystem of African-American college segregation was an important issue with regard to white authority over African-Americans.   It became an issue of contention among the new school's board members.   Southern white philanthropists such as Edgar B. Stern objected to the possibility of the new school having equal interracial social contacts between faculty and an African-American president as an authority over white faculty members.[106]   It was these institutional constraints which shaped Thompson's scholarly pursuits.

Scholars who were successful in African-American institutions, i. e., advanced to positions of monetary gain, power, and influence, mastered teaching and social skills which were not a part of "mainstream" scholarly communities.   These skills were related to a segregated world.   Since most of Thompson's career took place during the time of legal segregation, his career aspirations were shaped by the professional definitions of the time.   According to Linda M. Perkins, many married African-American academics "rarely thought of uprooting to move elsewhere" because of their limited professional opportunities.   Thus, Thompson's stay at Dillard may have reflected the employment constraints of the academic world as well as the familial living choices made by African-American academics.[107]

In addition, the inconveniences of research in segregated institutions prevented many African-American intellectuals from scholarly pursuit. Thompson suffered the same research constraints as colleagues in other disciplines such as John Hope Franklin in history.[108]   Thus, his obscurity reflected the fact that few African-American institutions placed emphasis on participation in white scholarly organizations. As a teaching institution, Dillard recognized the classroom contributions of its faculty. Faculty members were encouraged to devote their time and energy to projects which enhanced their relationships with students. Thompson's activities included serving as advisor of the E. Franklin Frazier Sociology Club. Many of his sociology club members continued on to graduate study such as Barbara Guillory who was one of two students named in the complaint against Tulane University's discriminatory admissions policies and later received her doctorate in sociology;[109] and Frank Pinto who received a social work degree. He served as a mentor to junior colleagues such as Monte Pilawsky. His students attended America's leading professional and graduate schools such as Harvard, Yale, and Georgetown.[110] His cultivation of student relationships, scholarly publications, and advancement through academic ranks aided in his mastery of the African-American college network. His publications provided the only element of his Dillard background assets which "mainstream" institutions valued as recognizable scholarly contributions. As a result, his recognition beyond the South and SSS was influenced by the disciplinary interpretation of adequate scholarly productivity and limited participation in minority organizations.

Despite Randall Kennedy's (b. 1954) recent use of a quote from John Hope Franklin (b. 1915) in an attack on African-American scholarly organizations such as ABS, the ASBS and its counterparts continue to serve an important role for African-American sociologists and other scholars.[111] Joyce Ladner provided the following explanation for such organizations:

> [T]he profound consequence of the drive toward assimilation and incorporation was abject tokenism. Otherwise, assimilation was a dismal failure. The return to parallel structures would provide [African-Americans] with a better opportunity to decide their own fate [and] expand the scope of professional participation through research concerning the [African-American] community. It could also serve as a protective or ego-safeguard function by shielding [African-Americans] from the negative aspects of subordinate roles.[112]

Ladner's comments were an accurate description of how African-Americans viewed their relationship with professional organizations during most of the 20th Century. According to Key, this was particularly true "for some [African-Americans], primarily the younger, more militant of the new sociologists" in the 1970's.[113]

Simpson reported accurately that many African-Americans chose the ASBS over the SSS because of the following: (1) willingness to accept papers from lesser known African-American scholars; (2) featuring topics of special interest to faculty of African-American colleges; (3) smallness, conviviality, and complete acceptance by ASBS members; (4) prohibitive cost of multiple memberships in professional associations; and (5) interdisciplinary approaches.[114] The ASBS played a significant role in recognizing the outstanding contributions of African-American sociologists. Jackson offered three reasons why the ASBS continued to hold significance for African-American social scientists (1) the need for a "black conscious" social scientific organization; (2) the need for an organization in which a large number of African-Americans participate; and (3) the need for an organization "which had some impact upon accumulating and utilizing knowledge about blacks and black-white relations."[115]

While Thompson may have played a minor role in African-American and white sociological organizations, he had a major role in the civil rights movement of New Orleans. He helped in organizing voter registration campaigns for the African-American community. He used his scholarship to document "irregularities in the [voter] registration procedures" of the state.[116] Through his research, he encountered many of Louisiana's leaders including such arch-segregationists as Leander Perez (b. 1891, d. 1969). Thompson's forthright character led him to a degree of frankness in an encounter with Perez. Thompson said reportedly:

> You may be able to keep all public facilities segregated. You can have racially separate schools, hospitals, parks and libraries. However, when [African-Americans] become a numerical majority *we* will run the local government. There can only be one mayor.[117]

Like Jones, he viewed his role as a scholar-activist. His research on youth and poverty resulted in work on several anti-poverty programs, including the establishment of an Upward Bound Program for teenagers on the Dillard campus.[118]

His greatest contribution as a scholar-activist was the founding and leadership of the Coordinating Council of Greater New Orleans (CCGNO). The CCGNO was a federation of African-American organizations with the purpose of "coordinating the resources and talents of the various types of [African-American] leaders in the solution of common problems."[119] It developed voter registration campaigns from 1961-1965. The CCGNO included a cross-section of groups such as social clubs, beauticians, barbers, prominent clergy, university professors, political personalities, and mainstream civil rights organizations. It received an endorsement from the local Roman Catholic Church authorities. The group's initial goal was to influence the 1962 mayoral election. Over the years, the CCGNO activities included the operation of voter education schools and observing local elections. The CCGNO sent matched pairs of applicants for voter registration to test the fairness of the process. Their test data were used as evidence in court cases to demonstrate voter discrimination. In addition, the CCGNO organized "Youth Voter Crusader Corps" comprised of high school and college students who canvassed the African-American community; and it staged a picket of the (New Orleans) Municipal Auditorium, the office of the voter registrar, and (New Orleans) City Hall[120] In 1960, Thompson assisted in designing the techniques used by the Consumers League of Greater New Orleans in a protest against white merchants in African-American business areas who refused to employ African-Americans.[121]

Thompson's political activism reflected the type of involvement which has been suggested by Kim Lacy Rogers as the "integrationist and political generations" due to their commitment in the late 1950's and early 1960's to an activist style which incorporated prominent middle-class African-American leadership who served as racial negotiators.[122] Their civil rights work was based on "progressive assumptions."[123] Many of these assumptions were incorporated in Thompson's scholarly work as a sociologist. They were a part of the middle-class character of Dillard's institutional life in juxtaposition to other African-American colleges in New Orleans such as working-class Southern University of New Orleans.[124] In addition, Thompson's civil rights involvement was similar to the pattern of protest reported by Charles U. Smith and Lewis Killian (b. 1920), i.e., indirect participation and protest related to publications.[125] Thus, his political activism made sociological organizational activity secondary to the greater struggle of civil rights.

Unlike Jones who was an ABS presidential candidate and was recognized by ASBS and ABS, Thompson never served as ASBS or ABS president. However, he was selected as a fellow at Oxford University and the prestigious Center for Advanced Study in Behavioral Sciences at Stanford University. In 1982, he received the ASA's DuBois-Johnson-Frazier Award. This recognition was achieved on national and international levels despite his limited attainments in

SSS or its African-American counterparts.

Solving Social Problems through an Interdisciplinary Approach: The Scholarship of Thompson and Jones

Their publishing productivity highlights the greatest distinction between the scholars. The normal publishing expectations for any scholar based in a small liberal arts teaching college is quite different from those based at large research institutions. When one considers the financial constraints of African-American institutions of higher learning and the intellectual isolation of some African-American schools, the issue of publishing becomes even more problematic. Thompson's publication record of five books and fifty articles stands in stark contrast to such expectations.

While Jones' community service record was outstanding, his publications were limited like many African-American sociologists of the second generation. The diverse focus of his publications reflected a pattern common to second generation African-American sociologists who integrated white schools such as Charles H. Parrish (b. 1899).[126] Prior to the 1950's, Jones' productivity was negligible. The absence of publications may be related directly to his employment. According to Thompson, scholars at African-American institutions of higher learning reported limited research support at their institutions and challenging teaching loads.[127] These institutional characteristics had a profound impact on the productivity of its faculty. Early in his career, Jones was employed in "teaching" institutions in the African-American community. After his move to OWU, his productivity gained some momentum. His publications focused on African-American historical figures, curriculum development, and civil rights law. Thompson's publications focused on stratification, African-American leadership, education, social movements, family, social psychology, and religion. The wide range of foci reflected their interdisciplinary perspective and the availability of publishing options. Their research was based in the African-American sociological tradition. Thus, a discussion of their scholarship must rely upon those critical differences which have been suggested as essential to understanding the African-American sociological tradition.

According to Edward G. Armstrong, there existed three critical differences in "conventional sociology" and black sociology: (1) the prior acceptance of a model; (2) the claim to value neutrality; and (3) the presence of paradigmatic biases--the practical consequences of research built upon the prior acceptance of a model and claim to value neutrality. These differences were influenced by the professional experiences of African-American sociologists.[128]

Ralph Hines looked at the extraordinary working circumstances of African-American sociologists. He reported their professional status made them susceptible to a quasi-elitist frame of reference. However, he encouraged the African-American sociologist not to identify with an in-group of only some sociologists such as the Chicago School. He felt sociologists should resist identification with in-groups which would "exclude[e] contact with theories and concepts from other disciplines." [129] Hines' early call for a unique African-American perspective was responded to by Wilbur Watson.

Watson presented a three-factor typology of race-related sociologies in an effort to "probe into the meanings of black sociology." (See Watson article in this volume)[130] He highlighted four aspects of black sociology: (1) a conduct of inquiry conducted by one whose racial identity is Black; (2) a subject matter--race relations--researched by Black sociologists; (3) a theoretical frame based on matters of concern to Blacks; and (4) a radical ideological stance.[131] He defined black sociology as follows:

> Black sociology means the conduct of inquiry initiated and implemented by a sociologist (1) whose social identity is Black, (2) whose ideological allegiance, as expressed in the formulation of research problems and interpretation research results, is for the release of Black people from race-related social oppression, and (3) whose primary research population is constituted by Black people.[132]

Thompson's and Jones' publications reflected each of the characteristics highlighted above. While they identified themselves as African-Americans and conducted research on race, they did not utilize a theoretical frame of reference based on racial assumptions; and they were not radical scholars. Their sociological work reflected the New Deal liberal scholarship of their white peers. An apt description of their views would be "liberal-integrationist." Although their scholarship may have challenged indirectly the system of segregation, it supported their liberal views rather than a radical view of society. Jones' scholarship was influenced by the liberalism which Washington suggested as a characteristic of the second generation. Jones explained his liberal-integrationist view in an unpublished manuscript by saying:

> Social science teaching should be directed toward the end that the

individual becomes aware of the basic points of agreement as well as the basic points of conflict in society. There can be no denying the fact that conflict is a common characteristic of modern industrial urban society. ...Conflicts between individuals competing for status, prestige, security, money, cannot and should not be overlooked or minimized. But there is yet another element in modern society not so obvious and thus quite likely to be overlooked and that is the existence of certain basic ideals which have tended to hold men together as human beings.[133]

Moreover, most of their scholarship focused on African-Americans descriptively rather than developing a new theoretical analysis of the community. This review of their scholarship will feature a select group of their publications and research papers. It will focus on those representative publications which were recognized by other sociologists as important contributions to the discipline.

Thompson's Views on Social Stratification: Leadership Styles in the African-American Community

In his work on social stratification, *The Negro Leadership Class*, Thompson used his research to explore the dimension of leadership skills found in New Orleans, Louisiana (Crescent City).[134] As in most of his work, his methodology incorporated a variety of instruments which aided in an explication of the critical variables. He utilized a literature review, personal interview data, "forum" interviews, participant observation, research staff meetings, and a leadership conference to ascertain pertinent information. As a long time resident and moderate leader in New Orleans, his insight regarding the special social, cultural, and political factors which shaped the Crescent City's sociological landscape made his utilization of these techniques an effective method of social analysis.

Thompson was a proud member of New Orleans' upper class African-American community. His identification with the community on personal and professional levels gave him access to many circles. In New Orleans' Afro-Creole society, racial identity was a complex aspect of a complicated culture. Although Thompson was a light brown-skinned person in a color conscious society and married to a solid member of the upper class African-American New Orleans community, the community was still a very closed society. Recent works have highlighted the community's exclusivity.[135] Thus, Thompson's ability to traverse the various levels of the Crescent City's leadership class demonstrated more than the scholarly capabilities of methodological acumen. An excellent example of his unique knowledge was demonstrated in his analysis of data.

While his research team conducted interviews with 318 subjects (139 African-Americans and 79 whites), only 100 subjects were selected as the focus of his final work. His keen eye evinced that 218 respondents provided information which "was too narrowly focused" or had questionable leadership credentials for his research purposes.[136] For Thompson, the sample selection process was not a mere methodological formality. It represented the crux of an approach to sociological inquiry on race relations which permeated his research. In this respect, his work on African-American leadership had a phenomenological perspective, i.e., a perspective which emphasized the basis of consciousness and subjective understanding in the analysis of social action.[137] By looking at the quality of responses, he examined the meaning offered by the subjects as a method of interpreting their awareness of African-American leadership. Thompson may have attempted unwittingly to select and analyze data with the phenomenological goal suggested by Armstrong, "a rigorous description of the intentionality of consciousness--the essential correlations between 'appearance and that which appears.' "[138] In his work, the inclusion of subjects was based on the study's focus. His study was concerned with the relationship of Gunnar Myrdal's concept of the American Creed to leadership in a segregated southern city.[139]

Thompson's work on leadership was published in the early 1960's. It was an important part of the published social science literature appearing in the incipient stages of the modern-day civil rights movement. He provided a thorough analysis of the major characteristics of New Orleans' leadership class. He highlighted some social characteristics which still persist among leaders, especially within the African-American community. These characteristics included a majority male leadership cadre, a diverse age cohort with the majority of the leaders over forty, self-made men, well-educated, and Protestant leaders. While some of these characteristics simply reflected the historical outgrowths of the African slave community's encounters with Europeans, they also demonstrated leadership within the African-American community reflected a sophisticated interplay between the American racial dynamics and the traditional definition of a leader, which Thompson defined as: "one...who initiates, stimulates, coordinates, and directs the activities of others, his followers, in the solution of some common problem or the achievement of some specific social goal [as well as] those who achieve high positions, or meet with notable success in any group, [by serving as] champions of the group's basic values[.]"[140]   Thus, he believed a leader was an individual who was "essential for [a group's] survival at a particular time and location, and in a given situation."[141]

Through his study of New Orleans leaders, he was able to define distinct leadership styles which influenced the community.   Within the white community, he reported that leadership was dominated by the segregationist perspective.   He found three distinct subtypes of segregationists: (1) white supremacists, (2) states' righters, and (3) culturists.[142]   Through a concise explication of the subtypes, Thompson showed Southern white ideological patterns influenced the social and political levels of discourse as well as social interaction on racial issues.   Most importantly, the discourse and interaction took place only in the context of segregationist perspective.[143]

Similarly, he defined three distinct leadership subtypes in the African-American community.   They were: (1) Uncle Toms, (2) Moderate--Racial Diplomat, and (3) Liberal--Race Man.   Thompson's description of African-American leadership subtypes continue to have salience in American society.   They transcend time and remain useful tools for political analysis of leadership styles in the African-American community.

His research in the area of stratification was not limited to African-American leadership.   His study of private African-American colleges provided an important data set about the environment that nurtured the growth and development of many African-American leaders.   Similarly, his last major work on stratification, *A Black Elite--A Profile of Graduates of UNCF Colleges*, explored the success of African-American college graduates in the post-civil rights era.   In this study, Thompson presented "a comprehensive profile of black college graduates as a distinct, self-conscious segment in American society."[144]

He attempted to offer a "systematic description and interpretation" of African-American college graduates' "socioeconomic origins, racial disadvantages, academic handicaps and successes, philosophies of human relations, levels and fields of post-baccalaureate education, career patterns, social class identities, community services, civil rights attitudes and activities, political persuasions, and leadership styles and achievements."[145]   His research utilized information derived from forty focused interviews, survey responses from a random sample of 2,089 United Negro College Fund (UNCF) alumni, a review of personal documents submitted by twenty-four subjects, and his forty plus years of experience and observations in UNCF schools.   He discovered that the graduates of the UNCF institutions comprised an "integral, creative element within this nation's college-educated [African-American] elite which diligently (sic) strives for personal success and racial advancement in American society."[146]

Thompson's Views on Professionalization: The Unique Character of the African-American College Professor

Similarly, Thompson's views on professionalization within the African-American community provided telling information for contemporary research. In his studies of the career patterns and morale of African-American college teachers, he presented some of the first and most extensive research data on this community. As in all of his work, he utilized a variety of research methods. He employed questionnaires, interviews, observations and a literature review. While his study focused on the descriptive features of this community, he attempted to interpret his findings in practical ways. Thompson suggested education was a valued commodity in the African-American community. He reported African-Americans lagged far behind the white community in educational attainment. Thus, he wanted to answer two critical questions: (1) Why there is a relative shortage of well-qualified [African-American], college teachers? (2) Why educated [African-Americans], particularly those who hold the doctorate or some significant academic administrative post, are usually assigned a higher status in African-American society than their [white counterparts]?[147]

Although Thompson's work followed closely a similar study by his Howard University colleague, G. Franklin Edwards (b. 1915),[148] it was a precursor to many of the 1960-1990 studies of African-American professionalization.[149] In his work, he reported many African-American college teachers met competence standards which were similar to whites, i.e., formal training, scholarship, and morality.[150] Yet, he felt the institutions provided little support for scholarly production. The lack of support had a political basis.

By looking at the politics of the period, he offered a standard for looking at the political dynamics of contemporary race relations. As a sociologist, he felt the academic enterprise was one which demanded high standards. He applied these standards to his analysis. He reported African-American college teachers acquired advanced degrees despite economic hardships. He suggested their economic situation forced them to work during graduate study. In a recent work, Meier and Rudwick said Thompson suggested African-American college teachers were retarded in their professional development and narrowed in their intellectual perspectives as a consequence of this situation.[151] Although his study was conducted during the Jim Crow era, his findings relate to contemporary society.

He found some measures of the African-American college teachers where they were struggling against almost insurmountable odds; on other measures, he found them demonstrating exceptional levels of competence and creativity. He reported that the overwhelming majority of the teachers were satisfied with their career choice. When he looked closely at their responses, he discovered their responses were linked to "a more or less realistic appraisal of existing estimable job opportunities."[152]   In addition, he reported teachers were flexible regarding teaching styles. Their flexibility was an important attribute in an academic community with students who share a diverse range of competencies. With regard to teaching, he reported a challenging teaching load which differed from many of their colleagues at white institutions. Similarly, the teachers reported frequent moves to other institutions in pursuit of better opportunities. The so-called "itinerant professors" were those who were at the top of the profession.

Since the majority of the African-American institutions were teaching institutions, it was not surprising that the college teachers in Thompson's study reported limited research support at their institutions. His study made the important contribution of interpreting the institutional racism of "mainstream" academic support networks such as publishing houses and scholarly journals.[153]   Recently, Manning and Stanfield have examined the institutional racism which related to philanthropic and research-based supporters of scholarly endeavor.[154]   Their studies merely confirmed Thompson's early comments in which he stated, "[African-American] colleges were accorded low status in the academic world."[155]   Similarly, his ideas mirrored Will Scott's discussion of the maintenance of a unique perspective by African-American sociologists despite the slights by the "mainstream" community and limited financial capacities of their departments.[156]

The most interesting examination element of African-American college teachers related to the contradictory relationship between their social status and economic earnings. According to Thompson, 1950's and 1960's African-American college teachers were members of the African-American upper middle class. Yet, their income precluded full participation in the group's activities. The contradiction between designated group status and realistic economic conditions of the group membership had a strong impact on the African-American college teacher. Similarly, Jones suggested the African-American in the sociological discipline was affected by this aspect of African-American academic life, especially in terms of many talented academics leaving the professorate to become administrators.[157]

Thompson stated it had an impact on faculty morale. In an insightful discussion of African-American college teachers' morale, he found low morale was influenced by the following: limited career options; segregated living and working communities; autocratic administrations; lack of opportunity to carry on individual research or creative scholarship; lack of academic freedom; uncertainty about promotion policies; low salaries; and lack of recognition and respect. In his conclusion, he said African-American college teachers had "a widespread feeling of insecurity, uncertainty and low morale."[158] His discussion not only addressed the pressing need for improved conditions for teachers in African-American colleges; but he addressed the needs of all teachers in small teaching colleges.

Thompson's and Jones' Views on Social Movements and Social Change

Thompson's interest in social movements was presented in several articles which focused on the historical development and maintenance of a protest movement within the African-American community. In his work on social movements, he focused on the conflictual relationship between the social controls which governed segregation in America through legal and corporal means with the moral and religious precepts which most white Americans identified. He suggested the development of the civil rights protest in the African-American community was a result of relative deprivations. He believed the African-American protest had been a mainstay of their cultural experience. The African-American protest was "a clear endorsement of the 'American Creed.'" By utilizing a method of interpretive analysis which relied on historical events and their relationship to the changing legal status of African-Americans, Thompson showed the continuity of protest thought and political action in the African-American community.[159] His interpretation of the civil rights movement placed it in the appropriate context for understanding the political changes which shaped the African-American experience of the latter 20th Century. Thompson's interest in contemporary African-American social movements was shared by Jones.

In his research on social movements, Jones showed the continuity of protest thought and political action in the African-American community. In 1953 and 1959, he wrote two articles which focused on the issue of civil rights. The six-year time differential placed the articles in political context. In 1953, he focused on the changing laws which were having an impact on the South. Although the article contained no footnotes, Jones cited numerous sources within the text. His study of African-American political participation was based on historical records, state data, census data, and national survey data. The article's basic sociological premise was an exploration of smaller issues related to Sumner's thesis of the subordination of law to mores.

His study had a twofold purpose: (1) to identify changes in the legal requirements which had an affect on the practices in the areas of politics and education; and (2) "to suggest the manner in which these requirements and the changes in practices...influenced basic patterns of race relations in the South."[160] The article describes the elimination of Southern African-Americans from the political process by such methods as literacy tests, poll tax, and character test requirements. He suggested the *Smith v. Allwright* decision, 321 U. S. 649 (1944), which declared all-white primaries illegal, would alter the course of African-American political participation in the South.

Jones' optimism was supported with documented evidence of an increase in African-American voter registration throughout the region. He examined and compared voter registration patterns in the relatively "progressive" Southern cities such as Atlanta, New Orleans and Miami and "progressive" Southern states with hard core segregation areas such as North Carolina and Tennessee. Even in the hard core areas, he found an increased level of African-American political participation. Jones tempered his optimism with the stinging statement that the propensity to use the "nigger issue" was still a means for soliciting support in a hard fought political battle of white Southern candidates.

According to Jones, "the new legal requirements [had an affect] on the political participation of [African-Americans] and the changes in political practices result[ed]...directly [in] challenge[s] [to] the southerner's belief in the political irresponsibility of the group."[161] In the article, Jones highlighted the impact of those challenges. He discussed the legal battles which were waged by African-Americans to enter and integrate graduate, professional, elementary, and secondary schools. The discussion focused on shifts in the legal challenge to segregation from a perspective of providing equality under segregation to "equality of opportunity within a single system."[162] He stated the litigation resulted in two new legal requirements which, (1) imposed "same training" for all citizens and (2) stated "the test of equality of educational opportunity at the graduate and professional levels [was] not confined to showing equality in physical facilities or money appropriations."[163]

As a result of the second requirement, Jones reported an increase in expenditures for African-American schools between 1940 and 1950 and an increase in the accreditation of African-American public schools. He concluded his discussion of the relationship between the changes in race relations and the new legal requirements by highlighting the financial costs of maintaining a "separate-but-equal" system and the conservative defensive methods used by segregationists to support their discriminatory practices.

In 1959, he examined the 1955 *Brown II* decision, 349 U. S. 294 (1955), the Supreme Court decision which focused on the implementation of the 1954 *Brown I* decision, 98 F. Supp. 797 (1951), 347 U. S. 483 (1954). After presenting the nine major elements of the decision, he noted the techniques used by Southern segregationists to thwart the school integration efforts. In essence, Jones stated *Brown II* gave segregationists the authority to make decisions regarding school integration. He discussed salary equalization suits by looking at the Atlanta (Georgia) School Boards' implementation of a "new" city-wide evaluation system. The system was designed and executed by the very segregationists who had operated a non-egalitarian school system. Although some African-Americans received advancements and higher pay, most African-American teachers were not favorably reviewed by their all-white evaluation groups. He discussed equalization of facilities cases by examining the famous cases which featured school inequities and the courts' role of the courts. He showed the inconsistencies in the behavior and decisions of Southern white judges regarding the need to provide equal school facilities. In the *Sweatt v. Painter* case, 399 U. S. 629 (1950), the judge suggested "no substantial advantage" to African-Americans' attendance in white law schools. In the *Pitts v. Board of Trustees of DeWitt School District* case, No. 1, 84 F. Supp. 975 (E. D. Ark., 1949), the court's role was not deemed as one of "interfere[nce] with the mores and customs of people in a matter as delicate and potentially explosive as race relations."[164]

Jones predicted the segregationists' use of obstructive tactics would maintain public school segregation from 1958 to 1970.[165] He concluded his discussion by calling for faster desegregation. He suggested the increase in African-American political power would have a positive benefit on the desegregation process. The 1953 and 1959 articles were derived from his on-going dissertation research which examined social issues and civil rights law. Most importantly, his work in the area of race and civil rights law offered a clear interpretation of their impact on the African-American community. This interpretation of the African-American community was useful when Jones examined other areas of sociological inquiry such as educational sociology.

Thompson's and Jones' Views on Education: An Examination of the African-American Student

In an article on developing social-civic competence within the Southern student population, Jones offered his views on the sociology of education. Since Jones was one of ten authors, it is not clear to what extent the article reflects his complete personal views. The article was penned as a result of participating in a Stanford University Summer Workshop.[166] Thus, the final article was riddled with footnotes which supported the segregationist perspectives of the South's racial history.

The article consisted of two parts: (1) a review of Southern social conditions which featured subheadings such as health, leisure, occupations, and inter-ethnic relations and (2) a practical guide for designing a curriculum. The article provided two key interpretive elements of education in the 1940's: (1) an endorsement of the utilization of innovative techniques in the classroom and (2) a benign acknowledgment of racial problems in the South. It presented educational policy which mirrored the conservative educational philosophies of the period.

Since the article was written during World War II, it was filled with language supporting democracy and the development of democratic and Christian ideals within the Southern student population. Despite these appeals to democratic and Christian principles, the authors steered a middle-of-the-road path on the issue of race. This ideological neutrality was most notable in the section on inter-ethnic relations. In this section, the South was described as having a bi-racial caste system which influenced the organizational structures of its institutions. The authors did not acknowledge the social inequities which resulted from a racial caste system. It was suggested timidly that some attention should be paid by educators to the possibility of "restrictions and discriminations" which might have an economic impact on the region's social progress. The section concluded with a typical 1940's appeal of

Southern white and African-American liberals to principles of goodwill. While the educational article was limited in its sociological depth, it provided a useful example of the interdisciplinary scope of Jones' scholarship and the strong impact of the assimilationist influences through the discipline's liberal orientation on second-generation African-American sociologists' work. Like Thompson, his writings spanned a galaxy of ideas and themes. This view allowed him the ability to work with whites in designing an educational curriculum as well as analyze important socio-political changes in American race relations.

Thompson's research in the sociology of education focused on an examination of the African-American students' experience. He was interested particularly in the "culturally disadvantaged" students as well as the college student. Thompson's understanding of the unique socio-cultural variables which created disadvantaged communities reflected the paternalistic condescension which Robert Washington suggests in this volume as an emergence within the African-American sociological tradition under the hegemony of white liberal ideology.[167] In a study of the "culturally disadvantaged," he examined experimental programs which were "designed to find ways of making quality education...available, appealing and estimable for all children."[168] He provided the following twelve characteristics of the socially disadvantaged children: (1) culturally deprived homes; (2) half of their homes had parental histories of alcoholism and criminality; (3) substandard and unkempt homes; (4) one fourth of children were born out of wedlock; (5) no family pride; (6) half of their homes had no male head; when the father was present, a female dominated; (7) parents did not plan children's futures; (8) parents did not teach children self-respect; (9) children were not taught aspirations; (10) children had no concept of success; (11) children suffered traumatic stresses, strains, and break-ups due to chronic illness, imprisonment, poverty, and separation; and (12) children were similar to parents.[169]

According to Thompson, the twelve characteristics were related to social class. While he agreed with studies suggesting most culturally deprived children came from "lower class families and suffer[ed] the same degree and kind of deprivation," he believed "the concept social class... divide[d] society into large, heterogeneous segments [which had] limited value as an instrument with which [to] study specific degrees and kinds of deprivations that influence[d] the lives, behavior and attitudes of individuals."[170] His ability to discern the individual distinctiveness of the culturally disadvantaged was highlighted in his discussion of the major ideal type of "different social worlds within the generalized lower class."[171]

He suggested four social worlds existed in the African-American community: (1) the matriarchy; (2) gangs; (3) nuclear family; and (4) marginality. In each social world, the experiences of individuals were shaped by their familial structure. He reported the female-headed family was the most prevalent, oldest, and "deeply rooted family structure" among lower-class [African-Americans].[172] While Thompson never had the forum of Frazier to promote his perspective on the African-American social world, his work provided another scholarly voice to a conception of African-American culture which Washington aptly described as being derivative of an explanation of slavery in which they were "decultured."[173] Like Frazier, Thompson said the dominant role of "feminine culture" in the African-American family structure began during slavery and continued because many of the social conditions which led to its development persisted in contemporary society such as limited economic opportunities for African-American males. He believed the matriarchal family structure had "two cardinal characteristics: 1) high degree of cooperation among females and 2) maleness as a symbol of distrust, disrespect and dishonor."[174] As a consequence, "girls were deprived of positive male contacts and opportunities to develop honest, creative attitudes toward maleness."[175] In his discussion of the gang social world, he found many African-American males had marginal identities; and some African-American males were misogynists who organized their lives around a "male principle" to replace their female dominated home life. For these young men, manhood was not ascribed but achieved through gang culture. Thompson described the matriarchy and gangs as two opposing world views in the African-American lower class community.[176]

Thompson's views on the lower class African-American nuclear family were based on the assumption it was structurally similar to the white middle class pattern. The only identifiable characteristics were: (1) dominance of the father and (2) ethnocentrism. Consequently, the African-American lower class nuclear families provided very "limited individuality" due to its extreme ethnocentrism.

The marginal social world was inhabited by individuals rather than families. Among the various types of marginal individuals were people who "broke away from some distinct social world" and those "who never quite achieved any stable self-identity."[177] Thompson attributed marginality to "a series of conflicting psychological pulls from two or more diverse social worlds."[178] He described   several methods used by marginals to deal with "their identity anxieties," i.e., "engag[ing] in vain efforts to synthesize certain social values that are basically inconsistent" and "renunciat[ing] all previous self-identities; a total uprooting of personal ties."[179]

Thompson's discussion of lower class African-Americans' social worlds had particular relevance in examination of African-American students from culturally disadvantaged backgrounds. In his studies of African-American students, he highlighted the universality rather than unique racial characteristics of the population. This was especially true of his studies on college students.

In his work on higher education, he gave a description of the African-American private colleges as institutions which provided students with training that emphasized universal social values.[180] He found the private African-American college was unlike the private white college which mainly catered to elite white Americans. While the private African-American colleges had been in the forefront of African-American higher education in the past, African-American higher education was not an educational process designed for the privileged.

Thompson described the private African-American college as suffering from the encroachment of white colleges and universities and public African-American colleges and universities on its most capable faculty members and recruiting their most talented African-American student prospects. According to Thompson, the private African-American colleges were relinquishing some of their historical role as the only alternative for a gifted African-American student. The advent of the 1964 Civil Rights Act changed the character of the African-American college student population.

Thompson found private African-American colleges still had very talented students but none on the proportion of past years. He discovered the academic programs of private African-American colleges were quite flexible and faculty members were given more freedom to exercise their interests than anywhere in academia. He saw this as both a help and hindrance in preparing African-American students for graduate study and careers.

The students in Thompson's study came from economically poor families. He also found a number of the students were poorly prepared for college. The private African-American colleges had high faculty turnover rates. Faculties were composed of a large white percentage. The administrators of most private African-American colleges were changed recently to African-American men. These men had a lot of power over their colleges and were chosen by their college board of trustees. They were selected because of their corporate image. Many of the college presidents had advanced from the ranks of the college business manager.

Thompson found the private African-American college boards of trustees were composed usually of white majorities with the exception of African-American religious denominational institutions.   Most trustees were over forty years old and resided in non-Southern states. The trustees, like the African-American college administrators and faculty, were interested mainly in the college's financial solvency. Thompson concluded the African-American colleges' future depended on their ability to maintain a high academic caliber and obtain financial stability.   Thompson's work on African-American colleges was purely descriptive.   It echoed an earlier generation's scholarship on African-Americans by African-Americans with little reflexive tension found in the discussion.   This pattern of scholarship was similar to Jones' descriptive studies in political science and history.

Jones and the Myrdal Study: His Views on African-American History and Southern Politics

Jones' views on Southern history and politics were highlighted in a memorandum prepared for Gunnar Myrdal's Carnegie funded research on American race relations.   Myrdal's research resulted in the classic work, *An American Dilemma*.   The Jones memorandum, "Negroes in Atlanta," was prepared in 1940.   In a descriptive study of African-American life in Atlanta, Georgia, he had a threefold purpose: (1) to describe the political status of African-Americans; (2) to describe the activities of African-American protest and civic organizations, and interracial groups; and (3) to discuss the African-American leadership of the city.

His discussion of Atlanta's African-American community began with an historical overview of the segregationist views held by leading white Georgia politicians and other racist demagogues such as Eugene Talmadge (b. 1884, d. 1947) and Tom Watson (b. 1856, d. 1922). According to Jones, the racist populist spirit of Tom Watson continued to be a potent force in Georgia politics ten years after his death.   The disarray of white Georgia politics after Watson's departure left the state as a one-party political entity controlled by the Democratic Party.   The Democratic Party used advantageously the state's form of political government.

By using the county unit system in which each county was entitled to twice as many votes in the State Convention as it had representatives in the lower house of the Georgia General Assembly, any political candidate such as governor and supreme court judges who received a majority of one in a county was the beneficiary of an entire county's vote. Thus, counties controlled Georgia politics during the period. The county officers and several local lawyers were dubbed by Jones as the "Court House Gangs."[181]

The Court House Gangs in local counties were linked by marriage, familial ties as well as business. They often had complete sway over local elections. Since the white primaries were a part of electoral politics, the Court House Gangs were exclusively white political machines who limited participation in the political process to their cronies.[182] The backdrop of the Court House Gangs' activities was used by Jones to mark the distinctions of Atlanta and Fulton County government. He highlighted the importance of job patronage as part of the city's and county's political process.[183] He described Atlanta as a vibrant and dynamic "commercial and financial" center which failed to garner local wealth commensurate to its other commercial ventures.[184] In his opinion, its wealth was generated from "foreign capital and outside control."[185] This characteristic of 1940's Atlanta made the city lack a "high degree of interest in civic life." With a large number of people failing to register to vote or participating in the city's politics, the city had an ineffectual government.[186]

Since the city had an ineffectual mayor-council form of government, the city's mayor "exercise[d] almost no power or control of city affairs."[187] Although he had appointment powers, the council had majority voting power over his vetoes. This situation placed Atlanta's mayor in the precarious predicament of depending on his personal influence to advance his political interests. He used his appointments to wield influence.[188] While the state did not keep adequate racial employment records, African-Americans received few political appointments.[189] Similarly, the Fulton County five member board of commissioners had limited power over county affairs beyond its appropriations.[190] The redistricting split the African-American population.[191]

The racial dynamics of the city/county ineffectiveness was not missed on Jones. He reported the city council consisted of eighteen members, i.e., two elected from six councilmanic wards and one from six aldermanic wards. The city council's composition was changed as a result of redistricting. The number of wards was reduced from thirteen to six. Although African-Americans made a numerical majority in only one of the six new wards, the Jim Crow era influenced the election patterns. Consequently, African-Americans were not elected to the city council.   Despite the fact two wards in the pre-1937 redistricting had numerical African-American majorities, Jones found no direct evidence of racial gerrymandering as the basis for the reduction in the council member numbers.[192]   The African-American elected political officials' absence was reported in a city where the African-American population's growth exceeded the white population, 43.4% to 30.8%.[193]   Yet, the city failed to expand segregated services to fit the growing community.   The city's recreational, cultural, educational, and medical facilities were inadequate for the African-American community.   In some instances, the inequities were so severe that whites acknowledged the problem such as the overcrowding in the African-American wing of Grady Hosptial which resulted in a five to six month delay in female operations or the presence of   only one African-American public high school.   The city's expenditures on education were disproportionately in favor of whites, i. e., $91.27 per white pupil versus $29.77 per African-American pupil.[194]

Although the African-American vote was diminished through redistricting,   the poll tax, and yearly registration, Jones claimed eligible African-American voters shared whites' political apathy.   He gave five reasons for African-American political apathy: (1) the exclusivity of the white one party system; (2) the poll tax with its cumulative features; (3) African-American clergy's failure to support political action; (4) the African-American intelligentsia's lack of leadership; and (5) the lack of organization within the African-American community.[195]

Jones reported the African-American political apathy was exacerbated by the one-party control of the state's politics by an all-white Democratic Party.   The state's Republican Party consisted of a "cabal" which "was revived every four years for the express purpose of electing a lily white group to attend the National Convention."[196]   The rise of Democrats in the region's politics eliminated the influence of the Republican cabal in 1937.[197]   The exception to African-American political apathy was found in the development of a Republican organization, Young Men's Republican Club (YMRC).   The YMRC was an Atlanta based organization with supporters around the state.   Its leaders included prominent citizens.   Some YMRC members made a public challenge of the racism found in the state's Republican Party during an interracial meeting.   In time, the YMRC became the "only continuously functioning" Republican Party in Georgia.[198]

In addition to the YMRC, John Wesley Dobbs (b. 1882, d. 1961) led the Atlanta Civic and Political League (CPL).   Although Dobbs was a leader of an influential African-American fraternal order, Jones believed he "lack[ed] an understanding of the complex problems besetting [African-Americans in Atlanta]."[199] Despite Dobb's relative degree of political sophistication, the CPL launched an unsuccessful mass voter registration effort. After its failure, he alienated some segments of the African-American community by verbally attacking it "for a lack of interest in their own political future."[200]

In Jones' opinion, the YMRC and CPL were part of the problem associated with the lack of "a well-organized, continuously functioning mechanism for the promotion of civic responsibility."[201] He hoped some of the African American organizations would have a permanent presence within the community.

He reported three types of African-American organizations in 1940's Atlanta regarding political status. They were: (1) organizations which were strictly racial in membership and whose programs were primarily political; (2) bi-racial organizations whose programs and attack were along political, social and economic lines; and (3) organizations which were racial in membership and political in purpose, but which sought to work within the already existing party.[202]

The CPL was reported as an example of the first type. With the purpose of promoting civic interest and creating an electorate to secure political equality for African-Americans, it claimed a 2,500 membership base. Jones disputed this claim and suggested an accurate count of CPL's membership would have been closer to 1,000 members of whom only a small number actively participated in the group. He described it as a non-partisan group with "New Deal" sympathies. Its greatest accomplishment was a successful fight to defeat a 1938 bond election. The CPL's strategies included: a mass meeting; publishing and distributing pamphlets; and providing transportation for voters.[203] A counterpart to the CPL was the Woman's Civic Club. The second type of organization was represented in mainstream civil rights organizations such as the National Association for the Advancement of Colored People (NAACP) and the Urban League. The third type of organization was represented in the YMRC.

Although Atlanta contained reportedly 200 African-American churches with over 15,000 members in the 1940's, Jones said there was "almost complete absence of a social program in the churches of Atlanta."[204] In Jones' opinion, the absence of ministers' political activity was due to their placing "more emphasis upon the life of the hereafter than upon present conditions."[205]

According to Jones, the political disfranchisement of Atlanta's African-American community was a direct consequence of a white

Georgia political campaign strategy which used anti-African-American rhetoric. He suggested anti-African-American rhetoric was a part of local, state, and national campaigns within the state. It was most effective in rural communities. Jones suggested "that a candidate's fitness for office [was] measured in large part by his hatred for [African-Americans]" in many rural communities."[206] Consequently, the Atlanta African-American community of the 1940's was not able to "exercise any appreciable influence upon the [community's] political life.[207] The lack of political influence was exacerbated by the level of interracial contact. According to Jones, interracial political contact in Atlanta featured two types of white personalities: (1) whites dedicated sincerely to "a very real interest in the spread of democracy" such as the members of the Southern Conference on Human Welfare; and (2) whites who solicited African-Americans voters for "ulterior motives" such as the "lily white Republicans" who participated in the YMRC meetings.[208]

Jones said the lack of African-American political influence resulted in a racist climate which was reflected in the popular culture. He highlighted three aspects of the racist climate: (1) arbitrary enforcement of an archaic curfew law against African-American citizens; (2) the lack of African-Americans as policemen and firemen; and (3) the use of racial epithets by local officials in daily commerce.[209] Despite their exclusion from state politics, the African-American community was not receptive to overtures from radical groups. Jones reported the Communist party attempted unsuccessfully to attract African-Americans through the distribution of literature and interracial gatherings with white women as lures. While they were unsuccessful, their presence was sufficient enough to contribute to the "red baiting" of all interracial movements by southern segregationists.[210]

Jones concluded the overview of Atlanta's African-American community by suggesting it maintained a political system based on Georgia's unique cultural pattern. In his opinion, this cultural pattern was derived from the restrictive "workings of the political parties and the [segregationist] conduct of [officials in] state, county and city governments."[211] It was part of a conflict between rural and urban white Georgia voters. With the county unit system providing an advantage to the rural white voters, the urban white voters were subjected to the political will of rural whites. He reported white voters were linked by the doctrine of white supremacy. Without an ideological link, Jones reported African-Americans found it difficult to engage in political action as a unified group. His examination and commentary of state racial politics during the period reflect the three key aspects of national political racism which Steve Valocchi highlighted as a part of the New Deal: 1) the key to the South's power in Congress lay in the Constitutional compromises that gave white Southerners disproportionate electoral power and in the realigning elections of the late nineteenth century that eliminated party competition and accelerated the political disenfranchisment of blacks in the South; 2) the concentration of blacks in the South and their subsequent disenfranchisement were due to racially biased policies and practices of the federal government which constrained blacks geographical mobility and economic emancipation; and 3) the political machines in the urban North which provided the only vehicle for black political mobilization developed practices that limited the voting power of and patronage for blacks who were beginning to migrate in large numbers to certain Northern cities in the early twentieth century.[212] Although he softened his critique of the dire Atlanta situation by providing optimism about the possibility of a changing community in future years, it still was a direct attack on the blatant racism in Southern New Deal politics.[213]

While the preparation of the memorandum was done independently of Myrdal's influence, the inclusion of the document in a subsequent publication highlights the significance of Jones' tone regarding the Myrdal perspective. Despite his severe comments regarding the strength and persistence of segregation in Georgia politics, Jones' final comments echoed the social morality and Myrdal's liberal equalitarian optimism. According to Robert Washington, Myrdal's commitment to liberal values and emphasis on the moral dimension of the race problem were an important part of *An American Dilemma*. Thus, Jones' memorandum placed emphasis on critical themes present in mainstream views of American race relations.

Jones Explores Reconstruction History

Jones' socio-historical analysis of the Atlanta political scene in the 1940's was a part of an inquiry into African-American history which surfaced in a few publications. With a master's degree in history, Jones maintained a keen interest in African-American history. One of his earliest publications appeared in the *Negro History Bulletin*. His essay discussed the prominent African-American Reconstruction congressman, Jefferson Frederick Long (b. 1836). Jones' description of Long's life was more than a simple statement of details. He attempted to highlight the man's conviction by stressing the difficulties which he encountered in his bid for a congressional seat. Long's brief stint in

Congress was recalled through his speeches on the House floor. Jones cited newspaper commentaries about Long as a method of corroborating facts. The use of Long's own words gave the reader a sense of intimacy regarding the brief historical account of his life. Jones' inquiry into African-American history was a small part of an interdisciplinary perspective which looked at social change.[214]

Conclusion

Thompson and Jones made unique contributions to the discipline by providing distinctive perspectives. While one would have to agree with Morgan's analysis of African-American sociological scholarship as mostly descriptive during the period of their greatest productivity, Thompson's and Jones' descriptive approaches to exploring important social phenomena provided a bench mark for contemporary research.[215] They examined elements of the African-American experience with an analytical perspective which focused on the community's evolution in a modern world. As William Phillips (b. 1923, d. 1992) suggested regarding their contemporary, Tilman C. Cothran (b. 1919, d. 1994), "he [was] not an innovator methodologically, but he [was] an empiricist."[216] Their work in the areas of race and civil rights highlighted this unique methodological flexibility.

It was this very flexibility which contributed to their greatest weakness. Their research appeared to lack analytical depth. This weakness may have been a result of the analytical quality of the major theoretical models applied to the study of race relations. As Morgan suggested, second generation Black sociologists' research reflected a descriptive tone which was indicative of African-American sociologists who were schooled in the [popular] caste and class tradition. According to Morgan, "[the] caste theory is accommodative and implies that [African-Americans] must change if they are to become acceptable to whites, the dominant group."[217] Thompson discussed the caste perspective in several papers.[218] Jones and Thompson were influenced greatly by the caste and class school. Since many of their publications appeared during the height of the caste and class school's influence, it appeared in some of their work, especially Jones' collaborative article on southern school curriculum development.

While it is difficult to show a clear link between the caste perspective and Thompson's work, his discussions of the culturally disadvantaged children lean heavily in that direction. Yet, Jones and Thompson were not proponents of the caste school. Like many scholars of the second generation, the caste school of thought was viewed as an interesting method of social investigation on American race relations.

Their research described patterns of African-American behavior and offered suggestions for research foci; but they provided few explanations of the social causes for problems in the African-American community. This characteristic of their research may be a result of what Robert Washington described as "the professional constraints on [early] employment opportunities and theoretical perspectives of [African-American] sociologists which prevented [them] from locating a paradigm that would have resonated with [their] sense of estrangement."[219] Thompson and Jones made personal choices about the type of analytical discourse in which they engaged regarding race. This choice may have reflected their own personal histories with the discipline.

Thompson's longtime association with Dillard may have had some impact on the descriptive nature of his research. As Scott suggested regarding the nature of all African-American college social science programs, the departmental structure of Dillard was far less rigidly defined than small white universities.[220] Sociology was subsumed under the social science division. The social science division incorporated various disciplines as well as pre-professional training programs. Like most African-American colleges and universities, research funding was limited at Dillard. The lack of funds influenced his work. He used archival material, personal observations, and interviews as his major sources for data. These were the research tools of a person with limited access to funding. Throughout the 1960's and 1970's, Thompson served as a consultant for a variety of agencies such as the United States Department of Education and Ford Foundation. It is not clear whether Thompson's articulation of what Washington described as the "New Deal ideological agenda" made him an appealing consultant in the eyes of 1960's white liberals. However, he received only limited philanthropic support for research from agencies such as the Ford Foundation. Similarly, Jones' employment at OWU provided limited research support. Most importantly, Jones' role as the only African-American scholar in a white community forced him to devote a critical amount of intellectual capital in race relations activities for local communities. Despite this major shortcoming, their work provided a substantive basis for the work of future scholars.

Unlike Cayton and other second generation African-American sociologists who were influenced by the Chicago School, Thompson questioned the assimilationist myth which permeated sociological research. It is not clear whether Thompson's views reflected his

Columbia training or represented an intellectual departure from the strong currents of the times. During his Columbia years, the sociology department was noted for its study of social phenomena by examining individual behavior or attitudes as the dependent variables to be explained. The Columbia sociologists such as Lazarsfeld were interested primarily in individual responses to mass stimuli.[221] Since most of Thompson's research had the community or an organization as the focus, the impact of the "new" 1950's Columbia perspective is debatable. His work reflected the methodological focus of Columbia prior to the arrival of Lazarsfeld.[222] Thompson's research incorporated the combination of a community study which mixed some of the new sample survey methods with the traditional Chicago School approach. While the Chicago School's methodological approach was a part of his sociological perspective, his questions regarding the assimilationist model were very atypical of the Chicago School.

His acceptance of the Chicago School meant he acknowledged its fundamental interpretation of the social structure. Andrew Abbott described the Chicago School's interpretation as follows:

> The Chicago writers believed social structure to be a set of temporary stabilities in a process of flux and determination. The social world was made up of actors mutually determining each other in ways sometimes deliberate and sometimes quite unforeseen. But the cornerstone of the Chicago vision was location, for location in social time and space channeled the play of reciprocal determination. All social facts were located in particular physical places and in particular social structures. They were also located within the temporal logic of one or more processes of succession, assimilation, conflict, and so on. This meant that the Chicago vision was of a social structure embedded in time, a structure in process.[223]

Throughout Thompson's work, one can find the Chicago School's notion of social structural location. His studies on African-American leadership in New Orleans, African-American college professors, African-American colleges, social movements in the 1960's, and lower-income youth placed emphasis on the social location of the participants in society, especially in relationships to institutions and organizations. However, his writings on the African-American experience were his best applications of the Chicago School concept of location.

Thompson's later work attempted to offer sociological scholarship a new context for inquiry, the African-American experience. The use of the African-American experience was the beginning of Thompson's

intellectual effort to provide a paradigm that was useful in developing a theoretical interpretation of African-Americans. This was his closest attempt to veer away from doing "sociology by an African-American" to constructing an African-American sociological framework that Watson required of "black sociology."
His paradigm consisted of four levels. They were:

Level 1
> *The extent to which the [African-American] presence has influenced the ideology, structure and function of specific social organizations, movements, and ultimately, the overall nature of the American social system.*[224]

Level 2
> *The concept of the [African-American] experience should be defined so that it would include experiences resulting from conditions imposed upon [African-Americans] by the direct and indirect actions of white (or non-African-American) individuals, groups, institutions, and special social power arrangements.*[225]

Level 3
> *The [African-American] experience includes the nature and consequences of responses [African-Americans] have made and continue to make, to their unique condition in American society.*[226]

Level 4
> *The [African-American] experience includes contributions [African-Americans] have made, and continue to make to their own survival and progress, and to the enrichment of the culture of the wider society of which they are an integral part.*[227]

The "four distinct levels of the [African-American] experience" were suggested as tools for conducting empirical and theoretical research based on his assumption that "to understand the nature and meaning of [African-American] contributions must be based on a realistic understanding of subcultures in American society."[228] In keeping with his "liberal-integrationist" perspective, he believed that "indigenous subcultures in this society tend to vary from that of the dominant group to about the same degree as that group experiences social isolation from the dominant group."[229] In his opinion, African-American subculture was a "variation on a major, common cultural continuum or arc."[230] He believed the basic methodological aspects of studying African-Americans were twofold (1) the country had always been biracial; and (2) African-Americans and whites had always interacted. Thus, Thompson believed interracial interaction was the context for the study of race.

He suggested valid research on African-Americans must employ three distinct categories (1) the extent to which [African-Americans] have selected and elaborated otherwise neglected traits, themes, and ideas in American culture; (2) the extent to which [African-Americans] have selected common traits from the general culture and have transformed, reshaped, and adapted them to serve the peculiar needs and goals of their community; and (3) the extent to which [African-Americans] have contributed to the development of common aspects of American culture.[231]

Thompson's use of the African-American experience as a methodological paradigm for social analysis was employed in a later study on the African-American underclass. In this study, he offered "a prophetic analysis" of the African-American underclass' growing isolation which would lead to "a degree of class consciousness...developing in the [African-American] underclass."[232]

> This consciousness grows out of both the physical and psychological isolation experienced by those who are trapped, even imprisoned in the [African-American] ghetto. To them, their own limited environment with its distinct subculture is a source of whatever dignity, respect and social support available to them. Consequently, instead of removing the "invisible wall" which separates them from the outside world there seem to be deliberate efforts to reinforce this division through their esoteric dress, peculiar "Black English" and a nurturing of values they know conflict with those in our national culture.[233]

Although Key suggested Thompson's views were a part of the accommodationist/assimilationist perspective of the second generation sociologists, his queries regarding the validity of the assimilationist assumption that "every good American can get a job if he or she wanted one" and other "researchable sets of questions regarding [African-American] poverty," clearly debunk that categorization.[234] In level two of his paradigm, Thompson's research and observation of the African-American experience lead him to question such an idealistic presentation of reality.

He suggested sociologists should investigate questions regarding white support for improving African-American conditions; and sociological emphasis on the pathological elements of the African-American experience with its corollary being an explanation of African-American pathology as a derivative of the African-American community's failures. He believed the African-American experience was distinguished by conditions imposed on it "as the object of social action by whites."[235] According to Thompson, "[African-Americans] do not possess the structured authority necessary to resist or alter decisions made for them, or the ultimate consequences of these decisions."[236]

Thompson's four levels of the African-American experience provided the basis for the type of intellectual inquiry which Antonio Gramsci (b. 1891, d. 1937) encouraged Europeans to explore, i. e. intellectual work based on their unique group experiences. Gramsci's beliefs were based on his examination of the relationship of the European working-class movements to intellectuals. These intellectuals shaped their work around interpreting social processes.[237] Thompson's paradigm of the African-American experience was based on his idea that research on the African-American community should be linked to an African-American experiential methodology which highlighted working class African-American life as an interpretive dynamic. Gramscian ideas of developing a distinctive intellectual discourse may have not been his motive for introducing the four levels. However, it provided unwittingly an important tool for subsequent generations to consider in the development of "black sociology." Thompson's discussion of an experiential base for sociological inquiry demonstrated the type of intellectual flexibility which he shared with Jones. While this methodological tool was conceived as a part of Thompson's integenerationist political perspective, which was shared by Jones and others in the second generation, it provided continuity between the younger and older generations of African-American sociologists. The generational continuity came from Thompson's paradigm being a part of his articulation of a political viewpoint regarding race. Like Jones, his viewpoint reflected the moderate approach of racial negotiators from the New Deal era. Their moderation challenged the entrenched segregation of the times. With the institutional dynamics of racism continuing to have a strong influence on minority participation in the discipline, the intellectual styles of the second generation African-American sociologists gave the younger generation a critical role model for scholarship.

As second generation African-American sociologists, Thompson and Jones contributed to the African-American sociological tradition through their research and political activism. It reflected an intellectual style unique to the discipline. Despite their shortcomings, their work stands as a monument to "African-American sociology." It provided a younger generation with a clear interpretive voice regarding the changing African-American community.

Bibliography Of Selected Works By Daniel Calbert Thompson

Books

1986. *A Black Elite--A Profile of Graduates of UNCF Colleges.* Westport, CT: Greenwood Press.

1974   *Sociology of the Black Experience.*   Westport, CT: Greenwood, Press.

1973   *Private Black Colleges at the Crossroads.*   Westport, CT: Greenwood Press.

1963   *The Negro Leadership Class.*   Englewood Cliffs, NJ: Prentice Hall.

_____, John Rohrer and Monro Edmonson, editors
1960   *The Eighth Generation.* New York: Harper and Brothers, Publishers.

Thesis
1944   "The Social History of a Religious Cult." Master of Arts Thesis, Atlanta University.

Dissertation
1956   "Teachers in Negro Colleges: A Sociological Analysis." Ph.D. Dissertation, Columbia University.

Articles
1984   "Research Areas for Black Colleges." *Black Colleges and Universities--Challenges for the Future.* Antoine Garibaldi, editor. New York: Praeger.

1980   "Leadership: The Challenge of 'A More Perfect' Social Order." *Vital Speeches.*

1979   "Black Colleges: Continuing Challenges." *Phylon*, 40:
183-88.

1978   "Black College Faculty and Students: The Nature of
Their Interaction." *Black Colleges in America: Challenge, Development,
Survival*. Charles V. Willie and Ronald R. Edmonds, editors. New York:
Teachers College Press, Columbia University , pp. 180-194.

1976   "The Black Elite." *The Boule Journal*. 39: 10-18.

1975   "Radicalizing   the   Black   Church."   *Experiences,
Struggles, and Hopes of the Black Church*. James S. Gadsden, editor.
Nashville, TN: Tidings.

1973   "Caste and Negro Protest." *University English*. Volume
8.

1972   *Urban Values and the Church*. New Orleans, LA: Loyola
University Publication.

1971   *The Role of Leadership in School Desegregation*.
Washington, DC: United States Commission on Educational Resources
Information Center.

1970   "Patterns of Race Relations Leadership." *Perspectives
on Black America*. Russell Endo and William Strawbridge, editors.
Englewood Cliffs, NJ: Prentice-Hall.

1969   "The Civil Rights Movement." *In Black America:
1968 The Year of Awakening*. Pat W. Romero, editor. Washington, DC:
United Publishing Corporation.

1968   "The History of Black Americans." *Faculty Forum*.
Feature Article. Volume 46.

1968   "New Orleans and the Riot Report." *New Orleans
Magazine*. June.

1968   "Career Patterns of Teachers in Negro Colleges."
Sociology of Education: A Book of Readings. Ronald M. Pavalko, editor.
Itasca, IL: F. E. Peacock.

1968   "Cut Red Tape, Rebuild Cities." *U. S. News and World
Report*. April 22.

1967   "Teaching the Culturally Disadvantaged." *Speaking about Teaching*. Floyd Rinker, editor. New York: College Entrance Examination Board.

1966   "The New South." *The Journal of Social Issues*. 22: 7-19.

1966   "College Teacher." *Readings on Professionalization*. Donald Mills and Howard M. Vollmer, editors. Englewood Cliffs, NJ: Prentice-Hall.

1966   "Our Wasted Potential." *The Teacher and Integration*. Gertrude Noar, editor. Washington, DC: National Education Association.

1966   "The Formation of Social Attitudes." *Racial and Ethnic Relations*. Bernard E. Segal, editor. New York: Thomas Y. Crowell.

1965   "Poverty Re-examined: Old Problems, New Challenges." *Clarion Herald*. February 11.

1965   "The Rise of the Negro Protest." *Annals of the Academy of Political and Social Science*. 357: 18-29.

1965   "The Problem of Communicating with the Culturally Deprived Student." Paper presented at Harvard University, Summer Session for Advanced Study in English.

1964   "The Socio-Psychological Effects of Rejection." *The Journal of Louisiana Education Association*. September.

1964   "Negro Leadership." *Contemporary Society*. Jackson Toby, editor. New York: John Wiley and Sons.

1964   "Evaluation as a Factor in Planning: The Education of the Disadvantaged Child." *Journal of Negro Education*. 33: 333-340.

1964   "The Socio-Cultural Dimensions of Race Relations." *Proceedings of the New York University Seminar on Education and Race Relations*.

1964   "Negro Leadership." Comments in Robert Hutchins and Mortimer Adler, editors, *The Great Ideas Today*.

1963   "Race Relations--New Directions." *Proceedings of the Michigan Conference on Intergroup Relations*.

1963   "Civil Rights Leadership (An Opinion Study)," *Journal of Negro Education*. 32: 426-436.

1963   "Our Wasted Potential." *Integrating the Urban School*. Gordon J. Klopf, editor. New York: Teachers College, Columbia University.

1962   "The Formation of Social Attitudes." *American Journal of Orthopsychiatry*. 31: 74-85.

1961   *The Case for Integration*. Atlanta, Georgia: Southern Regional Council.

1961   "The Role of the Federal Courts in the Changing Status of Negroes Since World War II." *Journal of Negro Education*. 30: 94-101.

1961   "Negro Minister: Community Leader." *The Central Christian Advocate*. January.

1961   "The Role of Leadership." *The New Orleans School Crisis. A Report of the Louisiana State Advisory Committee on Civil Rights*.

1960   "Our Wasted Potential." *The Dillard Bulletin*. Volume 24.

1960   "The Problem of Faculty Morale." *Journal of Negro Education*. 29: 37-46.

1958   "Career Patterns of Teachers in Negro Colleges." *Social Forces*. 36: 270-276.

1957   "The Changing Status of Negroes in New Orleans." *The Journal of Social Science Teachers*. May.

1956   "Social Class Factors in Public School Education as Related to Desegregation." *American Journal of Orthopsychiatry*. Volume 26.

1956   "The Essential Dignity of All Labor." *The Central Christian Advocate*. September.

1956   "A Profile of Social Classes in the Negro Community." *Proceedings of the Louisiana Academy of Sciences*.

_____ and Barbara G. Thompson
1983/84 "The Black Underclass: A Continuing Saga." *The Black*

Southerner. Volume 1 & 2.

_____ Robin Williams and Oscar Cohen
1964   *Social Action and the Social Scientist.* Public Affairs
Research Center. University of Houston.

Book Reviews
1964   Review of *Negro Thought in America, 1880-1915* by
August Meier. *American Journal of Sociology.* 70: 491.

1966   Review of *An African Bourgeoisie: Race, Class, and
Politics in South Africa* by Leo Kuper. *Social Forces.* 44: 426.

1966   Review of *Dark Ghetto* by Kenneth B. Clark. *American
Journal of Sociology.* 71: 454-455.

1965   Review of *Dark Ghetto* by Kenneth B. Clark. *The
Progressive.* September. 29: 47-49.

1974   Review of *Marginality and Identity: A Colored Creole
Family Through Ten Generations* by Sister Frances Jerome Woods. *The
Journal of American History.* 61: 763-764.

Bibliography Of Selected Works By Butler A. Jones

Jones, Butler A.
1940   "A Memorandum on the Political Participation of
Negroes in Atlanta and Georgia." Prepared for the Carnegie-Myrdal Study
of the Negro in the United States.   Schomburg Center.   New York.
(Typescript)

1942   "Workers of Merit in Georgia: Jefferson F. Long." *The
Negro History Bulletin.* 5, 6: 129.

1953   "New Legal Requirements of Race Relations in the
South." *Phylon.* 13: 97-106.

1959   "The Case Is Remanded." *Social Problems.* 7: 27-34.

1961   "Introduction." Sarah Bradford, *Harriet Tubman: The
Moses of Her People.* New York: Corinth Books.

1974   "The Tradition of Sociology Teaching in Black

Colleges: The Unheralded Professionals." *Black Sociologists--Historical and Contemporary Perspectives*. James E. Blackwell and Morris Janowitz, editors. Chicago: University of Chicago Press.

Mary L. Anderson, Robert E. Cureton, Newell D. Eason, Butler A. Jones, Evelyn Lawlah, Charity Mance, Albert E. Manley, James E. Pierce, Jennie B. Ramsey and John T. Robinson
1945   "Improving Education for Social-Civic Competence in the Southern States." *The Southern Association Quarterly*. 9, 1: 90-109.

Thesis
1938   "The Diplomatic Relations of the United States and Chile, 1810-1823." Master of Arts. Atlanta University.

Dissertation
1955   "Law and Social Change: A Study of the Impact of New Legal Requirements Affecting Equality of Educational Opportunities for Negroes Upon Certain Customary Official Behaviors in the South, 1938-1952." Doctor of Philosophy. New York University.

References
Anderson, Mary L., Robert E. Cureton, Newell D. Eason, Butler A. Jones, Evelyn Lawlah, Charity Mance, Albert E. Manley, James E. Pierce, Jennie B. Ramsey and John T. Robinson. 1945. "Improving Education for Social-Civic Competence in the Southern States." *The Southern Association Quarterly*. 9, 1: 90-109.

Armstrong, Edward G. 1979. "Black Sociology and Phenomenological Sociology." *The Sociological Quarterly*. 20: 387-97.

Aurbach, Herbert. 1997. Telephone Interview. January 7.

Banks, William M. 1996. *Black Intellectuals--Race and Responsibility in American Life*. New York: W. W. Norton and Company.

Bell, Caryn Cossé. 1997. *Revolution, Romanticism, and the Afro-Creole Protest Tradition in Louisiana, 1718-1868*. Baton Rouge, LA: Louisiana State University Press.

Black, Albert W. Jr. 1976. "Whose Interests Are Served by Black Sociologists." *The Black Sociologist*. 5: 4-6.

Blackwell, James E. 1981. *Mainstreaming Outsiders, The Production of*

Black Professionals. New York: General Hall.

_____ 1974. "Role Behavior in a Corporate Structure: Black Sociologists in the ASA." *Black Sociologists--Historical and Contemporary Perspectives*. James E. Blackwell and Morris Janowitz, editors. Chicago: University of Chicago Press.

_____ _ and Morris Janowitz. 1974. *Black Sociologists-- Historical and Contemporary Perspectives*. Chicago: University of Chicago.

Blasi, Anthony J. 1997. "Using Pragmatist Sociology for Praxis: The Career of Charles H. Parrish, Jr." Paper presented at the Association of Social and Behavioral Scientists meeting, Nashville, Tennesssee.

Bond, Horace Mann. 1972. *Black American Scholars: A Study of Their Beginnings*. Detroit: Balamp.

Bowser, Benjamin P. 1981. "The Contribution of Blacks to Sociological Knowledge: A Problem of Theory and Role to 1950." *Phylon*. 42: 180-193.

Bracey, John, August Meier and Elliott Rudwick. 1971. *The Black Sociologists: The First Half Century*. Belmont, California: Wadsworth Publishing Company.

Buckley, Gail Lumet. 1986. *The Hornes--An American Family*. New York: Alfred A. Knopf.

Butler, Addie Louise Joyner. 1977. *The Distinctive Black College-- Talladega, Tuskegee, and Morehouse*. Metuchen, NJ: The Screcrow Press, Inc.

Bunche, Ralph J. 1973. *The Political Status of the Negro in the Age of FDR*. Dewey W. Grantham, editor. Chicago: University of Chicago Press.

Burns, George W. 1960. Letter to Butler A. Jones. May 2. Butler A. Jones Papers. The Western Reserve Historical Society. Cleveland, OH.

_____ 1960. Letter to Butler A. Jones. January 27. Butler A. Jones Papers. The Western Reserve Historical Society. Cleveland, OH.

_____ 1958. Letter to Butler A. Jones. January 24. Butler A. Jones Papers. The Western Reserve Historical Society. Cleveland, OH.

Carson, Clayborne. 1992. *The Papers of Martin Luther King, Jr., Volume*

I: Called to Serve, January 1929-June 1951. Berkeley, CA: University of California Press.

Cobb, Henry E. 1976. "Mission, Status, Problems, and Priorities of Black Graduate Schools." *Minority Group Participation in Graduate Education.* Washington, DC: National Academy of Sciences.

Coleman, James S. 1990. "Columbia in the 1950s," *Authors of Their Own Lives--Intellectual Autobiographies by Twenty American Sociologists.* Bennet M. Berger, editor. Berkeley, CA: University of California Press.

_____ 1990. "Robert K. Merton as Teacher," *Robert K. Merton--Consensus and Controversy.* London: Falmer Press.

Conyers, James. E. 1992. "The Association of Black Sociologists: A Descriptive Account from an Insider." *The American Sociologist.* 23: 49-55.

_____ 1986. "Who's Who Among Black Doctorates in Sociology." *Sociological Focus.* 19: 77-93.

_____ 1968. "Negro Doctorates in Sociology: A Social Portrait." *Phylon.* 29: 209-223.

_____ and Joseph W. Scott. 1992. *A Brief History of the Association of Black Sociologists, 1970-1990.* Privately published by the Association of Black Sociologists.

Cox, Oliver C. 1951. "The Leadership of Booker T. Washington." *Social Forces.* 30: 91-97.

Cromwell, Adelaide M. 1994. *The Other Brahmins--Boston's Black Upper Class, 1750-1950.* Fayetteville, AR: University of Arkansas Press.

Davidson, Douglas. 1977. "Black Sociologists: A Critical Analysis." *Contributions to Black Studies.* 1: 44-51.

Davis, Walter L. 1979. "Predicting Minority Student Performance in the First Medical School Year." *The Journal of the National Medical Association.* 71: 661-664.

Dent, Tom. 1997. *Southern Journey--A Return to the Civil Rights Movement.* New York: William Morrow and Company.

Edgcomb, Gabrielle Simon. 1993. *From Swastika to Jim Crow: Refugee Scholars at Black Colleges.* Malabar, FL: Krieger Publishing Company.

Epps, Edgar. 1997. Telephone Interview. January 7.

Edwards, G. Franklin. 1959. *The Negro Professional Class.* New York: Free Press of Glencoe.

Fairclough, Adam. 1995. *Race and Democracy--The Civil Rights Struggle in Louisiana, 1915-1972.* Athens, GA: University of Georgia Press.

Ficken, Clarence E. 1956. Letter to Butler A. Jones. January 9. Butler A. Jones Papers. The Western Reserve Historical Society. Cleveland, OH.

Franklin, John Hope. 1988. *Race and History--Selected Essays, 1938-1988* . Baton Rouge, LA: Louisiana State University Press.

Gatewood, Willard B. 1990. *Aristocrats of Color--The Black Elite, 1880-1920.* Bloomington, IN: Indiana University Press.

Gramsci, Antonio. 1977. *Selections from the Prison Notebooks.* Quintin Hoare and Geoffrey N. Smith, editors and translators. New York: International Publishers.

Gray, Fred. 1995. *Bus Ride to Justice--Changing the System by the System, The Life and Works of Fred Gray.* Montgomery, AL: The Black Belt Press.

Green, Harry Washington. 1946. *Holders of Doctorates Among American Negroes.* Boston: Meador Publishing Company.

Haskins, James. 1984. *Nat King Cole.* New York: Stein and Day.

Hines, Ralph H. 1967. "The Negro Scholar's Contribution to Pure and Applied Sociology." *Journal of Social and Behavioral Sciences.* 8: 30-35.

Hunter, Herbert M. and Sameer Y. Abraham. 1987. *Race, Class, and the World System--The Sociology of Oliver C. Cox.* New York: Monthly Review Press.

Jackson, Jacquelyne Johnson. 1996. "Obituaries--Charles Goode Gomillion, 1900-1995." *The Southern Sociologist.* 27: 33-34.

_____ 1995. "Charles Goode Gomillion, Ph.D.: A Mighty Social Force." Paper presented at the Southern Sociological Society.

_____ 1974. "Black Female Sociologists."

Black Sociologists--Historical and Contemporary Perspectives. James E. Blackwell and Morris Janowitz, editors. Chicago: University of Chicago Press.

_____ 1972. "Black Professional Organizations: A Case Study." *The Journal of Afro-American Issues.* 1: 75-91.

Johnson, Guy Benton and Guion Griffis Johnson. 1980. *Research in Service to Society--The First Fifty Years of the Institute for Research in Social Science at the University of North Carolina.* Chapel Hill, NC: University of North Carolina Press.

Johnson, Tobe. 1971. "The Black College as System." *Daedalus.* 100: 798-812.

Jones, Butler A. 1997. Telephone Interview. January 25.

_____ 1993. Telephone Interview. March 20.

_____ 1974. "The Tradition of Sociology Teaching in Black Colleges: The Unheralded Professionals." *Black Sociologists--Historical and Contemporary Perspectives.* James E. Blackwell and Morris Janowitz, editors. Chicago: University of Chicago Press.

_____ 1964. Letter to Mr. Schultz, R. E. Glendening, George Wolfe, Grover Gatton, Edward Flahive and Henry Chaney. January 9. Butler A. Jones Papers. The Western Reserve Historical Society. Cleveland, OH.

_____ 1953. "New Legal Requirements of Race Relations in the South. *Phylon.* 23: 97-106.

_____ 1940a. "Workers of Merit in Georgia--Jefferson Frederick Long." *Negro History Bulletin.* 5: 129.

_____ 1940b. "Negroes in Atlanta." Report prepared for Ralph J. Bunche. Atlanta University.

_____ N. d. "The Functions of Social Science Teaching in Negro Colleges." Unpublished paper. Butler A. Jones Papers. The Western Reserve Historical Society. Cleveland, OH.

Jones, Maxine D. and Joe M. Richardson. 1990. *Talladega College--The First Century.* Tuscaloosa, AL: University of Alabama Press.

Kennedy, Randall L. 1989. "Racial Critiques of Legal Academia." *Harvard Law Review.* 102: 1745-1819.

Keith, Verna M. and Cedric Herring. 1991. "Skin Tone and Stratification in the Black Community." *American Journal of Sociology.* 97: 760-778.

Key, R. Charles. 1978. "Society and Sociology: The Dynamics of Black Sociological Negation." *Phylon.* 39: 35-48.

Killian, Lewis M. 1994. *Black and White: Reflections of a White Southern Sociologist.* Dix Hills, NJ: General Hall.

Kilson, Martin. 1993. "Harvard and the Small-Towner." *Blacks at Harvard--A Documentary History of African-American Experience at Harvard and Radcliffe.* Werner Sollors, Caldwell Titcomb, and Thomas A. Underwood, editors. New York: New York University Press.

Kilson, Martin. 1986. "Harvard and the Small-Towner." *Varieties of Black Experience at Harvard--An Anthology.* Werner Sollors, Thomas A. Underwood, and Caldwell Titcomb, editors. Cambridge, MA: Harvard University, Department of Afro-American Studies.

King, Martin Luther. 1980. *Daddy King--An Autobiography.* New York: William Morrow and Company.

Ladner, Joyce. 1973. *The Death of White Sociology.* New York: Random House.

Lewis, David Levering. 1993. *W. E. B. DuBois--Biography of a Race, 1868-1919.* New York: Henry Holt.

McBride, David and Monroe H. Little. 1981. "The Afro-American Elite, 1930-1940: A Historical and Statistical Profile." *Phylon.* 42: 105-119.

Manning, Kenneth. 1983. *Black Apollo of Science--The Life of Ernest Everett Just.* New York: Oxford Press.

Meier, August. 1992. *A White Scholar and the Black Community, 1945-1965--Essays and Reflections.* Amherst, MA: University of Massachusetts Press.

_____ and Elliott Rudwick. 1986. *Black History and the Historical Profession, 1915-1980.* Urbana, IL: University of Illinois Press.

Mommsen, Kent G. 1974. "Black Doctorates in American Higher Education: A Cohort Analysis." *Journal of Social and Behavioral*

Scientists. 20: 101-117.

_____ 1973. "On Recruiting Black Sociologists." *The American Sociologist*. 8: 107-116.

_____ 1973. "Professionalism and the Racial Context of Career Patterns Among Black American Doctorates: A Note on the 'Brain Drain' Hypothesis." *Journal of Negro Education*. 42: 191-204.

Morgan, Gordon. 1994. *Tilman C. Cothran--Second Generation Sociologist*. Bristol, IN: Wyndham Hall Press.

_____ 1973. "First Generation Black Sociologists and Theories of Social Change." *Journal of Social and Behavioral Sciences*. 19: 106-119.

Myrdal, Gunnar. 1944. *An American Dilemma--The Negro Problem and Modern Democracy, Volume I*. New York: Harper and Row.

Natanson, Maurice. 1962. *Literature, Philosophy and the Social Sciences*. The Hague: Martinus Nijhoff.

Norrell, Robert J. 1985. *Reaping the Whirlwind: The Civil Rights Movement in Tuskegee*. New York: Alfred A. Knopf.

Pearson, Willie. 1985. *Black Scientists, White Society, and Colorless Science: A Study of Universalism in American Science*. Millwood, NY: Associated Faculty Press.

Perkins, Linda M. 1996. "For the Good of the Race: Married African-American Academics, A Historical Perspective." Unpublished working draft to appear in *Academic Couples: Problems and Promises*, Marianne A. Ferber and Jane W. Loeb, editors. Urbana, IL: University of Illinois Press, forthcoming).

Phillips, William M. Jr. 1982. "Doing Sociology with Tilman C. Cothran: Some Reminiscences." *Phylon*. 42: 249-252.

Pilawky, Monte. 1995. "Dan Thompson: Scholar, Activist, Mentor, Friend." Paper presented at Southern Sociological Society.

Pitts v. Board of Trustees of DeWitt School District. No. 1. 84 F. Supp. 975. Eastern District of Arkansas. 1949.

Platt, Anthony M. 1991. *E. Franklin Frazier Reconsidered*. New Brunswick, NJ: Rutgers University Press.

298   *Confronting the American Dilemma of Race*

Pomerantz, Gary M. 1996. *Where Peachtree Meets Sweet Auburn--The Saga of Two Families and the Making of Atlanta.* New York: Scribner.

Raushenbush, Winifred. 1979. *Robert E. Park--Biography of a Sociologist.* Durham, NC: Duke University Press.

Robbins, Richard. 1996. *Sidelines Activist--Charles S. Johnson and the Struggle for Civil Rights.* Jackson, MS: University Press of Mississippi.

Rogers, Kim Lacy. 1993. *Righteous Lives--Narratives of the New Orleans Civil Rights Movement.* New York: New York University Press.

Schweninger, Loren. 1990. "Prosperous Blacks in the South, 1790-1880." *American Historical Review.* 95: 31-56.

Scott, Nolvert P. 1976. "On the Advantage Arising from the Incorporation of the Caucus of Black Sociologists." *The Black Sociologist.* 5: 6-7.

Scott, Will. 1979. "A Perspective on Perspective." *The American Sociologist.* 14: 91-95.

Sewell, William H. 1992. "Some Observations and Reflections on the Role of Women and Minorities in the Democratization of the American Sociological Association, 1905-1990." *The American Sociologist.* 23: 56-62.

Simpson, Ida Harper. 1985. *Fifty Years of the Southern Sociological Society--Change and Continuity in a Professional Society.* Athens, GA: University of Georgia Press.

Smith, Charles U. and Lewis Killian. 1974. "Black Sociologists and Social Protest." *Black Sociologists--Historical and Contemporary Perspectives.* James E. Blackwell and Morris Janowitz, editors. Chicago: University of Chicago Press.

Stanfield, John H. 1985. *Philanthropy and Jim Crow in American Social Science.* Westport, CT: Greenwood Press.

Sztompka, Piotr. 1986. *Robert K. Merton--An Intellectual Profile.* New York: St. Martin's Press.

Taper, Bernard. 1962. *The Tuskegee Gerrymander Case--Gomillion versus Lightfoot.* New York: McGraw-Hill.

Thompson, Barbara Guillory. 1990. "In Memoriam--Daniel Calbert

Thompson, 1912-1988." *National Journal of Sociology*. 4: 1-14.

Thompson, Daniel C. 1986c. *A Black Elite--A Profile of Graduates of UNCF Colleges*. Westport, CT: Greenwood Press.

_____ 1979. Interview. May 23. Kim Lacy Rogers-Glenda R. Stevens Collection. Amistad Research Center, New Orleans, LA.

_____ 1974. *Sociology of the Black Experience*. Westport, CT: Greenwood Press.

_____ 1973m. "Caste and Negro Protest." *University English*. 8.

_____ 1973d. *Private Black Colleges at the Crossroads*. Westport, CT: Greenwood Press.

_____ 1970b. "Patterns of Race Relations Leadership." *Perspectives on Black America*. Russell Endo and William Strawbridge, editors. Englewood Cliffs, NJ: Prentice-Hall.

_____ 1969l. "The Civil Rights Movement." In Pat W. Romero, editor, *In Black America: 1968 The Year of Awakening*. Washington, DC: United Publishing Corporation.

_____ 1966i. "The New South." *The Journal of Social Issues*. 22: 7-19.

_____ 1965g. "The Rise of the Negro Protest." *Annals of the Academy of Political and Social Science*. 357: 18-29.

_____ 1964. "Evaluation as a Factor in Planning: The Education of the Disadvantaged Child." *Journal of Negro Education*. 33: 333-340.

_____ 1963h. "Civil Rights Leadership (An Opinion Study)," *Journal of Negro Education*. 32: 426-436.

_____ 1963a. *The Negro Leadership Class*. Englewood Cliffs, NJ: Prentice Hall.

_____ 1961j. "The Role of the Federal Courts in the Changing Status of Negroes Since World War II." *Journal of Negro Education*. 30: 94-101.

_____ 1960f. "The Problem of Faculty Morale." *Journal of Negro Education*. 29: 37-46.

_____ 1958e. "Career Patterns of Teachers in Negro Colleges." *Social Forces*. 36: 270-276.

_____ and Barbara Guillory Thompson. 1984. "The Black Underclass: A Continuing Saga." Part II. *Black Southerner*. 11: 48, 50-54.

Valocchi, Steve. 1994. "The Racial Basis of Capitalism and the State, and the Impact of the New Deal on African Americans." *Social Problems*. 4: 347-362.

Washington, Robert. 1981. "Horace Cayton and the Problem of Arrested Black Sociological Productivity." Paper presented at the Eastern Sociological Society Meetings.

Watts, Jerry Gafio. 1994. *Heroism and the Black Intellectual--Ralph Ellison, Politics and Afro-American Intellectual Life.* Chapel Hill, NC: University of North Carolina Press.

_____ 1983. "On Reconsidering Park, Johnson, DuBois, Frazier and Reid: Reply to Benjamin Bowser's 'The Contribution of Blacks to Sociological Knowledge.'" *Phylon*. 44: 273-91.

Watson, Wilbur H. 1976. "The Idea of Black Sociology: Its Cultural and Political Significance." *The American Sociologist*. 11: 115-123.

Willie, Charles V. 1982. "Walter R. Chivers: An Advocate of Situation Sociology." *Phylon*. 43: 242-248.

Winston, Michael R. 1971. "Through the Back Door: Academic Racism and the Negro Scholar in Historical Perspective." *Daedalus*. 100: 678-719.

Young, Andrew. 1996. *An Easy Burden--The Civil Rights Movement and the Transformation of America.* New York: Harper-Collins.

Endnotes

1. While all errors in this discussion are the author's, the discussion of second generation African-American sociologists was developed with the able assistance and consultation of the premiere expert on African-American sociologists, James E. Conyers. The author acknowledges his support and encouragement.

2. Benjamin P. Bowser, "The Contribution of Blacks to Sociological Knowledge: A Problem of Theory and Role to 1950," *Phylon*, 1981, 42: 180-193; Jerry G. Watts, "On Reconsidering Park, Johnson, DuBois, Frazier and Reid: Reply to Benjamin Bowser's `The Contribution of Blacks to Sociological Knowledge,'" *Phylon*, 1983, 44: 273-291; Douglas Davidson, "Black Sociologists: A Critical Analysis," *Contribution to Black Studies*, 1977, 1: 44-51; Wilbur H. Watson, "The Idea of Black Sociology: Its Cultural and Political Significance," *The American Sociologist*, 1976, 11: 115-123; Edward G. Armstrong, "Black Sociology and Phenomenological Sociology," *Sociological Quarterly*, 1979, 20: 387-397.

3. John Bracey, August Meier and Elliott Rudwick, *The Black Sociologists: The First Half Century*, (Belmont, California: Wadsworth Publishing Company, 1971), p. 1.

4. Gordon Morgan, "First Generation Black Sociologists and Theories of Social Change," *Journal of Social and Behavioral Sciences* (*JSBS*), 1973, 19: 106-119; Jacquelyne Johnson Jackson, "Black Female Sociologists," *Black Sociologists--Historical and Contemporary Perspectives*, James E. Blackwell and Morris Janowitz, editors, (Chicago: University of Chicago Press, 1974), pp. 267-295; Butler A. Jones, "The Tradition of Sociology Teaching in Black Colleges: The Unheralded Professionals," *Black Sociologists--Historical and Contemporary Perspectives*, James E. Blackwell and Morris Janowitz, editors, (Chicago: University of Chicago Press, 1974), pp. 121-163; R. Charles Key, "Society and Sociology: The Dynamics of Black Sociological Negation," *Phylon*, 1978, 39: 35-48; James E. Conyers, "Negro Doctorates in Sociology: A Social Portrait," *Phylon*, 1968a, 29: 212; Charles V. Willie, "Walter R. Chivers: An Advocate of Situation Sociology," *Phylon*, 1982, 43: 242; Harry Washington Green, *Holders of Doctorates Among American Negroes*, (Boston: Meador Publishing Company, 1946), p. 64.

5. William M. Banks, *Black Intellectuals--Race and Responsibility in American Life*, (New York: W. W. Norton and Company, 1996), pp. 93-100.

6. Henry E. Cobb, editor for the Conference of Deans of Black Graduate Schools, "Mission, Status, Problems, and Priorities of Black Graduate Schools," *Minority Group Participation in Graduate Education*, National Board of Graduate Education, (Washington, DC: National Academy of Sciences, 1976), pp. 192-193, 195.

7. According to William Banks, Columbia University produced 144

African-American Ph.D.'s between 1930 and 1962. New York University, Ohio State, and the University of Chicago followed Columbia in Ph.D. production.
Banks, 1996, p. 130.

8. James E. Conyers, "Negro Doctorates in Sociology: A Social Portrait," *Phylon*, 1968, 29: 216; Telephone Interview with Dr. Butler A. Jones, March 20, 1993.

9. Like her talented sibling, Louise P. Jones was a young scholar who encountered the racism of the segregated South. She had an aspiration of becoming a lawyer. She attended Ohio State University's Law School and the University of Toledo's Law School. However, her goal was thwarted by the segregationist authorities of Alabama who reneged on their promise to finance her legal studies. This experience helped to shape Jones' views regarding race relations.
Letters from E. B. Norton to Louise P. Jones, January 18, 1946, August, 1945; Letters from A. R. Meadows to Louise P. Jones, June 12, 17, 18, 1946; July 13, 24, 1946; Letters to A. R. Meadows from Louise P. Jones, July 27, 1946; November 2, 18, 1946, Container 1, Folder 1, Butler A. Jones Papers, The Western Reserve Historical Society, Cleveland, OH.

10. James E. Conyers, "Negro Doctorates in Sociology: A Social Portrait," *Phylon*, 1968, 29: 216; Telephone Interview with Dr. Butler A. Jones, March 20, 1993.

11. Ibid.

12. Ibid.

13. James E. Conyers, "Negro Doctorates in Sociology: A Social Portrait," *Phylon*, 1968, 29: 216; Telephone Interview with Dr. Butler A. Jones, March 20, 1993; Letter, Butler A. Jones to Ralph Bunche, November 11, 1939, Ralph Bunche Papers, Box 36, Folders 7, 8, Schomburg Center for Research in Black Culture, The New York Public Library, New York, New, York.

14. Ibid.

15. Ibid.

16. Ibid.

17. According to Butler A. Jones, Clayborne Carson's report of Martin Luther King Jr.'s "failing grade in social studies" was incorrect. As an experimental and progressive school, Jones stated the Atlanta University's Laboratory School did not award grades. Students were given reports which summarized their progress in areas of study. As he recalls, King received a good report in eighth grade social studies.
Telephone Interview with Dr. Butler A. Jones, January 25, 1997; Telephone Interview with Dr. Butler A. Jones, March 20, 1993; Clayborne Carson, senior editor, *The Papers of Martin Luther King, Jr.*, *Volume I: Called to Serve, January 1929-June 1951*, (Berkeley, CA: University of California Press, 1992), p. 32, fn. 103.

18. Ibid.

19. Addie Louise Joyner Butler, *The Distinctive Black College--Talladega, Tuskegee, and Morehouse*, (Metuchen, NJ: The Scarecrow Press, Inc., 1977), p. 43.

20. David Levering Lewis, *W. E. B. DuBois--Biography of a Race, 1868-1919*, (New York: Henry Holt and Company, 1993), p. 61; Telephone Interview with Dr. Butler A. Jones, March 20, 1993.

21. Jones' Talladega experience was enhanced by the school's faculty housing support. According to Jones' mother, J. A. Jones, the school provided the family with a modern home, including a very nice kitchen. This allowed Jones' first wife, a musician, to offer private music lessons.
Letter, J. A. Jones to Louise P. Jones, January 6, 1945, Container 1, Folder 1, Butler A. Jones Papers, The Western Reserve Historical Society, Cleveland, OH.

22. Telephone Interview with Dr. Butler A. Jones, March 20, 1993.

23. Although Maxine D. Jones and Joe M. Richardson have suggested Jones' 1953 departure from Talladega College was due to displeasure with the administration of Daniel A. Beittel, Jones denied emphatically their explanation in an interview with the author.
Maxine D. Jones and Joe M. Richardson, *Talladega College--The First Century*, (Tuscaloosa, AL: The University of Alabama Press, 1990), p. 162; Informal Interview with Dr. Butler A. Jones, American Sociological Association meetings, 1992, Pittsburgh, Pennsylvania; Gabrielle Simon Edgcomb, *From Swastika to Jim Crow: Refugee Scholars at Black Colleges*, (Malabar, FL: Krieger Publishing Company, 1993), pp. 92-93;

Telephone Interview with Dr. Butler A. Jones, March 20, 1993.

24. Ibid.

25. Ibid.

26. Ibid.

27. Letters, George W. Burns to Butler A. Jones, May 2, 1960, January 27, 1960, January 24, 1958; Letter Clarence C. Ficken to Butler A. Jones, January 9, 1956, Butler A. Jones Papers, The Western Reserve Historical Society, Cleveland, OH.

28. Telephone Interview with Dr. Edgar Epps, January 7, 1997.

29. Ibid.

30. Butler A. Jones, "The Function of Social Science Teaching in a Negro College," no date, unpublished paper, Butler A. Jones Papers, The Western Reserve Historical Society, Cleveland, OH.

31. Ibid.

32. Ibid.

33. Ibid.

34. Telephone Interview with Dr. Butler A. Jones, January 25, 1997.

35. Ibid.

36. Ibid.

37. In addition to Jones' Washington trip, Talladega students took trips to places such as Mexico, Cuba, Canada, Europe, and Broadway.
     Maxine D. Jones and   Joe M. Richardson, *Talladega College--The First Century*, (Tuscaloosa, AL: The University of Alabama Press, 1990), p. 154.

38. Maxine D. Jones and Joe M. Richardson, *Talladega College--The First*

Century, (Tuscaloosa, AL: The University of Alabama Press, 1990), p. 161.

39. Telephone Interview with Dr. Butler A. Jones, January 25, 1997.

40. Telephone Interview with Dr. Edgar Epps, January 7, 1997; Telephone Interview with Dr. Butler A. Jones, January 25, 1997.

41. Robert Park often used the services of African-American college students and faculty members as chauffeurs. Many of these individuals were recognized as scholars such as Earnest E. Neal, a rural sociologist at Tuskegee and the father of the Black Panther Party activist, Kathleen Neal Cleaver. Neal worked as Park's chauffeur during his graduate study at Fisk University.
    Winifred Raushenbush, *Robert E. Park--Biography of a Sociologist*, (Durham, NC: Duke University Press, 1979), p. 157; Telephone Interview with Dr. Butler A. Jones, January 25, 1997.

42. Robert Park's harsh comments to Lewis Jones regarding the Jewish community may have been a result of his complex racial views on cultural hybrids *vis-a-vis* his race relations cycle which John Stanfield (*Philanthropy and Jim Crow in American Social Science*, Westport, CT: Greenwood Press, 1985, p. 49) explained as seeing "marginal people, like Jews, as adherents to an outmoded cultural past and not quite incorporated into the host society."

43. Telephone Interview with Dr. Butler A. Jones, January 25, 1997.

44. Bernard Taper, *The Tuskegee Gerrymander Case--Gomillion versus Lightfoot*, (New York: McGraw-Hill, 1962); Fred Gray, *Bus Ride to Justice--Changing the System by the System, The Life and Works of Fred Gray*, (Montgomery, AL: The Black Belt Press, 1995); Tom Dent, *Southern Journey--A Return to the Civil Rights Movement*, (New York: William Morrow and Company, 1997).

45. Jacquelyne Johnson Jackson, "Charles Goode Gomillion, Ph.D.: A Mighty Social Force," a paper presented at the Southern Sociological Society, 1995, p. 7; Jacquelyne Johnson Jackson, "Obituaries--Charles Goode Gomillion, 1900-1995," *The Southern Sociologist*, Winter 1996 27, 3: 33-34.

46. Telephone Interview with Dr. Butler A. Jones, January 25, 1997.

47. Oliver C. Cox, "The Leadership of Booker T. Washington," *Social Forces*, October 1951, 30, 1: 95; Herbert M. Hunter and Sameer Y. Abraham, editors, *Race, Class, and the World System--The Sociology of Oliver C. Cox*, (New York: Monthly Review Press, 1987), pp. xxv-xxvii.

48. Daniel C. Thompson Interview, May 23, 1979, Kim Lacy Rogers-Glenda R. Stevens Collection, Amistad Research Center, Tulane University, New Orleans, LA.

49. Daniel C. Thompson Interview, May 23, 1979, Kim Lacy Rogers-Glenda R. Stevens Collections, Amistad Research Center, Tulane University, New Orleans, LA.

50. .In an interview with Kim Lacy Rogers, Daniel C. Thompson states his father provided Martin Luther King Sr. with basic literacy.   King's autobiography does not support the claim.   In his autobiography, King said his first teacher was Mrs. Low, the wife of the Reverend W. H. Low of Stockbridge, Georgia. Mrs. Low had 234 pupils in her school.
     Daniel C. Thompson Interview, May 23, 1979, Kim Lacy Rogers-Glenda R. Stevens Collections, Amistad Resarch Center, Tulane University, New Orleans, LA; Martin Luther King, Sr., *Daddy King--An Autobiography*, (New York: William Morrow and Company, 1980), pp. 37-38; *The Papers of Martin Luther King, Jr., Volume I: Called To Serve, January 1929-June 1951*, Clayborne Carson, Series Editor, (Berkeley, CA: University of California Press, 1992), pp. 22-23.

51. Ibid.

52. Hubert served in a number of capacities in the Atlanta University Center, including as dean of the Morehouse School of Religion.   His kindness to indigent students has been heralded by former students such as Martin Luther King, Sr.
     Addie Louise Joyner Butler, *The Distinctive Black College: Talladega, Tuskegee and Morehouse*, (Metuchen, NJ: The Scarecrow Press, 1977), p.126.

53. Barbara Guillory Thompson, "In Memoriam--Daniel Calbert Thompson, 1912-1988," *National Journal of Sociology*, 1990, 4, 1: 1-4; Daniel C. Thompson Interview, May 23, 1979, Kim Lacy Rogers-Glenda R. Stevens Collections, Amistad Research Center, Tulane University, New Orleans, LA.

54. Ibid.

55. Monte Pilawsky, "Dan Thompson: Scholar, Activist, Mentor, Friend," a paper presented in a special Southern Sociological Society session to posthumously bestow the Charles S. Johnson Award, "A Southern Race Man: The Sociological Contributions of Daniel C. Thompson," April 7, 1995.

56. Barbara Guillory Thompson, "In Memoriam--Daniel Calbert Thompson, 1912-1988," *National Journal of Sociology*, 1990, 4, 1: 1-4; Dorothy Cowser Yancy, "William Edward Burghardt DuBois' Atlanta Years: The Human Side--A Study Based Upon Oral Sources," *Journal of Negro History*, 1978, 63, 1: 59-67..

57. Piotr Sztompka, *Robert K. Merton--An Intellectual Profile*, (New York: St. Martin's Press, 1986), pp. 28-30.

58. Daniel C. Thompson Interview, May 23, 1979, Kim Lacey Rogers-Glenda R. Stevens Collection, Amistad Research Center, Tulane University, New Orleans, LA.

59. Martin Kilson, "Harvard and the Small-Towner," *Blacks at Harvard--A Documentary History of African-American Experience at Harvard and Radcliffe*, Werner Sollors, Caldwell Titcomb, and Thomas A. Underwood, editors, (New York: New York University Press, 1993), pp. 491; Martin Kilson, "Harvard and the Small-Towner," *Varieties of Black Experience at Harvard--An Anthology*, Werner Sollors, Thomas A. Underwood, and Caldwell Titcomb, editors, (Cambridge, MA: Harvard University, Department of Afro-American Studies, 1986), pp. 156.

60. Kilson, 1993, p. 492; Kilson, 1986, p. 157.

61. Ibid.

62. Kilson, 1993, pp. 492-493; Kilson, 1986, p. 157.

63. According to Adelaide M. Cromwell, Boston's African-American upper class society was determined by four factors: (1) the pattern of African-American and white relations and the effect they have on attitudes and behaviors of African-Americans as well as whites; (2) the restricted economic opportunities for themselves which was an aspect of a saturated community life; (3) the political impotency; and (4) the general

conservatism of the larger community. These factors resulted in African-American upper class status being accorded to five categories of Bostonians: (1) a small and distinct group with national prominence such as opera singer, Roland Hayes; (2) a group who had local distinction such as local political figures; (3) a group of social leaders, i. e., party givers and attenders; (4) a group of "old families"; and (5) a group of families that were "just old" and respectable members of New England's African-American historical community but may not have maintained the economic resources over generations to stay in prominent community social positions. In addition, she described a sixth marginal group, i. e., the "whities." They were composed of light-to-fair complected African-Americans who preferred to live and intermarry with whites. They were not well-educated or professionals and had a passing social interaction with the African-American elite via fraternity and sorority dances, debutante balls, and other elite social functions.

Adelaide M. Cromwell, *The Other Brahmins--Boston's Black Upper Class, 1750-1950*, (Fayetteville, AR: University of Arkansas Press, 1994), pp. 189-194.

64. In her family history, Gail Horne Jones Lumet Buckley said her upbringing was devoid of many African-Americans after age nine or ten. She described herself as a "totally lapsed member of the black middle class." (p. 227) She attributed her "cosmopolitan" perspective to her mother, Lena Horne. According to Buckley:

> Lena's remarriage, as well as her post war politics caused her to re-examine the bourgeois life-style. She found it shallow and frivolous. As far as Lena was concerned, the "uplifting" bourgeoisie of Cora and Edwin's (her ancestors) turn of the century black America, and the "creative" bourgeoisie of Harlem's 1920s and '30s, was now just black Babbittry." (p. 227)

Buckley took this condescending attitude toward the African-American middle class with her to Harvard. She said her attitudes reflected her mostly white upbringing rather than a conscious rejection of African-Americans.

Using a set of Harvard student categories offered by a 1950s sociology student, she divided Harvard students into three groups: "Clubbies," "Bohos," and "Other Ranks." She described herself as a member of the Bohos who were literary, arty, Beat, and "acceptably" Jewish, black, or foreign. (p. 231) Unlike Martin Kilson, Buckley did not see a critical mass of African-Americans at Harvard. She considered herself a part of a small group of token African-Americans in 1950s Harvard. Her Harvard years were similar to her pre-Harvard white upbringing.

Since African-American children of Hollywood stars have not been the subject of a systematic analysis, it is unclear to what extent Buckley's experiences were representative of the group. It should be noted Nat King Cole's daughter, Carol Cole was presented as a debutante in a glittering ball sponsored by the African-American women's civic group, the Links. The Cole debut was made before presidential candidate John Fitzgerald Kennedy at the Hollywood Biltmore. Although Cole shared many of Buckley's experiences and was ten years her junior, her Links debut indicates that some African-Americans of her social class maintained greater ties to the African-American middle class.

Gail Lumet Buckley, *The Hornes--An American Family*, (New York: Alfred A. Knopf, 1986), pp. 227, 231; James Haskins, *Nat King Cole*, (New York: Stein and Day, 1984), pp. 151-52.

65. James S. Coleman, "Robert K. Merton as Teacher," *Robert K. Merton-- Consensus and Controversy*, Jon Clark, Celia Modgil and Sohan Modgil, editors, (London: Falmer Press, 1990), pp. 25-32.

66. One of the more interesting coincidental connections between Merton and Thompson was their New Orleans backgrounds. Merton served as chairman of the Tulane University sociology department from 1939 through 1941. Since Thompson was a student in Atlanta during those years, he did not meet Merton.

Daniel C. Thompson Interview, May 23, 1979, Kim Lacy Rogers-Glenda R. Stevens Collections, Amistad Research Center, Tulane University, New Orleans, LA.

67. James S. Coleman, "Columbia in the 1950s," *Authors of Their Own Lives--Intellectual Autobiographies by Twenty American Sociologists*, Bennett M. Berger, editor, (Berkeley, CA: University of California Press, 19990), p. 75.

68. Coleman, p. 77.

69. Unwittingly, Coleman's essay provides an unusual glimpse of his Midwestern/Southern ethnic/racial sensitivity and upbringing. He uses the pejorative, " a couple of Puerto Ricans," in reference to individuals who purchased his 1947 Chevrolet without noticing "an ominous sound in the

differential." (Coleman, 1990, p. 98) Thus, it is not surprising African-American colleagues or 1950's Negro colleagues were not significant in his discussion of 1950's Columbia.

While the author realizes the absence of African-American sociologists' names from an autobiographical essay may be a result of many factors, including memory lapses, the quantitative emphasis of Coleman and many of his contemporaries suggest a different methodological focus from Thompson. Thompson's interest in racial topics was not a major focus of "Charlie Glock's Young Turks". On the other hand, a more critical reviewer of Columbia's African-American sociology graduate students might suggest their absence from Coleman's discussion was a reflection of their limited impact on the important intellectual activities of the department's elite students.

Coleman, p. 77.

70. Coleman, pp. 79, 82.

71. Barbara Guillory Thompson, "In Memorian--Daniel Calbert Thompson, 1912-1988," *National Journal of Sociology*, 4: 1-14; Daniel C. Thompson Interview, May 23, 1979, Kim Lacy Rogers-Glenda R. Stevens Collections, Amistad Research Center, Tulane University, New Orleans, LA.

72. Although Thompson scaled the ranks of the Dillard administration, his success was not without its moments of tension. On one occasion, the son of a former colleague witnessed Thompson's absolute expression of disillusionment upon being unable to satisfy the unreasonable demands of the university's chief administrator.

Barbara Guillory Thompson, "In Memoriam--Daniel Calbert Thompson, 1912-1988," *National Journal of Sociology*, 4: 1-14; Daniel C. Thompson Interview, May 23, 1979, Kim Lacy Rogers-Glenda R. Stevens Collections, Amistad Research Center, Tulane University, New Orleans, LA.

73. Within recent years, Richard Robbins has taken some of Charles Johnson's critics to task regarding their interpretation of his dominance over the philanthropic community and degree of intellectual independence. According to Robbins, Johnson's czar status was a result of the following:

The foundations had the money, and they allocated it. They had confidence in Johnson. He needed their resources to get the work done; he went to them. If the relationship was criticized as "too conservative," "to safe" with respect to such issues as head-on commitment against segregation, that had to be. And nowhere is there any record of Johnson being compelled to submit his work to censorship imposed by the foundations. In the milieu of his time, in an era of extreme racism, he managed to obtain the grants, get the studies done, and conceivably, advance the understanding of racial oppression and what strategies could be deployed against it. ..Johnson's options were far more limited during that long period, from the 1930s to the 1960s, before the civil rights revolution began to shatter rigid racial segregation.

Thus, Robbins believed the czar label did not accurately describe the socio-political context of Johnson's role as a second generation scholar.
Richard Robbins, *Sidelines Activist--Charles S. Johnson and the Struggle for Civil Rights*, (Jackson, MS: University Press of Mississippi, 1996), p. 9; August Meier, *A White Scholar and the Black Community, 1945-1965--Essays and Reflections*, (Amherst, MA: The University of Massachusetts Press, 1992), pp. 73-87.

74. Anthony M. Platt, *E. Franklin Frazier Reconsidered*, (New Brunswick, NJ: Rutgers University Press, 1991), pp. 94, 105-108.

75. William H. Sewell, "Some Observations and Reflections on the Role of Women and Minorities in the Democratization of the American Sociological Association, 1905-1990," *The American Sociologist*, 1992, 23: 57.

76. Jacquelyne J. Jackson, "Black Professional Organizations: A Case Study," *The Journal of Afro-American Issues*, 1972, 1: 75-91.

77. The official Association of Black Sociologists (ABS) history places emphasis on its role in changing the nature of the American Sociological Association's institutional racism. In Lewis M. Killian's autobiography, he takes issue with this view. According to Killian, the New Left radicals and the emerging Sociologists for Women in Society were in the vanguard as reformers of the ASA. For many ABS founders, Killian's comments were an insult to their valiant work to change the ASA; and it demonstrated the liberal perspective which minimized African-American contributions .
While the Conyers and Scott history provides a concise history of the Association of Black Sociologists (ABS), Jones' bid as ABS president is conspicuously absent. John Sibley Butler is listed as president during the Jones years. According to the author's personal records, Jones won the presidency with twenty-three votes and his challenger, John Sibley Butler, received eighteen votes. While this memorandum may have been in error,

the author never received a corrected memorandum.
     James E. Conyers, "The Association of Black Sociologists: A Descriptive Account from an Insider," *The American Sociologist*, 1992, 23: 49-55; James E. Conyers and Joseph W. Scott, *A Brief History of the Association of Black Sociologists, 1970-1990*, (Privately published by the Association of Black Sociologists, 1992); Memorandum from Wilbur H. Watson, ABS President to all members of the Association of Black Sociologists, regarding "results of the recent election of officers," March 18, 1979 (While this memorandum may have been inaccurate, it contained the number of votes cast as cited above.); Letter from Wilbur H. Watson to ABS Board of Directors, June 1, 1979; Lewis M. Killian, *Black and White: Reflections of a White Southern Sociologist*, (Dix Hills, NJ: General Hall, 1994), p. 176.

78.   During his Talladega years, his participation in predominantly African-American organizations may have been curtailed by the college's policy regarding non-integrated groups. Beittel maintained a policy of allowing faculty members to attend all-African-American groups such as the Association of Social Science Teachers (the predecessor to the interracial Association of Social and Behavioral Scientists) but he would not pay membership dues or an institutional membership.
     Jones' professional associations have included memberships in American Studies Association, Alpha Kappa Delta, Law and Society Association, Society for Applied Anthropology.
     Maxine D. Jones and Joe M. Richardson, *Talladega College--The First Century*, (Tuscaloosa, AL: The University of Alabama Press, 1990), p. 289.

79.   Butler A. Jones, "The Tradition of Sociology Teaching in Black Colleges: The Unheralded Professionals," *Black Sociologists--Historical and Contemporary Perspectives*, James E. Blackwell and Morris Janowitz, editors, (Chicago: University of Chicago Press, 1974), p. 129.

80.   Telephone Interview with Dr. Herbert Aurbach, January 7, 1997.

81.   Telephone Interview with Dr. Herbert Aurbach, January 7, 1997.

82.   Ibid.

83.   Ibid.

84.   Ibid.

85. Ibid.

86. Ibid.

87. Jerry Gafio Watts, **Heroism and the Black Intellectual--Ralph Ellison, Politics, and Afro-American Intellectual Life**, (Chapel Hill, NC: University of North Carolina Press, 1994), p. 15.

88. The faculty and students were concerned about a variety of issues including the college board's failure to appoint Dean James T. Cater as president; the diminution of the College Council's power; the closing of the interracial Drewry Practice High School to support the segregated public school system; Beittel's failure to reinstate the intecollegiate athletic program; lack of enrollment in which 86 of 105 scholarship recipients rejected Talladega; the low salary scale for faculty; and complaints about the campus food service.
    Maxine D. Jones and Joe M. Richardson, **Talladega College--The First Century**, (Tuscaloos, AL: The University of Alabama Press, 1990), pp. 143-167.

89. Maxine D. Jones and Joe M. Richardson, **Talladega College--The First Century**, (Tuscaloosa, AL: The University of Alabama Press, 1990). p. 162. 167).

90. Ibid.

91. Telephone Interview with Dr. Butler A. Jones, January 25, 1997.

92. Telephone Interview with Dr. Herbert Aurbach, January 7, 1997.

93. Ibid.

94. As a member of the Delaware Civil Rights Committee, Jones sent a letter to a white civic group who sponsored an annual minstrel show in a public junior high school auditorium which demeaned African-Americans. Through activities of this nature. Jones' organizational life influenced race relations.
    Letter to Mr. Schultz, Dr. R. E. Glendening, Mr. George Wolfe, Mr. Grover Gatton, Mr. Edward Flahive and Mr. Henry Chaney from Butler A. Jones and Thomas E. Liggins for the Delaware Civil Rights Committee. January 9, 1964, Bulter A. Jones Papers. The Western Reserve Historical Society, Cleveland, OH.

314   *Confronting the American Dilemma of Race*

95. Ida Harper Simpson, *Fifty Years of the Southern Sociological Society--Change and Continuity in a Professional Society*, (Athens, GA: University of Georgia Press, 1985), p. 210.

96. The institutional power base of the Atlanta, Fisk, and Tuskegee triumvirate stemmed from their close scholarly relationships with some of the Southern Sociological Society's leading white scholars, i.e., Walter Chivers of Atlanta University assisted Arthur Raper of Agnes Scott College in his 1930's studies *Lynchings and What They Mean* and *The Tragedy of Lynching*; Ira de Augustine Reid of Atlanta University collaborated with Raper on *Sharecroppers All* (1941). Both research projects were sponsored by the University of North Carolina's Institute for Research in Social Science.

Guy Benton Johnson and Guion Griffis Johnson, *Research in Service to Society--The First Fifty Years of the Institute for Research in Social Science at the University of North Carolina*, (Chapel Hill, NC: University of North Carolina Press, 1980), pp. 139-40, 142-43, 220-21.

97. Simpson, pp. 205-208.

98. James E. Conyers, "Negro Doctorates in Sociology: A Social Portrait," *Phylon*, 1968a, 29: 222; James E. Conyers, "Who's Who Among Black Doctorates in Sociology," *Sociological Focus*, 1986b, 19: 77-93.

99. Simpson, op cit., pp. 180, 186, 210; Key, op cit., pp. 35-48.

100. Simpson, op cit., p. 184.

101. Informal comments of Dr. Charles U. Smith, Symposium: On an African American Sociologist's Pursuit of Excellence--The Life and Scholarship of Daniel C. Thompson, Southern Sociological Society, April 10, 1992.

102. Tobe Johnson, "The Black College as System," *Daedalus*, Summer 1971, 100, 3: 799.

103. Ibid.

104. Ibid.

105. Johnson, 1971, p. 800.

106. Fairclough, pp. 38-41.

107. Although this work does not discuss their marriages, each scholar's success was supported by their spouse. According to Linda Perkins, professional couples maintained support for their partner's professional career. She highlighted as an example of this relationship the careers of second generation African-American sociologist and his physician wife, Charles and Margaret Lawrence.
Linda M. Perkins, "For the Good of the Race: Married African-American Academics, A Historical Perspective," an unpublished working draft, *Academic Couples: Problems and Promise*, Marianne A. Ferber and Jane W. Loeb, editors, (Urbana, IL: University of Illinois Press, forthcoming), pp. 19-20, 25.

108. John Hope Franklin, "The Dilemma of the American Negro Scholar," *Race and History--Selected Essays, 1938-1988*, (Baton Rouge, LA: Louisiana State University Press, 1989), pp. 295-308; Margaret Walker Alexander, "Black Women in Academia," *Words of Fire--An Anthology of African-American Feminist Thought*, Beverly Guy-Sheftall, editor, (New York: The New Press, 1995), pp. 454-460..

109...Daniel C. Thompson, *The Negro Leadership Class*,(Englewood Cliffs, NJ: Prentice-Hall, Inc., 1963), p.163.

110...Pilawsky, p. 8.

111...Randall L. Kennedy, "Racial Critiques of Legal Academia," *Harvard Law Review*, 19 ,102: 1766.

112. Joyce A. Ladner, *The Death of White Sociology*, (New York: Random House, 1973), p. xix.

113. Key, op cit., pp. 46-47.

114. Simpson, op cit., p. 207.

115. Jacquelyne J. Jackson, "Black Professional Organizations: A Case Study," *The Journal of Afro-American Issues*, 1972, 1: 80; James E. Blackwell, "Role Behavior in a Corporate Structure: Black Sociologists in the ASA," *Black Sociologists--Historical and Contemporary Perspectives*, James E. Blackwell and Morris Janowitz, editors, (Chicago: University of Chicago Press, 1974), pp. 341-367; Albert W. Black, Jr., "Whose Interests

Are Served by Black Sociologists," *The Black Sociologist*, 1976, 5: 4-6; Nolvert P. Scott, Jr., "On the Advantage Arising from the Incorporation of the Caucus of Black Sociologists," *The Black Sociologist*, 1976, 5: 6-7.

116. Pilawsky, p. 4.

117. Pilawsky, p. 4.

118. Pilawsky, p. 6.

119. Daniel C. Thompson, *The Negro Leadership Class*, (Englewood Cliffs, NJ: Prentice-Hall, Inc., 1963), p. 170.

120. The CCGNO's voter registration activities had contact with over two hundred schools, pool halls, beauty salons, barbershops, and churches. It had mixed success in voter registration. With 300 student volunteers, it encouraged 1,000 African-Americans to register; only 350 applicants were registered successfully.

Pilawsky, p. 6; Adam Fairclough, *Race and Democracy--The Civil Rights Struggle in Louisiana, 1915-1972*, (Athens GA: University of Georgia, 1995), pp. 272-73, 275-76, 278, 281; Kim Lacy Rogers, *Righteous Lives--Narratives of the New Orleans Civil Rights Movement*, (New York: New York University Press, 1993), pp. 67, 77-78, 85, 105-106.

121. The Consumers League of Greater New Orleans (CLGNO) was founded in 1959 with the purpose of developing African-American retail employment, especially in African-American neighborhoods such as Dryades Street. The CLGNO's leaders included Dr. Raymond B. Floyd of Xavier University, Dr. Henry Mitchell, and the Reverend Avery Alexander.

Rogers, pp. 67-69; Pilawsky, p. 6; Fairclough, p. 272; August Meier, *CORE--A Study in the Civil Rights Movement, 1942-1968*, (New York: Oxford University Press, 1973), p. 114.

122. Although the CCGNO has been labeled by some civil rights activists such as Tom Dent as a figurehead organization, its records reported a proposed budget of over $25,000. It maintained a complex organizational structure which consisted of 12 committees, executive board, members-at-large, treasurer, secretary, staff, vice chairman, and chairman. The voter registration staff received salaries, i. e., a director, assistant director, office secretary, part-time secretarial service for hire, and part-time field workers. Thus, the CCGNO functioned as efficiently as any civil rights organization of the period.

Report of the Subcommittee on Structure and Procedure of the Voter Education Committee of the CCGNO, Giles A. Hubert Papers, Box 8, Folder 2, Amistad Research Center, Tulane University, New Orleans, LA; Coordinating Council of Greater New Orleans (CCGNO) [Flow Chart], Giles A. Hubert Papers, Box 8, Folder 2, Amistad Research Center, Tulane University, New Orleans, LA; CCGNO Proposed Budget, January 1 - December 31, 1963, Giles A. Hubert Papers, Box 8, Folder 2, Amistad Research Center, Tulane University, New Orleans, LA; Constitution of the CCGNO, Giles A. Hubert Papers, Box 8, Folder 2, Amistad Research Center, Tulane University, New Orleans, LA; Program Planning and Membership Involvement, Giles A. Hubert Papers, Box 8, Folder 2, Amistad Research Center, Tulane University, New Orleans, LA; Rogers, pp. 11-12, 199-207.

123. Ibid.

124. While a few students from Dillard University and Xavier University joined the civil rights protest, Rogers reports their middle class values prohibited movement participation. On the other hand, Southern University of New Orleans (SUNO) students who came from working class families were very active in the early days of the New Orleans civil rights movement. Rogers, p. 115.

125. Charles U. Smith and Lewis Killian, "Black Sociologists and Social Protest," *Black Sociologists--Historical and Contemporary Perspectives*, James E. Blackwell and Morris Janowitz, editors, (Chicago: University of Chicago Press, 1974), pp. 206-209.

126. Anthony J. Blasi, "Using Pragmatist Sociology for Praxis: The Career of Charles H. Parrish, Jr.," paper presented at the Association of Social and Behavioral Scientists meeting, Nashville, Tennessee, 1997.

127. Daniel C. Thompson, "Problems of Faculty Morale," *Journal of Negro Education*, 1960, 29: 37-46; Daniel C. Thompson, "Career Patterns of Teachers in Negro Colleges," *Social Forces*, 1958, 36: 270-276.

128. Edward G. Armstrong, "Black Sociology and Phenomenological Sociology," *Sociological Quarterly*, Summer 1979, 20: 387.

129. Ralph H. Hines, "The Negro Scholar's Contribution to Pure and Applied Sociology," *JSBS*, 1967, 8: 30-35.

130. Although African-American is the current term of identification used
by contemporary sociologists, the term "black sociology" is used in the
text because the phrase was coined for application to a specific type of
sociological scholarship during a specific socio-historical time which was
separate and distinct from "American" white sociology. Thus, the phrase
conveys a special meaning.

Wilbur H. Watson, "The Idea of Black Sociology: Its Cultural and
Political Significance," *The American Sociologist*, 1976, 11: 118.

131. Armstrong, op cit., p. 388.

132. Watson, 1976, p. 118.

133. Butler A. Jones, "The Function of Social Science Teaching in a Negro
College," no date, Butler A. Jones Papers, The Western Reserve Historical
Society, Cleveland, OH.

134. Daniel C. Thompson, *The Negro Leadership Class*, (Englewood Cliffs,
N J: Prentice-Hall, 1963a).

135. Kim Lacy Rogers has suggested that Catholic Afro-Creole society
maintained the following characteristics:

> [Catholic Afro-Creoles had] a different cultural tradition than
> Protestant [African-Americans] of New Orleans. In the twentieth
> century, [Afro-] Creoles formed an aristocracy in New Orleans'
> [African-American] community.   Educated [Afro-]Creoles in
> private or Catholic institutions...assumed positions of social and
> political leadership in the city. ...[T]hey were political moderates
> who favored negotiation over confrontation, and who deeply
> believed in an individualistic ethic of social mobility.

Similarly, Andrew Young discussed the color conscious Afro-Creole
society in New Orleans. In his autobiography, he described his social circle
of "bourgeois friends" who "were so comfortable, while so many other
blacks were so poor." Young reported relatives who were *passe blanc*,
passing for white. Similarly, Rogers reported numerous civil rights
activists with Louisiana *passe blanc* relatives.

Adam Fairclough suggested the civil rights movement in Louisiana
was shaped by the complicated racial dynamics of Afro-Creole southern
Louisiana which included a history with 41% of its antebellum *gens de
couleur libre* (Afro-Creoles or free people of color) owning slaves and

substantial amounts of property; the *placage* system which gave legitimacy to common law interracial marriages; and a tripartite society of whites, slaves, and *gens de couleur libre*. A recent historical work by Caryn Coss_ Bell (*Revolution, Romanticism, and the Afro-Creole Protest Tradition in Louisiana, 1718-1868*, Baton Rouge, LA: Louisiana State University Press, 1997) has attempted to disassemble fact from fiction about Afro-Creole culture. Yet, her work confirms the complicated political and opportunistic dimension of their racial and ethnic ambiguity toward the descendants of the darker-complected Africans who they later dubbed in postbellum years as the "Americans."

Andrew Young, *An Easy Burden--The Civil Rights Movement and the Transformation of America*, (New York: Harper-Collins, 1996), pp. 10, 30-31; Adam Fairclough, *Race and Democracy--The Civil Rights Struggle in Louisiana, 1915-1972*, (Athens, GA: University of Georgia, 1995), pp. 2-3, 5-6, 15-16; Kim Lacy Rogers, *Righteous Lives--Narratives of the New Orleans Civil Rights Movement*, (New York: New York University Press, 1993), p. 4-6, 16-17, 21, 82.

136. Thompson, 1963a, pp. 2-4, 7.

137. Maurice Natanson, *Literature, Philosophy and the Social Sciences*, (The Hague: Marinus Nijhoff, 1962), p. 157.

138...Edward G. Armstrong, "Black Sociology and Phenomenological Sociology," *Sociological Forum*, 1979, 20: 394.

139. In his classic study of American race relations, Gunnar Myrdal's concept of the American Creed stated: Americans believed in freedom, justice, equality, and a fair opportunity for all citizens.

Gunnar Myrdal, *An American Dilemma--The Negro Problem and Modern Democracy, Volume I*, (New York: Harper and Row Publishers, 1944); Thompson, 1963a, pp. 2-4, 7.

140. Thompson, 1963a, p. 3.

141. Thompson, 1963a, p. 3.

142. Thompson, 1963a, pp. 331-334.

143. Daniel C. Thompson, "Patterns of Race Relations Leadership," *Perspectives on Black America*, Russell Endo and William Strawbridge, editors, (Englewood Cliffs, NJ: Prentice-Hall, 1970b), pp. 330-352.

320   *Confronting the American Dilemma of Race*

144. Daniel C. Thompson, *A Black Elite--A Profile of Graduates of UNCF Colleges*, (Westport, CT: Greenwood Press, 1986), p. xv.

145. Ibid.

146. Daniel C. Thompson, *A Black Elite--A Profile of Graduates of UNCF Colleges*, (Westport, CT: Greenwood Press, 1986c), pp. xv, xvi, xvii; Daniel C. Thompson, *Private Black Colleges at the Crossroads*, (Westport, CT: Greenwood Press, 1973d).

147. Daniel C. Thompson, "Career Patterns of Teachers in Negro Colleges," *Social Forces*, 1958e, 36: 270.

148. G. Franklin Edwards, *The Negro Professional Class*, (New York: Free Press of Glencoe, 1959).

149. James E. Blackwell, *Mainstreaming Outsiders--The Production of Black Professionals*, (New York: General Hall, 1981); Horace Mann Bond, *Black American Scholars: a Study of their Beginnings*, (Detroit: Balamp, 1972); James E. Conyers, "Who's Who Among Black Doctorates in Sociology," *Sociological Focus*, 1986b, 19: 77-93; James E. Conyers, "Negro Doctorates in Sociology: A Social Portrait," *Phylon*, 1968a, 29: 209-223; Walter L. Davis, "Predicting Minority Student Performance in the First Medical School Year," *The Journal of the National Medical Association*, 1979, 71: 661-664; Willard B. Gatewood, *Aristocrats of Color--The Black Elite, 1880-1920*, (Bloomington, IN: Indiana University Press, 1990); Barbara M. Guillory, " The Career Patterns of Negro Lawyers in New Orleans," Master of Arts Thesis, Louisiana State University, Baton Rouge, 1960; Butler A. Jones, "The Tradition of Sociology Teaching in Black Colleges: The Unheralded Professionals," *Black Sociologists--Historical and Contemporary Perspectives*, James E. Blackwell and Morris Janowitz, editors, (Chicago: University of Chicago Press, 1974), pp. 121-163; Verna M. Keith and Cedric Herring, "Skin Tone and Stratification in the Black Community," *American Journal of Sociology*, 1991, 97: 760-778; David McBride and Monroe H. Little, "The Afro-American Elite, 1930-1940: A Historical and Statistical Profile," *Phylon*, 1981, 42: 105-119; Kent G. Mommsen, "Black Doctorates in American Higher Education: A Cohort Analysis," *JSBS*, 1974, 20: 101-117; Kent G. Mommsen, "On Recruiting Black Sociologists," *The American Sociologist*, 1973, 8: 107-116; Kent G. Mommsen, "Professionalism and the Racial Context of Career Patterns Among Black American Doctorates: A Note on the 'Brain Drain'"

Hypothesis," *Journal of Negro Education*, 1973, 42: 191-204; Willie Pearson, *Black Scientists, White Society, and Colorless Science: A Study of Universalism in American Science*, (Millwood, NY: Associated Faculty Press, 1985); Loren Schweninger, "Prosperous Blacks in the South, 1790-1880," *American Historical Review*, 1990, 95: 31-56; and Michael R. Winston, "Through the Back Door: Academic Racism and the Negro Scholar in Historical Perspective," *Daedalus*, 1971, 100: 678-719.

150.   Daniel C. Thompson, "Problems of Faculty Morale," *Journal of Negro Education*, 1960f, 29: 38.

151.   August Meier and Elliott Rudwick, *Black History and the Historical Profession, 1915-1980*, (Urbana, IL: University of Illinois Press, 1986), p. 131.

152.   Thompson, 1958e, p. 272.

153.   Thompson, 1958e, p. 273.

154.   John H. Stanfield, *Philanthropy and Jim Crow in American Social Science*, (Westport, CT: Greenwood Press, 1985); Kenneth R. Manning, *Black Apollo of Science—The Life of Ernest Everett Just*, (New York: Oxford University Press, 1983), pp. 114-163.

155.   Thompson, 1958e, p. 273.

156.   Will Scott, "A Perspective on Perspectives," *The American Sociologist*, 1979, 14: 91-95.

157.   Butler A. Jones, "The Tradition of Sociology Teaching in Black Colleges: The Unheralded Professionals," *Black Sociologists--Historical and Contemporary Perspectives*, James E. Blackwell and Morris Janowitz, editors, (Chicago: University of Chicago Press, 1974), p. 129.

158.   Thompson, 1960f, p. 46.

159.   Daniel C. Thompson, "The Rise of Negro Protest," *Annals of the American Academy of Political and Social Science*, Arnold M. Rose, special editor, 1965g, 357: 18-29; Daniel C. Thompson, "Civil Rights Leadership (An Opinion Study)," *Journal of Negro Education*, 1963h, 32: 426-436; Daniel C. Thompson, "The New South," *The Journal of Social*

Issues, 1966i, 22: 7-19; Daniel C. Thompson, "The Role of the Federal Courts in the Changing Status of Negroes Since World War II," *Journal of Negro Education*, 1961j, 30: 94-101; Daniel C. Thompson, "The Civil Rights Movement," *In Black America: 1968 The Year of Awakening*, Pat W. Romero, editor, (Washington, DC: United Publishing, 1969l).

160.   Butler A. Jones, "New Legal Requirements of Race Relations in the South," *Phylon*, 1953, 13: 97-106.

161.   Butler A. Jones, "New Legal Requirements of Race Relations in the South," *Phylon*, 1953, 23 (2): 101.

162.   Ibid.

163.   Ibid., p. 102.

164.   *Pitts v. Board of Trustees of DeWitt School District*, No. 1, 84 F. Supp. 975 (E. D. Ark., 1949), p. 984.

165.   In 1958, the author enrolled in a segregated Mississippi elementary school. In 1970, he graduated from a segregated Mississippi high school. Thus, Jones' prediction was accurate.

166.   Mary L. Anderson, Robert E. Cureton, Newell D. Eason, Butler A. Jones, Evelyn Lawlah, Charity Mance, Albert E. Manley, James E. Pierce, Jennie B. Ramsey and John T. Robinson, "Improving Education for Social-Civic Competence in the Southern States," *The Southern Association Quarterly*, 9 (1): 90-109.

167.   Robert Washington, "Sociology by Blacks versus Black Sociology: Revisioning Black American Social Reality," see last chapter in this volume.

168.   Thompson, 1964, pp. 333-340.

169.   Daniel C. Thompson, "Evaluation as a Factor in Planning Programs for the Culturally-Disadvantaged," *Journal of Negro Education*, 1964, 33, 3: 333-340.

170.   Thompson, 1964, pp. 333-340.

171. Ibid.

172. Thompson, 1964, pp. 333-340.

173. Robert Washington, "Sociology by Blacks versus Black Sociology: Revisioning Black American Social Reality," see final chapter of this volume.

174. Thompson, 1964, pp. 333-340.

175. Ibid.

176. Ibid.

177. Daniel C. Thompson, *Sociology of the Black Experience*, (Westport, CT: Greenwood Press, 1974), p. 338.

178. Ibid.

179. Ibid.

180. Thompson, 1973d.

181.. Butler A. Jones, "Negroes in Atlanta," a research report prepared for Ralph J. Bunche, Atlanta University, May 1940, pp. 1-3, Ralph Bunche Papers, Box 36, Folders 7, 8, Schomburg Center for Research in Black Culture, The New York Public Library, New York, New York.

182. Jones, "Negroes in Atlanta," pp. 4-5.

183. Jones, "Negroes in Atlanta," pp. 5-6.

184. Jones, "Negroes in Atlanta," p. 6.

185. Jones, "Negroes in Atlanta," p. 7.

186. Jones, "Negroes in Atlanta," p. 7.

187. Jones, "Negroes in Atlanta," p. 7.

188. Jones, "Negroes in Atlanta," pp. 7-8.

189. Jones, "Negroes in Atlanta," p. 33.

190. Jones, "Negroes in Atlanta," pp. 5-6.

191. Jones, "Negroes in Atlanta," p. 12.

192. Jones, "Negroes in Atlanta," p.8

193. Jones, "Negroes in Atlanta," pp. 11-12; Ralph J. Bunche, *The Political Status of the Negro in the Age of FDR*, Dewey W. Grantham, editor, (Chicago: University of Chicago Press, 1973), p. 485.

194. Jones, "Negroes in Atlanta," p. 13; Bunche, p. 485.

195. Jones, "Negroes in Atlanta," p. 13; Bunche, p. 486.

196. Jones, "Negroes in Atlanta," p. 16; Bunche, p. 487.

197. Jones, "Negroes in Atlanta," p. 16.

198. Jones, "Negroes in Atlanta," p. 18; Bunche, p. 487.

199.. Jones, "Negroes in Atlanta," pp. 20-21.

200.   Jones, "Negroes in Atlanta," p. 21; Gary M. Pomerantz, *Where Peachtree Meets Sweet Auburn--The Saga of Two Families and the Making of Atlanta*, (New York: Scribner, 1996), pp. 125-127, 147-153

201.. Jones, "Negroes in Atlanta," p. 21.

202. Jones, "Negroes in Atlanta," pp. 21-22.

ii)   In 1938, the Atlanta City Council floated a $7,500,000 bond issue to be used in improving various city institutions and city services, such as, Grady Hospital, libraries, etc. The city council did not designate funds from the proposed bond to aid African-Americans, e. g., monies for a new high school or an addition to the old high school. The CPL developed a negotiation committee which investigated the racial inequities of the bond's appropriations; and it engaged in early discussions with the mayor and city council. It only took action against the bond when it became apparent that the white "City Fathers" had no desire to provide services to the African-American community.

Jones, "Negroes in Atlanta," p. 25.

204. Jones, "Negroes in Atlanta," p. 24.

205. Jones, "Negroes in Atlanta," p. 24.

206. Jones, "Negroes in Atlanta," p. 28.

207. Jones, "Negroes in Atlanta," p. 28.

208. Jones, "Negroes in Atlanta," p. 32 (sic 29); Bunche, p. 491.

209. Jones, "Negroes in Atlanta," pp. 28-29.

210. Jones, "Negroes in Atlanta," pp. 29-30; Bunche, pp. 492-493.

211. Jones, "Negroes in Atlanta," pp. 30-31.

212. Steve Valocchi, "The Racial Basis of Capitalism and the State, and the Impact of the New Deal on African Americans," *Social Problems*, 1994, 41: 359.

213. Jones, "Negroes in Atlanta," pp. 30-31; Bunche, p. 493.

214. Butler A. Jones, "Workers of Merit in Georgia--Jefferson Frederick Long," *The Negro History Bulletin*, 1940, 5 (6): 129.

215. Gordon Morgan, "First Generation Black Sociologists and Theories of Social Change," *JSBS*, 1973, 19: 106-119.

216. William M. Phillips, Jr., "Doing Sociology with Tilman C. Cothran: Some Reminiscences," *Phylon*, 1982, 42: 250.

217. Morgan, op cit., p. 112.

218. Daniel C. Thompson, "Caste and Negro Protest," *University English*, 1973m, 8;Thompson, 1965g, pp. 18-29.

219. Robert Washington, "Horace Catyon and the Problem of Arrested Black Sociological Productivity," quote taken from transcription of a paper presentation at the Eastern Sociological Society meetings, March 22, 1981.

220. Scott, op cit., p. 92.

221. James S. Coleman, "Columbia in the 1950s," *Authors of Their Own Lives--Intellectual Autobiographies by Twenty American Sociologists*, Bennett M. Berger, editor, (Berkeley, CA: University of California Press, 1990), pp. 90-91.

222. Coleman, op cit., p. 90.

223. Andrew Abbott, "Of Time and Space: The Contemporary Relevance of the Chicago School," *Social Forces*, 1997, 75, 4: 1158.

224. Daniel C. Thompson, *Sociology of the Black Experience*, (Westport, CT: Greenwood Press, 1974), p. 43.

225. Ibid., p. 46.

226. Ibid., p. 50.

227. Ibid., p. 53.

228. Ibid., p. 57.

229. Ibid., p. 57.

230. Ibid., p. 57.

231. Ibid., pp. 58-59.

232. Pilwasky, p. 5.

233. Pilawsky, pp. 5-6; Daniel C. Thompson and Barbara G. Thompson, "The Black Underclass: A Continuing Saga," Part II, *Black Southerner*, 1984, 11, 2: 50..

234. Thompson, 1974, pp. 48-49.

235. Daniel C. Thompson, *Sociology of the Black Experience*, (Westport, CT: Greenwood Press, 1974), p. 46.

236. Ibid.

237. Antonio Gramsci, *Selections from the Prison Notebooks*, Quintin Hoare and Geoffrey N. Smith, editors and translators, (New York: International Publishers, 1977); Banks, pp. 336-337.

PART THREE

Conclusion:
An Overview on Black Intellectual
Encounters with Sociology

Robert E. Washington

In this conclusion section, Robert Washington revisits the issue concerning the defining characteristics of black sociology. By reformulating and expanding its meaning, Washington proposes a new definition of black sociology that moves beyond liberal integrationist ideology, which has operated as a central assumption underlying sociological writings by black Americans. Rather he calls for a new black sociology, rooted in the reality of segregated black American community life, with an analytical perspective that resonates black American culture.

Chapter 12

SOCIOLOGY BY BLACKS VERSUS BLACK SOCIOLOGY: Revisioning Black American Social Reality

Robert E. Washington

Our search for understanding through social analysis is conditioned by how we resolve long-standing controversies, not the least of which is the relationship between ideology and science. In the case of Africans captured in the West (particularly in the United States of America), that has all too often been resolved by black intellectuals acquiescing to a white social science. This has meant swallowing the most favorable white positions without piercing through to the implicit ideological assumptions really used to guide history with white interests. Many black social scientists seemingly have not really known the extent to which science is inevitably a hand servant to ideology, a tool for people to shape, if not create, history.
Gerald McWorter (1968)

Introduction

In the above incisive declaration, Gerald McWorter calls attention to ideology in the work of black sociologists. While agreeing with McWorter, I want to go beyond his general argument and focus on the problem of liberal ideology, which has oriented the work of most black sociologists. Specifically, I want to argue that black sociologists on the eve of the 21st century are adrift because they have failed to recognize the shortcomings of liberalism and the need move on to a new, realistic vision of black American social reality. As the concluding chapter of a volume focused on lesser known black sociologists, this seems an especially appropriate place to address this problem of the future direction of black sociologists.

If any one tendency characterized the outlook of earlier black sociologists during the first half of the 20th century, it was their faith in liberal racial reform. In the words of Morris Janowitz, these black sociologists saw in the discipline of sociology "the intellectual tools for the redefinition of race relations, and, in turn, a positive element for social change." (Janowitz 1954: xiv) Thomas Pettigrew made a similar point in reference to the writings of W.E.B. Dubois, Charles Johnson, E. Franklin Frazier, and the other earlier black sociologists he included in the book he edited on the history of the sociology of race relations. Highlighting their commitment to racial reform, Pettigrew noted: "Different as their varied approaches are, the common thread among them is their emphasis upon positive structural change in American race relations." (Pettigrew xxiv) In short, they regarded their liberal sociological writings as instruments of rational enlightenment that would effect improvements in black American life.

While the suppositions of their liberal outlook changed in emphasis over time, several beliefs remained central: (1) the equation of racism with ignorance of modern scientific biology; (2) the view of education as the solution to the problem of racial prejudice; and, (3), the belief that government must play an active part in alleviating the poverty, unemployment, slum housing, sub-standard education, and other social problems that plagued the black community. This last belief in the activist state, which became the foundation of what we can term "the transformative liberal vision," emanated from President Franklin Roosevelt's New Deal program. In fact, it was the New Deal political coalition, comprised of intellectuals, progressive churches, labor unions, blue collar white ethnics, and black Americans, that spearheaded liberal reforms in the United States between the 1930s and the mid-1960s. If that New Deal coalition failed to achieve fully the policies of a European style social democratic party, it was because one of its major components, the conservative white South, persistently resisted and undermined its most progressive initiatives.

Nevertheless, this period of New Deal liberal ideological dominance witnessed many impressive racial reforms: desegregation of the armed forces; racial integration of professional sports; constitutional prohibition against state mandated school segregation; desegregation of public facilities throughout the South; federal legislation guaranteeing blacks the right to vote; affirmative action hiring practices in public and private sector institutions; and the emergence of a new and greatly expanded black middle class.

Yet with much remaining to be done, that liberal period in American political culture abruptly ended in the late1960s. As a disillusioned white electorate turned against liberal social reforms, the dominant political attitude toward disadvantaged minorities shifted from compassionate concern to distrust and hostility. The complex causes that brought about that change need not concern us here, but one thing is indisputably clear: beginning with the Nixon and Ford administrations in the late1960s and early 1970s, and then gathering greater momentum under the Reagan and Bush administrations in the1980s, a reactionary political climate enveloped the United States. Legitimating and reinforcing that reactionary political climate, a neo-conservative intellectual movement surfaced in sociology and other social sciences, spearheading an intellectual backlash against1960s liberal racial reforms, with the result that school busing, affirmative action, Headstart, and other compensatory programs encountered a barrage of criticism. We will examine this conservative intellectual movement in greater detail later.

Though many black sociologists hope to revive the spirit of the1960s, that hope is delusional. The era of liberal ideological dominance in American political life has past. In particular, the liberal ideological vision of a racially integrated and harmonious American society, the vision that energized the work of most earlier black sociologists, no longer seems a realistic expectation. At least for the foreseeable future, several trends in black American life seem incontrovertible: (1) most black Americans will continue to live a segregated community life; (2) most black Americans will continue to inhabit inner city ghetto neighborhoods; (3) most black American workers will continue to earn substantially less than their white American counterparts; (4) most black American children will continue to grow up in poverty; (5) most black American children will continue to receive substandard public school educations; (6), and, finally, black Americans -- especially black American males -- will continue to be over represented among the jobless, the drug addicted, the imprisoned, and the murdered populations in the United States. These are the unpleasant facts we must face as we approach the 21st century.

The challenge confronting black sociologists is not to do more research that further documents black America's problems; we hardly need more data about social problems affecting black Americans. Rather the challenge confronting black sociologists is to formulate a new ideological perspective on black American social realities, a new ideological perspective that creatively utilizes existing data, to articulate ideas and strategies for solving black American problems within a politically conservative American society. In short, we must recognize the obsolescence of liberal ideology and move on to develop a black American centered sociology that resonates black American social realities.

My objectives in writing this essay are threefold: (1) to provide a brief historical overview of liberal ideological hegemony that reigned over sociological writings on black Americans from world war one to the mid-1960s; (2) to retrace the events that resulted in the current crisis confronting that liberal ideological hegemony; (3) and, finally, to suggest guidelines for a genuine black sociology.

I. The Pre-Civil Rights Era

I want to begin by drawing a distinction between what I term "'sociology on blacks by blacks" (henceforth to be referred to as "sociology by blacks") and "black sociology," which corresponds roughly to the distinction Karl Marx drew between a class on itself (an sich) and a class for itself (fur sich). (Bottomore:186)That is to say, it contrasts the ideologically unconscious and unreflexive black sociological writings of the past to the ideologically conscious and reflexive black sociological writings that, I maintain, we must develop in the future.

Sociology by blacks developed from an early intellectual marriage between black sociologists and liberal white sociologists, with the result that liberal ideology dominated black sociological writings. Put somewhat differently, we might say, sociology by blacks emerged under the hegemony of white liberal ideology. However, to say that the relationship between black sociologists and liberal white sociologists was hegemonic is not to suggest that its effects were necessarily bad. As we can see in Karl Marx's assessment of European colonialism in Asia, hegemonic relationships sometimes may have positive effects. (Marx 1969) The question about whether the effects of a given pattern of hegemony are positive or negative can be determined only by analyzing the prevailing historical conditions, particularly the subordinate community's phase of socio-economic development. Based on this criterion, we can say, the liberal ideological hegemony exercised over black sociological writings was largely positive. Emerging at a time when most black Americans lived in the rural South, where they existed in a state of social and economic backwardness and isolation from the mainstream white society, that liberal ideological hegemony played a major part in transforming white America's racist culture by promoting ideas that challenged crude biological doctrines on racial groups differences. Also, and perhaps most important, that liberal ideological hegemony created opportunities for blacks to pursue professional careers in sociology. Nevertheless, as I will later make clear, the benefits accruing from that liberal ideological hegemony -- like the benefits yielded by colonialism in the third world -- possessed definite historical limits.

W.E. B. DuBois' <u>Philadelphia Negro</u> -- A Forerunner
of Liberal Sociology By Blacks

Before turning to the central development of that hegemonic liberal ideology and its consequences for sociological writings about blacks, we must examine briefly the place in this history occupied by DuBois' Philadelphia Negro. (DuBois 1967)The forerunner of liberal sociology by blacks, Dubois' study derived from liberal white Protestant sponsorship. As Digby Baltzell points out, "W.E.B. DuBois was brought to Philadelphia largely on the initiative of Susan P. Wharton, a member of one of the city's oldest and most prominent Quaker families. She had long been interested in the problems of Negroes and was a member of the Executive Committee of the Philadelphia College of Settlement, which had been founded in 1892. It is important to see." Baltzell goes on to add, "that The Philadelphia Negro was a product of the New Social Science and Settlement House movements, both of which grew up in this country and in England during the closing decades of the nineteenth century." (Baltzell: xvi) During the time of that study's publication in1896, the United States was steeped in a narrow minded racist culture, based on a set of beliefs Baltzell termed "the Anglo-Saxon complex."

> The Anglo-Saxon complex .(reflected) the inevitable racial implications in Social Darwinism, which was the over- whelmingly dominant ideology in America at that time. In an age when men thought of themselves as having evolved from the ape rather than having been created in the image of angels, the Negro, it was almost universally agreed among even the most educated people, was definitely an inferior breed and situated at the very base of the evolutionary tree. (Baltzell:xxi)

This outlook was hardly limited to the popular culture but was manifested also in the dominant sociological outlook of the day. As E. Franklin Frazier later pointed out, sociological theory in the late 19th and early 20th centuries "was not unrelated to public opinion and the dominant racial attitudes of the American people. The racial conflict in the South had subsided and the North had accepted the thesis that the South should solve the race problem . . . . The famous formula of Booker T. Washington, involving the social separation of the races and industrial education, had become the accepted guide to future race relations. The sociological theories which were implicit in the writings on the Negro problem were merely rationalizations of the existing racial situation." (Frazier1968: 35-36)

DuBois' study, it is important to emphasize, did not emanate from the sponsorship of *liberal white sociologists*.. Liberal white sociologists in the late19th century constituted a fractional group that existed at the margins of the newly forming discipline. Thus in contrast to later sociology by blacks, DuBois' study surfaced as a small oasis of liberal thinking in a desert of racist sociological discourse.

The liberal ideology DuBois espoused in The Philadelphia Negro hardly resembled the liberalism of the post World War two period. Rather it expressed a tepid, if not to say, defensive outlook on racial reform, which evidenced several primary features: laissez faire assumptions which looked to charity and private philanthropy for assistance; appeals to whites (re: the white Protestant elite) by skillfully blending moral rhetoric and pragmatic argument; and exhortations to blacks stressing the Protestant ethic virtues of self-help and moral uplift.

An example of DuBois' appeal to whites, along with his implicit assimilationist stance, is revealed in a passage where he discussed black inferiority.

> Men have a right to demand that members of a civilized community be civilized; that the fabric of human culture, so laboriously woven, be not wantonly or ignorantly destroyed. Consequently a nation may rightly demand, even of a people it has consciously and intentionally wronged, not indeed complete civilization in thirty or one hundred years, but at least every effort and sacrifice possible on their part toward making themselves fit members of the community within a reasonable length of time . . . (DuBois:398)

In short, DuBois accepted the prevailing white view of black cultural inferiority. His deference to the dominant white culture's superiority was indicated clearly in his argument for desegregation.

The little decencies of daily intercourse can go on, the courtesies of life be exchanged even across the color line without any danger to the supremacy of the Anglo-Saxon or the social ambition of the Negro.

Sharply contrasted to this appeal for sympathetic concern from whites was his implied exhortation to blacks. (Dubois: 397)

It can be rightly demanded that as far as possible and as rapidly as possible the Negro bend his energy to the solving of his own social problems -- contributing to his poor, paying his share of the taxes and supporting the schools and public administration. (DuBois:389)

But in setting forth this black self-help argument, DuBois was careful not to over do it and risk discouraging external aid. About which he wrote:

Such aid must of necessity be considerable, it must furnish schools and reformatories, and relief and preventive agencies; but the bulk of the work of raising the Negro must be done by the Negro himself... (DuBois:389-90)

This rhetorical melody counter-balancing emphases on black self help and white philanthropy winds throughout the pages of The Philadelphia Negro, as DuBois subtly invoked the ethical principles of a religiously rooted liberalism.

Embracing a naive faith in a positivist "scientific sociology," DuBois carefully compiled empirical data to support his arguments, because he believed, once those findings were clearly presented, they would alter white attitudes toward blacks. But he soon became disillusioned. When he realized the white sociological community was ignoring his book, which was the most sophisticated empirical sociological study, up to that time, undertaken in the United States, DuBois began to have second thoughts about the efficacy of scientific sociology. Though he continued his sociological work for another thirteen years under difficult financial conditions at Atlanta university, he eventually threw in the towel and abandoned his liberal sociological career to become a political activist. Devoting his efforts to advocacy and agitation rather than to sociological research as the means to effect racial reform, DuBois sustained his activist role, albeit from a variety of ideological perspectives, throughout the remainder of his long life.

While DuBois' study evidenced liberal ideology, it is important to emphasize, its liberalism did not derive from the influence of liberal white sociologists. We can only speculate what might have happened if the incisive and strong willed DuBois had embarked on his sociological career a decade or so later, after the liberal ideological hegemony had crystalized in sociology. No doubt both DuBois' intellectual career and sociology by blacks would have taken a different direction.

Robert Park and The Chicago School : Institutionalizing Paternalistic Hegemony

It was Robert Park, the leading figure of the Chicago School of sociology, who played the key role in institutionalizing both the sociology of race relations and the liberal ideological hegemony over sociology by blacks. The initial phase of that development was manifested in what I term the the paternal hegemonic pattern, which consisted of sociological writings on blacks by whites. Not surprisingly, the writings emanating from this early liberal paternalistic pattern of sociology on blacks by whites featured white American conceptions of black American life. For example, Park's theoretical formulations such as the race relations cycle and civilizational process, which derived from his white American Protestant world view, pioneered this hegemonic discourse. (Hughes) While liberal in the sense that it harbored no biological notions of black inferiority, Park's sociology differed from progressive forms of liberalism, such as that espoused by Jane Adams, Lincoln Steffins, and John Dewey, because he ignored political power. In effect, Park believed that social life developed through natural processes of evolution, an idea resembling in some ways Adam Smith's economic notion of the "hidden hand," that operated independent of political institutions. Indeed, it suggested that political intervention would harm rather than advance these natural processes. We see this clearly in his theory of the race relations cycle, with its phases of contact, conflict, accommodation, and assimilation, which incorporated laissez-faire assumptions. "Were blacks demanding social equity with whites only to be refused at every turn? Then their demands must be out of kilter with the times. They were simply unaware that they were living in an age of accommodation and that social equality was reserved for the next stage of their relations with whites." (Lyman:31)Matters pertaining to legal and constitutional processes as potential sources of racial reform Park simply ignored.

Park's naturalistic, evolutionary conception of race relations attracted him to Booker T. Washington's work, and, though less well known, caused him to sympathize with the activities of European colonialists like Cecil Rhodes in South Africa. (Matthews:57) Concomitantly, that evolutionary perspective turned him against the work of liberal political activists, who he regarded as little more than rabble rousers and propagandists. Projecting this stoical brand of liberalism, Park achieved considerable influence in American sociology. As Stanford Lyman has pointed out,"two generations of sociologists had for the most part accepted not only the general principles of the original cycle but also its promise of an eventual racelessness in the world." (Matthews 35) This was especially true of black sociologists.

Despite the weaknesses in his circular and apolitical theory of race relations change, Park brought to the study of black Americans in particular, and encounters between racial groups in general, a systematic analytical perspective that superseded a legacy of crude biological ideas in sociology. In that sense, his work constituted an advance. Moreover, resulting directly from his enormous influence as the foremost sociological race relations theorist between the two world wars, Park had a major hand in training Charles Johnson and E. Franklin Frazier, that generation's two leading black sociologists, who initiated the liberal sociology by blacks that dominated the modern period.

<u>Charles Johnson and E. Franklin Frazier</u> : The Co-optive Hegemonic Pattern of Black Sociological Writings on Blacks

Notwithstanding the outstanding intellectual achievement of DuBois's <u>Philadelphia Negro</u>, it was the work of Charles Johnson and E. Franklin Frazier that established the dominant liberal ideological paradigm for sociology by blacks . Though Johnson and Frazier began their sociological careers before the New Deal, they eventually embraced the liberal New Deal ideological agenda, with its emphasis on the welfare state. It is impossible to exaggerate the importance of the New Deal, for its policies transformed American political culture. As Talcott Parsons has correctly observed, "the New Deal brought the first major governmental entry into the field of guaranteeing the social components of citizenship through labor and social welfare legislation, establishing a trend which could readily be extended into the field of protecting minority groups. Combined with various other measures of governmental control, this entailed both a strengthening of the federal government's administrative machinery and a general increase in popular support for such strengthening." (Parsons: xxi)

Though the New Deal's depression-era policies ignored civil rights, blacks benefited from the economic assistance programs brought about by those policies.

The most important New Deal contribution to black Americans . . . was its creation of relief and welfare programs. Few such programs made special provisions for blacks, and some permitted substantial discrimination against them. But the New Deal did give significant economic assistance to many African Americans, and Roosevelt received overwhelmingsupport from black voters in return. (Brinkley:166)

In consequence, this New Deal conception of the activist state became a central premise in the ideological vision of sociology by blacks.

In contrast to Park's writings about blacks, which never incorporated New Deal influence, Johnson's and Frazier's sociological writings, as did the writings of other black sociologists, subsumed potential welfare state initiatives. Even so, Park's influence on their sociological outlook remained strong. This can be seen particularly in their cultural suppositions. Though their writings exhibited greater empirical depth than Park's writings on blacks, their conceptions of black American life were not grounded in black American culture. When describing aspects of black American culture such as its religious practices or family patterns, they invariably 'bracketed' or subsumed these within a theoretical framework derived from white American culture. As Richard Robbins has noted in reference to Charles Johnson's Shadow of the Plantation, which focused on the lives of six hundred Mississippi black families: "At the outset in the "folk" material, there are traces in Johnson's approach of that defensiveness, that accommodation to white definitions of "the Negro problem," which marked some of the social science research of the time." (Robbins:68)

Robert Park's influence on Charles Johnson was especially strong. From the beginning of Johnson's sociological career, Park closely steered his work. Park got Johnson appointed to his first major job, as research director of the Chicago Riot Commission, shortly after that city's tragic1919 race riot. Though Johnson is credited with writing the Commission's report, Park was heavily involved in the study. " Park's role in the research study and the later recommendations was crucial. Eighteen staff researchers were hired; three, like Johnson, were Park's students. Of the seven who later wrote drafts of the Commission report, three had studied under Park." (Carey:78)

Bearing the imprint of Park's views, the report suggested that the police should curb their discrimination toward blacks and increase their control on the actions of white juvenile gangs, the main instigators of anti-black violence. Yet it recommended no enforcement machinery. In the words of one analyst of the report, "the Chicago Commission on Race Relations, as an experiment in sociology-policy-making partnership, was a failure, if implementation of recommendations is the measure." (Carey:80) Nothing came of the report. It was the first in what was to be a long line of officially sponsored liberal reports on major racial disturbances over the ensuing decades, reports that created expectations of major reforms, only to be relegated to the dustbins of history.

In many ways, Charles Johnson's career exemplified the co-opted hegemonic pattern. As we can see from what Robbins has termed "the astonishing range of Johnson's involvement with commissions and foundations concerned with public policy (i.e. from the Chicago period of his work with the Urban League to the Post-World War II period of his service with President Truman's commission for the reorganization of education in Japan)," Johnson became the first 'token' black American academic to gain entry into the white American establishment. As Robbins notes:

> In 1930 he was a member of the League of Nations commission to investigate forced labor in Liberia. . . . In 1931 he coordinated President Hoover's special commission on Negro housing and home building. During the New Deal period there was other advisory and research work for the Tennessee Valley Authority, the Southern Commission on the Study of Lynching, and the Southern Regional Council. Other commission responsibilities concerned farm tenancy, national health priorities, and national manpower needs. He served as well on the advisory board of the National Youth Administration (NYA) in Tennessee in the early forties and, in the same period, participated actively in the White House Conference for Children. _

Small wonder that Johnson found it difficult to criticize the white power structure. In Robbins' words: "Johnson continued to work so closely with the white philanthropic and governmental establishment over so many years that he could not bring himself to a dramatic challenge in print against the real white power structure that sanctioned the whole system of discrimination and segregation."(Robbins:73)

Much the same can be said about E. Franklin Frazier's work, at least until the last few years of his sociological career. More than any other black scholar of the 1930s and 1940s period, Frazier was responsible for the propagating dubious conceptions about black American culture. Regarded for several decades as a leading authority on slavery, Frazier argued that slavery had de-cultured blacks, leaving them without a distinctive set of values and traditions that could operate as the basis of an organized community life. Though not all of Frazier's views are traceable to Robert Park and the Chicago School, the theoretical framework of his sociological writings on black American culture reflected the influence of Park and Ernest Burgess. We see an example of the way the Chicago School legitimized and reinforced Frazier's distorted conception of the black family in a review Burgess wrote praising Frazier's The Negro Family in the United States, the work which argued that black family disorganization resulted from the destruction of black culture under slavery. In what can only be described as an act of intellectual arrogance, Burgess, who knew even less than Frazier about the black family, anointed the study as "the most important contribution to the literature on the family since the publication of the Polish Peasant. . . " (Edwards:94) This reflected the way in which liberal white sociologists routinely valorized liberal sociology by blacks; Frazier's study immediately acquired the aura of canonical authority.

This Frazierian legacy of misconceptions about the black family took odd turns. It was partly the influence of Frazier's writings on the black family that prompted Daniel Patrick Moynihan to write his essay on black illegitimacy, which turned out to be one of the most controversial sociological works on black Americans published in the post world war two period. In the words of one author, ". . . the Moynihan Report came to be viewed as an attack upon the Negro family and its author was widely criticized for his views. The fact that much of the subject matter treated in the Report had been addressed by Frazier in The Negro Family in the United States, coupled with Moynihan's frequent citation of the volume, established a linkage between the two works." (Edwards:97)

But probably the most serious charge against Frazier's liberal sociology came from the anthropologist, Charles Vallentine, who accused "Frazier of having established a pejorative tradition by concluding that the Negro masses do not live by any coherent cultural patterns and that 'the existence of the modern Negro poor is an immoral chaos brought about by the disintegration of black folk culture under the impact of urbanization'. " (Vallentine:29)

As a co-opted hegemonic discourse, Frazier's perspective on black Americans, like that of Johnson, failed to resonate black American culture. Critiquing Frazier's theoretical suppositions, Vallentine highlights this cultural distortion .

> An essential element in Frazier's reasoning is one that is perpetuated
> by later thinkers. This is a direct logical step from social statistics,
> which are deviant in terms of middle class norms, to a model of
> disorder and instability. Such reasoning effectively eliminates
> consideration of possible cultural forms that, in spite of differing

from Frazier's assumed standard, might have their own order and function. (Vallentine:29)

Frazier's Black Bourgeoisie was in many ways the most egregious example of this cultural distortion. (Frazier 1957) Quite apart from the issue of the accuracy of his description of the black middle class, the question arises: whose conception of a middle class life was Frazier using as his standard of comparison? Though Frazier never said so explicitly, he obviously was using a white American middle class standard of reference. In charging that the black middle class was not behaving as it should, he was betraying his allegiance to white middle class norms, which he believed, without ever saying so, defined the universal standard in terms of which the black middle class could be validly compared. This was consistent with Frazier's liberal ideological supposition, which then regarded black America's eventual assimilation into the mainstream white society as the ideal.

Frazier acknowledged Park's influence. As Franklin Edwards has pointed out in his discussion of Frazier's career: " He credits Park with changing the study of race relations from a social problems approach to a sociological approach which made for a more objective analysis of behavior in this area. His framework for the study of race and culture contacts is taken over from Park, although . . . with some modification; and his natural history approach to the Negro family and the concepts of the lack of influence of the African background on Negro American experience owe much to Park." (Edwards, 1974:111) Though Frazier acknowledged Park's intellectual influence, he seemed oblivious to its ideological implications.

Why did Johnson, Frazier and most other black sociologists of the modern period fail to incorporate black American conceptions of black reality in their analytical perspectives on black American life? It was because they identified with the liberal ideological perspective, which, in their view, embodied universally valid ethical and scientific principles of social organization. It is important to recall that this preceded the influence of cultural relativist ideas. Hence these black sociologists, having internalized a naive scientific positivism, never questioned mainstream sociology's cultural suppositions. Their acquiescent attitude bore testimony to the strength of the liberal ideological hegemony. This was not unusual, for as Antonio Gramsci pointed out, hegemonic ideology becomes so deeply internalized in the subordinate group's consciousness that it operates as common sense. (Gramsci, 1971)

Though that liberal ideology hardly turned out to be the panacea black sociologists supposed, it did effect progressive social and racial reforms, as noted above. In fact, from the period of World War I to the early 1960s, most black sociologists regarded liberalism and black American interests as being synonymous. So much so, a foreign observer would have found it difficult to discern significant disagreement or debate between white liberal sociologists and most black American sociologists.

If Johnson and Frazier seemed disinclined to apologize for ignoring black American culture in their theoretical conceptions of black American life, it was because they regarded black American culture as essentially a folk culture, emanating from a past mired in poverty and substandard education, which blacks would eventually grow beyond. Racial integration and assimilation into the mainstream white society were destiny.

The Golden Era of Liberal Sociology on Blacks: 1945-1965

At no time in the history of liberal sociology on blacks did the future of racial integration and assimilation appear to be more inevitable than during the two decades following the second world war. Gunnar Myrdal's An American Dilemma marked the beginning of this new era in liberal sociology on blacks. (Myrdal, 1964) As Meier, Bracey and Rudwick have noted, "the   publication of this opus in 1944 . . . " symbolized "the hegemony of the racial equalitarian point of view among sociologists of race relations." (Bracey, 1971) Sociological writings on blacks abandoned the the cautious and tentative Chicago school perspective. And for the first time, due in large part to Myrdal's An American Dilemma, the plight of black Americans gained national recognition as a major social problem. Grounding his analysis on American culture, Myrdal argued that white America's treatment of blacks contradicted the nation's most cherished democratic ideals, which he termed the American Creed.

This landmark work departed from pervious sociological writings on blacks in several significant ways. Unlike the earlier sociologists who had written about blacks and the racial problem, Myrdal was a foreigner, a European scholar from a non-colonizer nation, who it was assumed lacked the racial prejudices that permeated American culture, as well as the cultures of European imperialist nations such as Britain, France, and Holland. Also in contrast to previous sociological works on blacks, Myrdal's study received generous financial support. The result of a grant from the Carnegie Foundation, its ample financial resources made it possible for the study achieve another unprecedented feat --- the incorporation of contributions from the most eminent black sociologists of the day. In an effort to broaden the range of his inquiry, Mrydal hired Charles Johnson, E. Franklin Frazier, Ira De Augustine Reid, and Alison Davis, along with many other talented black American social scientist research consultants, to write reports on various aspects of black American life. (Bracey, 1971: 20) It is important to recognize that this arrangement, aside from eliciting invaluable contributions from these black social scientists, continued even more directly the co-optive hegemony we noted above. No previous sociological writings on blacks had drawn on such a large and talented pool of black social scientists. One consequence of their participation was their conspcicuous silence in reference to the study's shortcomings, and particularly Myrdal's liberal conception of American race relations. It was hardly coincidental, though somewhat surprising, that the most penetrating criticism of Myrdal's view of black culture came not from black American social scientists, but from Ralph Ellison, a black American literary artist. (1964)

Another feature that distinguished the study from earlier sociological writings on blacks was its imposing scholarly apparatus: forty-five chapters of 1,024 pages; ten appendixes of over a hundred pages; a bibliography of 37 pages; and over 250 pages of footnotes. This, in addition to the author's foreign background and extensive collaboration with black specialists, undoubtedly contributed to the study's aura of authority.

As for the study's liberal ideological argument, what stood out most clearly, in contrast to previous sociological studies of blacks, was its concern with the role of values in social science research. Unlike the Chicago School, Myrdal refused to hide behind the rhetoric of scientific objectivity. Rather he responded directly to the issue of value bias, not by claiming immunity through professional detachment or training but by acknowledging frankly the role of values in sociological discourse. In his words: "There is no other device for excluding biases in social sciences than to face valuation and to introduce them as explicitly stated, specific, and sufficiently concretized value premises." (Frazier, 1980: 160) In light of the controversy surrounding the American race problem, the study made a suprisingly bold stand in setting forth its liberal value commitment. It is doubtful that an American sociologist would have dared be so forthcoming about the problem of value bias in such a study.

This was not lost on E. Franklin Frazier who, in reviewing the book for The American Journal of Sociology, noted: "This position in regard to value judgments in social science will certainly be opposed by most American sociologists. But when one considers this position in relation to the author's statement that 'the value premises should be selected by the criterion of relevance and significance to the culture under study,' it would be difficult to challenge the author's position." (Frazier, 1980: 160) But whose culture would be the frame of reference for those value premises-- black Americans' or white Americans' ? This question Frazier failed to raise.

Myrdal does not use the term 'ideology' in his discussion of values, but there can be no doubt he embraced a liberal equalitarian ideology. Where Park and his Chicago school proteges avoided raising moral concerns in their discussions of race relations, Myrdal placed the issue of morality -- liberal morality -- at the very center of his analysis. "The Negro problem is essentially a moral problem, not because of a conflict between valuations held by different persons and groups, but because it is a moral struggle within people themselves." (Frazier, 1980: 161) The higher democratic ideals of the American people, Mrydal argued, consisted of a liberal morality of fairness and inclusion. This emphasis on the moral dimension of American racial relations, it should be noted, foreshadowed the strategy of moral engagement that Martin Luther King would use to mobilize public support for black civil rights roughly a decade later.

Similarly prescient, and departing from previous liberal sociological writings on blacks, was Myrdal's global perspective. For Mrydal, it was not sufficient to inject liberal morality into analysis of the race problem; that problem had to be viewed within the context of the international political arena, and linked to pragmatic considerations of national interests, by calling attention to its ramifications for the cold war. In the words of one historian,

> The book was a factor in drawing white liberal attention to problems of race -- precisely because Myrdal himself discussed racial injustice as a rebuke to the nation's increasingly vocal claim to be the defender of democracy and personal freedom in a world measured by totalitarianism. (Brinkley: 169)

Myrdal argued that the United States, in its competition against communism in Asia and Africa, had to solve its race problem, if it hoped to demonstrate the superiority of its way of life. Which is to say, Myrdal correctly anticipated that the collapse of European colonial empires and the rise of new post colonial states would create pressures to change the status of black Americans. By discussing the American race problem in terms of the United States' struggle against communism, Myrdal introduced a new dimension in the liberal sociological perspective on blacks.

In concluding his study, Myrdal expressed optimism because he believed America's liberal values would prevail. We can see this optimism still beaming some eighteen years later. In the introduction he wrote to the 1962 edition of The American Dilemma, Myrdal paid tribute to Frederick Keppel, the head of Carnegie Foundation, who had commissioned the study. Referring to Keppel as a true liberal, Myrdal noted that:

> As long as America has men like Keppel placed   in responsible positions . .The trend toward greater fulfillment of the liberalideals cannot be reversed, and America will remain a bastion of intellectual freedom and social progress. (Myrdal: xxvi)

That optimistic liberal equalitarian view was incorporated into the outlook of the post war sociology of race relations. Indeed, the last three features of Myrdal's study that we noted above -- its open commitment to liberal values, its emphasis on the moral dimension of the race problem, and its view of that problem in terms of the international political arena -- operated as a virtual ideological paradigm for post war sociological writings on blacks.

Even so, despite its vaunted optimism, Myrdal's study possessed several major weaknesses, which distorted its view of American race relations. The first consisted of its suggestion that racial injustices against blacks was "on the conscience of white America." This misrepresented black-white relations. As E. Frazier pointed out in his review, many blacks passively accepted their inferior status, and the whites they encountered hardly felt guilty when they encountered such subservient black behavior. Quite the contrary. That behavior tended to confirm their attitudes about black inferiority. Frazier then went on to clarify the issue of white moral guilt that Myrdal apparently misunderstood. "For many whites the Negro lives in an entirely different social world or is not part of the same moral order. It is when the Negro emerges as a human being and a part of the moral order that discrimination against him is on the conscience of the white man" (Frazier, 1980: 161). When precisely this occurs, Frazier did not say. But the conditions of racial segregation in the United States hardly conduced to white moral engagement, in the absence of black protest.

Second, Myrdal's liberal sociological ideology placed too much faith in moral ideals. What becomes of those moral ideals when they conflict with economic, familial, and self interests?   Mrydal presented a palatable moral critique with a painless solution, that is, a solution that would avoid challenging the dominant institutional structure and conflicting with prevailing white American interests. Such a critique was far more likely to appeal to American corporate and foundation elites than was one that advocated major changes in the American political economy, residential neighborhoods, job hiring practices, and legal sanctions for racial discrimination.

In effect, Mrydal's study amounted to a "feel good" moral critique. And as such it presented an attractive alternative to Marxist, black nationalist, and other "unsettling" radical perspectives on American race relations. But that rosy prognosis was achieved by ignoring the actual demons behind American racial inequality, namely, those interests that benefited from the racial status quo, which would abandon liberalism if its racial reforms that demanded major white American sacrifices.

Third, and closely related to the above point, the study tended to draw sharp contrasts between the North and the South. Indeed, the South was scripted to perform the role of pariah in this liberal morality play.

> In the South the supremacy and impersonality of the law do not exist so far as the Negro is concerned. Negroes are constantly subject to the brutality of white policeman, usually ignorant and poorly paid, who do not only maintain caste rules but also protect whites in their aggressions against Negroes. Consequently, Negroes do not have the feeling of personal security they have in the North. Likewise, the 'vicious circle' of discrimination and poverty is analyzed in connection with the rationalizations which the South uses to justify its treatment of Negroes as former slaves. (Myrdal: 533-534)

This heavy emphasis on southern racism turned out to be overdrawn not because the South was being misrepresented -- blacks did experience the South as a facist region -- but because it caused Myrdal and his followers to underestimate racial problems in the North, the regional base of liberal ideology. Northern cities also had serious racial problems, but these were more intertwined with the industrial capitalist economy, which liberals were not inclined to criticize. Hence the postwar liberal ideological paradigm failed to anticipate the racial tensions and violence that erupted in northern ghettoes.

While the study's underestimation of the North's racial problems constituted a serious weakness, it was its liberal hegemonic cultural premises, its ethnocentrism, that revealed perhaps its greatest flaw. As Stanford Lyman has noted:

> Myrdal sees the black as existing in the shadow of American culture, dependent on its slow but inexorable changes, subject to its cultural, social and idiosyncratic whims, to be liberated by eventual absorption into the American system, which will then have triumphed in the final solution of the black problem.(Lyman: 120)

This flaw Myrdal shared with his liberal predecessors, because he measured developments in black American life from the perspective of assimilation.

While Myrdal's An American Dilemma had a large hand in fostering the new liberal equalitarian sociological perspective on blacks, that study was by no means the only influential liberal sociological work of the period. We should note a few examples. Among these liberal sociological works there was a study by Bruno Bettlehiem and Morris Janowitz which went beyond Mydral's moral argument by suggesting a link between ethnic prejudice and economic insecurity, specifically downward economic mobility. Pointing to the policy implications of their findings, the authors noted, "It seems reasonable that, as long as anxiety and insecurity persist as a root of intolerance, the effort to dispel stereotypes by rational propaganda is at best a half-measure." (Bettlehiem and Janowitz: 178). This suggested potential problems in attempting to change the racial prejudices of whites who were experiencing, or feeling threatened by, a decline in their economic status.

But aside from that specific finding, the Bettleheim-Janowitz study evidenced another significant feature: the suggestion that outgroup prejudices were often generalized to several minority groups. We see this theme in other liberal post war social psychological studies of prejudice. As Stanford Lyman has noted in reference to Gordon Allport's The Nature of Prejudice and T. W. Adorno, et. al. Authoritarian Personality, these studies emphasized "the psychological characteristics of American society in general and white men in particular. . . . They see the black, together with the Jew and other members of minorities, as the victim of white men's mental problems; only with the elimination of these mental problems will the race problem become stable." (Lyman:121) This tendency to equate the racial oppression of blacks with the oppression experienced by other minority groups, expressed an equalitarian view of victimhood that would characterize liberal sociological ideology until the mid-1960s.

Liberal sociology on blacks marked perhaps its greatest achievement in its influence on the1954 Supreme Court school desegregation decision. That influence emanated primarily from two sources. First was the research done by Kenneth and Mamie Clark demonstrating the psychologically damaging effects of racially segregated schools on black children. Lawyers from the NAACP Legal Fund contacted the Clarks because they had heard about the research they were doing on black children in segregated southern schools. As Clark later recalled, the

NAACP lawyers "were seeking the repeal of the Plesssy v. Ferguson doctrine of 'separate but equal' which required or permitted racial segregation in the public schools. They were seeking to demonstrate to the courts that even if the conditions were adequate, racially separate schools could never be equal." (Clark: 15) The second influence on the court's decision derived from expert testimony given by a number of liberal social scientists, later summarized in the <u>Social Science Appendix to the Legal Brief</u>, which was accepted by the Supreme Court and cited in footnote 11 of the Brown decision.

It is impossible to overstate the importance of that Supreme Court decision, which broke through the tradition of legalized segregation like a sudden rupture in a dike, unleashing a flood of long pent up black American aspirations. That decision, prompted by the Court's acknowledgment of the American democratic ideals Myrdal had emphasized, set in motion liberal social forces that transformed the landscape of American race relations. Starting with the Montgomery bus boycott and black college students' demonstrations that launched the civil rights movement in the South, then followed by the Congressional Civil Rights Acts of 1964 and 1965 and the War on Poverty legislation, and, finally, culminating with demise of the anti-poverty programs in the early 1970s, American race relations experienced the most dynamic period of reforms since the end of slavery. And liberal sociological influence had a large hand in effecting those reforms. In fact, never before or since has American sociology exercised so much influence on national public policy.

The Conservative Backlash in National Political Life

If the1960s ushered in unprecedented liberal racial reforms, that decade also marked the beginning of a conservative backlash, evidenced in mounting opposition to black demands for equality, that cast a cloud over the future of liberalism. Many factors contributed to that backlash. First, there was the increased tension in race relations in the North which resulted from a series of ghetto riots and the emergence of a radical black nationalist movement, events that reflected the increased frustrations felt by many poor northern blacks living in inner city ghettos. Second, there was the southern white reaction to the Voting Rights Act, a development that spelled a political realignment in the South. In fact, President Lyndon Johnson had anticipated this change, saying as he signed the new law: "I have just handed over the white South to the Republican party for the next half century." This turned out to be a prescient political observation, as we can see today, roughly three decades later: The white South has become the most solidly Republican region in the country.

Third, there was the impact of Title VII, the anti-job discrimination provision in the Civil Rights Act of 1964, which encountered opposition from labor unions. Although these unions were key groups in the New Deal coalition, their liberalism did not extend to hiring and promotion practices in the workplace. Most unions historically had operated to protect white workers' privileges.

> As unions in many sectors of the economy had become the institutional expression of white employment expectations, based upon the systematic subordination of black labor, white workers for generations had taken for granted the assumptions of discriminatory racial norms and bitterly resisted any alteration or deviation. Thus many unions supported the actions of whites against black workers who were challenging discriminatory practices. (Hill: 328)

Because it provided black workers legal redress from racial discrimination, the Civil Rights Act of 1964 provoked racist reactions among white workers in the North, racist reactions that weakened the Democratic party in the 1968 presidential campaign. In the words of the labor scholar, Herbert Hill:

> The adoption of the Civil Rights Act of 1964, and its subsequent enforcement by the federal courts, was a major factor in the defection of the northern white working class from the coalition that had constituted the Democratic party. Race redefined political relationships and there emerged a racist populism that fueled the retreat on civil rights.(328)

The most immediate manifestation of this white working class defection from the Democratic party could be seen in the surprising surge of George Wallace's popularity. " . . . Running on a racist platform," in the 1968 presidential campaign, Wallace "garnered 10 million votes, receiving significant support in many northern industrial areas with large concentrations of white union members. " (328)

This conservative backlash led to Richard Nixon's election to the presidency in 1968. Throwing aside all moral scruples, Nixon cynically exploited the white racist sentiments that Wallace had galvanized in both the North and the South. Thinly veiling his racial messages in such code words as "law and order," "silent majority," and "southern strategy," Nixon not only gave a new respectability to white racism; he helped to set back American race relations perhaps half a century.

Though few observers then anticipated major changes, the 1968 presidential election foreshadowed the future   direction of American politics. As Herbert Hill accurately notes:

> Race supplanted class as an organizing principle of American politics in the postreform period that began after judicial enforcement of the civil rights legislation enacted in the 1960s, and given the white hostility to black advancement, racism became the decisive factor in determining the politics of the nation. Para- doxically, the coalition formed in the period of Franklin D. Roosevelt's New Deal was shattered by its last major victory: the adoption of the civil rights act of 1964. (329)

In its effort to translate liberal ideals into public policies of racial reform, the Democratic party leaders alienated a substantial part of its power base, because they failed to recognize that many northern whites had vested interests in the society's racial stratification. For these whites, racial reforms were fine as long as they occurred in distant places like Montgomery and Little Rock, and did not affect their lives.

> There was intense opposition by white workers to compliance with the law, especially in regard to job security, affirmative action, and school desegregation. These issues clearly affected the lives of urban whites. Earlier civil rights struggles were largely concentrated in the South, and advances were for the most part of a limited, symbolic nature that required no change in the daily lives of white people, especially those living in northern states. But after 1964 institutional changes in the status of blacks directly impinged on the lives of white workers who sought to maintain their race-connected privileges.(328-329)

Liberal ideals were cast aside as the political system soon began to accommodate these white anxieties and, thereby, impose brutal -- if not to say, insurmountable -- constraints on further racial reform. In recognizing this situation, Derrick Bell, the black American legal scholar and former civil rights activist, has articulated what might be termed the "new American Dilemma" confronting efforts to redress white racial injustices against blacks. In a political system based on white interests, as Bell puts it: "Black gains must not translate into direct or indirect white losses."(80) Policies of racial reform not only should be just; they must avoid threatening white interests. This was the unpleasant lesson of American society's failure to solve its race problem, marking the demise of the liberal ideals that had generated the New Deal coalition.

The Rise of the Neo-Conservative Movement

While a number of forces contributed to liberalism's decline, none did so with as much determination as did the neo-conservative movement. (Steinfels, 1979) Surfacing in the early 1970s amid increasing disillusionment with liberalism within mainstream white America, the neoconservative movement soon grew into a major political force. Conservatism was hardly a new phenomenon in American politics. A conservative American political tradition can be traced back to the founders of the nation such as George Washington, Alexander Hamilton, and James Madison. But by the end of the 19th century, conservatism had lost its intellectual vitality. Its European philosophical roots having atrophied, conservative ideology became associated with the provincial values of Main Street and the economic ideology of American business, stressing Protestant ethic values of religion, self-reliance, and individualism.

In contrast to this provincial and business tradition of conservatism, neoconservatism constituted a genuine intellectual movement. Comprised mostly of academic intellectuals, many having defected from liberalism in the late 1960s and early 1970s, the neoconservative movement set out not just to criticize liberal public policies but to demolish their intellectual rationale, their commitment to compassion and assistance for the disadvantaged, as misguided social engineering.

To say that this neoconservative movement differed from the older strain of conservatism is not to say there were no links between them. Neoconservatives embraced many of the older conservative values celebrating business enterprise and the free market. But even more important, it harvested considerable financial support from the older conservative sources, financial support that soon transformed the movement into a prosperous and highly effective intellectual machine.

From the early 1970s, self-identified neo-conservatives had, in fact, developed close ties with the Scaife, Smith Richardson, and John M. Olin foundations. All of these institutions, which have devoted their resources to upholding traditional American values, have become reliable sources for funding neoconservative (as well as other conservative) enterprises. The Hoover Institution, the Heritage Foundation, and the American Enterprise Institute also include neo-conservatives among their trustees and resident scholars. Significantly, all three of these think tanks, which have multimillion dollar annual operating budgets, began as vehicles for old right movement conservatives. (Gottfried: 73)

The most important dividend yielded by the movement's financial resources was media influence. As Peter Steinfels observes:

> Neoconservatives have frequently complained of a liberal "oppositionist" bias in the media. Their own position in the media, however, has never been weak, and now grows increasingly stronger. Besides Commentary, and The Public Interest, they have long-standing ties with Encounter, The New Leader, American Scholar, and Foreign Policy. They turn up in T. V. Guide as well as Reader's Digest, Fortune, Business Week, and U.S. News and World Report. (Steinfels: 8)

Also, neoconservative journalists and intellectuals have appeared regularly on television news programs such as the Brinkley show, Nightline, McNeil Leherer, and CNN news programs, assailing liberal public policies and advocating a return to conservative American values.

Without question, the public policy issue that most preoccupied neoconservatives has been that of race. Their opposition to the post civil rights liberal programs targeted for black Americans prompted most neoconservatives to abandon liberalism.

If one belief set neoconservatives apart from most black Americans, as well as others committed to liberal ideology, it was their belief that the problems of racial discrimination in the United States were solved by the 1960s civil rights legislation. For instance, in a November 1985 Commentary magazine article, the neo-conservative sociologist Peter Berger hailed what he termed "the gigantic political efforts to ensure that no group within (America) is excluded from the cornucopia of industrial capitalism" and then went on to marvel "at how racial discrimination was abolished in the span of a few years." (Gottfried and Fleming: viii)

Following directly from this belief that racial discrimination ended in the United States in the 1960s, neoconservatives opposed compensatory liberal programs aimed to redress the effects of past discrimination against blacks, on the grounds that such programs unfairly victimized whites.

To understand the deeper rationale for their opposition to compensatory liberalism, we must comprehend the neoconservative conception of equality. In the words of Peter Steinfels, " one of the most perplexing aspects of neoconservatism is its apparent belief that America is in the grip of implacable equalitarianism." To illustrate this point, Steinfels quotes the neoconservative sociologist Nathan Glazer, who "gloomily contemplates the 'awesome potency' of 'the revolution of equality . . . the most powerful social force in the modern world." This social force, according to Glazer, "not only expresses a demand for equality in political rights and in political power; it also represents a demand for equality in economic power, in social status, in authority in every sphere . . . . There is no point at which the equality revolution can come to an end'. "(Steinfels: 214)

As can be seen in Glazer view, neoconservatives embrace a narrow conception of equality, which they define in terms of formal equality of opportunity. Thus in their view, if no barriers to black access are visible, racial discrimination is nonexistent. Because they assume that racial discrimination is always observable, they refuse to acknowledge covert, informal, and insidious forms of discrimination which, because they are harder to detect, may require affirmative action and other forms of official monitoring to counteract.

In effect, neoconservatives have no response to problems such as the virtual absence of blacks in upper level executive positions in banking, insurance, communications, advertising, and other areas of the private sector -- except to say that blacks apparently lack sufficient talent or motivation. Neoconservatives do not write about racism as a social problem; rather they write about what they term "reverse racism," arguing that the black demands for government programs to counter entrenched habits of racial discrimination violate the American norms of meritocracy. As Daniel Patrick Moynihan has put it: "The point of semantics is that equality of opportunity now has a different meaning for Negroes than it has for whites. It is not (or at least no longer) a demand for liberty alone, but also equality -- in terms of group results." (Steinfels: 217) In Moynihan's view, blacks are demanding not equal opportunity but something approximating socialism, giving them a "distribution of achievements roughly comparable to that among whites."

What is especially noteworthy about this neoconservative characterization of black demands for affirmative action and similar programs is their refusal to acknowledge the persisting problem of racial discrimination. Corresponding to their disregard of racial barriers, they also oppose the post civil rights anti-poverty programs, seeing them as threatening to the American class system. We see a typical example of their contempt for these programs in Nathan Glazer's vitriolic attack on Lyndon Johnson's Great Society initiatives.

> The Great Society was part of that "decade of rubbish"; it proved that the negative, unintended consequences of social intervention would out-weigh the positive, intended ones; it increased social conflict without relieving social ills; the burden of political commentary should

be to oppose any movement toward similar programs rather than revive the spirit of that period. (Stenfels: 219)

Cracks in the Liberal Sociological Community

Running parallel to the neoconservative movement in the political arena was an anti-liberal neoconservative reaction in sociology and other social sciences. This was particularly significant in sociology, where a number of former liberal sociologists assumed prominence in the neoconservative ranks. Though most regard themselves as detached scholars, they have operated in sociology, as well as other social sciences, primarily as polemicists, seeking to intellectually legitimate conservatives social policies. A few examples will illustrate this point.

The first neoconservative crack in sociology's liberal ideological paradigm on blacks appeared relatively early, in 1965, when Daniel Patrick Moynihan wrote what turned out to be an infamous report on the black American family. (Moynihan) Attributing black poverty to the relatively high prevalence of female headed households in the black community, Moynihan placed the blame for this situation on black males. This report, which provoked anger and a feeling of betrayal among black sociologists, who had regarded Moynihan as a liberal, violated a sacred tenet of the liberal sociological paradigm: It placed the blame for poverty on its victims rather than the social system. Hence Moynihan's report surfaced as one of the earliest signs that some white sociologists were beginning to retreat from the liberal paradigm on blacks, with its emphasis on racism and discrimination as primary causes of black American social problems.

Following the Moynihan report, James Coleman's attack on busing was the next most significant crack in the dominant liberal sociological paradigm on blacks. (1966) As the author of the most comprehensive empirical study of school inequality ever undertaken in the United States, Coleman was widely regarded as a leading authority on school integration. But he soon retreated from his earlier support of integration policies. Influenced by the white backlash, evidenced in the movement of whites out of urban neighborhoods targeted for busing, Coleman argued that busing was counterproductive. What was ideologically significant about Coleman's stance was not his opposition to busing on tactical grounds, for some blacks, as well as some liberal whites, had also expressed misgivings about busing. Rather it was Coleman's failure to articulate an alternative means to achieve the goal of school integration. Such alternatives as neighborhood desegregation, housing subsidies to allow blacks live in suburbs, or some non-residential criterion for assigning students to public schools were simply ignored. Hence Coleman's objection to busing left segregated public schools as the only alternative, effectively abandoning the era's most important racial reform, in order to accommodate white racial sentiments. Coleman's opposition did not stop with busing; he soon began criticizing the federal courts' role in desegregating schools, arguing that those decisions violated democratic process. Throughout his involvement in the busing controversy, Coleman failed to see the issue of school desegregation as a matter of securing black American constitutional rights to quality public school education in a society that was unprepared to alter its tradition of racially segregated housing. His position exemplifed the 'new American Dilemma' I alluded to above. Though Coleman's argument provoked outrage among many liberal and leftist sociologists, it helped to sway lay public opinion and legitimate the retreat from school desegregation in the North.

Following Coleman's attack on busing, the anti-liberal sociological work that ignited the next most bitter conflict was Nathan Glazer's Affirmative Discrimination. (1975)   Attacking affirmative action programs, the most far reaching post civil rights liberal reforms, Glazer argued that they unfairly victimized whites. Though affirmative action programs also benefited women and other minorities, the public discourse attacking the programs typically targeted blacks. And this race linkage no doubt had a large hand in increasing the programs' unpopularity. While Glazer's book did not of course create the hostile sentiments against affirmative action; it provided those sentiments an intellectual rationale, and, thereby, made it easier for those motivated by bigotry to rail against the programs without being stigmatized as racists. Perhaps the most visible evidence of the effect of the growing neoconservative influence on anti- affirmative action policy was the Bakke decision, in which the Supreme Court overruled a medical school admissions program and ordered the school to admit a previously rejected white male applicant.

The neoconservative works of these three sociologists were hardly alone in attacking liberal racial reform. Among the other works that resonated neo-conservative ideology, there were: Edward Banfield's Unheavenly City, (1970) which attacked urban anti-poverty programs; Arthur Jensen's controversial article in the Harvard Educational Review, which attacked Head Start programs and revived the racist biological argument that blacks possessed a lower level of intelligence than whites; (Jensen) Jonathan Reider's Carnarsie, which sympathetically portrayed a racist white ethnic community in Brooklyn, N.Y. (1985) and Charles Murray's and Richard Herrnstein's The Bell Curve, which attacked compensatory liberal programs and once again revived biological racism, ala' Jensen, arguing that blacks were intellectually inferior to whites.(1995)

These are only a few examples of the anti-liberal reaction that surfaced in sociology and the other social sciences. One hardly needed to be a race relations scholar to realize that these works departed sharply from Myrdal liberal equalitarian paradigm. Not only did these neoconservative works dismiss white racial prejudice and discrimination as barriers to black American social mobility and prosperity; they placed the responsiblity for black American disadvantages on black Americans themselves. Bluntly stated, this marked the dawning of a new pessimistic era of race relations.

Efforts to Resuscitate the Liberal Paradigm on Blacks in a Revised Form

Despite the increasingly beleaguered state of the liberal sociological paradigm on blacks, some sociologists managed to keep alive the liberal flame, because they regarded liberalism as the only hope for improving the economic condition of urban lower class blacks. Especially noteworthy in this regard was William Julius Wilson's The Declining Significance of Race. (1978) This book, it would hardly be an exaggeration to say, remains the most acclaimed book written by a black American sociologist. It constituted a momentous intellectual achievement which appealed across the ideological spectrum. Though Wilson had intended to revive the New Deal liberal tradition, the book's argument—and especially its title—was appropriated by neoconservatives. Most neoconservatives saw the phrase "declining significance of race" as an affirmation of their view that racial discrimination had ceased to be an obstacle to black American upward mobility.

Wilson, however, was actually saying something very different from this. In a political climate that had grown hostile to social programs targeted for blacks, Wilson decided to stress poverty in universalistic rather than race specific terms. This was a practical political strategy for mobilizing public support for liberal social programs that would benefit the most devastated sectors of the black community, social programs that Wilson knew would not be forthcoming if they were presented as had the 1960s programs, as race specific remedies. Simply put, he sought to shift the focus from issues of race to issues of class.

Though it was well intentioned, we might reasonably question the success of that strategy. In a political climate where increasing numbers of whites tended not only to deny the existence of racism, but also to oppose social welfare programs because they perceived welfare programs as benefiting 'undeserving' blacks, any policy proposals de-emphasizing the problems of racial discrimination were likely to have the unintended consequence of reinforcing individualistic conservative explanations of black poverty. While in his subsequent book Wilson devoted much attention to the problems of inner city poverty, he failed to present a corresponding analysis of the political climate and the ways it could be changed to accommodate his liberal policy proposals. Simply put, Wilson needed to present more than a liberal class oriented analysis of poverty; he also needed to present a political sociology of American society that explained how, in a conservative political culture, his liberal proposals could be implemented. (1987) .[1]

We see another example of an effort to revive the liberal ideology on blacks in A Common Destiny, a comprehensive overview of black American life sponsored by National Research Council and co-edited by Robin Williams and Gerald Jaynes (1985). This book was published in 1989. Drawing on the collaborative efforts of some 40 scholarly experts in education, employment and income, health and demography, politics and criminal justice, and social and cultural change, it sought to achieve an overview roughly approximating that of Myrdal's An American Dilemma. However, given the auspices under which the study was done, the outcome was decidedly more bland. It avoided the issue of value bias. Also, it avoided putting forward a theoretical formulation to explain American race relations. Rather it remained focused on empirical trends. Despite its efforts to project a rhetoric of value neutrality through antiseptic prose, its liberal ideological suppositions were obvious, as can be seen from their policy stance. They recommended:

1. Provision of education, health care, and other services to enhance people's skills and productive capabilities;
2. Facilitation of national economic growth and full employment;
3. Reduction of discrimination and involuntary segregation; and
4. Development and reform of income-maintenance and other family social welfare programs to avoid long term poverty. (29)

These liberal recommendations had no realistic prospect of being enacted into public policy.

Again, as in the case of Wilson's efforts to resuscitate the liberal paradigm, William's and Jaynes failed to provide a political sociology to explain how those liberal policies could be enacted in a conservative political climate. Lacking such an analysis, their liberal policy recommendations amounted to little more than rhetorical gestures.

In a recently published article, Paget Henry highlights sociology's shortcomings in analyzing race and ethnic relations, and suggests that its former virtual monopoly in these fields is being usurped by the new fields of cultural and ethnic studies. (Henry) While Henry accurately depicts many of sociology's failures in the area of race relations, he sees these failures as the result of a narrow positivist epistemology rather than liberal ideological assumptions. In fact, Henry ignores the role of ideology; and, in consequence, the problematic role of integrationist objectives. Thus in his discussion of the sociology of race relations the problem created by liberal ideological assumptions remains unresolved.

The Need to Abandon the Liberal Paradigm and Revision Black American Social Reality

In the wake of American society's political changes, the liberal paradigm on blacks is not simply in crisis; it is moribund. As I stated at the outset of this paper, black sociologists must stop deluding themselves. They can not resuscitate the liberal political climate. The beneficial phase of the liberal sociological hegemony on blacks reached its historical limits when the conservative white backlash surfaced in the 1970s. And, in consequence, the liberal ideology no longer offers a viable vision of black American social reality. To achieve that vision we must develop a genuine black sociology.

It is noteworthy that E. Franklin Frazier arrived at a similar conclusion about the liberal vision of race relations shortly before his death in 1962 (Frazier, 1968) In a penetrating critique of the black American intellectual scene, Frazier expressed pessimism about the future demise of social barriers separating blacks and whites. Though he focused on the predicament of black American intellectual life, rather than just the problems of black American sociologists, his comments anticipated many concerns addressed in this paper.

We can only speculate why Frazier never wrote a critique of black American sociologists. Perhaps it was because such a critique would have hit too close to home, casting a cloud over his own earlier work, as well as rupturing many long standing professional relationships with white sociologists he still valued. Or maybe he simply felt that the problems plaguing black sociologists were so similar to those plaguing other black intellectuals that a general -- rather than a disciplinary --

focus was warranted. In this connection, it should be noted that Frazier's essay appeared in <u>Negro Digest</u>, a publication oriented to an educated black American audience.

I will begin with the three themes that Frazier emphasized about black intellectuals in that essay, themes that are linked to black sociologists' historical commitment to the liberal ideological paradigm. The first theme Frazier addressed was what I term <u>the black intellectuals' co-optation and hegemonic dependency.</u> Though he avoided reference to his Chicago School oriented writings in this regard, Frazier suggested that most black intellectuals were dependent on whites:

> ...educated Negroes or Negro intellectuals have failed to achieve any intellectual freedom. In fact, with the few exceptions of literary men, it appears that the Negro intellectual is unconscious of the extent to which his thinking is restricted to sterile repetition of the safe and conventional ideas current in American society. (272)

Frazier is referring to black intellectuals across the board, but his observations here are especially pertinent to the works of black sociologists. With a few notable exceptions, black sociologists embraced the prevailing white sociological conventions in not only their ideas about black American life but also their conceptions of their professional roles. Moreover, they have evidenced a conspicuous lack of <u>theoretical creativity</u>. Frazier suggested that these co-optive and hegemonic tendencies derived from the black intellectual's economic dependence on whites. Recalling the origins of the black American educated and intellectual class in American society, he noted that they

> emerged as the result of white American philanthropy.
> Although the situation has changed and the Negro intellectuals are (today) supported through other means, they are still largely dependent upon the white community. There is no basis of support for them within the Negro community. And where there is economic support within the Negro community it demands conformity to conservative and conventional ideas.(272)

In effect, black intellectuals were obliged to work within white controlled institutional structures that determined virtually every aspect of their careers, from their graduate school training and job placement to the recognition and rewards that defined their standards of professional achievement. This dependency, to a large extent, was inevitable during the early years when black Americans entered the profession of sociology. And this was not necessarily bad. As I noted above, the liberal sociological hegemony yielded important benefits. Liberalism helped to erode the racist political culture during the first quarter of the 20th century and eventually fostered significant changes in race relations, as I indicated in the discussing Myrdals' An American Dilemma and the post war reforms. But the limits of liberalism's positive contributions to blacks were reached shortly after the passage of the civil rights legislation and the dismantling of the Great Society programs. Frazier does not incorporate this dialectical concept of limits in his discussion, but it is consistent with his dependency argument.

If Frazier's first theme drew attention to the constraints that had been imposed on black intellectuals, his second theme highlighted the voluntary aspect of their conformity to white norms, which reflected what he termed the black intellectual's obsession with assimilation. In Frazier's words, the black intellectual "must rid himself of his obsession with assimilation. He must come to realize that integration should not mean annihilation--self effacement, the escaping from his identification." (279) These assimilationist aspirations, Frazier argued, derived from the post war new black middle class.

...there has been an implied or unconscious assimilationist philosophy, holding that Negroes should enter the mainstream of American life as rapidly as possible leaving behind their social heritage and becoming invisible as soon as possible.

This has been due, I think, to the emergence of a sizable new middle class whose social background and interests have determined the entire intellectual orientation of educated Negroes. (270)

These black middle class aspirations reflected the optimistic post war liberal ideology, which viewed assimilation as a gradually unfolding, inexorable force of social rationality in American life. Frazier was hardly as sanguine. While he expected increased integration of blacks into mainstream American institutional life, through desegregation of schools, recreational facilities, hospitals, business enterprises, and the like, he nevertheless expressed pessimism about the prospect of black American assimilation, which would entail whites accepting blacks into the more intimate spheres of their associational life (i.e. informal fraternal and family relations). This, Frazier suggested, white Americans would resist. Indeed, Frazier thought it was delusional for black intellectuals to persist in their pursuit of assimilation, a pursuit that had diverted them from the critically important tasks of revitalizing black American culture.

This point is closely related to Frazier's third, and final, theme, which can be termed the need for a black American centered epistemology.

Though he articulated this theme in philosophical terms, he was actually arguing that black intellectual works be grounded in black American culture.

We have no philosophers who have dealt with these and other problems from the standpoint of the Negro's unique experience in this world. . The philosophy implicit in the Negro's folklore is infinitely superior to the opportunistic philosophy of Negro intellectuals who want to save their jobs and enjoy material comforts. (273-274)

What about the work of black sociologists? Have their analyses of black American life been written "from the standpoint of the black American's unique experiences"? Did they ground their theoretical conceptions of black American life in the philosophy or worldview implicit in black American ethnic culture?

If any single deficiency plagued the works of most black sociologists -- including ironically Frazier -- it was their failure to develop a black American theoretical discourse, that is, a theoretical discourse centered in black American cultural perspectives. (This point was implicit in Vallentine's critique of Frazier's work, which was quoted earlier.)There is no question that such black cultural perspectives exist. All one needs do is listen to black jazz, blues, and rap music, read the poetry of Langston Hughes, Gwendolyn Brooks, and Don Lee, or see the jitterbug, mash potatoes, breakdance, and other black dance forms. Visit a working class black church, a local black barber shop, or beauty parlor in virtually any city in the United States and you will discover a cultural universe that black sociologists have failed to creatively transmute into a theoretical discourse on black American life. That is, a discourse centered in black American experiences of social reality.

The liberal ideological paradigm could not provide this. Despite its equalitarian ideals, liberal ideology remained centered in white American perspectives on black American life, which seemed reasonable so long as assimilation appeared to be predestined. Though the prospect of assimilation faded over two decades ago, black sociologists have persisted in producing work predicated on assimilationist assumptions, works not only ungrounded in black experiences of realty, but bereft of a conception of black American culture. While one may agree with the policies those works sought to promote, they failed to resonate the prevailing reality of American race relations.

What is different about racial segregation today in contrast to the 1950s? Today we can recognize the historical limits of liberalism. This recognition is hardly restricted to sociology. In fact, intellectual movements fostering African American centered discourse have emerged in such fields as history, literary studies, anthropology, musicology, philosophy, and politics.

We see an example of this in a recent article by Eugene Rivers. Acknowledging the demise of liberalism, Rivers calls for a black centered political agenda.

> But even if it (liberalism) could have worked at the time, its time has passed. The Civil Rights movement assumed the health of Black communities and churches, and the integrationist approach to racial equality built upon them (and upon a widespread commitment to an activist national government). But we can no longer make that assumption (nor is there the commitment to activist national government). Given current conditions in inner cities, a strategy for ending a racial caste system in which color fixes life chances now needs to focus on rebuilding black institutions . . . (17-18)

Similarly noting liberalism's demise, Ronald Walters advocates the development of a black political party.

> Blacks vote at about the same rate as whites; it is fallacious to think that Blacks now have reasons to turn out in much larger numbers than whites. Taking a cue from the past is a better idea. In 1932, when Blacks began to vote Democrat, they changed 65 years of political history. African-American journalist T. Thomas Fortune, editor of New York Age, said that it was time for Black people to go home and "turn their picture of Abraham Lincoln to the wall." Maybe now it is time to do the same with Roosevelt. (98)

To extend Walters' metaphor with specific reference to black sociologists, I think it is time we turned Myrdal's picture to the wall. In its stead, we would do well to hang the picture of W. E. B. DuBois, not the young eager to assimilate DuBois who wrote the Philadelphia Negro, but the older, more chastened and intellectually mature DuBois, who relocated in Ghana. I think the elder DuBois symbolizes the spirit of awakening to the realization that blacks must see through the mirage of assimilation and devise strategies for reconstructing the foundations of a viable community life.

Toward a Genuine Black Sociology

Before setting forth the guidelines for this New Black Sociology, I should point out several pitfalls it must avoid. First, it must avoid the repeating the mistakes of the 1960s Black Sociology Movement.

Started amid the rancor and racial polarization of the 1960s by the Black Sociology Caucus at the1968 American Sociological Association Meetings, that Black Sociology Movement constituted more a polemical than a scholarly enterprise. (Ladner: 22) And in consequence, it failed to evidence the theoretical and analytical developments needed to generate and sustain a new scholarly field. Among the factors responsible for its shortcomings, perhaps none were more crucial than its failure to produce a journal that could have served as a vehicle for consolidating the movement and cultivating its distinctive sociological perspective. That movement had other major weaknesses, which we need not elaborate here. Suffice it to say, the 1960s movement failed to take off, in large part, because its participants lacked both the historical perspective and the intellectual commitment to establish a new scholarly discourse.

Second, this New Black Sociology must avoid confusing the liberal assimilationist conception of race relations with the liberal principles of civil society. If liberal assimilationist ideology has become outdated and irrelevant, liberal principles of civil society remain essential to the stability of a democratic and multicultural American society. Unfortunately, the 1960s Black Sociology Movement failed to observe this distinction in their denunciations of liberalism. But respect for civil liberties, democratic procedures of governance, and tolerance of other cultural groups are principles that black Americans, as well as other Americans, must promote and uphold as the foundational precepts of citizenship.

Third, and closely linked to this last point, this New Black Sociology must reject racism, anti-Semitism, and sexism. Indeed, all forms of essentialism must be excluded from any enterprise claiming intellectual respectability as sociological discourse. Just as it is possible for black Americans to produce works of White Sociology, it is perfectly possible (though less likely) for white Americans to produce works of Black Sociology, insofar as that work is grounded in black American culture and reflects the interests of the black community. Though lacking an explicit critique of the liberal assimilationist ideology, such works by white Americans as Charles Keil's Urban Blues, Carol Stack's All Our Kin, Ulf Hannerz's Soulside, and Herbert Gutman's The Black Family In Slavery and Freedom possess methodological ingredients of a Black Sociology. There are of course more works by black Americans evidencing some of these ingredients, such as Andrew Billingsley's Black Families in White America, Robert Staples' Black Masculinity, Patricia Hill Collins'

Black Feminist Thought, and Charles Payne's I've Got The Light of Freedom, to name only a few.

Now, shifting to more concrete programmatic issues, we can ask: what substantive attributes should this New Black Sociology possess? First, and foremost, as I have emphasized throughout this paper, it must be grounded in black American experiences of reality. That means its analytical perspectives should resonate a black American world view. Take for example an event such as the American Revolution. Seen from the perspective of white American experiences, this was a glorious event because it marked the birth of American democracy. And that is the way the event is represented in public schools. But that hardly reflects a black American worldview. Seeing that revolution as an event that shifted power from one group of white men to another group of white men while leaving blacks in slavery, black Americans are less inclined to celebrate it as a momentous occasion. Which is to say, from the standpoint of black American experiences of reality, the American Revolution does not symbolize freedom. We might point to other examples such as the black American experiences of the Statue of Liberty, the American Dream, Hollywood, the Founding Fathers, corporate capitalism, the criminal justice system, the media, and the like.

Second, because this New Black Sociology privileges black American experiences of reality, it must emphasize the use of ethnographic methodology. While other methods may be needed to fully execute an inquiry, they should be used to complement, not supplant, ethnographic grounding. In addition to facilitating a holistic perspective that reveals black Americans' humanity, ethnography permits the expression of black American voices, communicating their distinctive experiences of reality, in a society where blacks are all too often "talked about" but seldom heard.

Three, this New Black Sociology must develop theoretical explanations of both black American behavior and white American behavior from the vantage point of black American experience. "Every way of seeing," noted the philosopher Kenneth Burke, "is a way of not seeing." There is much about life in American society that sociology grounded in white American experiences *failed to see* .   And this is where the New Black Sociology promises to generate new creative developments.

Let 's take the example of the American South, alluded to earlier. The United States throughout its history has been defined as a political democracy. Yet for many black Americans living in the South prior to the 1960s, the United States -- at least the part they inhabited--

constituted a fascist political order. Had black sociologists grounded their work in black American rather than white American experiences of reality, they would have been obliged to challenge the conception of the United States as a democracy. Indeed, from a black American perspective, Leopold's Belgian Congo, Lugard's British colonial Africa, Stalin's Soviet Union, Franco's Spain, Hitler's Germany, and Mussolini's Italy constituted the most relevant models for comprehending the experience of living in a political order where people lacked basic human rights and were subject to brutal violence. But when one turns to the works of black sociologists writing about the American South during the first half of this century, one searches in vain for references to such models. In fact, black sociologists never produced a political sociology of the South from the vantage point of black American experiences. This is just one example of their failure to evidence theoretical independence.

Fourth, this New Black Sociology must possess a scholarly journal. It is impossible to overemphasize the importance of this point, because a journal is essential if we are to sustain a new black American centered sociological discourse. That journal should contain articles debating pertinent methodological and theoretical issues, presenting empirical analyses of varied black American experiences, and reviewing books that deal with issues pertinent to black American life and American race relations. While the journal should be open to different theoretical orientations insofar as they are centered in black American experiences of reality, it should also impose exacting editorial standards to assure high quality in the articles it publishes.

Finally, this New Black Sociology should be committed to communicating its work to the larger black American community. Which is to say, black sociologists should develop the habit of writing shorter versions of their research work for mass circulation black magazines and newspapers. Moreover, we should become involved in local community groups, giving them the benefit of our expertise in dealing with various problems. This means we should strike a better balance between our professional careers and our responsibilities as members of the black American community. If the black American community is going to solve its problems and continue to develop in this post liberal age, black sociologists, as well as other black social scientists, must become more involved in supporting, and devising strategies to rebuild, local black institutions.

In closing, I should reiterate this paper's central thesis that now, at the beginning of the 21st century, we must recognize that liberal sociology by blacks is obsolete and move on to accept the challenge of developing a genuine black sociology—rooted in black American experiences of reality.

References

Baltzell, Digby. 1967. "Introduction." <u>Philadelphia Negro</u>. W.E.B. DuBois. New York: Shocken Books.

Banfield, Edward. 1970. <u>Unheavenly City</u>. Boston: Little Brown

Bell, Derrick. 1993. "Rembrance of Racism Past." <u>Race In America</u>. Herbert Hill and James E. Jones. editors. Madison, Wisconsin: University of Wisconsin Press.

Bettelheim, Bruno and Morris Janowitz in <u>The Sociology of Race Relations</u>, ed. Pettigrew.

Billingsley, Andrew. 1968. <u>Black Families in White America</u>. Englewood Cliffs, N.J.: Prentice Hall.

Bottomore, T. B. and Maximillen Rubel. 1963. <u>Karl Marx: Selected Writings in Sociology and Sociology</u>. Middlesex, England: Penguin Books.

Blackwell, James and Morris Janowitz <u>Black Sociologists</u>. 1974. Chicago:U. of Chicago Press.

Bracey, John, August Meier, and Elliot Rudwick. "The Black Sociologists: The First Half Century." <u>The Death of White Sociology</u>. Joyce Ladner, editor.

Brinkley, Alan. 1994. <u>The End of Reform</u>. New York: Alfred Knopf.

Carey, James. 1975. Sociology and Public Affaris: The Chicago School. Beverly Hills, Ca.: Sage Publications.

Clark, Kenneth. 1993. "Racial Progress and Retreat: A Personal Memoir." <u>Race In America</u>. Herbert Hill and James E. Jones.

James Coleman. 1966. <u>Equality and Educational Opportunity</u>. Washington, D.C.: U.S. Department of Health, Education, and Welfare.

_____ 1990 . <u>Equality and Advancement in Education</u>. Boulder, Colo: Westview Press.

Collins, Patricia Hill. 1990. Black Feminist Thought. Boston: Unwin Hyman

DuBois, W.E. B. 1967. Philadelphis Nego. New York: Shocken Books.

Ellison, Ralph. 1964. Shadow and Act. New York: Random House.

Frazier, E. Franklin. 1957. The Black Bourgeoisie. Glencoe, Ill.: Free Press

_____. 1968. "Sociological Theory and Race Relations." E. Franklin Frazier on Race Relations. G. Franklin Edwards. editor. Chicago: U. of Chicago Press.

_____ 1968. "The Failure of the Negro Intellectual." E. Franklin Frazier on Race Relations.

_____ "Review of Myrdal's An American Dilemma." The Sociology of Race Relations. Thomas Pettigrew. editor.

Glazer, Nathan. 1975. Affirmative Discrimination. New York: Basic Books

Gottfried, Paul and Thomas Fleming. 1988. The Conservative Movement. Boston: Twayne Publishers.

Gramsci, Antonio. 1971. Selections From the Prison Notebooks. Quintin Hoare and Geoffrey Nowell Smith. New York: International

Guttman, Herbert. 1976. The Black Family in Slavery and Freedom. New York: Pantheon

Hill, Herbert. 1993. "Black Workers, Organized Labor, and Title VII of the 1964 Civil Rights Act." Race In America. Herbert Hill and James E. Jones. editors. Madison, Wisconsin: U. of Wisconsin Press.

Hughes, Everett C. 1950. The Collected Papers of Robert Ezra Park. Glencoe, Ill.: Free Press.

Janowitz, Morris. "Introduction." Black Sociologists. James Blackwell and Morris Janowitz. editors. U. of Chicago Press.

Jensen, Arthur. 1969. "How Much Can we Boost I.Q. and Scholastic Achievement." Harvard Educational Review 39.

Keil, Charles. 1966. Urban Blues. Chicago: U. Chicago Press

Ladner, Joyce. 1973. The Death of White Sociology. New York: Vintage

Lyman, Standford. 1973. The Black American in Sociological Thought. New York: Capricorn

Marx, Karl. 1969. On Colonialism and Modernization. Garden City,N.Y.: Anchor Books

McWorther, Gerald. 1973. "The Ideology of Black Social Science." The Death of White Sociology.

Matthews, Fred. 1977. Quest For An American Sociology: Robert E. Park And The Chicago School. Montreal: McGill-Queens U. Press.

Moynihan, Daniel P.1965. The Negro Family: The Case For National Action. Washington: U.S. Department of Labor.

Murray, Charles and Richard Herrnstein. 1994. The Bell Curve. New York: Free Press.

Parsons, Talcott. 1965. "Why Freedom Now, Not Yesterday." Talcott Parsons and Kenneth Clark. editors. The Negro Americans. New York: Houghton Mifflin.

Payne, Charles. 1995. I've Got The Light of Freedom. Berkeley,Ca.: U. Calif. Press

Pettigrew, Thomas. 1980. "Introduction." The Sociology of Race Relations. Thomas Pettigrew. editor. New York: Free Press.

Reider, Jonathan. 1985. Canarsie. Cambridge, Ma.: Harvard U. Press

Rivers, Eugene F. 1995. Boston Review. Summer.

Robbins, Richard. 1975. "Charles Johnson." Black Sociologists. Blackwell and Janowitz.

Staples, Robert. 1980. Black Masculinity. San Francisco: The Black Scholar Press.

Steinfels, Peter. 1978. The Neo-Conservatives: The Men Who ARe Changing American Politics. New York: Simon and Schuster

Vallentine, Charles. 1968. Culture and Poverty: Critique and Counter Proposals. Chicago: U. of Chicago Press.

Walters, Ronald. Feb.,1996. "Third Party Chasm." Emerge Magazine.

Williams, Robin and Gerald Jaynes. 1985. A Common Destiny. Washington, D.C.: Natinal Academy Press.

Wilson, William Julius. 1978. The Declining Significance of Race. Chicago: U. of Chicago Press.

_____. 1987. The Truly Disadvantaged. Chicago: U. of Chicago Press.

Endnotes

[1] I am pleased to note that William Julius Wilson published just such a political sociological analysis several years after this chapter was written. See: The Bridge over the Racial Divide: Rising Inequality and Coalition Politics, University of California Press, 1999.

About the Contributors

Anthony J. Blasi is an Associate Professor of Sociology at Tennessee State University.

Benjamin P. Bowser is an Associate Professor of Sociology at California State University, Hayward.

Donald Cunnigen is an Associate Professor of Sociology at the University of Rhode Island.

Robert E. Washington is a Professor of Sociology at Bryn Mawr College.

Wilbur H. Watson, the late sociologist was a member of the Morehouse Medical School faculty.

Jerry G. Watts is an Associate Professor of American Studies at Trinity College in Hartford, Connecticut.

Charles V. Willie is Charles William Eliot Professor of Education (Emeritus), Graduate School of Education, Harvard University.

Alford A. Young, Jr. is an Assistant Professor of Sociology at the University of Michigan, Ann Arbor.